D0464699

DEEP BLACK

ALSO BY WILLIAM E. BURROWS

ON REPORTING THE NEWS
(a textbook)

VIGILANTE

RICHTHOFEN

DEEP BLACK

SPACE ESPIONAGE AND NATIONAL SECURITY

WILLIAM E. BURROWS

RANDOM HOUSE/NEW YORK

TO LARA JULIE
with love, respect, and hope

Grateful acknowledgment is made to Harcourt Brace Jovanovich, Inc.,
for permission to reprint excerpts from *Flight to Arras* by Antoine
de Saint-Exupéry, translated from the French by Lewis Galantière.
Copyright 1942 by Harcourt Brace Jovanovich, Inc. World English
language rights excluding the United States and Canada
administered by William Heinemann Ltd., London.
Reprinted by permission of the publishers.

Library of Congress Cataloging-in-Publication Data

Burrows, William E., 1937–
Deep black.
Includes index.
1. Space surveillance—United States. 2. United
States—National security. I. Title.
U6475.B87   1986   358'.8   86-10220
ISBN 0-394-54124-3

Designed by Richard Oriolo

Manufactured in the United States of America
9

What espionage people have not accepted is that human espionage has become a complement to technical systems. Espionage either reaches out into voids where technical systems cannot probe or double-checks the results of technical collection. In short, human intelligence today is employed to do what technical systems cannot do.

—Admiral Stansfield Turner
Former director, Central Intelligence Agency

This stuff is black, black, black!

—John Pike
Federation of American Scientists

Preface

"I wouldn't want to be quoted on this," Lyndon Johnson told a small group of local government officials and educators in Nashville in March 1967, "but we've spent thirty-five or forty billion dollars on the space program. And if nothing else had come out of it except the knowledge we've gained from space photography, it would be worth ten times what the whole program has cost. Because tonight we know how many missiles the enemy has and, it turned out, our guesses were way off. We were doing things we didn't need to do. We were building things we didn't need to build. We were harboring fears we didn't need to harbor."

By "space photography," Johnson had in mind the broader system of space reconnaissance and surveillance with which the United States each day takes the measure of the world electronically, monitoring vital signs from Soviet missile tests, Chinese and French nuclear weapons facilities, Nicaraguan ports and airfields, the Afghan army, terrorists training in Iran, Libya, and Syria, North Korean radar installations, and a large number of other places and activities in order to be able to assess developments that could figure prominently, if not decisively, in the fortunes of the United States and its allies.

To be sure, the technical intelligence systems are extraordinary, whether they are low-orbiting satellites that silently record images of events with remarkable clarity and relay them even as the action itself is occurring, or whether they are other spacecraft, some parked a tenth of the way to the moon, that point their mechanical ears in directions allowing them to listen to and pass on a crescendo of military and civilian communication signals and even eavesdrop on conversations taking place deep within the walls of the Kremlin.

But this is not solely the story of spaceborne robots and other exotic hardware. It most concerns the people who conceive, produce, and control the various intelligence-collection systems, who interpret and analyze the "product," and who formulate national policy accordingly. In one sense, cutting-edge technology drives the system, in that a stagnant intelligence-collection apparatus would soon be overwhelmed by events with which it could no longer cope and at the same time become increasingly vulnerable to exposure and countermeasures—to being fooled, spoofed, or simply missing the action. And not so incidentally, high-tech spy systems are challenging to design, prestigious to build, and carry a low-keyed, but unmistakable, panache that those who operate them and are privy to their secrets give every appearance of thoroughly enjoying. There is a kind of reconnaissance club, an unofficial secret society composed of "black hats" from the various contractors, military services, and the intelligence agencies and divisions, all of whom carry the appropriate clearances and are scrupulous about remaining in deep shadow. But they know who they are and they like it.

Yet in another, more fundamental sense, space reconnaissance and surveillance is about politics at the highest level. And politics is passionate stuff. While it is true that the photo and signals interpreters have honed their specialties into precise and coolly practiced arts, for example, those who use their pictures and taped intercepts to hammer out foreign policy—to shape responses to a threatening world—often do so with opposing convictions that on any number of occasions have aroused rage and set the stage for long-standing feuds. Those who use technical intelligence almost always do so with preconceptions that they bring to the analytical process. There is rarely disagreement over what a picture shows, for example, but what it *means* is often the subject of intense debate.

Arms control is but one case in point. The process depends upon detailed agreements that specify what is permitted, qualitatively and quantitatively, in maintaining and developing certain kinds of weapon systems. Since the benefits of successful cheating on a large scale can be considerable, arms control agreements stipulate that their provisions be verifiable by so-called national technical means:

that is to say, by assorted sensors on earth, in the air, and in space that listen, watch, and record vibrations in the mantle of the planet itself. Were it not for these machines, there could be no arms control because it is the technology that allows each side to satisfy itself that the various provisions are in the main not being contravened. But "cheating," particularly where treaty language is vague, is often very much in the eye of the beholder and tends to reflect his or her political inclination. Policymakers who are convinced that the U.S.S.R. is an evil empire bent on world domination at all costs view collected intelligence one way, while those who see the Kremlin somewhat more benevolently often interpret intelligence quite differently.

The sensors that are used to monitor compliance with arms control agreements are precisely the same that gather military intelligence, so the collection process would go on with or without treaties. Although the "take" is the same, however, the purposes for which it is used vary widely. The testing of a Soviet ballistic missile is a case in point. With an arms control treaty that limits ICBMs in effect, the State Department must know whether the weapon violates size, range, throw weight, and other restrictions. The CIA and the Air Force need to know about the missile's performance characteristics and about the silo in which it is kept so it can be jammed in flight, or perhaps intercepted, or even successfully attacked on the ground if possible. The sum of the intelligence—all of the collected data on that missile—is the same, though it is used for varying purposes.

In the case of arms control, it is important for the citizens of the Western democracies to grasp enough of the process of the national technical means of verification and about space surveillance in general so that they can make informed judgments on the matter, rather than abandon such an important subject to the whims of successive politicians and their subordinate ideologues. A basic understanding of the technical collection process leads to some pointed questions. There is an apparent contradiction, for example, in the frequent assertions by the Reagan administration that the Soviet Union has consistently cheated on strategic arms control agreements while simultaneously asserting that those agreements are not adequately verifiable. If the United States does not have reconnaissance and surveillance systems that are precise enough to monitor arms control treaties with reasonable certainty that they are being adhered to, how can it be so certain that those treaties have been violated?

That question and others need to be raised. But answers from Washington have not been forthcoming. Attempts to get to the heart of the matter quickly run headlong into the national security shibboleth, which has it that since arms control verification and the collection of pure military intelligence are part of the same process and involve the same systems, revelations about one must necessarily expose the other to a dangerous extent.

The rule, therefore, is not to talk about anything having to do with space reconnaissance, at least officially and for the record. Yet it must be noted that those who are the most vociferous about maintaining the absolute secrecy of U.S. space reconnaissance operations also tend to be the most persistently hostile toward arms control.

One of the places I visited for the preparation of this book was the North American Aerospace Defense Command headquarters in Cheyenne Mountain, outside Colorado Springs. There, one afternoon in late June 1984, I interviewed Brigadier General Paul D. Wagoner, who was in charge of NORAD's combat operations. Early in the conversation, I mentioned the names of some space reconnaissance systems (the KH-11 imaging satellite being one of them) and asked the general if he would provide some details about them that I did not have.

General Wagoner provided not a scrap of additional information about the systems I mentioned, yet the interview was one of the most interesting and instructive I had because it got to the heart of the politics of the situation.

The general began by explaining, in a polite and carefully modulated way, that the subject about which I was writing is so secret that it is governed by a classification system known as Sensitive Compartmented Information, or SCI, and that SCI is even more rigorously classified—is even "blacker"—than the top-secret category. "Compartmented" is the operative word. Those who hold SCI clearances, General Wagoner explained, have access to extremely important information but are permitted to know only what is necessary for them to do their jobs. That way, he added, damage to national security can be kept to a minimum in case some traitor or casual talker spills secrets (Colorado Springs is fairly infested with Communist agents who are assigned to pry sensitive information out of the unwary and turn the gullible or gluttonous into spies, General Wagoner warned, his voice rising).

He next turned to the danger that could come to the nation

because someone—a writer, for example—sifted through the open literature, talked with those knowledgeable on the subject, and then made inferences that might give away secrets and endanger the national security. General Wagoner was now angry and began whittling his words to a finer point. "That's what's so dangerous about guys like you having too much knowledge, because you don't really know what you might be giving away. You're still fishing and you're dangerous from that standpoint. *I'm* dangerous when people don't clear me into compartments," Wagoner added, "because I damned *near* know what's in there, but I don't, so I feel like I can speak from conjecture."

Next to actual espionage, it is conjecture that most worries those who guard the secrets of the strategic reconnaissance systems. They worry because of the possibility that a single individual doing in essence what they do—fitting thousands of pieces of information into a mosaic until a meaningful picture begins to materialize—will unintentionally hand the opposition secrets that it could not otherwise obtain.

I responded by explaining that my technical background was modest, that I possessed little hard information about secret space systems at that stage, and that since the Soviet Union has its own flourishing space reconnaissance program, the Russians must know quite a bit more about the subject than they would ever be likely to learn from my writing. "They've got electro-optical and real-time imaging capability," I pointed out. "So what are they going to find out from me?"

"Well," Paul Wagoner answered, a look of consternation on his face, "you've talked about a number of things here, and I don't know whether you know much or not. But you throw around terms that scare the shit out of me. I'm not trying to discourage you, but I'm telling you that what you're treading on is very, very dangerous to national security."

But did the general not think that the people of the United States ought to know at least enough about space reconnaissance and surveillance so that they could make intelligent decisions about arms control verification, rather than take political pronouncements about it as an article of faith?

Wagoner, a self-described "farm boy from Indiana" who was sitting deep inside NORAD's command bunker—a place almost certainly earmarked for obliteration by the first Soviet warheads to come down on the United States—grew alarmed at the subject and became shrill. "Any treaty with the Soviet Union is one-way," he snapped, his voice rising again as he skirted the question. "They do not honor treaties. You show me how goddamned many they do. And we honor treaties. Every time we sign something, we compromise; every time *they* sign something, it's because they've gained something. Goddammit, the Soviets have *never* given us anything that I can find in any of my readings," Wagoner said vehemently. "I have never seen them want anything that was to their disadvantage," he added, claiming that the United States, by comparison, has become a "socialist giveaway state" that is being victimized by the arms control process. Treaties are not verifiable, General Paul D. Wagoner insisted, because the Kremlin does not want them verified. "They lie *intentionally*," he said, unable to suppress his anger.

Hans Mark, who was under secretary of the Air Force in the Carter administration before becoming the chancellor of the University of Texas, takes a different view of arms control but not of national security considerations and the need for absolute secrecy where space reconnaissance is concerned. Mark believes that the provisions of SALT II, which was concluded during Carter's term in office, are verifiable, though he has reservations about future treaties, particularly those relating to cruise missiles, which are small, and anti-satellite weapons, which can appear ambiguous in space imagery.

Following a brief discussion we had in the spring of 1985, Mark sent me a letter expressing sympathy for this project and pointing out that publicizing some information about U.S. space reconnaissance systems "would make it very much easier for our political leaders to justify a number of important military and foreign policy initiatives if people really knew what our adversaries around the world are doing."

But Hans Mark went on to warn that publishing "classified" information would "give direct aid and comfort to our adversaries around the world" and therefore ought not be done. Others agree. Their concern, as most commonly expressed, comes down to this: we don't know what the other side knows about the systems we use to watch and listen to them, so prudence dictates keeping as much of that information as possible safely under wraps (or, at any rate, under the cloak).

Every nation, of course, has secrets that must be kept. Important elements of the U.S. strategic reconnaissance system certainly fall into that category and ought to be well protected, since laying them bare can only minimize their effectiveness and make the whole reconnaissance process pointless. Working details of how reconnaissance planes and spacecraft gather foreign data, including most of the frequencies and codes they use and specific ways in which they are hardened against attacks by nature and the political opposition, are not in this book. Such engineering data are not here because they are not needed to tell the story, they would encumber the average reader with useless minutiae, and they would provide valuable information to the nation's adversaries. To seek such information in order to publish it would be irresponsible.

At the same time, Washington's penchant for classifying almost everything military, which began in earnest even before World War II, has grown to such overwhelming proportions that it has long been the butt of jokes. At last count, more than two million American citizens were either stamping assorted documents as classified or were almost arbitrarily cleared to read them. Christopher Boyce obtained a high-level security clearance with ludicrous ease and went on to sell operational data about Rhyolite, one of the nation's most secret reconnaissance satellites, to the KGB. Ronald W. Pelton, a highly knowledgeable National Security Agency technician who sold the Kremlin a wealth of information about secret U.S. communications intelligence activities, possessed far more "compartmented" operational data than his mid-level rank justified; the blunder was compounded by the fact that counterintelligence ignored him after he left the NSA even though, by his own admission later, he was "broke and desperate." And the John A. Walker, Jr., Navy spy-ring case so underscored the excesses of this madcap process that even Pentagonians were finally moved out of sheer embarrassment to trim the number of persons having access to classified documents and reappraise the notoriously ill-defined rules governing what really needs to be classified and what does not. The current system's pervasiveness and often arbitrary nature have had a numbing effect and has therefore become counterproductive. So many documents are classified top secret and higher that the designations tend to be shrugged off and even ridiculed. To classify almost everything is to classify almost nothing.

In 1955, James R. Killian's Technological Capabilities Panel produced a report on national strategic intelligence requirements that laid the foundation for the U-2 aerial reconnaissance and early space reconnaissance programs. Details of the report remain classified to this day despite the fact that the Soviet Union recovered Francis

Gary Powers's U-2 (including its camera system and exposed film) in 1960 and the early satellite reconnaissance operation was heavily publicized by the government at its inception. General Wagoner, to take another example, steadfastly refused to allow even the name KH-11 (one of the reconnaissance satellites whose mere mention scared "the shit" out of him) to pass his "zipped" lips while almost simultaneously Admiral Stansfield Turner, the former director of Central Intelligence, referred to the same spacecraft by name in a memoir that was allowed to be published only after a long (and bitterly contested) censoring by the CIA. A satellite that does or does not exist, depending upon which source is consulted, is reduced to the role of a mere prop in the theater of the absurd and makes a mockery of the bloated, though leaky, system in which it functions.

The most frequently heard response to the suggestion that the Kremlin must surely know a great deal more about U.S. space reconnaissance activities than are described in these pages is that we really don't know what the opposition knows in this game of cat and mouse. It is therefore better to write nothing, the argument goes, than to chance the accidental disclosure of information that the Kremlin does not already possess. This is yet another misleading notion.

In fact, the national technical intelligence establishment does know just about everything the Russians know about its collection systems, according to several knowledgeable sources who were interviewed for this book.

Space reconnaissance has quietly evolved into an immense and extremely intricate electronic contest that elite intelligence organizations on both sides of the East-West political chasm play by a gentleman's agreement that excludes their respective citizenries. The contest's purpose, of course, is to gather useful intelligence and in the process be able to monitor compliance with arms control agreements. The means of accomplishing those goals entails the use of many diverse collection systems, some of which masquerade as other things, in order to obtain specific information. A ferret satellite is orbited to establish certain characteristics of some type of Soviet radar, for instance. Since the Russians don't want their radar's characteristics established, they change frequencies as soon as they discover the ferret and guess its mission. (They might also maintain the frequency to fool the ferret's operators into believing that they had not guessed its mission and instead prepare to change frequencies suddenly in the event of war. The alternate frequency would have to be tested, though, and that too would probably be picked up.) Were that ferret to remain in orbit and do its job for five or six years without the radars it was monitoring changing frequencies or testing for an emergency change, it might reasonably be supposed that the ferret, or at least its mission, had gone undetected.

What, then, do the Russians know about American space reconnaissance systems in general? As it turns out, they know quite a bit about U.S. low-orbiting spacecraft, such as the reconnaissance types that constitute the core subject of this book. The low orbiters are easier to see, easier to listen to, and easier to track than satellites higher up. In the case of the obsolescent KH-11, which takes pictures and taps into some communications signals, they also own an operations manual purchased from a CIA traitor for a paltry three thousand dollars. Finally, the Kremlin has its own long-standing space reconnaissance program, and although Washington's systems are in general superior technologically, the basic hardware is more similar than different. The opposition knows a fair amount about the medium orbiters, which include most of the radar ferrets, ocean surveillance types, and some of the eavesdropping signals intelligence satellites. It knows relatively little about the high orbiters out at 22,300-mile geosynchronous range and beyond, which carry the brunt of surveillance for early warning of attack, navigation, communications relay, missile telemetry and electronic signal interception, and specialized ABM radar ferreting. This appraisal was made by one who has good reason to know.

Then there is the matter of national security. "I have a feeling you're going to write an exciting book," said General Wagoner, "but I hope it is one that adds to national security, rather than detracts from it." So do I. Yet "national security" is an exceedingly ambiguous term and one that, paradoxically, has come to have abidingly pernicious implications. The late Charles Yost, a gentle, perceptive, and cultured diplomat who spent a lifetime pondering relations among nations, observed that the more tenaciously the superpowers grapple for national security through arms stockpiling, the less secure they become. Adults, and many children, throughout the industrialized world carry with them the persistent (though usually sublimated) fear of a nuclear attack and annihilation that could come at any time. We are in fact not very secure at all.

But space-based reconnaissance and surveillance play a key role in three areas that really do relate to national security in its truest sense.

First, to echo Lyndon Johnson, the technical collection systems provide in abundant detail information on what the opposition has in the way of weapons (not to mention industrial productivity, agricultural output, civil projects, and so forth) and also what it does not have. To the extent that an effective defense posture is necessary, space and related intelligence systems provide sufficient data so that real threats can be checked. At the same time, they also help us to decide what not to build because of the absence of a threat, thereby saving untold billions of dollars. Technical intelligence pointing to a curtailed Soviet strategic bomber force in the 1970s, for example, allowed the Air Force to cut back on its fighter-interceptors and put the funds it saved elsewhere.

Second, the system virtually eliminates the possibility of a surprise attack by the Soviet Union or any other major power (nuclear terrorism by some Third World nations is a different matter, however, and is taken more seriously than the Soviet threat by many in the intelligence community). The remote sensing systems with which each side monitors the other and most of the rest of the world are so many, so redundant, and so diffuse that no preparation for an all-out attack could take place without triggering multiple alarms, many of them coming from space. Orders for armies to march, planes to fly, and civilians to hide must be communicated relatively quickly over vast areas, and what is communicated can be intercepted; everything necessary to wage the war must be moved, and what is moved can be photographed. Similarly, the technical collection systems permit effective crisis management and in the process can prevent the sort of runaway escalation that has often propelled other generations into war almost by accident. Surprises tend to make generals jumpy; space reconnaissance and surveillance reduce the element of strategic surprise to practically nil, which, as was the case during the Cuban missile crisis, gives each side time to take the other's measure and consider responses rationally.

Finally, even the anemic level of arms control that currently exists, denigrated and undercut as it has been of late, would be impossible without the space-based monitoring capability described here. This is no place for a discussion of arms control. But there are two arguments against it, both currently gaining fashion, which relate to the subject of this book and therefore bear challenge.

There is the allegation that arms control is dangerous because it rewards the cheater to the point of making an attack against the side that adheres to the agreement seem feasible. Therefore, the argument goes, both sides ought to build as many weapons as they deem necessary in order to ensure an indefinite standoff. This presumes that cheating on a significant scale can go undetected, which is untrue, and that the more nuclear weapons there are in the world, the safer it will be, which is absurd. Further, there is the assertion that smaller weapons—cruise missiles and mobile ICBMs, for example—make treaty verification virtually impossible. Those weapons make monitoring more difficult, it is true, but far from impossible. To the contrary, the record shows that reconnaissance and surveillance technology have kept pace with weapons technology and give every indication of continuing to do so.

A freeze on weapons testing, on the other hand, would accomplish the stated purpose of the Strategic Defense Initiative—to make nuclear weapons obsolete—at relatively minuscule cost and without the provocation that "Star Wars" will necessarily entail. So would effective mutual strategic force reduction. It may be determined that neither of these is in the best interest of the United States. But the assertion that neither is possible because the nation's technical intelligence systems are unequal to the task of guaranteeing adequate compliance is blatantly false. Like SDI itself, publicly stated concern regarding the alleged inadequacy of U.S. verification capability smacks of nothing less than a desire to disrupt and destroy arms control once and for all. But treaties or not, the world will continue to be scrutinized by a pervasive, highly advanced armada of spaceborne sentinels that constitutes the Western alliance's first line of defense. This book is an account of how they came to be, what they are, and who controls them.

—W.E.B.
Stamford, Connecticut
June 1, 1986

Acknowledgments

The material in this book came from five basic kinds of sources. The preponderance of historical, political, and technical detail derived from open literature, including books, reports, congressional hearings, newspapers, trade and professional journals, a doctoral dissertation, and scholarly papers delivered at meetings I attended, including those sponsored by the American Association for the Advancement of Science, the American Institute of Aeronautics and Astronautics, and the New York Academy of Sciences. All of these are cited.

I also received a great deal of help with technical data from scientists who had no security clearances at the time I interviewed them but were working in the forefront of technology that is so analogous to that in the black systems that reasonable inferences could be made about the latter based on knowledge of the former ("You're getting this stuff *before* it's classified!" quipped one of the scientists).

In addition, I interviewed many of those who had been in technical intelligence collection in any of several capacities, as some of the names listed below will readily indicate. Several participated in the earliest stages of modern overhead reconnaissance. I was always conscious during these interviews (which were taped) that time is exacting its relentless toll on their memories, so I made every effort to dredge up missing pieces of historical detail before they became lost forever. Being able to do that was quite a privilege. Each agreed to participate, I might add, because he believed in the validity of the project.

Much valuable material, in addition to a variety of helpful perspectives, came from political scientists and others with expertise in the governmental as well as technical ramifications of space reconnaissance and surveillance.

Finally, there were those who provided a little technical information and generous amounts of backgrounding on how the political aspect of space reconnaissance works from the inside with the proviso that their anonymity be respected. Each had good reason to know that he gave away nothing that the opposition does not already have.

My deepest appreciation, then, goes to Moustafa T. Chahine, Charles Beichman, John Ford, and James Janesick of the Jet Propulsion Laboratory in Pasadena, James Gunn of the Department of Physics at Princeton University, Jerry Nelson of the Department of Physics at the University of California at Berkeley, Patrick Huggins of the Department of Physics at New York University, Joel Bregman of the National Radio Astronomy Observatory, Ted Greenwood of Columbia University, George Rathjens of MIT, Merton E. Davies of RAND, Amrom H. Katz of R&D Associates, Edwin H. Land of the Rowland Institute of Science, James R. Killian, Jr., of MIT, Hans Mark of the University of Texas, Clarence E. ("Kelly") Johnson and Ben Rich, lately of the Skunk Works, Nicholas Durutta of Lockheed California, Nicholas L. Johnson of Teledyne Brown Engineering, Harold E. Nash, formerly of the Naval Underwater Systems Center, D. G. King-Hele of the Royal Aircraft Establishment, Allan A. Needell of the National Air and Space Museum, Ruth Hurt of the United States Air Force Museum, Ann Collins of the New York Academy of Sciences, Desmond Ball of the Strategic and Defence Studies Centre of the Australian National University, Nils Petter Gleditsch of the International Peace Research Institute, Richard Coltart of *Jane's Defence Weekly*, Richard M. Bissell, Jr., William E. Colby, and E. Henry Knoche (all formerly of the Central Intelligence Agency), Robert Behler, Jerry Glasser, and Tom Ross of the 9th Strategic Reconnaissance Wing, Beale Air Force Base, Brigadier General Paul D. Wagoner (United States Air Force), General George J. Keegan, Jr. (USAF, retired),

McGeorge Bundy of the Department of History at NYU, and the late George B. Kistiakowsky of Harvard University and the Eisenhower White House. John Pike of the Federation of American Scientists proved to be a reliable, energetic, and always available source of information, as did Robert Windrem of the NBC Nightly News.

My special gratitude goes to the late Herbert ("Pete") Scoville, Jr., at one time head of the CIA's Directorate of Science and Technology and later president of the Arms Control Association, who devoted many hours to reconstructing the formative years of space reconnaissance and putting various developments into perspective. Pete also read the relevant chapters for accuracy despite an illness that caused him severe pain, and provided encouragement to the end. He was a courageous and indefatigable savant and a model for us all.

To acknowledge the support of those immediately involved in a project as long and often arduous as this is to risk turning profound gratitude into banality. It must nevertheless be said that the book owes a great deal to Sarah Whitworth, who ministered to my graduate students and bore many burdens that were rightfully mine while I wrote, and to Bob Loomis, whose patience, confidence, taste, and intellect have earned him a place on the editors' endangered species list.

Joelle, who endured years of triumph and tribulation at close quarters, and remained unflaggingly supportive and enthusiastic throughout, must be thanked in other ways.

Contents

A WORD ABOUT NOMENCLATURE

"Reconnaissance" and "surveillance" are not synonymous where technical intelligence collection is concerned. Generally, reconnaissance has to do with the active pursuit of specific information, such as the performance characteristics of a ballistic missile. Surveillance entails the passive, systematic watching or listening for something to happen, such as a ballistic missile being fired. For the sake of simplicity, I have occasionally used the term "reconnaissance" for both systems.

DEEP BLACK

1

The Need to Know

"You can have no idea how big this is," Major General George J. Keegan, Jr., United States Air Force (retired), explained with a weariness he made no effort to conceal. "Reconnaissance and its elements have become an immense source of power and control. It's at the center of the maelstrom."

Keegan slouched on a sofa in the sunken living room of his modest ranch house, located on a cul-de-sac in Oxon Hill, Maryland. The community, like many others that surround Washington, is a tidy but plain feeder colony for the federal government. The house, in fact, was not far from his old office at the Pentagon (which, ironically, had also turned out to be a cul-de-sac for him).

Now his hands were clasped over a modest paunch and his alert eyes—the constantly searching eyes that are the mark of the professional intelligence officer—wandered past sandaled feet, which rested on the coffee table, to the far wall. Keegan was tired, and by his own admission had grown sour. Yet he was as disgruntled and impassioned as always. Even after all the years since he relinquished active duty because of less than encouraging prospects for promotion, there remained in George Keegan an abiding anger that was fueled by the conviction that the nation's eyes and ears were being dangerously manipulated in the naïve hope that détente with the Soviet Union could be made to work; that a freeze on nuclear weapons testing, for example, is adequately verifiable, and that significant cheating can therefore be detected. In order to accomplish this stupendous exercise in self-deception, he explained in slow, measured tones that rang with bitterness, control of the nation's vast, intricate, and supersecret space reconnaissance system becomes imperative. In Keegan's opinion, maintaining an iron grip on this most important of all intelligence programs so that the flow of information taken from the Soviet Union and elsewhere can be altered or misdirected as political requirements dictate becomes crucial.

The former chief of Air Force intelligence does not believe for a moment, as he has accused the Central Intelligence Agency of believing, that the wily men in the Kremlin have finally given up the idea of inflicting Marxist-Leninist hegemony on the world and have now merely settled for trying to guarantee the safety of the motherland. No. He bristled at the mention of mutual assured destruction, or MAD, which has it that since neither side would survive a nuclear war, the very nature of such a conflict acts as a deterrent. It might deter the United States, warned George Keegan, but it will in no circumstance deter the U.S.S.R. MAD, he maintained, is a theory hatched by John F. Kennedy, McGeorge Bundy, and all of the other liberals who have chosen, for reasons Keegan cannot quite fathom, to sleepwalk through a time of steadily growing danger while assuring themselves and the American public that each nation holds the other hostage to catastrophic retaliation and therefore has no alternative to accepting coexistence.

But the Kremlin is under no such delusion, Keegan said darkly, his eyes still fixed on the wall. The Soviet leaders believe, as they have always believed, that given proper preparation the citizens of the Soviet Union would in the main be able to withstand a nuclear war, riding it out in relative safety, and that such a war is therefore taken to be entirely feasible. George Keegan is unshakably sure of this. He has spent more than two decades studying "massive" evidence relating to Soviet civil defense. He has read everything he could lay his hands on, he explained, including Marshal V. D. Sokolovskii's seminal *Soviet Military Strategy*, which exhaustively discusses the importance of civil defense in the nuclear age. More important, he has studied highly classified satellite reconnaissance photographs showing Soviet civil defense activities in consummate detail. George Keegan has seen the pictures and they do not lie.

In 1971, not long after he ended a tour as chief of Air Force intelligence in the Pacific and returned to Washington to assume command of all of Air Force intelligence, Keegan claims to have read a top-secret report prepared under the direction of the Central Intelligence Agency. The single volume, which had been a year in the making, amounted to a briefing aid for the State Department negotiators who had been instructed to conclude an anti-ballistic missile treaty with the Soviet Union if at all possible.

The thrust of that report, Keegan asserted, was that there existed "no substantial, centrally-directed, civil defense effort [in the U.S.S.R.] that would impinge on the negotiation of an ABM treaty." The agreement, which was signed and ratified the following year, is generally taken to be the linchpin of all of the arms control treaties. It severely restricts the number of anti-ballistic missiles and attendant radar each side can have, thereby leaving each vulnerable to the other's ballistic missiles. This too is a manifestation of the principle of mutual assured destruction. But if one of the signatories was even partially protected by effective civil defense while the other had no comparable program, the former would have a considerable, perhaps decisive, advantage, ABMs or no ABMs, according to Keegan. His study of military history, part of which was undertaken at Harvard, left no doubt in his mind that a nation having such an advantage would be sorely tempted to use it.

When he finished reading the CIA's report, Keegan recalled, he wasted no time going into action. He ordered his staff to search the already vast data bank for any satellite photography that could in any way relate to civil defense activity in the Soviet Union. The pictures his young lieutenants and captains soon began bringing back "in armsful" were electrifying, he recalled, angrily.

"There were incredible photographs of civil defenses of all types going up all over the Soviet Union. They showed the basements of every new apartment house in construction, with the foundations being made up of massive civil defense shelters—blast doors, reinforced walls—as good photographs as you could find anywhere," said Keegan, evidently still marveling at the quality of the pictures, most of which had been taken from altitudes of more than a hundred miles in the late 1960s. Then, he continued, he and his staff scrutinized the imagery in order to answer such "ancillary" questions as what types of civil defenses they were and where they were being installed.

"We examined thirty-nine of the largest cities and found that every apartment house built after 1955 had a massive nuclear-bomb shelter in the basement. Secondly, we found large tunnels interconnecting every one of these buildings. And *in* these tunnels, we found water, electric power conduits, and a vast storage of medical supplies: hospital-type facilities."

Next, said Keegan, his junior officers turned their attention to industrial civil defense. With the help of Russian defectors in New York, some of whom had been engineers who participated in the civil defense construction program, further details began to emerge about the extent of Soviet preparations to survive a nuclear war. Once the defectors had described industrial shelters for Keegan and his staff, he said, another computer search of the records stored in the data bank was undertaken. The Air Force photo interpreters soon discovered that "every factory in the Soviet Union, in the thirty-nine-odd cities examined, had a massive shelter," George Keegan asserted, his voice rising in mild astonishment fourteen years after the purported discovery. "What we did, primarily, was to research old photography to find out how long this had been going on so we could get a better perspective. And then, the biggest shock was to find that the *factories* also had shelters. So, then, they are going to protect the work force."

Finally, Keegan recalled, he focused on preparations that had been made to protect Soviet political and military leaders. "By this time, my team had grown to thirty or forty people. I had a whole group of Army volunteers; *this* excited the U.S. Army. They graciously gave me a lot of photo interpreters and really banged into it because civil defense was an Army mission for years, and still is, for all I know. Then we got an exception to the law about reservists working on top-secret satellite photography, so I got a number of civil engineers whose business the building of shelters is. Then we went into the military structure," Keegan added, "and we never got over what we found."

The photo interpreters began searching the area inside the Moscow beltway, a highway some eighty miles long that rings the city the way the Capital Beltway circles Washington. They manipulated the photographs, applied false colors, and used other techniques to fine-search the resurrected satellite pictures for details that had previously gone unnoticed for lack of interest. The imagery, very good by 1971 standards in that objects two feet long and even a bit smaller could be distinguished, reran through Keegan's mind like a classic film he relished watching over and over again. He began to speak more slowly, drawing the flavor out of each syllable as he savored what he clearly considered to be one of the great intelligence triumphs of his career.

The interpreters found seventy-five huge underground command posts. "How big were they?" George Keegan asked rhetorically. "Roughly the size of the Pentagon. How deep were they? They were completely covered and were underground," he added, referring to moundlike structures about seven hundred feet across whose dimensions could be measured through "good shadow photography," which provides photo interpreters with a means of ascertaining size. Knowledge of a satellite's position and the time of day at which the photograph was taken allows a skilled interpreter to calculate an object's size to a matter of inches by measuring shadows. "Filled and covered with what?" Keegan asked the wall. "One, with a hundred feet of reinforced concrete and four hundred feet of earth fill. That's two or three times the strength of the Hoover Dam. Not one, but seventy-f-i-i-i-ve. . . ." He drew out the last word for emphasis. "A number of them had large steel stairs covered with concrete. The giant shelters contain storage tanks for water and for diesel fuel to power generators," Keegan continued. "Many of them were very posh—landscaped—with beautiful barracks around them."

Then, he went on, "with a little detective work for which we all deserved a medal, but that we got reprimanded for, we eavesdropped on the Soviets in Moscow and used a few other tricks to find out who was occupying them," Keegan said in reference to who was supposed to use the giant shelters in the event of war. "We confirmed who the occupants of these incredible facilities were, and that was members of the Politburo, chiefs of the industrial ministries headed by Communist party members: the *brass*. There were two for the KGB, two for the GRU—military intelligence—and on, and on, and on, and on.

"Then we went into the field—Leningrad, Vladivostok, Novosibirsk, Gorki—and found that throughout the military chain of command, in every city in every military district, were replications of the Moscow giant underground facilities, but smaller. Then we called in the engineers to help us determine how tough they are. How much overpressure can they withstand? How much blast pressure? And then we had the civil engineers come in and estimate what it would cost to build one shelter like any of the Moscow shelters. The figure was so staggering that I never published it for fear that I would have no credibility left: five hundred billion dollars to build *one!*" George Keegan exclaimed.

Food. "It doesn't make any sense if there's no food," the former intelligence officer recalled thinking. He went on to recount the interrogation of yet another Russian defector who provided a wealth of detail on how food shelters the size of three or four football fields were dug at minimum depths of sixty feet ("That's pretty goddamned deep," the general noted). And the food storage shelters, he went on to explain, are compartmentalized and stocked with oats, barley, greens, American wheat. He told of still other satellite pictures showing trucks and railroad cars disgorging two or three million metric tons of foodstuffs onto conveyors at each of the shelters, at all thirty-nine of them. Yes, Keegan emphasized, "there was one in each of the thirty-nine cities on which we already had a data base. We would ask the computer: 'Is there a facility that looks like so-and-so-and-so?' The computer would tell you, and then you'd take out some sample photographs," he explained matter-of-factly.

"*That's* the kind of evidence we had," said Keegan, his voice rising with renewed bitterness as the CIA once again came to mind. George Keegan worries about the Russians and deeply mistrusts them. But he despises the CIA. "And to this day, after five studies, the CIA is telling the Congress that it's not quite so," he said in feigned wonder. " 'Yes, there *are* sophisticated structures,' they now admit reluctantly," he said, mimicking the agency, " 'but it doesn't make any difference because none of them will survive a nuclear war.' " Keegan was deeply angry now. The old rage was beginning to well under the hawk's frustration and fatigue. Each word became clipped and articulated with the utmost care. Each word was shaped by profound disgust. "That is total . . . bowdlerized . . . balderdash."

George J. Keegan, Jr., born in Houlton, Maine, on the Fourth of July, is by all odds a brave man. By the time he left the Air Force to enter self-imposed exile just twenty days before Jimmy Carter's inauguration, the tempestuous airman had accumulated more than thirty-four hundred hours of flying time, including fifty-six combat missions against Japan. He is a veteran of six campaigns in World War II—from New Guinea to Okinawa—and holds various medals with clusters for his flying skill. He was also awarded the Distinguished Service Cross by the Republic of Vietnam for planning the defense of Khe Sanh during the Tet offensive in 1968. The evidence suggests that armed combat never fazed Keegan, who went on to graduate from Harvard in 1947 and then built a generally respected reputation within the highest levels of military intelligence as a professional almost without equal in being able to anticipate problems a decade or more ahead of time.

But George Keegan was also to evolve into a political hard-liner who is not easily given to changing his opinion after it has been formed. His detractors—and there are now many of them among the moderates in the U.S. intelligence establishment—maintain that he has an irritating habit of arranging observations to conform to a world view which holds that the Soviet Union is unalterably committed to the destruction of the United States by whatever means possible. And chief among the Kremlin's allies in this endeavor are the unwitting détentenik drones in the State Department and the Central Intelligence Agency.

In order to promote the myth that Moscow will accommodate Washington honestly if only Washington will do the same, Keegan grumbled, it is of the utmost importance that the means by which the U.S.S.R. is perceived be closely controlled: whoever has his fingers around the choke points through which the data flow can control those data as political whim dictates. And that, he contends vehemently, is precisely what the long and often acrimonious competition for control of space reconnaissance has been about.

George Keegan, among others, wants the military services to have decisive control over their own space "assets," as the satellites and related systems are euphemistically called, as well as a primary role in the interpretation and analysis of the "product" those systems gather. Interpretation and analysis of the raw data—determining what's in a given picture or transmission and then trying to divine what it means—can have the most profound effect on what the United States knows about its adversaries' (and allies') military and economic capabilities, and also on whether the various arms control agreements are being observed. The decision-makers at the highest levels of government, including those who sit on the National Security Council, view the world in large measure according to what a huge and staggeringly expensive technical intelligence establishment tells them is out there, beyond the horizon. Who controls that establishment therefore in effect makes policy.

"Are they, or are they not, building submarines secretly?" Keegan wondered aloud. "The judgment I want above all others is that of the foremost submariner in the United States Navy. I want *that* Navy captain evaluating *that* photography and making the primary judgment," he said emphatically. "I *don't* want some GS-16 in CIA who's never been to war, never been to sea, never been on a submarine, and who knows nothing of the [military] operational arts. I don't want that guy to have a monopoly judgment going to the president that says the Soviets are not building submarines."

Control. "Every guy in the CIA on the executive level will fall on his sword on this one—on the absolute need to have total control," Keegan continued. And through control, he went on, reconnaissance is being used to rationalize a serious lack of military preparedness and a potentially perilous lack of assured safety positions in arms control agreements with the Soviet Union. However good U.S. reconnaissance and surveillance systems are, Keegan maintained, there is a negative aspect to them that is deeply dangerous where arms control is concerned. That is the misguided assumption that what *must* be seen *will* be seen. Those who negotiate with the Kremlin in the belief that what needs to be verified can be verified are indulging in baseless optimism at best and willful malfeasance at worst, the former head of Air Force intelligence charged. There are almost endless candidates to fit this description, in Keegan's view, but at that moment he was thinking about one in particular: William E. Colby, who directed the Central Intelligence Agency while Keegan was running Air Force intelligence.

"Now, he's typical of what's happened to the George McGoverns that I can't explain," said Keegan, who seemed genuinely perplexed. He summoned up the name of the former Democratic senator from South Dakota and onetime presidential candidate as a kind of generic model of the war hero who has mysteriously metamorphosed into a disoriented liberal dodo. McGovern flew thirty-five combat missions in bombers with the Fifteenth Air Force in Italy and won the Distinguished Flying Cross for bravery. Keegan returned to the subject of William Colby.

"Here's a liberal," said the airman, taking a long pause between each accolade. "Dyed in the wool ... superb education ... absolutely brave ... Congressional Medal of Honor type* ... performance in World War II was just . . . parachuting behind German lines ... You name it," Keegan said of the man who went on to head the CIA from 1973 to 1976. "The guy has earned the right to wear the medal; a great, great American in the best sense.

---

*Colby did not win the Congressional Medal of Honor. He was in the Office of Strategic Services (OSS) in World War II, parachuting behind occupied French and Norwegian lines. He was awarded the bronze and silver stars and the Croix de Guerre.

"But here's a guy who, over a period of years, I sent the photographs to because his own staff wouldn't show him: of specific Soviet [treaty] violations. I fed him a mountain of hard, incontrovertible evidence, *which he accepted,*" Keegan explained. The pictures embarrassed the CIA and the State Department, he added, because they provided evidence that Moscow was cheating. That, in turn, could only "perturb" arms control negotiations. The intelligence was therefore suppressed.

"Today," said George Keegan with apparent disbelief, "Bill Colby, in the face of all that, gets on the platform with me—we've debated at the Waldorf-Astoria and a number of other places—and says that the Soviets have never violated arms control agreements, that the Soviets were always true to their word!" Colby continues to insist that the United States must have the arms control process and has even called for a freeze on the testing of nuclear weapons, Keegan added disgustedly.

"But he's wrong, he knows he's wrong, and when you get right down to it—and that's on the record—he's *lying*!" The grizzled, aging hawk paused for a moment, there in the cul-de-sac in Oxon Hill, Maryland, a look of bewilderment on his face. "What makes these people do it?" General George J. Keegan wondered. "Is the hope for peace so blinding . . . ?"

William E. Colby returned to Washington from Saigon in the summer of 1971 to make the transition from handling clandestine CIA field operations to becoming the agency's executive director-comptroller (its third-ranking officer, at least on the organization chart). The move amounted to the governmental equivalent of a top salesman's being brought back from the field for promotion to the home office. For Colby, who had studied political science at Princeton, graduated from Columbia Law School, and spent most of his career in intelligence engaged in cloak-and-dagger operations from Scandinavia to Southeast Asia, the job in the home office brought with it a series of revelations, including new management techniques and exposure to other parts of the federal bureaucracy. And there was a great deal more.

"Perhaps the most impressive lesson I learned in the new job was that an incredible revolution in the technology of intelligence had occurred during all those years in which I had been running operations in the jungles of Southeast Asia," he recalled in his memoir.

"I had, of course, been aware of the wonder of the U-2 spy plane, if for no other reason than its noisy downing in Russia in 1960 and the vital role it had played in the Cuban missile crisis. But during my orientation briefings for my new post in the fall of 1971, I went on a tour of the aerospace technology factories on the West Coast and there had my eyes opened to the veritable science-fiction world of space systems, radar, electronic sensors, infrared photography, and the ubiquitous computer, all able to gather intelligence from high in the sky to deep in the ocean with astounding accuracy and precision."

Colby found himself dazzled, he recalled, by a reconnaissance system that could produce "exquisitely detailed" reports of secret experiments and tests undertaken at remote locations in Asia, of barracks and truck parks in Eastern Europe, and of many other scientific and military goings-on that allowed analysts in Washington to maintain a "stunningly accurate reading of foreign military forces." He went on to describe his amazement when shown electronic systems that provided highly detailed data on existing and experimental missiles and airplanes, on the volume and pattern of communications of Soviet and other nations' offensive and defensive forces, and, perhaps most impressive of all, even on political and social events in the "hard target" areas. Colby expressed particular amazement at the massive data banks that shuffled the secret intelligence "take" with openly available information like a deck of several billion cards to produce extraordinary tableaux showing what the opposition was up to.

"It is impossible to overstate the importance of these astonishing technological advances. They were not just bigger and better toys for spies but the instruments of a profound change in the profession of intelligence, adding immeasurably to the volume of available information from which wise assessments could be made," he observed.

In his memoir, Colby also made passing reference to the new technology's having forced the various parts of the intelligence community to work more closely together. "It would have been grossly wasteful, if not in fact impossible, for each intelligence service to have, for example, its own costly space system. One for any particular job obviously was enough so long as the information it gathered was effectively distributed to all the services. But which service should have it under its control? This question," William

Colby noted in passing, "was a subject of constant debate with every new technological advance." As will be seen, "debate" isn't the word for it.

Colby became director of Central Intelligence (DCI)* in 1973, even as Vietnam war protesters were nailing up posters in Washington that depicted a sinister likeness of him above a skull and cross-bones and called him a "murderer" and war criminal for his role in overseeing Operation Phoenix, in which about twenty thousand Vietcong suspects were killed in an effort to positively identify them so they could be either recruited to work for Saigon or thrown in prison. He spent a great deal of time during the next two tumultuous years embroiled with House and Senate select committees on intelligence and with the Justice Department, each of them digging into actual or merely alleged CIA abuses overseas and at home involving the war protesters and the Watergate break-in. Gerald Ford finally responded to the heat in the time-honored way of politicians who need to have things cooled off. He sacked his director of Central Intelligence in early November 1975 and then, just before Colby cleaned out his desk to make way for George Bush, pinned the National Security Medal on him.

Eight years later William Egan Colby, at age sixty-four, was still in Washington, like so many of his colleagues who had also parted from the agency or the Defense Department. He now worked for International Business Government Counsellors, a consulting firm with a suitably ambiguous name, which occupied a suite on the seventh floor of a building at 16th and I streets, N.W. He was still the traditional "gray man," as he had been called, who is "so inconspicuous that he can never catch the waiter's eye in a restaurant."

One afternoon in April 1984 Colby sat in his office and mused about reconnaissance, surveillance, and arms control, much as George Keegan had. The office was not a twenty-minute drive from Keegan's home, though in view of the conversation taking place in it, it might as well have been on Jupiter. The former head of Central Intelligence, wiry and athletic-looking, wore a conservatively cut tan suit, white button-down oxford shirt, and a modestly patterned

---

*The title makes its holder not only the director of the CIA but also the head of all of the nation's foreign intelligence collection organizations, including the National Security Agency, Defense Intelligence Agency, and the various military security bodies. As any number of DCIs have discovered, however, maintaining authority over all of the competing fiefdoms has proved to be virtually impossible.

maroon tie. His eyes, framed by ordinary translucent plastic glasses, were pale blue and gave the impression of being almost opaque: they seemed to take in a great deal while resisting penetration.

"If you look at the way we do our normal intelligence work today on matters that are not controlled," Colby said in reference to all intelligence collected by reconnaissance over the Soviet Union, and not just to data relevant to arms control, "I think you'd have to say that the last strategic surprise we had was Sputnik in 1958.* We haven't had a strategic surprise in hardware since that time." He made the further point that U.S. space reconnaissance and its related ground and sea systems are easily good enough to monitor a freeze on nuclear weapons testing by both of the superpowers. Colby is an outspoken advocate of such a freeze.

"What I'm participating in is the debate as to whether we should go for a nuclear freeze, and I hasten to say that my position is very clear. We *could* verify a substantial arms control treaty, or a freeze, or whatever, *if* you look at what verification is really about. Now, if you focus on whether you can identify the last quarter inch of the fin on some missile, and you think that's verification, then you're wrong," Colby said emphatically. "Verification is nothing more than the continuation of our normal intelligence process. We're going to cover Soviet weaponry whether there's a treaty between us or not; we have to in order to protect our country against surprise.

"Overhead reconnaissance has hugely increased our total fund of knowledge of the world," Colby added. "It's opened up areas that were totally forbidden. We can look down into the test center and see some test going on of some device that isn't going to be operational for five years, and we can tell quite a lot about it, and watch how it's doing. That's what this technology has given us: an enormous increase in our total knowledge.

"The Defense Department issued a booklet a couple of days ago: *Soviet Military Power.* † You'll find in there detailed descriptions of

---

*The satellite to which he apparently referred, Sputnik 1, was launched on October 4, 1957. Herbert Scoville, Jr., who was the CIA's assistant director for scientific intelligence from the late 1950s through 1961, and who in that capacity was responsible for selecting targets for coverage by the U-2 aircraft and Discoverer reconnaissance satellites, maintained that Sputnik's inaugural flight was no surprise at all. Scoville claimed that his office predicted Sputnik's launch a year before it occurred and even estimated the political consequences. "Nobody paid attention," he said. "It was a good example of the right kind of intelligence being ignored."
†The periodical, first released by the Pentagon in September 1981, had grown to 156 pages in its 1986 edition.

Soviet weapons systems, forces, and all the rest of it, much of which is nonverifiable in a precise, exact sense," Colby added as a preface to again returning to arms control. "But you'll find in there an estimate of the number of Soviet tanks in Europe. Now, you can hide them under barns, can't you? You could hide them so there could be ten more. But we came up with a perfectly adequate estimate for our defense planning on the number of tanks because we had to do that. And we gather that information by the process of central intelligence, which means bringing all the indicators to- gether and then making an informed estimate. A treaty makes all this easier because it has provisions which ease the process of moni- toring: nonconcealment, notification of tests, declaration of forces —a whole variety of things—that are designed to make that moni- toring process easier.

"What is the purpose of verification? Is it to prove a breach of contract, or is it to protect our country?" Colby asked. "I think it's to protect our country," he said, warming to the subject. "If they have twenty-five thousand nuclear weapons, and they make five more, is that going to hurt our country? No," the Columbia-trained lawyer answered himself without giving his interviewer a chance to speak. "It's a marginal violation. There are all sorts of potential violations. There are traffic-ticket-level ones. There are misdemean- ors. There are felonies. And there are capital crimes. You have to think in terms of the violation and what threat that violation poses to our country."

As William Colby went on about the need for verifiable arms control and the system that he steadfastly maintained can guarantee it, he became more animated, his voice more imploring. "You get back to the fundamental question: Is the treaty and the restraints it will impose on Soviet behavior going to do more to protect our safety than continuing the present arms race? I think that in most cases, at the risk of a marginal violation, the answer's obvious. A marginal violation would not be strategically significant. We are debating today whether that radar out in Siberia is a technical viola- tion or not. But that radar is not part of a nationwide scheme that stops our missiles. We caught it at the earliest stages and we're debating it and arguing about it long before it becomes a strategic factor in our relations with the Soviets."

The radar to which Colby referred has itself become a cause célèbre in the arms control debate since its discovery was made public in the summer of 1983. The giant radar, still under construc-

tion at Abalakova in south-central Siberia, was interpreted as having
been designed for use in an ABM defense system. The Kremlin has
maintained that the radar is intended solely to track objects in space.
But its location, near SS-11 and SS-18 ICBM silo complexes, has
only further convinced opponents of arms control that the Russians
willfully disregard treaties when they believe it is in their best
interest to do so. The ABM treaty of 1972 prohibits construction of
such radars except along borders, where they may be pointed only
outward. Not many arms control proponents dispute the nature of
the radar. They contend, however, that it was picked up by reconnaissance satellites long before it could be completed, let alone
turned on, and that amounts to convincing evidence that U.S. strategic reconnaissance, including the various space systems, are up to
monitoring compliance. Opponents of arms control counter by
pointing out that the huge device had been under construction for
more than a year before it was spotted, indicating that space reconnaissance cannot be relied upon to keep up with such developments.
Proponents rebut by maintaining that construction was under observation practically from its beginning, but that it simply took time
before the radar's shape, power supply system, and other characteristics could be definitively established, and so on.

George Keegan and William Colby have a great deal in common.
Both devoted long years in the service of their country, occasionally
risking their lives to do so. Both are educated, thoughtful, and
articulate. Both are unquestionably patriotic in the generally accepted sense of the word. Both spent years immersed in different
parts of the same intelligence stream, being briefed by many of the
same interpreters, poring over many of the same reports and estimates, dealing with the same technical collection systems, meeting
with the same colleagues from other intelligence services, agencies,
or departments, and looking at the same pictures.
   Yet for all that, they could not be more dissimilar in political
outlook or in the way their world view influences their attitudes
concerning the intelligence from space and what that intelligence
portends. Colby, for example, does not even recall seeing the imagery of fallout shelters along the Moscow beltway that so disturbs
Keegan. Yet he dismisses it out of hand. The leaders in the Kremlin
hold no hope whatever that such shelters would make an appreciable
difference in an all-out war, Colby maintained, but there were

nonetheless highly pragmatic reasons for building them. Because the country was invaded by Mongols, Teutons, Napoleon, and the Third Reich (the last with devastating destruction), the presence of shelters, complete with food, water, and clothing, gives a sense of security to the people, according to Colby. In addition, merely constructing the shelters was a useful exercise in promoting discipline and therefore in maintaining social order and cohesion. The motivations for building the immense bunkers are therefore valid, Colby observed, but they have little or nothing to do with a belief that the structures will make a real difference in the event of nuclear war.

Both men agree that U.S. reconnaissance systems are very good. But they profoundly disagree as to what they are good for. It is imperative to find out because George Keegan and William Colby speak for many in the debate over whether the system is up to the tasks of providing adequate intelligence to maintain effective U.S. military strength while also monitoring arms control agreements. Their conflicting views about the same system also speaks to how that system can be politicized and, most dangerously, how it can be made to find only what those who control it want it to find and nothing more.

The system is many systems, most of which overlap, and all of which collectively produce something called TECHINT, which stands for technical intelligence. The other kind is known as HU-MINT, or human intelligence, and it has to do with the more traditional methods of espionage that involve people photographing documents, hiding microfilm in pumpkins and garbage bags, and so forth. As is the case with everything relating to strategic intelligence, TECHINT and HUMINT are often used together as part of one process. In testimony before the Senate in 1979, Secretary of Defense Harold Brown said that the U.S. intelligence community knew of four ICBM design bureaus in the Soviet Union and that it monitored the "nature of the projects and the technologies pursued" at those bureaus. This suggests—and it has been mentioned by others in a position to know—that information relating to Soviet ballistic missile design is gathered while it is still on the drawing boards (and in some cases even before it is placed on the drawing boards) and passed out of the country. This hints at an espionage apparatus inside the U.S.S.R. that is extremely effective and is the very blackest of all black operations conducted by U.S. intelligence. Once the missile's components have been built and brought together for assembly into a finished weapon that can be tested, the TECHINT systems are turned on. Similarly, terrorist deployment sites, staging areas, and training centers in North Africa and the Middle East are routinely scrutinized by U.S. reconnaissance satellites, but usually only after informants have pinpointed their locations, according to one highly knowledgeable source. It is those systems, not the "spooks" who supply HUMINT, that are the subject of this book.

TECHINT, in turn, comprises several other INTs* which have to do with the kind of information that is gathered, not with the system that does the gathering. SIGINT, which stands for signals intelligence, is a major subsystem that itself divides into COMINT (communications intelligence), which has to do with intercepting messages of one sort or another, ELINT (electronic intelligence), which concerns such noncommunication electronic signals as radar jammers, and TELINT (telemetry intelligence), which entails listening to the telemetry, or data, transmitted by missiles during testing. The other major system is sometimes called PHOTINT, or photographic intelligence, but since standard photography has in most cases given way to digitally transmitted electro-optical systems, the aircraft and satellites that take pictures are lumped into a broad category that is known simply as "imaging." Finally, there is RADINT, which in one intelligence service may mean the gathering of intelligence about radar, while in another it may mean the use of radar to gather intelligence. Given the fabulous cost of building and flying intelligence-gathering planes and satellites (which are collectively called "platforms" or "assets" by their users), it is customary to send more than one system up at the same time. Although KH-11 reconnaissance satellites are primarily imaging platforms, for example, they also carry COMINT antennas and related equipment so they can eavesdrop on communication activity as they pass over their targets.

The aircraft and satellites are both known as "overhead" reconnaissance systems (the term "aerial reconnaissance" was largely abandoned with the advent of satellites, which do not fly through air), and they span the globe in a never-ending search for bits and

*The acronyms are defined on page 351.

pieces of information that can be fitted into the national foreign intelligence mosaic.

Of the planes, there are the lumbering, dependable EC-135s and RC-135s, the venerable U-2s and their TR-1 derivatives, and the blisteringly fast SR-71s. The EC-135s and RC-135s, which are military versions of Boeing's 707 airliner, prowl just off the Siberian coast, over the Barents Sea, and elsewhere along the Soviet frontier, soaking up communication signals, radar emissions, and missile test telemetry. One of these planes, based at Shemya Island in the Aleutians, was in the vicinity of the Korean Air Lines 747 the night it was shot down in September 1983. It had been sent there to gather telemetry from a scheduled Soviet ballistic missile test. The graceful midnight-black U-2s, with their long, tapering wings and unpretentious engines, soar fifteen miles high as their cameras record the activity of those far below who can neither see nor hear them. And there are the sleek, manta-shaped SR-71s, popularly known as Blackbirds, which can fly at four times the speed of sound—faster than the proverbial speeding bullet—and photograph up to one hundred thousand square miles an hour from altitudes well above one hundred thousand feet.

The satellites are even more diverse. There have been low earth orbiters that could take standard photographs and then send them down in capsules whose parachutes were snared in midair by aircraft trailing special cables, and others that image in "real time"— as the action is taking place—and send what they see by simultaneous digital transmission. Above them, in the intermediate orbits between one thousand and ten thousand miles, still other space platforms "ferret" Soviet, Chinese, and other nations' radars, making highly detailed measurements of their frequencies, ranges, power levels, and other operational characteristics. There are ocean reconnaissance satellites that travel in groups and follow the movement of foreign naval vessels. Still higher, along the 22,300-mile-high orbit known as geosynchronous because satellites sent there move in time with the earth to remain over fixed spots, there are still other spacecraft that monitor missile telemetry and intercept communication traffic, including microwave telephone conversations. Some satellites parked on this orbit use infrared sensors to watch for the telltale heat blasts that would signal a missile attack, while others are used to relay data from their intelligence-gathering cousins. Beyond geosynchronous, at sixty thousand miles—about a quarter of the way to the moon—aged U.S. spacecraft named Vela stare down and register each double flash that signals a thermonuclear explosion. There are even satellites that travel in highly elliptical orbits disguised as data transmission types, but which really take the pulse of Soviet ABM radars so they can be nullified in the event of war.

When the people involved in technical intelligence collection refer to particular systems, they rarely mean only a type of aircraft or satellite. Space reconnaissance systems are wholly dependent on a vast network of ground facilities that, like the platforms themselves, span the globe. Spacecraft, and particularly those in low orbit, tend to become disoriented and wander unless they are cared for by people on the ground. They require a variety of in-orbit maintenance operations, known as "housekeeping," in order to function properly. They must also be tracked so their whereabouts are always known and "uplinked" and "downlinked" in order that instructions can be sent up to them and they can, in turn, send their intelligence take down where it can be used.

Accordingly, there are U.S. reconnaissance and surveillance aircraft and satellite-related facilities in the District of Columbia and in several states—notably, Alaska, California (where the spacecraft are made), Colorado, Hawaii, Maryland, North Carolina, and Virginia—and in a number of other nations, including Australia, Great Britain, Norway, and Turkey. The KH-11, to take that example again, is therefore more than a type of satellite: it is the entire system in which the satellite functions, including the specialized facility at Fort Belvoir, Virginia, where the spacecraft's imagery is sent.

The cost of all this as it now exists is incalculable. That is partly because some of the people and equipment are used for purposes other than reconnaissance, partly because research and development programs that did not have reconnaissance requirements as a goal have contributed hardware to it, and partly because many of the system's costs have been so well camouflaged over the years due to its black nature that no one knows where to find them. What is currently in place is easily worth more than $100 billion, however.

The data from this immense system arrive in torrents every day. There is so much of it, mostly routine, that great quantities have to be stored without analysis. Imagery judged to be important and which has been specially requested, or "tasked," receives priority attention from the photo interpreters in the National Photographic Interpretation Center in Washington and from whichever intelligence agency or branch is designated to perform other analysis. The National Security Agency, or SIGINT City, as it is sometimes called, at Fort George C. Meade in Maryland does the same with intercepted signals intelligence.

The giant computers at the National Photographic Interpretation Center, or NPIC (En-pick), constitute an enormous data bank for the storage of millions upon millions of bits of imagery that can be called up to assemble the sort of composite picture George Keegan had in mind when he talked about fallout shelters in the U.S.S.R. Similarly, the digital system can be made to display highway, railroad, or canal networks, missile silos, air bases, grain storage facilities, bridges of various sizes, weapons factories of one sort or another, nuclear reprocessing plants, and everything else that is considered by the national intelligence establishment to be of immediate or potential interest. Images are stored in the massive data banks so that they can be compared with newer ones, because being able to discern and measure change is an essential part of the technical intelligence professional's stock-in-trade. The picture of a railroad spur where there was none before can speak volumes.

Overhead reconnaissance and surveillance mechanisms and those who operate them are charged with three basic responsibilities. They are supposed to discover and keep track of every military and economic development throughout the world that can impact in one degree or another upon the United States and its allies. This obviously includes the development of new military equipment and the whereabouts of the opposition's army and navy. But it also has to do with maintaining an accurate inventory of foreign agricultural and industrial levels, oil and gas production, and other economic factors that could have an important effect on a particular nation's status. Second, the air and space systems, together with others on the ground (and under it) and on the high seas, constitute the nation's so-called national technical means (NTM) of arms control verification. They are deemed to be so important in the arms control process that interfering with them is specifically prohibited by each treaty. Finally, the systems act as a kind of alarm that is supposed to go off when any of many indicators signaling a possible attack against the United States or any of its allies is observed. The sudden movement of scores of Soviet ballistic missile submarines from their berths at Severomorsk and elsewhere into the North Atlantic would be one such indicator. Taken by itself, the mass sailing might be interpreted as nothing more than a large-scale exercise. It would cause great concern in the National Security Council, however, if it coincided with such other indicators as Russians heading for their fallout shelters and the country's ballistic missile and bomber forces going on full alert.

The opposition's possession of accurate information regarding the true extent and full capability of this vast and intricate system, much of which has been engineered to be redundant for multiple coverage and backup capacity in case one element malfunctions, would amount to a decisive intelligence coup for the opposition and most probably a severe, if not fatal, loss for the West. U.S. intelligence would be practically deaf, dumb, and blind, and the nation would be commensurately vulnerable.

It is for this reason that the system that does all of this watching and listening is so pervasively secret—so black—that no individual, including the chairman of the Joint Chiefs of Staff and the director of Central Intelligence, knows all of its hidden parts, the products they collect, or the real extent of the widely dispersed and deeply buried budget that keeps the entire operation functioning. The system's operators, technicians, and taskmasters inhabit a carefully encapsulated netherworld whose provinces are identified by acronym, whose secrets are shared only by the relatively few having one or more special clearances, and whose existence is publicly either played down or denied outright.

The provinces are, or have been, named the Committee on Imagery Requirements and Exploitation (COMIREX), Committee on Overhead Reconnaissance (COMOR), Defense Special Missile and Astronautics Center (DEFSMAC), Intelligence Producers Council (IPC), Joint Reconnaissance Center (JRC), Naval Reconnaissance Center (NRC), National Intelligence Council (NIC), National Foreign Intelligence Board (NFIB), National Foreign Intelligence Council (NFIC), National Reconnaissance Office (NRO), and the Weapons and Space Systems Intelligence Committee (WSSIC), among others.

Those engaged in U.S. space reconnaissance and related aeronautical activities work in a Byzantine world that is carefully ordered by a security system known as Sensitive Compartmented Information, or SCI. The reconnaissance establishment uses no daggers, of course, but its cloak is large and black. Compartmented intelligence became institutionalized during World War II, when the United

States and Great Britain broke the Axis codes. Words such as MAGIC, ULTRA, PEARL, and THUMB were used to denote particularly sensitive intelligence, and access to it was tightly restricted by category. SCI functions on the theory that damaging security leaks can be kept to a minimum if those in the system know only what they need to know in order to perform their jobs. Security people are always talking about the "need to know." Compartmentalizing information is the way they restrict what is known. SCI, then, is supposed to do for national security what the watertight doors do on a naval vessel: limit the amount of water entering the ship to a single compartment rather than allowing the entire hull to be flooded.

There are at present more than thirty SCI categories used by the U.S. intelligence community, three of which pertain directly to technical intelligence collection: Special Intelligence (SI), Talent-Keyhole (TK), and Byeman. Special Intelligence and Talent-Keyhole concern data that are the product of signals intelligence collection and/or overhead reconnaissance. Talent-Keyhole, by itself, relates strictly to information obtained by overhead reconnaissance, by both airplanes and satellites. SI and TK clearances are almost always given jointly, however. They allow their holders access to the product of particular overhead reconnaissance systems, but not automatic access to details about the collection systems themselves. Thus interpreters in the National Security Agency, the National Photographic Interpretation Center, and the CIA, for example, have SI-TK clearances that permit them to hear taped intercepts or to study imagery, but they are not supposed to know how the planes and satellites that do the collecting work, or even their names, because they do not need to know.

Clearances for access to information about the collection platforms themselves are given on a system-by-system basis within the Byeman compartment—again, based on who needs to know what. Byeman is itself compartmentalized according to the particular type of plane or satellite. When they were fully classified, for instance, the U-2's Byeman code name was Idealist, while the SR-71's was Oxcart. Reconnaissance satellites carry, or have carried, such Byeman code names as Corona, Argus, Aquacade, Rhyolite, Chalet, Magnum, Vortex, Indigo, and Jumpseat. Some of these names have been changed after being made public.

All imaging reconnaissance, whether by plane or satellite, comes under the rubric of a program called Keyhole, which is further divided, according to branch of service and specific type of mission: Air Force imaging reconnaissance, for example, is designated Senior Keyhole. Such satellites carry Keyhole, or simply KH, numbers: KH-7, KH-8, KH-9, KH-11, and KH-12 (there was a planned satellite designated KH-10, but it was superseded so quickly by the KH-11 that it never made it off the drawing board). And each Keyhole satellite, in turn, not only has its own Byeman code name but a separate number as well. This compartmentalizes the system even more, according to who designs them and their components, who builds them, who operates them, and who actually receives the data as they come down. Some people with SCI clearances therefore know the KH-11 only as the KH-11. Others know it only by its Byeman code name, which is Kennan. Still others know it only as part of a series of satellites that are numbered 5500. Anyone having clearance for the last designator would know at a glance what 5504 means: 5000 is the number that refers to imaging satellites; 500 means that it is a KH-11; and the final digit tells which particular KH-11 it is (5504 was launched from Vandenberg Air Force Base in California on September 3, 1981). Similarly, all 7000 series satellites are dedicated primarily to gathering signals intelligence (SIGINT). The designator 7500 refers to a SIGINT satellite that gathers electronic intelligence (ELINT), while 7600 is carried by Rhyolite, a spacecraft that collects telemetry intelligence (TELINT). The Rhyolite that was orbited on the night of April 8, 1978, then, would have been 7605, or the fifth in that series.

This is not to say that SCI is foolproof. Far from it. As Robert Lindsey has noted, Christopher Boyce's successively higher security clearances for work in TRW's Rhyolite program were granted almost whimsically, and security breaches in the plant's supersecret Black Vault were commonplace. Less than a year after the first KH-11 went into orbit, William Kampiles, a watch officer at the CIA's Operations Center, sold a copy of its technical manual to the KGB for three thousand dollars. Dr. Leslie Dirks, whose Directorate for Science and Technology helped develop the satellite for the CIA, later bemoaned the fact that the manual contained the KH-11's "characteristics, capabilities and limitations . . . describes the process of photography employed and illustrates the quality of photos and the process used in passing the product along to users of the system . . . and describes the limitation in geographic coverage." No one believes that such disclosures are wholly preventable, but those involved in the highest levels of space reconnaissance think that SCI at least limits the amount of damage that can be done. How much it does so is a matter of some conjecture.

The technology of the machines that watch and listen from the edge of space and beyond has become extraordinary. And as William Colby has observed, that technology "is accelerating, not merely growing." Yet it is the political dimension of this high-tech black art that remains its most fascinating aspect.

At its narrowest, the politics of space reconnaissance—its control and use—has occasionally degenerated into squalid contests over turf as one bureaucrat or another, in uniform and out of it, tried to expand his roost's influence on U.S. foreign relations with the basest of motives. At its grandest, the system has fostered temperance among nations that possess an unprecedented capacity for destruction, and on at least one occasion, the Cuban missile crisis, almost certainly averted catastrophe. With it all, space reconnaissance is every bit the immense source of power and control that General Keegan said it is, and it is becoming more so as its technology continues to be extended both qualitatively and quantitatively. Perhaps the best way to express this is by updating a dictum pronounced in 1919 (with apologies to Sir Halford Mackinder):

Who controls reconnaissance watches the enemy;
Who watches the enemy perceives the threat;
Who perceives the threat shapes the alternatives;
Who shapes the alternatives determines the response.*

*Mackinder postulated the notion that whoever controlled Eastern Europe would control the Eurasian "heartland," and therefore the "World Island," consisting of Europe, Asia and Africa. Control of that, he maintained, meant control of the world. The idea was given a certain amount of credence at the time.

2 .

Denied Territory

●━━━━━━━━━━━━━━━━━━━━━━━━━━━━

On the afternoon of May 26, 1940, Antoine de Saint-Exupéry, a captain in the French Air Force's Group 2-33, was ordered to fly a reconnaissance mission from his unit's temporary base at Laon, a town in the heart of the department of Aisne, to the city of Arras, a little more than sixty miles to the northeast.

The German army, which had smashed through the Maginot Line less than two weeks earlier, was advancing on the city Saint-Exupéry was supposed to reconnoiter. Arras's defenders needed to know the enemy's strength and whereabouts, the aviator was led to understand, so it was up to him, a photographer named Dutertre, and a gunner to fly to the burning city and find out. That dangerous and futile mission (the Third Republic was at the moment being overrun by German panzers and already had virtually collapsed) was immortalized by Saint-Exupéry in his *Flight to Arras*, which describes an attempt to gather intelligence from the air in murderous circumstances because the French generals were blind without it ("The Staffs appeal to us as if we were a tribe of fortune-tellers," Saint-Exupéry lamented in the way of reconnaissance pilots the world over).

"172°."
"Right! 172°."
Call it one seventy-two. Epitaph: "Maintained his course accu-

rately on 172°." How long will this crazy challenge go on? I am
flying now at two thousand three hundred feet beneath a ceiling
of heavy clouds. If I were to rise a mere hundred feet Dutertre
would be blind. Thus we are forced to remain visible to the
anti-aircraft batteries and play the part of the archer's target for
the Germans. Two thousand feet is a forbidden altitude. Your
machine serves as a mark for the whole plain. You drain the
cannonade of a whole army. You are within range of every caliber. You dwell an eternity in the field of fire of each successive
weapon. You are not shot at with cannon but beaten with a stick.
It is as if a thousand sticks were used to bring down a single
walnut.

The dread of antiaircraft fire is well known to reconnaissance
pilots, who often have to hold their aircraft absolutely steady and in
a straight line in order to get their photographs, and in the process
offer themselves as relatively easy targets. Francis Gary Powers's
U-2 was knocked out of the sky by a surface-to-air missile high over
Sverdlovsk almost exactly twenty years later as he flew straight and
level while the plane's camera clicked away. But for Saint-Exupéry
it was fighters, not guns on the ground, that evoked the deepest
dread. The fighters thrive where the reconnaissance planes are so
vulnerable.

The fighters come down on you like lightning. Having spotted
you from fifteen hundred feet above, they take their time. They
weave, they orient themselves, take careful aim. You know nothing of this. You are the mouse lying in the shadow of the bird of
prey. The mouse fancies that it is alive. It goes on frisking in the
wheat. But already it is the prisoner of the retina of the hawk,
glued tighter to that retina than to any glue, for the hawk will
never leave it now.
    And thus you, continuing to pilot, to daydream, to scan the
earth, have already been flung outside the dimension of time
because of a tiny black dot on the retina of a man.
    The nine planes of the German fighter group will drop like
plummets in their own good time. They are in no hurry. At five
hundred and fifty miles an hour they will fire their prodigious
harpoon that never misses its prey. A bombing squadron possesses
enough fire power to offer a chance for defense; but a reconnaissance crew, alone in the wide sky, has no chance against the

seventy-two machine guns that first make themselves known to it by the luminous spray of their bullets. At the very instant when you first learn of its existence, the fighter, having spat forth its venom like a cobra, is already neutral and inaccessible, swaying to and fro overhead.

In describing this rather typical wartime mission, Saint-Exupéry immortalized all reconnaissance crews whose seemingly inglorious, but often crucial, task it is to return not with spent ammunition canisters, empty bomb racks, and tales of inflicted destruction, but with the most precious of all military commodities: information about the enemy. The perils of the reconnaissance sortie were well known to such aviators as Manfred von Richthofen, who flew two decades before Saint-Exupéry, and Francis Gary Powers, who came two decades after him (both the Red Baron and Powers flew intelligence-gathering missions against Russia and narrowly survived to tell about them). Even today's orbiting reconnaissance robots have been targeted for attack by anti-satellite weapons whose assignment would be to "kill" them before they can send back meaningful information in time of war.

The idea of getting high enough for a good view of the enemy has always been irresistible. Military commanders have therefore sent observers into the sky in a variety of contraptions for centuries so they could spy on the opposition. Chinese and Japanese folklore mention the use of spotters who either went up in baskets suspended from giant kites or else were strapped right onto them. France is credited with being the first Western nation to use aerial reconnaissance. It organized a company of *aérostiers* in April 1794, during the revolutionary wars, and is said to have kept one balloon aloft for nine hours while the group's daring commander, Colonel Jean Marie Joseph Coutelle, made continuous observations during the battle at Fleurus in Belgium. Napoleon used a company of *aérostiers* in the siege of Mantua in 1797 and the following year took a balloon corps on his expedition to Egypt. This time, though, the balloonists saw no action. They were disbanded in 1800 for reasons that remain unclear.

The invention of the photographic camera in the late 1820s opened new possibilities for aerial reconnaissance because it promised to provide tacticians on the ground with detailed photographs they could study, rather than with impressionistic sketches or oral descriptions of what was happening beyond their line of sight. It was not until 1860, however, that the two infant technologies were married in the United States. On October 13 of that year, Samuel A. King and James W. Black took the first American aerial photograph when they shot South Boston from the basket of the balloon *Queen of the Air* at an altitude of twelve hundred feet.

On April 20, 1861, Thaddeus S. C. Lowe, a New Hampshire meteorologist, took off from Cincinnati in a balloon in order to make weather observations. But the hapless Yankee was soon carried by high winds to South Carolina, where he was promptly arrested as a Union spy. Lowe was released after he convinced his captors that he had been conducting legitimate scientific experiments, but at some point in the adventure he apparently became convinced that tethered balloons would make excellent platforms from which to observe Confederate positions. He therefore arranged a demonstration ascent for President Lincoln on June 18, during which he managed to send the first air-to-ground telegraph message. The president was sufficiently impressed to authorize the creation of an Army Balloon Corps with "Professor" Lowe in command.

Cameras and hydrogen balloons did not prove to be compatible. Balloon baskets were relatively small and the cameras of the day were large and bulky. Furthermore, they used glass plates that had to be coated with a light-sensitive emulsion in the field and then quickly used. In addition, the photographs had to be developed soon after being taken or their image would fade. Since it was impractical to repeatedly send up and then pull down the large balloons, there was little aerial photography of battlefields during the war. Instead, Lowe depended upon the human eye and the sketch pad. On December 8, 1861, one of his balloons, tethered where General Joseph Hooker's troops were on the Maryland side of the Potomac, was used by a Union officer to make accurate sketches of rebel infantry camps and artillery batteries on the Virginia side of the river.

The following May the new reconnaissance unit, with Professor Lowe as its "chief aeronaut," went into action with General George McClellan's Army of the Potomac as it advanced on Richmond. The Balloon Corps consisted of Lowe, a captain, fifty noncommissioned officers and privates, two generators drawn by four horses each, and a sulfuric acid wagon pulled by two more horses. The hydrogen used to inflate the balloons was made by combining the sulfuric acid with scrap metal that was gathered along the route of march. After a balloon had been filled with the light gas, the Union Army's chief aeronaut, standing precariously in a red, white, and blue box-shaped basket whose sides were only about two and a half feet high and perhaps three wide, would rise slowly to about a thousand feet as four groups of NCOs and privates let out the balloon's lines a little at a time. From his elevated vantage point, about a mile behind the front lines, Lowe could watch the enemy with little fear of either being hit by hostile fire or being overrun.

The professor maintained that the observations he made at the Battle of Fair Oaks barely averted a Union defeat. That may be so. On the whole, however, the effectiveness of balloon reconnaissance during the Civil War seems to have been marginal at best. During the last week of May 1862, for example, McClellan's hundred thousand men were poised along the Chickahominy River only seven miles from Richmond and required accurate intelligence about the Confederate deployment. Yet one Union captain was to recount the following November that Lowe's reports were too ambiguous to be worth much, that encampments and fortifications could be seen plainly enough but the number of soldiers protecting them could not be determined because of distance and foliage cover. Since other Union generals showed little or no interest in balloon reconnaissance, the North deactivated its air force in 1863, though not before Mathew Brady had taken many fine photographs of it as part of his pioneering war coverage.

Serious experiments with airborne cameras were well under way by the end of the century. The British conducted balloon photography at Woolwich Arsenal, not far from London, throughout the 1870s and 1880s. One imaginative method involved the use of eight cameras arranged around the periphery of a balloon's basket, resulting in panoramic pictures of the surrounding terrain.

Kites carrying remotely controlled or timed-release cameras were used by both the U.S. and British armies in the waning years of the nineteenth century and even into the twentieth because they were less expensive than balloons, easier to transport, and less apt to be put out of action when hit by enemy fire. Their glaring disadvantage, of course, had to do with the fact that they would not go up without wind. Some kites carried cameras whose shutters were snapped by an electrical impulse coming through wires running to the ground, while others used ordinary fuses or clock mechanisms. By 1895 the U.S. Army's 9th Infantry Regiment, based in the Madison Barracks on New York's Governors Island, was using seventeen- by sixteen-foot versions of the ordinary "plane-surface" or "two-stick" diamond-shaped kites sold almost everywhere. Once one of the huge kites was in the air, a box camera was sent up the restraining line. It was then triggered either by a timer or by pulling a second line, after which it was made to slide back down the tether so its film could be taken out and processed. Aerial reconnaissance of this sort is supposed to have been used in Puerto Rico during the Spanish-American War.

No doubt the most bizarre aerial photography technique involved the use of pigeons. Visitors to the International Photographic Exhibition in Dresden in 1909 could buy picture postcards of the fair taken by pigeons. The birds would flap over the exhibition area with two-and-a-half-ounce cameras strapped to their breasts, taking automatically timed photographs every thirty seconds of the goings-on below. The exposed film was then hastily developed and turned into postcards by Julius Neubronner, who had patented the pigeon camera in 1903. Neubronner understood that since homing pigeons could fly over great distances relatively quickly, cameras that were attached to them and were timed to shoot at carefully determined locations had some military value, at least in theory. Nothing seems to have come of pigeon reconnaissance, however.

Although balloons carrying men were used for aerial photography as soon as cameras were made smaller and easier to operate (Washington was photographed with impressive clarity from a high-flying balloon in 1907 and the Army had a balloon unit stationed at Fort Myer, Virginia, the following year), it was the airplane that really got reconnaissance off the ground in every sense of the phrase. Military establishments in the United States and in Europe were quick to understand that airplanes added two incalculably important dimensions to aerial reconnaissance: speed and range. Airplanes, which did not have to be held captive by restraining ropes, could go virtually anywhere in search of information and then get back speedily. This was seen for what it was almost from the very beginning: a military weapon of staggering value. It took time for airplanes to be produced and distributed, but once that had been done, their adaptation to reconnaissance was swift and apparently unquestioned.

In January 1911, barely seven years after the Wright brothers' inaugural flight, the first American photograph from an airplane was taken of the San Diego waterfront by someone on a Curtiss hydroplane. That same year the U.S. Army Signal Corps opened a flight training school at College Park, Maryland, and at the outset put aerial photography on the curriculum.

The airplane's debut in war also came in 1911, when an Italian reconnaissance flight was used to make observations of Turkish positions during Italy's attempt to gain a foothold in North Africa by invading Tripolitana. Both visual and photoreconnaissance missions were flown by the U.S. Army between 1913 and 1915 in the Philippines and along the Mexican border. In the spring of 1915, in fact, reconnaissance aircraft supported General John J. Pershing in his pursuit of Pancho Villa along the Rio Grande. By the eve of World War I airplanes had so established themselves in reconnaissance, an activity traditionally undertaken by cavalry, that air units were even given cavalry names: squadrons.

The Royal Flying Corps's No. 3 Squadron began extensive experiments with aerial photography in 1914, though government funds were so short that the British aircrews had to use their own cameras, and finally devised one that remained in use during the first year of the war. They were also mindful of the need to get the information they carried to the ground forces as quickly as possible and soon came up with one effective way of accomplishing that. "They would develop negatives in the air, and, after a reconnaissance, would land with the negatives ready to print," Walter Raleigh noted in *The War in the Air*, the official account of British air operations in World War I. "In one day, at a height of five thousand feet and over, they took a complete series of photographs of the defences of the Isle of Wight and the Solent."

If the camera and airplane were the mother and father of photoreconnaissance, then World War I was its midwife. The great cavalry sweeps and infantry marches of wars past gave way to sluggish, writhing armies dug deep in French soil, hammering at each other remorselessly from fixed positions. The lack of movement, together with an abiding concern that the other side was preparing some new way to break the deadlock by inflicting sudden, terrible damage, forced the general staffs on both sides to make certain that they could peer well beyond the smoke and ruin of the front lines to see what was going on behind them.

"The single use in war for which the machines of the Military Wing of the Royal Flying Corps were designed and the men trained was (let it be repeated) reconnaissance. . . . The Military Wing was small—much smaller than the military air forces of the French or

Germans—it was designed to operate with an expeditionary force and to furnish that force with eyes," Raleigh continued.

As the war of attrition began to congeal along parallel trench systems dug across northeastern France in the autumn of 1914, both sides took to the air with balloons and airplanes for artillery spotting, observation, and reconnaissance. Although the balloons' shapes had changed from onion to sausage, fins had been added to increase stability, and mechanical winches had in many instances replaced the lines of privates and NCOs who had to play tug-of-war to get the gas bags up and down, they remained essentially what they had always been: vulnerable, limited-range observation platforms whose restraining lines forever made them captives of the earth. Still, the thousands of "kite" balloons (so named because their fat stabilizing fins gave them the handling characteristics of kites in the wind), which bobbed suspended five hundred feet or higher in the acrid air over the western front, were valuable enough to be lucrative targets for fighter pilots, some of whom specialized in attacking them. Frank Luke, Jr., the Arizona "balloon-buster," sent eight Hun balloons down in flames during one five-day period in September 1918 before being killed later that month after destroying three more.

Reconnaissance planes abounded during the war as their importance became established in each nation's operational plans. There were French Morane-Saulniers, Breguets, REPs, Nieuports, Blériots, Dorands, and Farmans; German DFWs, Aviatiks, Albatroses, AEGs, Halberstadts, Gotha-Taubes, LVGs, AGOs, and Rumplers; British RE 5s, BE 2s, BE 8s, Martinsydes, and Avros; Austrian Aviatiks, Phönixs, Hansa-Brandenburgs, UFAGs, Lloyds, and Lohners; Italian SAMLs, SIAs, Ansaldos, Pomilios, and Fiats; Russian Antras and Lebeds. Since many aircraft were used for dual purposes, including bombing and pursuit, there are no meaningful numbers relating to those that were turned out exclusively, or even primarily, for reconnaissance. Yet many hundreds were used for that purpose, and their intelligence product was prodigious, both quantitatively and qualitatively.

By the end of 1917 German reconnaissance planes were bringing back about four thousand photographs a day and in the process completely covering the entire western front every two weeks. Combined British and French operations probably about equaled those of the Germans. In March 1918 Germany had 505 out of a total of 2,047 planes on the western front dedicated to reconnaissance missions. In addition, it was also fighting in the Near East, where its pilots and observers carried out extensive reconnaissance flights against British bases on the islands of Imbros and Tenedos in the eastern Aegean and, operating out of Beersheba and El Arish, against British forces in Palestine, the Sinai, and the Cairo area. (In November 1916 two German lieutenants named Falk and Schultheiss bombed the Cairo railroad station and took reconnaissance photographs from over the side of their Rumpler. Then, unable to resist the urge to do a little sightseeing, they also photographed the pyramids before returning to Beersheba.)

In the war's early stages, observer-photographers were considered to be the more important members of the two-man reconnaissance team, with pilots playing the strictly supportive role of getting their passengers to the place that was supposed to be observed or photographed and, in the case of the latter, holding the plane steady enough so that clear pictures could be taken. Reconnaissance pilots in Germany's Military Aviation Service were actually called chauffeurs.

The cameras used by both sides weighed between thirty-five and a hundred pounds and were usually hand-held by the photographer. Since it was easier to shoot at an angle while resting the camera on the rim of the cockpit than it was to lean out into the violent slipstream and point it straight down, many of the photographs taken during World War I were "obliques," as opposed to perpendicular "verticals." Both terms are still in use. Sometimes the camera was bolted to the metal cockpit ring that was supposed to hold a machine gun. The technique steadied the camera, but the loss of the weapon made the aircraft far more vulnerable to attackers. Lord Douglas of Kirtleside, an innovative British military photographer, disdained over-the-side picture-taking altogether. He simply cut a rectangular hole in the floor of his BE 2a biplane; when the target area appeared in the hole, he pushed his camera into it, clicked the shutter, and flew away.

The shortest of the camera lenses had focal lengths of 8.5 inches, while the longest were on the order of 40 inches. Most film still came in the form of photo plates, which had to be changed by hand, though some were attached in belts for quicker loading. In some instances roll film even began to appear. Plate film used by the Allies returned negatives that were 7 by 9.5 inches, while roll film measured 4 by 5 inches. On the whole, the quality of photographs was quite good, particularly given the still-primitive state of the equipment and the constant engine vibration, which, then as now, caused blurring unless dampened.

The reconnaissance plane's effectiveness early in the war was such that it soon became a victim of its own success. "Pursuit," or "scout" planes (later to be called fighters) carrying guns evolved over a short period because of the need to shoot down the prying reconnaissance planes before they could return to their bases with collected intelligence. Fighters came into being for the express purpose of destroying reconnaissance planes—of in effect putting out the enemy's eyes—and they often did this with savage skill. "Fighting in the air," Raleigh noted dryly, "had by 1916 become a regular incident of reconnaissance work."

The air forces on both sides of the trenches responded to enemy interceptors in three ways: they sent up their own fighters to protect the reconnaissance planes (which led to the fierce, swirling battles that came to be known as dogfights); they armed their reconnaissance planes; and they tried to get them to fly higher in order to keep them out of enemy fighters' gunsights. Operating at higher altitudes not only produced photographs of smaller scale, however, but also caused condensation to develop, which fogged lenses, cracked film and the emulsion on glass plates, and froze lubricants. But as so often happens in war, the problem quickly became the incubator of the solution. The Germans responded to the bitter cold impeding their high-altitude photography by inventing the electrically heated camera.

Throughout the war, interpreters analyzing the photographs on the ground kept pace with those who took them in the sky. Comparative coverage, which remains a cornerstone of imaging analysis, was developed relatively early. It involved comparing pictures of the same target that were taken on successive days or weeks in order to spot such changes as troop buildups or withdrawals, bridge or road construction, armament stockpiling, the laying of railroad tracks, and other indicators of enemy intentions. Interpreters were taught not only to spot points of interest in the photographs but to "exploit" what they saw: that is, to use it to draw valid conclusions about the enemy's plans. They used stereo viewers for a three-dimensional effect that helped them to notice objects of interest and determine their size, and they learned how to assemble many photographs into large photomosaics depicting entire combat areas.

Aerial reconnaissance had assumed mammoth proportions by the autumn of 1918. During the Meuse–Argonne offensive that September, for example, fifty-six thousand aerial reconnaissance prints were delivered to various U.S. Army units within a four-day period. The total number of prints produced between July 1, 1918, and Armistice Day the following November 11 came to 1.3 million, according to the United States Air Force's official account. "Toward the closing months of the war aerial photographs were handled so efficiently that many cases were recorded where only twenty minutes elapsed from the time an important photograph of enemy territory was taken until it had been brought to ground, developed, printed, interpreted and used as a basis for giving American batteries the proper range for artillery fire."

The imagery was channeled to the various specialized units needing it, including specific air, artillery, armor, and infantry commands. However well each used the imagery it received, cooperation in analyzing the amassed intelligence product, much less the development of a central intelligence organization that could coordinate the data and focus them for maximum use, was not realized in World War I. In that regard, no less than in the lack of development of highly specialized equipment and interpretive skills, a precedent was set that was to linger for many years.

The value of aerial reconnaissance having been established in World War I, low-keyed research, much of it significant, continued throughout the twenties and thirties despite shrunken military budgets and a concomitant competition for funding among all commands within the military services. Where the Army was concerned, the Air Corps (as the Air Service was renamed in 1926) was far back in line behind the other fighting commands, and even behind the Corps of Engineers, in competing for precious dollars. Even within the Air Corps itself, pursuit and bomber wings, and the research that went into them, had priority over reconnaissance. And there was another wrinkle. Since top commands in air forces throughout the world traditionally went to pursuit and bomber pilots, just the way most ground Army generals and Navy admirals came from the infantry, cavalry, artillery, and the dreadnought flotillas, respectively, there were no delusions among career-minded junior officers in the Army Air Corps that specializing in reconnaissance—in picture-taking and interpretation—would put stars on their shoulders. The few who didn't care, however, tended to be zealots, and the foremost among them was named George W. Goddard.

Even before the war ended, Goddard had made a name for himself as an irrepressible champion of photoreconnaissance. His aptitude for combining flying and photography got him into the Army's new aerial photography school at Ithaca, New York, late in 1917. After graduation the following March, Goddard was commissioned a second lieutenant and made an instructor in aerial photographic interpretation. Since the armistice came just before he was to take three aerial reconnaissance sections to France, Goddard was rerouted to Carlstrom Field, Florida, where he earned his pilot's wings, and then to McCook Field, Ohio, where he was put in charge of the Air Service's aerial photographic research.

In the years immediately following, George Goddard experimented with infrared and long-distance photography, did extensive ground mapping for the civilian Federal Board of Surveys and Maps, organized the first Army Aerial Photographic Mapping Unit, and worked extensively on developing the very long focal-length camera lenses that were to prove so valuable in the war that General Billy Mitchell repeatedly, but ineffectually, warned was coming.

Late on the night of November 20, 1925, after months of failure, Goddard flew over Rochester, New York, and dropped a fourteen-foot-long, eight-inch-wide wood-shelled "bomb" suspended from a parachute. The device held eighty pounds of tightly packed flash powder that was compressed between two oak plugs at either end. Four timing fuses were pulled as the explosive canister was dropped from Goddard's twin-engine Martin bomber, and twenty seconds later, most of downtown Rochester was bathed in dazzling light. The illuminated streets and buildings were etched on film in a camera whose shutter had been opened moments before by someone on the bomber, resulting in the first night aerial photograph. More than a decade later, Goddard and Dr. Harold E. Edgerton of MIT invented a safe, reusable electronic flash that used energy generated from the airplane's engines and was synchronized with the cameras.

Goddard anticipated the development of real-time photography —of transmitting televisionlike pictures of events as they occur—in 1927, when he photographed the federal prison at Fort Leavenworth from the air, developed the pictures in the plane, and then sent them by telephoto transmission over telegraph wires so that they arrived in New York twenty-three minutes later. He went on to do major work on haze-reduction techniques and the use of color film for aerial photography, and experimented with the triple-lens camera that led the way to the trimetrogon system that was used extensively in World War II and afterward. A trimetrogon camera takes left and right obliques and a vertical—outward to the left and right and straight down—at the same time. This produces a photograph of the target area that is panoramic, in some cases from horizon to horizon, which therefore provides interpreters with a view not only of the primary target area below the plane but of that area's periphery, where other important developments might be occurring.

But Goddard's most important invention was probably the stereoscopic twin-lens strip camera, which he labored over between 1936 and 1939. Until it was perfected, airplanes on tactical reconnaissance missions that took low-altitude, high-speed oblique pictures with cameras pointing straight out from behind windows in their sides returned with blurred images. That was because stationary objects were recorded as blurs as the speeding camera passed by. This precluded photographing enemy gun emplacements, for example, which had to be approached parallel to the line along which they were strung out, at altitudes as low as twenty-five feet ("on the deck," as the pilots put it) to see beneath the camouflage nets usually spread over them, and very quickly to hinder the gunners who would try to shoot down the reconnaissance plane.

Goddard got the idea for the strip camera at the Agua Caliente racetrack in California, where he saw that the camera used to do the photo finishes held film that was electronically synchronized to move at the same speed as the horses as they charged past its lens. He eventually developed a shutterless camera whose heart was an automatic electronic image-synchronizing mechanism that matched the film speed to the plane's ground speed, which took pictures in both color and black and white, and used two lenses for a stereoscopic effect.

"In the summer of 1942," Goddard was to recall in his memoir, "we installed one in an F-5 [the reconnaissance version of Lockheed's P-38G/H Lightning fighter], and tests were flown at speeds between 350 and 400 miles per hour at an altitude of 200 feet. A picture was taken of an old wooden bridge which actually showed the knotholes and the grain of the planks. On the windshield of a car parked close by, the letter 'A' on the gasoline ration ticket stood out clearly." Strip cameras were used on "dicing missions"* in both theaters in World War II, including reconnaissance missions along the beaches in Normandy prior to the invasion, and by Air Force and Navy tactical reconnaissance planes during the Cuban missile crisis in 1962.

Elsewhere, work continued in fits and starts on improved cameras, films, and related hardware. Cameras were put inside airplanes once and for all during the interwar period, and the ensuing vibration problems were for the most part overcome by using specially designed cushioned, vertically stabilized mounts (which replaced tennis balls and inner tubes). Multilens cameras, which produced wide-angle pictures that were less distorted than those made by single lenses, were heavily tested throughout the 1930s. Fairchild's T-3A five-lens mapping camera, first used in 1928, was made the standard Army Air Corps camera in 1931. It could produce high-quality photographs of 225-square-mile chunks of terrain from twenty thousand feet and cover 20-mile-wide bands of territory along a single, continuous, line of flight. Roll film spooled in magazines with electronic drives replaced plates and was operated by remote control mechanisms that could adjust the speed at which the film moved. Cameras were also made that took interchangeable lenses. And the lenses themselves not only were up to three feet long but also produced less distortion than their predecessors.

Meanwhile, filmmakers—largely Eastman Kodak—were working on aerial films that were increasingly light-sensitive and had smaller silver molecule emulsion grains. Looked at in cross section under a microscope, film grains resemble a mountain range, with light falling on the peaks registering a different quality than that hitting the valleys. A grainy film having many peaks and valleys produces an image having both light extremes and is therefore less clear than a flatter film, which is struck more uniformly by the light. The finer-grained films, combined with the longer, more distortion-free lenses, produced photographs whose resolution improved steadily. And resolution, which is the ability of an optical system to

*Low-level reconnaissance runs were so dangerous because of often heavy enemy fire at close range that they were known to World War II American and British pilots as "dicing missions" after a grim British joke about "dicing [gambling] with the devil." A greater percentage of pilots were lost on such missions than on high-altitude sorties.

distinguish separate objects that are close together, was and remains
the cornerstone upon which imaging reconnaissance is built.

A surge of vitality and derring-do spread through U.S. military
aviation practically before the guns of August had cooled. This may
have been caused in part by an excess of energy and spirit that were
no longer being channeled into combat. It was certainly prompted
in large measure by anemic defense budgets that spurred the drive
for favorable public relations by services competing for scarce funds.
And related to that was General Billy Mitchell's relentless prodding
of his aircrews to break records in order to demonstrate in the most
dramatic way that military aviation deserved a role in its own right,
not merely as an appendage of land and naval forces. The Byrds,
Posts, Earharts, and Lindberghs were not to have the field to themselves. Following the first transatlantic flight in 1919 by a Navy
NC-4, Army pilots set and broke scores of speed, altitude, and
endurance records as they pushed their airplanes to the limit. The
most spectacular feat came in 1923, when Lieutenants John Mac-
ready and Oakley Kelly made the first nonstop flight across the
United States in a Fokker monoplane. That same year a new technique, aerial refueling, helped two other Army lieutenants, Lowell
Smith and John Richter, remain in the air for a record-breaking
thirty-six hours. And two years later the Schneider Trophy race was
won in an Army Curtiss biplane flown by another young lieutenant
named James Doolittle.

There were implications for reconnaissance in much of this. On
October 10, 1928, Captain St. Clair Streett and Captain A. W.
Stevens, a photographer who was another of the reconnaissance
zealots, set an unofficial world altitude record for airplanes with
crews of more than one when they climbed to 37,854 feet. The
following year Stevens, who championed long-distance photography because it kept the vulnerable reconnaissance planes as far as
possible from enemy fighters and antiaircraft guns, photographed
Mount Rainier from a distance of 227 miles, breaking the long-
distance aerial photography record by 50 miles.

In 1934 another Army aviator, Lieutenant Colonel Henry
("Hap") Arnold, led a flight of new Martin B-10s from Bolling Field
in Washington, D.C., to Fairbanks, Alaska, in a spectacular demonstration of the Air Corps's ability to send heavy planes where they
were needed in a hurry. George Goddard was a passenger on one

of the bombers. In three days of intensive flying with five crews, Goddard managed to photo-map twenty thousand square miles of Alaskan wilderness. In 1935 two other airmen rode in the specially built, pressurized cabin of a balloon that rose to a record altitude of 72,395 feet. When they got as high as they could go, they proceeded to take thousands of photographs of the terrain below. They took their pictures from almost exactly the same altitude at which U-2s were to operate, beginning in 1956.

But there was a dark side to the military's competitiveness that had to do not with the breaking of records but with the securing and protecting of turf. Both the Army and the Navy saw long-range aerial reconnaissance as falling within their respective provinces. The Army Air Corps believed that since it had the long-range airplanes, and since its primary responsibility was flying, it ought to be able to fly those planes for the collection of intelligence. The Navy, on the other hand, was responsible for control of the two oceans that insulated North America, and it took long-range reconnaissance to be an inseparable part of that responsibility. This increasingly stubborn contest for control of reconnaissance in turn bubbled just over a deeper enmity: the admirals had never forgotten that Mitchell's two-thousand-pound bombs had sunk the supposedly impregnable *Ostfriesland* in the summer of 1921 and sent the myth of the invincibility of the dreadnought to the bottom with her.

It was not that the Navy Department did not believe in air power. On the contrary, it placed so much stock in the value of warplanes that it wanted most of them for itself. The admirals were convinced that pursuit "ships" properly belonged on aircraft carriers so that they could protect the nation's sea-lanes far from the coasts or be efficiently transported anywhere in the world if necessary. And they wanted their own bombers, reconnaissance planes, and airships for long-range coastal defense, too. This made perfect sense to the admirals, but it enraged many of the senior officers in the fledgling Air Corps. The political skirmishes that went on during the mid-1930s for control of reconnaissance were among the first in which the young pilots who would lead a future Air Force became embroiled, but they were by no means the last. In any case, relations between the admirals and the Air Corps generals had become so venomous by the summer of 1937 that an exasperated Franklin Roosevelt ordered both sides to settle the coastal defense and reconnaissance issues once and for all. The result was Joint Air Exercise No. 4.

The exercise, which took place on August 12 and 13, pitted Air Corps bomber crews against the battleship *Utah*. The Air Corps, using twin-engine B-10 and B-18 bombers and the first of the new four-engine B-17 Flying Fortresses to be delivered by Boeing, was supposed to locate and "bomb" the naval vessel, which would be cruising somewhere in a hundred thousand miles of ocean between the latitudes of San Francisco Bay and the San Pedro Channel off Los Angeles.

That would have been a formidable enough undertaking, but there were other complications. The West Coast had been selected over the East Coast by the War Department, despite Air Corps objections, even though there is a great deal of offshore fog there at that time of year. As if that weren't bad enough, the Army aviators had only two half-days—from noon to sunset on the first day and from dawn to noon on the second—to find their quarry, and they were prohibited from flying under one thousand feet, fog or no fog, to do so. The fifty-pound water bombs they were supposed to drop on the *Utah* belonged to the Navy; they had never been used by the airmen prior to the trip to California and, inexplicably, were unavailable for practice until shortly before the exercise began. The B-10s and B-18s were next to useless, it turned out, because their limited range was insufficient to cover the search area, particularly in fog. The mission therefore rested on the B-17s. Finally, the B-17 crews were to rely on thirty Navy scout planes to actually spot the *Utah* and then radio her coordinates to them. The scouts were also limited to the noon-to-sunset, sunrise-to-noon time frame.

For their part, the Army aviators answered a Navy request for information on the B-17's top speed by giving it as 190 miles an hour. They reasoned that if they provided the heavy bomber's real maximum speed, which was about 250 miles an hour, the Navy would keep the *Utah* so far out to sea that finding her would be impossible within the time limitation.

Sure enough, fog, extending two hundred miles out, covered the entire length of the exercise area on the appointed day. While the B-17 crews fidgeted helplessly beside their silent planes, the Navy scouts spent more than three hours in an apparent search for the *Utah*. Finally, at 3:37 P.M., they reported spotting the battleship, but it was four o'clock before the message was routed through First Naval District Headquarters. Soon after taking off, the Air Corps pilots were told by the Navy that the *Utah* was actually forty miles east of the original sighting, so they changed direction only to find empty sea where the ship was supposed to be. The lead Air Corps navigator, a lieutenant named Curtis LeMay, frantically rechecked his calculations and swore that he had made no error. The forlorn airmen got word at nine-thirty that night that the Navy scouts had admitted making a tiny navigational mistake of only one degree. On the exercise's chart scale, though, it translated to sixty miles.

The B-17s were off again when the sun came up, this time without waiting for the Navy. General Delos C. ("Lucky") Emmons, the commander of the bomber group, got it into his head that the *Utah* was going to feint toward San Francisco and then steam south, so he instructed his crews to fly a course that would intercept her. The first Navy sighting came in at 11 A.M., which not only would have been too late had the airmen been waiting for it on the ground, but was off once again by exactly sixty miles. It didn't matter; the Navy's coordinates were ignored.

At 11:55 A.M., just five minutes before Joint Air Exercise No. 4 was scheduled to be concluded, Emmons's B-17s, now flying abreast, dropped below the prohibited thousand-foot level into clear sky. Suddenly, the crews became ecstatic at what they saw: there, dead ahead, lay the *Utah* with lounging sailors plainly visible on her deck. Moments later, with the gobs scattering for hatches and battle stations, three water bombs slammed into the *Utah*. Had they been the real thing, the lumbering warship would have gone to the bottom, or at the very least been made dead in the water.

The admirals responded by insisting that the exercise hadn't really proved anything because their ship had been the victim of a sneak attack. The generals parried by challenging the Navy to a one-day extension of the exercise and baited their offer by adding that the bombers would remain at altitudes between eight thousand and eighteen thousand feet, thus ensuring that there would be no question of sneaking up on the *Utah*. The Navy reluctantly agreed, and on the appointed day, despite vigorous evasive maneuvering, the *Utah* was pelted by thirty-seven more water bombs (23 percent of the total dropped) and was therefore theoretically blown out of the water.

The Navy Department's final word on Joint Air Exercise No. 4 was to remind the participants and the War Department that the test had been conducted solely for the benefit of the president of the United States and for the secretaries of war and the navy, and that the results were therefore strictly classified.

"I've got some pretty important news," newscaster Boake Carter told his radio audience with unconcealed amazement almost immediately after the Navy's secrecy order had been issued. "The Air Corps can not only find battleships with Flying Fortresses, it can put bombs on them; enough bombs to sink them. What's more, it can put bombs on a towed sled that's only about one third the size of a ship. I know what I'm talking about," Carter added. "I've got photographs right here in front of me to prove it." Official queries put to Emmons, LeMay, and the other fliers as to how the results of the exercise came to be leaked to the press were answered with shrugs and straight-faced expressions of bewilderment. But the point had been made: Air Corps bombers could find targets at sea, even under adverse conditions (logistically as well as meteorologically), and successfully photograph and attack them.*

For all the schoolboy mischievousness attending competitions like Joint Air Exercise No. 4, their purpose remained serious and by no means entirely political. Every nation able to do so conducted aerial reconnaissance throughout the interwar period on the reasonable assumption that clear aerial maps of every area were good to have. Military intelligence apparatuses throughout Europe and in the United States and Japan collected reconnaissance imagery with steadily increasing fervor. They wanted to fill their folders with pictures of strategically important targets, to be sure, but apparently no opportunity to get even marginally useful photographs was ignored. As early as 1923, for example, Goddard and a colleague had been sent over Mexico on secret reconnaissance flights to photograph places thought to be of potential interest. There never seemed to be enough pictures.

As another world war approached, however, those who collected intelligence from the sky did so with an increasingly clear idea of what really required coverage. Not long after he was dismissed as commander in chief of the German army in 1938 because of a

---

*The following year the Air Corps sent three more B-17s on a coastal reconnaissance mission from Long Island's Mitchel Field to intercept the Italian liner *Rex*, which was more than six hundreds miles at sea. In addition to George Goddard, the bombers carried a three-man NBC radio news team, C. B. Allen of *The New York Herald Tribune*, Harris Hull of *The Washington Post*, and Hanson W. Baldwin of *The New York Times*. "FLYING FORTS, 630 MILES OUT, SPOT ENEMY TROOP SHIP / 8 Hour Reconnaissance Locates Liner Rex at Sea / Generals elated by success of defense," blared a headline in the next day's *Herald Tribune*. The Navy Department was somewhat less than elated, however, with the result that the Air Corps soon found itself restricted to ocean reconnaissance operations within a hundred miles of the coast.

trumped-up scandal, General Werner von Fritsch predicted that the side having the best photoreconnaissance would win the next war. He was certainly in a position to know. The German Condor Legion fighting in Spain in 1936 came with a reconnaissance squadron. That same year a highly secret Luftwaffe unit commanded by the Third Reich's own reconnaissance genius, Theodor von Rowehl, was using Zeiss cameras in specially adapted twin-engine HE 111K bombers to fly over parts of Poland, Czechoslovakia, France, England, and the Soviet Union. And George Goddard does not think it farfetched that the *Graf Zeppelin*, a flying luxury liner that plied the airways of the world during the 1930s, carried reconnaissance cameras at least part of the time. Goddard also has no doubt, based on personal observations, that the Japanese carried out extensive aerial reconnaissance of U.S. installations in the Pacific before the war.

Britain's zealot was an Australian adventurer named Frederick Sidney Cotton, the unquestioned father of Allied photoreconnaissance in World War II. Cotton, who had been a Royal Naval Air Service pilot in the Great War, was a mechanically gifted inventor who went into several businesses during the twenties and thirties, many of them combining his two principal interests—flying and photography. He established an airmail service in Newfoundland, did aerial surveys, and started a commercial color film company. He also invented the windproof Sidcot, a warm flight suit for use at high altitude.

Early in 1939 a small company named Aeronautical Research and Sales was formed in London with the quiet support of the Royal Air Force. The firm, with an office on St. James's Square and Cotton as its president and chief sales representative, quickly set up routes crisscrossing much of Europe and leading, in particular, to Berlin. The object of such elaborate cover was to conduct secret photoreconnaissance over much of Europe and the Mediterranean. And the vehicle for doing this was a sky spook's dream.

Cotton got hold of a twin-engine Lockheed 12A corporate airplane and had it fitted with all of the posh accoutrements that would be expected of a successful businessman. He even had it painted a mildly flamboyant duck-egg green, a color that the proprietors of dozens of aviation-related businesses around Europe were soon associating with Aeronautical Research and Sales and with its affable chief executive. But what was not apparent to anyone who casually looked over the lovely Lockheed monoplane, even from up close, was that extremely tight-fitting port covers in its belly concealed a brace of three RAF F.24 cameras with five-inch lenses that were fanned so they could take left and right obliques and a vertical at the same time. This allowed Cotton to photograph an 11.5-mile-wide ribbon of earth from twenty thousand feet. He kept the cameras and other equipment from freezing at that altitude by running hot air over them. He also increased the 12A's range to sixteen hundred miles by installing extra fuel tanks. Even the plane's color scheme had been chosen with high-altitude reconnaissance in mind after Cotton had watched another plane painted similarly disappear as it climbed into the sky.

Cotton's business trips were conducted feverishly during the spring and summer of 1939. He left Heston airport, his growing organization's real home, in the spring for a swing around the Mediterranean that took him to Malta, Eritrea, Libya, Sardinia, and Sicily (whose airfields he committed to film). The Aussie's trips to Berlin, occasionally made somewhat circuitously, took him over naval facilities at Wilhelmshaven, the Dutch frontier, fortifications along the Rhine, the industrialized areas of the Ruhr, and elsewhere. On the assumption that the Nazi-Soviet nonaggression pact meant that German panzers would eventually be running on Russian petroleum and that its flow would therefore have to be cut by aerial bombardment, Cotton took superb photographs of the oil fields at Baku twice in late March 1940.

By then the "company" had been renamed the Photographic Development Unit and owned three stripped-down Spitfires that carried additional fuel tanks as well as cameras. It became clear once the shooting started and Luftwaffe fighters prowled the skies in menacing numbers that the Lockheed's service life was over. But the Spits were another matter. Their speed, ceiling, and maneuverability made them more than a match for the ME 109s that hunted them. One of Cotton's young colleagues, in fact, described what he considered to be the ideal reconnaissance plane in a historic memorandum to his boss:

The best method appears to be the use of a single small machine, relying on its speed, climb and ceiling to avoid destruction. A machine such as a single-seater fighter could fly high enough to be well above Ack-Ack fire and could rely upon sheer speed and height to get away from enemy fighters. It would have no use for armament or radio and these could be removed to provide room for extra fuel in order to get the necessary range. It would be a very small machine painted so as to reduce its visibility against the sky.

But Cotton's contribution to Allied photoreconnaissance went well beyond his customized planes, special cameras, and distinctive, high-quality photographs. The quasi-official Photographic Development Unit also refined photo interpretation by target specialty so that pictures of tanks or naval vessels, for example, were sent to interpreters who knew most about them. Photo processing was centralized to enhance speed and efficiency. So was the entire management structure. Cotton understood that there would be many customers for the fruits of aerial reconnaissance in the war just then beginning, each having different requirements, so he fashioned a prototypical organization that was equipped to meet those requirements.

Sidney Cotton was rewarded for his efforts by the Royal Air Force in mid-June 1940, when he was informed by official letter that his Photographic Development Unit was to be incorporated as a regular arm of the RAF, that it would have a regular RAF wing commander as its leader, and that his services were therefore no longer required.

George Goddard's and some others' efforts notwithstanding, U.S. photoreconnaissance capability was probably in even worse condition than that of the military as a whole when war finally came. The Navy had no capability to speak of. Its scout planes, whose range over ocean expanses was pathetically short, were used for visual observation, not photography. And that applied to the longer-range Consolidated PBY Catalinas and PB2Y Coronados, as well.

The Army was using three different kinds of flying units to gather information at the time of Pearl Harbor, none of them suited to the sort of photoreconnaissance that was suddenly required in a war whose fronts changed rapidly. There were observation units attached to ground forces that used light planes for close support, artillery spotting, and other missions that depended on visual sighting and a high degree of ground-air coordination. There was photomapping, which for the most part used commercial airliners that were wholly inadequate for combat. Finally, there were squadrons that were technically dedicated to reconnaissance, but these were really bomber units whose planes carried cameras in addition to guns and bombs. Training necessarily emphasized bombing and self-protection, while photography (largely for bomb-damage assessment) was secondary. Worse, the bombers —underarmed, obsolescent A-20s and plodding B-17s and B-24s— that ventured out on lone, long-range "recce" missions over denied territory, as enemy terrain is called, during the first months of the war often were decimated by enemy fighters. The high initial loss rate of B-17s sent on such operations, in fact, shocked U.S. airmen.

The U.S. Army Air Force (AAF), as the Air Corps was now known, had not learned, as had the RAF, that long-range, high-performance fighters were best suited to collecting photoreconnaissance. This changed quickly, though, in part because the British readily shared the knowledge gained from Cotton's Photographic Development Unit, and also because of the lessons learned through the exigencies of the war itself.

The AAF's 3rd Photo Group, which had arrived in England only in September 1942 to join the Ninth Air Force, was sent to North Africa two months later after the Allied landings. It thereby became one of the first American aerial reconnaissance units to see extensive action. The group's commander, Lieutenant Colonel Elliott Roosevelt, was also made commander of the Northwest African Photographic Reconnaissance Wing, which included South African Air Force and RAF units. Since the three air forces shared common facilities, including laboratories and readout rooms, hastily trained American photo interpreters learned many of the secrets of their trade from their more practiced British counterparts.

Typically, the 3rd Photo Group began operations with B-17s (called F-9s in their reconnaissance configuration) and P-38Es (or F-4s), but transitioned as soon as possible to exclusive use of the advanced, better-performing P-38G/Hs (known as F-5As). The later-model Lightnings could fly twenty miles an hour faster than their predecessors, four thousand feet higher, and, with two fuel tanks slung under their wings, four times farther. The distinctive twin-engine, twin-fuselage Lightning had been designed by Lockheed's Clarence L. ("Kelly") Johnson, a Michigan-born engineer who was destined to have more than a passing acquaintance with photoreconnaissance in the years ahead. The other fighter adapted to the photoreconnaissance role (though not by the 3rd Photo

Group) was North American Aviation's sleek P-51 Mustang, which was known as the F-6 in its recce variant. The plane's top speed of well over four hundred miles an hour made it especially popular with pilots who had to fly dicing missions at altitudes on the order of twenty-five feet, as was the case at Normandy. Indeed, speed was so prized by recce pilots that in at least one instance, that of the 10th Recon Group, paint was taken off fighters to reduce weight and many seams in their skin were filled and polished to boost speed by a few miles an hour.

Army fighter photoreconnaissance was done either by photoreconnaissance squadrons that used unarmed F-5As for aerial photography only, or by tactical reconnaissance squadrons that used F-6s whose guns had been left on so they could shoot either pictures or bullets. The latter frequently used fighters in pairs or in groups of four on so-called armed reconnaissance missions in which targets of opportunity were attacked more than photographed. Photo sorties, in fact, accounted for only about a tenth of the combat missions flown by one Ninth Air Force tactical reconnaissance squadron. This duality of roles could produce painful conflicts for pilots. An advanced fighter reconnaissance training manual written in August 1943, for example, exhorted tactical recce pilots to keep their guns blazing:

Fighter Reconnaissance Pilots must be thoroughly impressed with the fact that they are *fighter trained as well as reconnaissance trained* and must be capable of performing their duties in both roles in an excellent manner. Pilots must not only develop and perfect their reconnaissance skill, accuracy, speed in observing, but *they must also maintain at a high level the fighter tactics and techniques with which they were primarily indoctrinated* when they were graduated from the Fighter Command School. An *excellent* fighter reconnaissance crew by virtue of the additional training skill and technique will be, in general, equal to a *superior* fighter crew that had only fighter training.

Yet two years later a 15th Tactical Reconnaissance Squadron pilot narrowly averted a court-martial for shooting down three Stukas on the same day in a fit of exuberance. His escapade came on the heels of an order issued by fighter command headquarters telling recce pilots that they were not primarily fighter pilots and therefore ought to avoid scrapes so as not to jeopardize their primary task: returning with useful pictures.*

By the winter of 1944, each of the Army air forces had its own armada of reconnaissance aircraft. Three combat groups, each having three squadrons of twenty-five fighters, worked Italy and the Mediterranean. The Eighth and Ninth air forces in England, which were bombing the Continent on a massive scale, had twenty reconnaissance squadrons between them, for a total of nearly five hundred aircraft at strength (and that does not include the RAF's photographic reconnaissance units). Seven other squadrons flew photoreconnaissance missions in the China-Burma-India theater.

Although fighters and medium bombers, such as the B-25, were used extensively for reconnaissance in the Southwest Pacific, the great distances between the island bases from which Twentieth Air Force B-29s struck at the Japanese home islands required very heavy bomber reconnaissance by the Super Fortresses themselves (or F-13s, as they were called). The giant bombers were pressed into service to make detailed photographs of Japanese cities for target folders (B-29 crews making the initial attacks against Japanese industrial targets had been briefed using a 1928 ground plan and ground photos from that year and 1932), do bomb-damage assessment, pinpoint defensive installations and airfields for a possible Allied invasion, and conduct maritime surveillance.

The Navy also got into both tactical and long-range ocean reconnaissance as the end of the war approached, though none of its planes was ever modified for photoreconnaissance during the manufacturing stage as Army Air Force planes were. As a consequence, cameras were either hand-held or mounted on machine-gun rails, as they had been during World War I.

As the number of photoreconnaissance missions proliferated in both theaters, so, too, did qualitative improvements in the photographic equipment itself. As the war's end approached, there was a flood of technical innovations, some of them brilliant, whose effects were to extend far beyond the last vestiges of combat against an Axis already battered into near submission.

---

*Nor were planes the only targets attacked by tactical reconnaissance pilots. The unofficial history of the 10th Photo Recon Group in World War II notes that one of the unit's pilots strafed German soldiers who were trying to escape from the burning wreckage of a Junkers transport he had just shot down.

Color film of extremely high resolution was in widespread use by 1945, while heat-sensitive infrared film, which had first been field-tested aboard a National Geographic Society balloon in 1935, was in an advanced stage of development. Goddard's stereoscopic strip camera had overcome opposition by those in Army aviation who thought that using it where it worked best—on the deck—would cost unnecessarily high casualties. Dr. James Baker, a Harvard astronomer and optics expert, initiated the era of truly exotic photographic systems (in Goddard's view) by inventing cameras with 40-, 60-, 100-, and finally 240-inch focal lengths whose lenses automatically compensated for changes in air temperature and atmospheric pressure. This reduced the distortion that came when lenses changed shape slightly, and in the bargain allowed reconnaissance pilots to fly higher, where it was safer, and still return with the required imagery. During this same period, RAF Mosquitos became the first to use radar reconnaissance cameras that penetrated clouds and the blackness of night. Far from being relegated to the scrap heap after the war, these exotic gadgets and many others, including airborne radio interception equipment that allowed the collectors of aerial intelligence to hear the enemy as well as see him, would be pointed in yet another direction almost immediately.

Finally, whatever a photograph's quality, it is useless unless it can be made to yield information. Photo interpretation itself therefore had to evolve into an exacting, if arcane, skill whose practitioners —the photo interpreters, or PIs—could extract important information from pictures that to the untrained eye appeared utterly meaningless. Medmenham, a baronial estate on the Thames, became the principal place where hundreds of British PIs created highly refined ways to in effect get right into a picture and scour it for information. Most specialized in a particular piece of geography, weapons system, type of engineering, and so forth, and the best of them eventually got to know their area so well that they became intuitive: they could look at a photograph taken straight down from an altitude of forty thousand feet, for example, and know instinctively that something had changed: that a power line had been added or a small ship moved, or a V-1 "buzz-bomb" was poised for firing:

"This first excursion beyond the official bounds of the airfield encouraged me to try my luck in other directions," one noted British PI was later to recall as she scrutinized a photograph of the

German rocket test facility at Peenemünde. "I decided to follow the dead-straight road which led northward along the eastern boundary of the airfield toward the Baltic shore. . . . Right at the edge of the road there was something I did not understand—unlike anything I had seen before. . . . Rumors of 'launching rails' for secret weapons had reached me earlier; and ever since I had been briefed about pilotless aircraft I had been on the lookout for a catapult of some kind. . . . The quality of the photographs was poor, but even with the naked eye I could see that on the ramp was something that had not been there before. A tiny cruciform shape, set exactly on the lower end of the inclined rails—a midget aircraft actually in position for launching." In picking out that "cruciform" from all of the other equipment scattered around the large test facility, Constance Babington-Smith, one of Britain's most celebrated PIs, confirmed the existence of the V-1, the first of Hitler's vengeance weapons, thereby providing early warning of the desperate attacks that were soon to be launched against England from across the Channel.

"The photographs one brings back," Antoine de Saint-Exupéry reflected, "are submitted to stereoscopic analysis, as organisms are examined under a microscope; the interpreters of these photographs work exactly like bacteriologists. They seek on the vulnerable body of France traces of the virus which devours her. One can die from the effects of these enemy strongholds and depots and convoys which, under the lens, appear like tiny bacilli."

Early on the morning of July 31, 1944, Saint-Exupéry took off in a Lightning from Bongo, Corsica, to make a reconnaissance run north to Annecy and Grenoble. He never returned.

3.

Assets, Black and Skunky

"One of NASA's U-2 research planes, in use since 1956 in a continuing program to study gust-meteorological conditions found at high altitude, has been missing since about 9 o'clock Sunday morning (local time)," NASA press release 60–193 began matter-of-factly, "when its pilot reported he was having oxygen difficulties over the Lake Van, Turkey, area.

"The airplane had taken off from Incirlik Air Base, Turkey. The flight plan called for the first check point to be at 37 degrees, 25 minutes, North: 41 degrees, 23 minutes, East, and for a left turn to be made to the Lake Van beacon, thence to the Trabazon [sic] beacon, thence to Antalya, and return to Adana. . . .

"About one hour after takeoff, the pilot reported difficulties with his oxygen equipment. Using emergency radio frequency, he reported he was heading for the Lake Van beacon to get his bearings, and that he would return to Adana."

Then the Memo to the Press, as the handout was called, sounded an ominous note: "If the pilot continued to suffer lack of oxygen, the path of the airplane from the last reported position would be impossible to determine. If the airplane was on automatic pilot, it is likely it would have continued along its northeasterly course."

The city of Sverdlovsk, nine hundred miles east of Moscow, lies in a northeasterly direction from Adana, where the U-2 had purportedly taken off. And Sverdlovsk was precisely where the high-altitude "research" plane had been heading when it disappeared. In fact, even as Walter T. Bonney, the National Aeronautics and Space Administration's director of public information, was frantically pounding out a draft of the release, the U-2's crunched and twisted carcass was either still lying outside the city or was already on its way to the capital, where it would shortly go on display in Gorki Park.

The airplane's pilot, Bonney wrote, "as are all pilots used on NASA's program of upper atmosphere research . . . is a civilian employed by the Lockheed Aircraft Corporation, builders of the airplane." He went on to assert that overseas logistical support for the scientific program was provided by the Air Force's Air Weather Service, that Lockheed had designed the U-2 as a "flying test bed," and that it could stay in the air for a maximum of four hours at altitudes of up to fifty-five thousand feet. Bonney ended the release by lacing it with an impressive-looking conglomeration of weather-sampling equipment the ill-fated U-2 supposedly had been carrying, and even threw in a generally plausible assortment of sampling experiments it had purportedly been doing (an astute reporter might have wondered, however, how the airplane came to be collecting data on typhoons high over the Anatolian plateau).

NASA release No. 60–193, hurriedly written and distributed to an already skeptical press on the afternoon of May 5, 1960, was created to provide a cover story for the final episode of what was without question the most effective aerial reconnaissance program in history up to that time. In a perverse sort of way, Bonney might have been given credit for succeeding in misstating almost every-thing: the U-2 had not been on a scientific flight and carried no weather-sampling hardware; NASA had nothing to do with its operation; its endurance was more than three times what Bonney claimed, and it could fly at least fifteen thousand feet higher; and, of course, its pilot had not gotten lost at all. Bonney's press release was written five days after Francis Gary Powers was knocked out of the air in a hail of Soviet Surface to Air Missiles (SAM),* and on

---

*With a then maximum altitude of seventy-two thousand feet (it is currently more than eighty thousand), U-2s were impervious to attacks by Soviet fighters at that time and, until that day, to attacks by SAMs as well. According to Viktor Belenko, the MiG-25 pilot who defected to the West in his fighter in 1976, a "barrage" of SAMs was fired at Powers, which suggested that the Russians had become deeply frustrated by their inability to hit the high-flying spy planes. Belenko added that at least one MiG pursuing Powers was also caught and destroyed in the missile salvo.

the very day that Premier Nikita Khrushchev lambasted the Eisenhower administration for the "aggressive provocation" during a heated three-and-a-half-hour speech at the Supreme Soviet meeting in the Kremlin.

Two days later the United States took the unprecedented step of admitting that the U-2 "probably" had overflown Soviet territory while "endeavoring to obtain information now concealed behind the Iron Curtain." The revelation, which came only after a vigorous debate in the White House over the prudence of making such an admission, stressed that the plane had been civilian and unarmed and that the flight had been ordered by officials who remained anonymous; that "there was no authorization for any such flight" by authorities in Washington. But that too was untrue. Every flight made by a U-2 over the U.S.S.R. during the program's four-year existence had the personal blessing of the president, Dwight D. Eisenhower. It was Ike who wanted the reconnaissance planes operated by civilians, just as he wanted civilians to operate the space reconnaissance program, then barely getting under way, so as to foster the notion (which he tried mightily to promote) that the U.S. space program was essentially peaceful and thus avoid unnecessarily angering the volatile Soviet premier. And the U-2 pilots contracted with neither Lockheed nor NASA but with the CIA (which within the week was said by some smirking Washington wags to stand for Caught In the Act).

The statement of complicity also claimed that the Russians were engaged in their own reconnaissance operations, which was correct. Finally, it insisted that the U-2 flights had been undertaken in the first place only because Washington was worried about the "danger of surprise attack" by the Russians. That was perfectly true, too.

During the five years immediately following the end of World War II, American exhilaration at vanquishing a heavily armed and tenacious foe turned in rapidly successive stages from consternation to apprehension to outright alarm as yet another threat began to materialize from the rubble of the conflict that had barely ended: Stalinist Russia. In the course of a few years, all of Eastern Europe was locked behind an Iron Curtain; Greece nearly fell to the Communists in a civil war; West Berlin was blockaded by Soviet armor; the Kuomintang was chased off mainland China; the Hukbalahaps threatened the Philippines; South Korea was almost inundated by the North Korean army; and the Union of Soviet Socialist Republics exploded an atomic bomb. Evil was a hydra: for every fascist killed, two Communists seemed to spring up.

Of all the threats, the advent of a Soviet atomic bomb and the means to deliver it were taken to be the most dire. In 1946, with much of the Soviet Union still in ruin, the Kremlin ordered the creation of a Long Range Air Force equipped with TU-4s. The planes were exact copies of the propeller-driven B-29, three of which landed in Siberia after strikes against Japan in the closing days of the war and were never returned. In 1948 a defector, Colonel G. A. Tokayev, told Western intelligence that the Politburo was giving special attention to long-range bombing capability. This was quickly borne out. Three air bases in the western U.S.S.R. had TU-4s by 1949, and four years later there were a thousand of the bombers (not so coincidentally where U.S. strategic planners were concerned, 1953 also happened to be the year the Russians tested their first hydrogen bomb). Although the TU-4s had not the range to make round-trip attacks against the United States, nor even a one-way trip to most targets, bombers are offensive weapons, and their presence in substantial numbers was therefore taken not only as a menace in its own right, but as a sinister portent of Stalin's intentions.

In addition, there was also the disquieting fact that the Russians had captured or lured* several of the Peenemünde rocket alumni, and by 1946 had embarked on a priority program to reconstruct the full set of working drawings for the V-2 terror missile and start a production line for it. In such circumstances the need for reliable intelligence was considered crucial. But the Soviet Union was vast, repressive, and obsessively secretive.

"Our knowledge of what was going on inside the U.S.S.R. was desperately weak," the late Dr. George B. Kistiakowsky was to recall many years later. The Ukrainian-born Harvard chemistry professor had worked on the first atom bomb as the chief of the explosives division at Los Alamos and gone on to become Eisenhower's science adviser. "Much information had originally come

---

*Helmut Gröttrup, a guidance, control, and telemetry specialist of renown, declined to work for the Americans because he did not like the terms of his contract and wanted to remain in Germany. The Russians promised him a fine apartment in the Eastern Zone, the best of food and the equivalent of $1,250 a month. They kept their word.

from German engineers who had worked in the U.S.S.R. But they were never trusted very much [by the Russians], and as the Soviets got better at nuclear weapons and guided missiles, the Germans were separated and finally allowed to emigrate to the West. They were important sources of information in those days, but it didn't last long," the scientist explained. There were also repeated attempts to parachute spies into the Soviet Union and get them in by other means, including submarine landings, he said. "But that was a total failure. They were usually intercepted and liquidated. And the defectors, who came over by the thousands, were a decidedly mixed bag. Generally, it was pitiful. It was clear," said George Kistiakowsky, "that the time of Mata Hari had passed."

Kistiakowsky did not mean to imply that there no longer was a need for agents collecting HUMINT. Rather, he meant that under the circumstances spies were providing a mere trickle of useful information where a torrent was needed. In addition, there were many thousands of electronic "secrets" that even an effective spy network would have been ill suited—if not wasted—for trying to pry loose. Should there have been a major war, for example, attacking American aircraft crews would have needed to know the locations of hundreds of Soviet radars, what their ranges were, and what frequencies they operated on so they could be destroyed, skirted, or jammed. Obtaining such information from spies, even under ideal circumstances, would have been a waste of resources better used elsewhere. Accordingly, machines were used to bear the brunt of the espionage effort; in effect, they were pressed into service to spy on other machines.

Listening posts were set up at several points along the periphery of the U.S.S.R.; Liberty Ships and other kinds of vessels bristling with antennas were stationed off Soviet coasts, and many kinds of airplanes were stuffed with cameras, special radio receivers, air-sampling equipment, or all three, and dispatched to Moscow's far-flung frontiers.

In the case of radar, U.S. military aircraft known as ferrets probed along (and occasionally over) the Soviet border from Murmansk to Vladivostok in order to establish the Russians' radar characteristics. This was not new. The Army Air Force had conducted the first ferret mission early in World War II with a B-24D Liberator that operated out of the Aleutians to collect data on Japanese radar on

Kiska Island. Other ferrets, always flying alone at low altitude and at night, supported the invasion of Sicily in the summer of 1943.*

Planning for aerial reconnaissance of the U.S.S.R. began virtually as operations against the Axis ended. As early as December 1947, U.S. reconnaissance planes flying out of Alaska tried to photograph and ferret sections of the Chukotski Peninsula in order to gather information on airfields and radar installations there. Air Force intelligence feared that Soviet bombers operating from the peninsula, just on the other side of the Bering Strait, not only could reach targets in Alaska but could attack many other strategic locations in North America, if only on one-way "suicide" missions. No significant intelligence came of those early flights, partly because the focal length of the cameras was too short to capture meaningful detail, but the peripheral photographic and ferret reconnaissance program was at least under way. Subsequent photography by the 72nd Photo Reconnaissance Squadron using one-hundred-inch lenses turned up "very little activity" and no visible bases from which attacks against North America could be launched. At the same time, one report noted, there might well be elaborate inland bases on which no information is available or [for] which no photo coverage exists." Not having turned up a threat in the immediate vicinity of the Bering Strait, Air Force intelligence peered at the far horizon and wondered about the many secrets hidden there. Clearly, the denied territory had to be penetrated—overflown—in order to assess the threat accurately.

Deep penetrations were under way by the end of 1948. Richard Meyer, then a copilot in the 46th Reconnaissance Squadron at Ladd Field, in Fairbanks, Alaska, was to recall years later that during the summer of 1948 an all-volunteer crew was put together to fly a specially modified, stripped-down RB-29 into Siberia. The rear of the airplane was crammed with new electronic receivers operated by personnel who had not previously been in the squadron and were understood to be on hand for the special missions only.

The first penetration flight took off from Ladd on August 5, left Alaskan airspace at Point Barrow, flew deep into Siberia with its ferreting gear going, and landed at Yokota Air Base, near Tokyo, nineteen hours and forty minutes later. Three additional sorties

---

*That invasion also involved the first operational use of Carpet, which was one of the first radar jammers and was designed at Harvard's Radio Research Laboratory for use against the radar that directed German antiaircraft guns.

were made that summer, the first of which reversed direction, going from Yokota to Ladd in seventeen hours, forty-five minutes.

Two years later, other ferret missions, some of them penetration flights, were taking place from bases in Western Europe, notably Great Britain. Air Force RB-29s, RB-36Ds, RB-45s, and RB-50s, all modified bombers, were staging out of Burtoonwood, Manston, Lakenheath, and Brize Norton. The Air Force was responsible primarily for Eastern Europe, the Baltic, the Gulf of Bothnia, the Murmansk area, and the Caucasus. Meanwhile, the Navy ferreted the Mediterranean and the Black Sea with Privateers and Mercators operating out of Port Lyautey, Morocco.

Ferreting, even over international airspace, was a particularly hazardous business. Since Soviet radars were not generally kept on continuously, the ferrets had to force them on in order to tape their emissions. They often did this by boring straight in at the radar site until the jittery operators turned on the equipment (which soon was to include antiaircraft missile tracking radar) and then, at the last minute and with the tape recorders going, breaking off and heading back toward the apparent safety of open airspace. Many of those coastal and frontier radar stations were located near the air bases whose fighter-interceptors they were supposed to control, however. Ferreting could be extremely dangerous because once the radar started doing what the ferret wanted it to do—tracking the intruder —the fighters would sometime play their part by scrambling and actually going after the ferret.

The game could turn deadly when the fighters caught the recon-naissance planes. Almost forty U.S. aircraft, many of them ferrets, were lost on intelligence-gathering missions by the end of the 1940s as they flew up and down the Berlin corridors, prowled along the Kremlin's vast frontier, or actually made penetrations—some of them hundreds of miles deep—into Soviet airspace with camera shutters clicking and radio receivers and recorders turned on. When the stricken planes made the newspapers at all, which was rare, they were said to have wandered off course. Occasionally they were claimed to have been the victims of unprovoked attacks while flying some distance from Moscow's hotly denied territory. Crews that allegedly wandered off course were at first said to be on weather missions. But when it was realized that interrogations could quickly puncture such cover, they were told to tell their captors that they had been on long-range navigation training exercises. What could be more logical, after all, than fledgling navigators losing their way?

Much of the problem was due to the fact that the United States had no airplane specifically designed for reconnaissance. Elliott Roosevelt had asked for such a craft as early as 1943. That same year the AAF awarded contracts to Hughes and Republic for the development of an airplane specifically for long-range reconnaissance. Each built two prototypes for competitive testing. The Hughes entry, called the XF-11, held only a pilot and was sleek, along the lines of a fighter; its twin-fuselage, twin-engine configuration, in fact, made it reminiscent of Kelly Johnson's P-38. The XF-11 was plagued by development problems (the most embarrassing of which was the crash landing of one of the planes in Los Angeles with Howard Hughes himself at the controls) and was finally eliminated from competition.

Republic's XF-12 was designed by Alexander Kartveli, the company's vice president and the man who designed the P-47 Thunderbolt, one of the war's preeminent fighter-bombers. It was larger and more ambitious than the Hughes plane and was designed to be able to work in conjunction with the B-29s that were to span large areas of the Pacific in the raids against Japan. The XF-12 was therefore provided with four engines and a bullet-shaped fuselage, nearly ninety-four feet long, which was fully pressurized so that its sevenman crew could work without being restricted by umbilical-cordlike oxygen masks and hoses. Its aft section contained stations for vertical, split-vertical, and trimetrogon cameras, which were to operate from behind windows that were protected by electrically controlled sliding panels. The plane was also fitted with a bomb bay that held eighteen stacked flash bombs for night photography and a fully equipped two-table darkroom so that photographs could be processed en route from a mission in order to save time.*The XF-12 could cruise at 470 miles an hour at 40,000 feet and had absolute speed and altitude limits of 497 miles an hour and 49,000 feet, which was certainly equal to, if not a bit better than, the performance of the best of World War II's propeller-driven fighters.

But the end of the war marked the beginning of the transition from propellers to jets. German ME 262s, the world's first operational jet fighters, had been attacking Eighth Air Force bomber formations since the autumn of 1944, the same year the RAF Gloster Meteor first took to the sky. Meanwhile, in the United States, Bell

---

*The technique was invented by the British in World War I, as has been noted, and was used extensively by such U.S. bombers as B-17s and B-29s while on reconnaissance missions.

was building the jet-powered XP-59 Airacomet and Lockheed was putting the finishing touches on the even more advanced XP-80 Shooting Star. And in 1946, the year the XF-12 made its maiden flight, the Soviet Union produced its first three jet fighters: the Yak-15, Yak-17, and MiG-9 (which was a hundred miles an hour faster than the XF-12 at the same altitude). It is doubtful that the AAF knew much about the performance of the first Soviet jet fighters in 1946 (obtaining such information, after all, was what the reconnaissance frenzy was all about), but the advent of the high-speed jets and the consequent end of propeller-driven bombers and related aircraft was by then widely accepted.

In the autumn of 1947, after one of the XF-12s had nearly been totally wrecked while landing during a test at Wright Field and while the other was being tested at Republic's plant at Farmingdale, Long Island, the Air Force ordered twenty of the planes for use on "secret" missions.

"Operating from northern bases (Alaska, Canada), this 'flying photo laboratory' is capable of mapping broad stretches of territory in the Arctic regions and pinpointing new construction and movements of men and equipment with near-invulnerability," *Aviation Week* reported, though deliberately neglecting to mention the nationality of the men and equipment the planes were supposed to photograph. The writer may have been correct in hinting that the F-12s (as they were to be called once their testing, or experimental phase, had been completed) were wanted for sorties against Siberia and points south, but he was wrong in calling them nearly invulnerable. They were so vulnerable to the new fighters then rolling off Soviet assembly lines, and to more advanced models presumed to be on the drawing boards, that the contract was subsequently canceled, marking the end of the XF-12 and the suspension of the old dream of having a reconnaissance plane that could fly over denied territory with impunity. The dream was not to be realized until 1956.

Invulnerability to attack being one of the foremost requirements of a reconnaissance craft, it was only natural to consider building one that would go as high as possible, and that conjured up the notion of spaceflight. On May 2, 1946, the newly created RAND (Research and Development) Corporation, a think tank spin-off of the Douglas Aircraft Company, responded to an Army Air Force request to study the overall question of putting something in space with a

326-page engineering report titled "Preliminary Design of an Experimental World-Circling Spaceship." The authors of the document determined that, based on the then current technology, it was theoretically feasible to place a five-hundred-pound spacecraft in a 300- or 400-mile-high orbit around the earth provided a rocket was used that could fling the device up at a speed of 17,000 miles an hour.

Although the report mainly considered the scientific applications of such a "satellite" (as it was called), it did mention that such a vehicle "offers an observation aircraft [sic] which cannot be brought down by an enemy who has not mastered similar techniques." The cost of the project was estimated to be $150 million and would take five years to bring to fruition. The RAND engineers, a typically conservative, hardheaded group not given to superlatives, were clearly enthralled by the prospect of creating and launching a midget moon. In addition to calling it "one of the most potent scientific tools of the Twentieth Century," they went so far as to predict that "the achievement of a satellite craft by the United States would inflame the imagination of mankind, and would probably produce repercussions in the world comparable to the explosion of the atomic bomb." By 1948, however, budget cuts ordered by the Truman administration would force the military services to abandon such exotic projects in favor of bread-and-butter hardware. Report SM-11827, as the study was also called, would therefore be buried in closed files and largely forgotten.

Meanwhile, the national intelligence establishment made do with what it had, and in 1947 it had balloons as well as airplanes. On September 25 a camera-carrying, unmanned balloon was test-launched from St. Cloud, Minnesota, as part of a program to be code-named Moby Dick. The large balloons were developed by the Office of Naval Research (ONR); the high-altitude cameras were provided by the Air Force; and the project was one of the first to be sponsored by the Central Intelligence Agency, which had been created that year by the National Security Act. While some of the balloons were used for the collection of weather data, most were launched from Western Europe to drift over the Soviet Union, where their cameras recorded whatever the vagaries of the wind and the absence of clouds permitted. Some of them actually made it as far as Japan and the Pacific, where their camera pods were detached by radio command and retrieved. Others came down in the U.S.S.R.

itself and were sequestered. Not only were many of the balloons lost to the Russians in this way, but even those that successfully completed the transcontinental voyage often yielded photographs whose contents were unintelligible. Moby Dick was a singularly unsuccessful way to collect intelligence. The fact that such a haphazard scheme was tried at all is a measure of the desperation with which Washington wanted photo coverage of the Soviet Union.

As the 1950s began, the U.S. Air Force—which had become an autonomous service by virtue of the National Defense Act of 1947 —and the Navy used widely varying types of aircraft that had to be modified for the collection of intelligence, not only from the Soviet Union and its East European proxies but from the People's Republic of China and North Korea as well.

The Air Force adapted several of its fighters to recce operations during the early and mid-1950s, the most notable being the RF-84 Thunderflash,* which was a derivative of Republic's Thunderstreak fighter-bomber, and the RF-86 Sabrejet, a modification of North American's MiG-killing air superiority fighter that carried three cameras in a temperature-controlled compartment beneath the cockpit. Although the Sabrejet's range was limited, as was the range of all fighters before there was air-to-air refueling, its 650-mile-an-hour speed could be used to make sudden low-level penetrations a couple of hundred miles inside denied territory and then race back out before enemy interceptors had time to react. At one point RF-86s reportedly were carried to border areas slung under B-50 bombers and then released to fly in on recce runs. Being delivered to the border by a bomber conserved the fighter's fuel, which allowed a deeper penetration.

The brunt of long-range Air Force reconnaissance during that period, however, was borne by the fleet of modified bombers. There were the aging RB-29s and their larger, more powerful derivatives, the RB-50s. There were the huge, lumbering Convair RB-36Ds that were pushed by six propeller engines and pulled by a pair of jets suspended near either wing tip. RB-36Ds, their cavernous fuselages

*At the time the Air Force became a separate command, it began calling its pursuit planes fighters. The prefix P therefore gave way to F. P-51s, for example, became F-51s. In order to avoid confusion, the designating prefix for reconnaissance aircraft was changed from F to R and used before the letter indicating whether the plane was primarily a fighter, a bomber (B), or a cargo transport (C). F-80 Shooting Stars whose nose guns were replaced by cameras became RF-80s, for instance, and the rugged, dependable B-29s became RB-29s. Modifications for reconnaissance were made on the assembly lines as the planes took shape beside their sisters.

stuffed with electronic interception and ferret equipment in place
of monster bombs, flew repeated missions from England to the
vicinity of Soviet naval bases in the Barents Sea in what their crews
came to call Murmansk runs. Finally, there were the first of the
sweptwing bomber adaptations, Boeing's RB-47s. Of 1,614 B-47Es
built by the Seattle company, 255, or about one in six, were earmarked for reconnaissance.

The Navy depended for the most part on its ponderous Martin
P5M Marlin flying boats and Lockheed's versatile P2V Neptune
patrol planes (a decade later, however, the Navy would own North
American's RA-5C Vigilante, a relatively large but beautifully
streamlined carrier-based reconnaissance plane capable of speeds in
excess of Mach 2, or twice the speed of sound).

By the end of the 1940s, the reconnaissance crews' constituencies
had broadened to include the Atomic Energy Commission, which
had ultimate responsibility for keeping tabs on Soviet atomic and
hydrogen energy progress, including that in the weapons area. Although monitoring Soviet production of fissile materials and its test
program would eventually be undertaken in a variety of ways, the
earliest effort was made through high-altitude air sampling by the
Air Force's Long Range Detection Program. And it was here, rather
than in the areas of PHOTINT, COMINT, and ferreting, that
postwar U.S. aerial reconnaissance scored its first great triumph.

The Long Range Detection Program was created in 1947 at the
urging of AEC member Lewis Strauss, who pointed out in appeals
to Secretary of the Navy James Forrestal, Secretary of the Army
Kenneth Royal, and finally to Eisenhower that the United States
had no way of monitoring the Soviet nuclear program. As a consequence, the Air Force was authorized to establish a system that
would be able to determine without question the time and place of
any nuclear explosion anywhere in the world.

This was done by fitting B-29s with air-sampling boxes that contained filters about the size of an eight- by ten-inch photographic
plate, which would collect radioactive residue from the air as the
plane flew its course. The filters were ordinarily changed every hour
while the location of the area along which they were exposed was
recorded. By September 3, 1949, worldwide sampling by the B-29s
had been uneventful. But on that day Lewis Strauss's prodding paid
off. A WB-29 weather reconnaissance plane on routine patrol from
Japan to Alaska flying at eighteen thousand feet pulled in a record
amount of radioactive particulate matter. Other planes, including

one on a weather flight from Guam to Japan, registered even higher readings. The filters, which were analyzed at Los Alamos, the Naval Research Laboratory, and elsewhere, held traces of the same sort of radioactive debris that was produced by U.S. atomic tests. This left no doubt in the mind of J. Robert Oppenheimer and other top U.S. scientists who studied the evidence that the Soviet Union had detonated its first nuclear bomb. They concluded that the weapon had exploded between the twenty-sixth and twenty-ninth of August on the Asiatic landmass. That turned out to be correct. The Soviet Union's first atomic bomb had gone off at the test facility at Semipalatinsk on August 29.

As LeMay's Strategic Air Command began developing true intercontinental strike capabilities with its B-36s, B-47s, and soon-to-arrive B-52 Stratofortresses, its targeteers in turn developed an insatiable appetite for bombing data they could stick in target folders. They wanted to know exactly where SAC's targets were, what kind of explosives would be necessary to "take them out," how they were defended (including radar coverage), and what the terrain was like on the approach to the targets and along the way out. This required a massive amount of detailed photomapping, ferreting, and the kind of technical intelligence collection that would allow engineers, for example, to calculate the composition and thickness of buildings so that bombs appropriate for particular targets could be selected. The targeteers too became staunch clients of strategic reconnaissance. They took the relationship between reconnaissance and targeting to be so intimate, in fact, that they wanted SAC to control the former so that it could optimally serve the latter. LeMay agreed. The CIA did not. The result was an imbroglio, which began even before the last of the tired old propeller planes had been retired and which was to persist well into the space age.

Then there were the agencies, services, and departments that required regular technical intelligence: unadulterated data on the opposition's (and allies') various weapons, communication and transportation systems, industrial and agricultural facilities, capabilities, and output, atomic energy programs, and everything else that constituted a nation's vital signs. The CIA was solidly in this constituency, as was the National Security Agency (NSA), which was created by Truman in 1952 to handle the preponderance of SIGINT, the State Department's Bureau of Intelligence and Research (INR), and the military services themselves, including their respective intelligence branches. Seventh Fleet admirals wanted to know

how many submarines the Russians had in the Pacific and what their
operational characteristics were; generals of armor in West Germany wanted to know all about the Russian tanks they would face
in case of war; the generals who commanded the fighter-interceptors that were supposed to protect the United States from attack by
Russian bombers wanted to know how many there were, what their
flying qualities were like, and where they would be coming from.
There were a million questions.

Back in 1949, Stalin had ordered the development of a strategic
bombing force of airplanes capable of reaching targets in the United
States and then returning to the U.S.S.R. This resulted in the production of two big bombers: the four-jet-engine M-4—or Bison, as
it was code-named by NATO—which first flew in 1953, and the
TU-20 Bear, powered by four turboprops, which began testing
early the following year. As it turned out, neither plane was considered suitable for long-range bombardment, so they were eventually
relegated to reconnaissance, maritime patrol, and aerial refueling
missions. But Western intelligence did not know their ultimate fate
in 1952; they knew only that they were being developed to get atom
bombs to targets in the Free World.

And there was worse news. In September and October of that
year, many of the German engineers and technicians whom George
Kistiakowsky had referred to were carefully debriefed by American
and British intelligence teams. The sessions, one of which was held
at the Air Technical Intelligence Center at Wright-Patterson Air
Force Base, near Dayton, resulted in an Anglo-American report that
spelled out improvements the Russians had made in the V-2 terror
rockets they had liberated from Germany. The report went on to
describe work on a huge 240,000-pound-thrust rocket engine that
the Russians apparently believed would be able to propel a ballistic
missile 2,275 nautical miles by 1955 or, at the latest, by 1957. The
report was issued in 1953, the month before the Russians tested their
first thermonuclear bomb. The development by the Kremlin of
immensely destructive weapons, together with the means of getting
them to their targets, was becoming a central concern of the foreign
policy makers and defense planners in Washington. Collecting
every possible scrap of information about them was therefore
becoming an obsession in the intelligence establishment.

Shallow penetrations, or even some that went as deep as two
hundred miles, no longer would do. According to Robert Amory,
Jr., then the CIA's deputy director for intelligence, the Air Force

was asked to photograph Kapustin Yar, the first of the Soviet Union's three missile-test facilities, soon after its existence was discovered in 1953. Since the place was well north of the Caspian Sea, some sixty miles due east of Volgograd, General Nathan F. Twining, the Air Force chief of staff, told the CIA that it was out of effective reconnaissance range and that the Air Force therefore would not undertake the mission. The CIA then went to the RAF, which was more receptive. A twin-jet Canberra bomber carrying cameras was soon dispatched on what was probably the first trans-Soviet reconnaissance flight, and one that its crew would undoubtedly long remember. The plane took off from West Germany and then followed the Volga south to the target area. It overflew Kapustin Yar and continued on to Iran, where it landed with "some fair pictures" of the test area, according to Amory, as well as a spate of bullet holes. "The whole of Russia had been alerted to the thing, and it damned near created a major international incident," Amory was to recall later. The RAF responded to the CIA's congratulations by insisting that such a mission would never be repeated.

Still, the British had fared better than many of their American counterparts. On June 13, 1952, a Superfortress on a reconnaissance mission disappeared over the Sea of Japan. No trace of the plane or its thirteen-man crew could be found. On October 7 another Superfortress disappeared from ground-based radar screens after it was attacked by Soviet fighters fifteen thousand feet over Japanese territory. The Russians later claimed that the RB-29 had fired first. Another reconnaissance plane was jumped by MiGs on March 15, 1953, as it patrolled a hundred miles northeast of the Soviet naval facility at Petropavlovsk on the Kamchatka Peninsula. The U.S. Air Force plane returned fire and continued on to its base in Alaska. Four months later, however, an RB-50 was shot down by MiGs over the Sea of Japan; one of its crew was recovered and sixteen were lost. By 1954, reconnaissance planes on important missions in particularly dangerous regions were being escorted by fighters. On January 22 of that year, for example, a U.S. reconnaissance aircraft was attacked by MiGs over the Yellow Sea; sixteen Sabrejets flying close by drove off the attackers, shooting one down. Still, the losses mounted. On September 4 a Navy patrol bomber based at Atsugi, Japan, was shot down by two Soviet fighters forty miles off the Siberian coast; one of the crew was killed and nine survived.

Evidence of the growing Soviet nuclear threat seemed to increase even as the casualty rate among reconnaissance crews mounted. On

Red Air Force Day, 1955, Colonel Charles E. Taylor, the U.S. air attaché in Moscow, went to Tushino Airport to watch the annual military air parade, a flyby in which Soviet aircraft passed in review. Stunned, Taylor counted fully twice the number of Bison bombers as had flown past in the May Day parade earlier that year. The number of Bisons Taylor counted, in fact, amounted to four times that of the B-52s, which had only just started entering SAC's inventory. Taylor reported what he had witnessed. By the end of the year the number of Bisons scheduled to be in service by 1960 was estimated at between 600 and 800, while the production rate for Bear bombers was figured at 25 a month. The highly classified estimates were then leaked to the press, resulting in an apparent "bomber gap" and Senate hearings, which began in April 1956. Alone among the three military services, the Air Force issued dire predictions about the relative strengths of Soviet and American strategic bombing capability and in the process put the budget-minded Eisenhower administration on the defensive.

As it turned out, however, Colonel Taylor had been the victim of a shrewd hoax. No sooner had the first ten Bisons passed out of sight of the reviewing stand than they made a wide circle, were joined by eight more Bisons, and then made another pass over the crowd. The second formation evidently consisted of every M-4 capable of getting into the air that day. The result of the ruse was to show Taylor, the other air attachés, and the people of Moscow that the Kremlin had many more long-range bombers than it actually did. Since the stunt was pulled only weeks before Eisenhower, Khrushchev, and other world leaders were to meet in Geneva for a summit conference, it is likely that the wily Soviet premier was trying to inflate his country's military posture because he thought that doing so would enhance his political leverage.

As was to happen more than once during the arms race, though, Khrushchev's deception had the ironic effect of stimulating a weapons spurt in the United States. In this case, the flap raised by what appeared to be a bomber gap forced Eisenhower to authorize production of more B-52s than he wanted.

The trick also came as a prelude to the Open Skies proposal that Ike brought to Geneva in the hope of braking the costly and dangerous nuclear arms race that was already getting under way. The proposal, which had been inspired by a young Harvard political scientist named Henry Kissinger, called for nothing less than frequent, unimpeded inspection flights by U.S. and Soviet reconnaissance aircraft and an exchange of blueprints and plans for military installations. Such a reciprocal program, it was reasoned, would allow each side to monitor the other's military status and in the process ease tensions and reduce the sort of uncertainty about weapons levels that was driving the arms race. "I only wish that God would give me some means of convincing you of our sincerity and loyalty in making this proposal," Eisenhower told an impassive Soviet delegation. For his part, Nikita Khrushchev would scornfully dismiss Open Skies as a transparent attempt by the United States to commit sanctioned aerial espionage over the U.S.S.R. But the Russians were going to be overflown one way or another, Eisenhower knew, whether they liked it or not.

A year earlier the tenuous state of U.S. military preparedness and the growing threat from Moscow prompted J. Robert Oppenheimer to suggest to the Office of Defense Management's Science Committee (ODMSC) that a study of the situation and recommendations for improvement were warranted. The ODMSC, a collection of notables from the loftiest echelons of the nation's science and technology establishment (including James B. Conant and James R. Killian, Jr., of MIT), met with Ike on March 27, 1954, and was steered by him into a discussion on the danger of a surprise attack and on the high priority he thought ought to be given to preventing one. The fear of such a grim occurrence, given the nature of nuclear weapons, haunted Eisenhower throughout his presidency. And he was not alone. "This was at a time when the Pearl Harbor surprise attack was still very much on everyone's mind," Richard M. Bissell, Jr., was to recall three decades later. Bissell was shortly to play a major role in the events that developed as a result of the March meeting in the White House.

Eisenhower mandated his science brain trust to come up with solutions to the surprise-attack problem, and they, in turn, responded in the time-honored way of academicians the world over. They decided that Killian, then president of MIT, should form a subcommittee to study the feasibility of conducting a full-blown study. The subcommittee reported less than three weeks later that it believed a major study was indeed justified. Killian duly received a letter from Eisenhower on July 26 urging him to head the study. He accepted and had his forces deployed by summer's end.

The group, which went by the innocuous-sounding name of the

Technological Capabilities Panel (TCP), consisted of a steering committee, three project teams, a communications working group, and a military advisory committee. The fifty or so individuals who contributed their time to the TCP represented the cream of the nation's military, industrial, and scientific communities. They came from Bell Labs, Los Alamos, Brookhaven National Laboratory, RAND, the California Institute of Technology, Shell Oil, Polaroid, MIT, the Lincoln Laboratories, the Carnegie Institution, Harvard, Princeton, Washington University, the University of Wisconsin, Williams College, and elsewhere, including the CIA and the three armed services.

The TCP was an administrative tour de force, not only because of the caliber of the people Killian selected, but because he assembled them very quickly and had their combined report, titled "Meeting the Threat of Surprise Attack," in the White House on Valentine's Day, 1955—about a year after the project was conceived.

The three project teams—one devoted to offense, one to defense, and one to intelligence—were the heart of the TCP. Project 3, which concerned technical intelligence collection, was chaired by Edwin H. Land of Polaroid and included James G. Baker, the Harvard astronomer and optics expert who had done the highly innovative lens work for George Goddard.*

"We *must* find ways to increase the number of hard facts upon which our intelligence estimates are based, to provide better strategic warning, to minimize surprise in the kind of attack, and to reduce the danger of gross overestimation or gross underestimation of the threat," said Project 3's section of the report. "To this end, we recommend adoption of a vigorous program for the extensive use, in many intelligence procedures, of the most advanced knowledge in science and technology."

Eisenhower considered much of the material enumerated by the Land group to be so sensitive that he didn't even want the National Security Council to be informed of it for fear of leaks. Instead, the president was briefed in private by Killian and Land, who described several reconnaissance systems they and their colleagues considered promising, including earth satellites of the sort first mentioned in RAND's Report SM-11827. Not only was satellite technology still

---

*The others were Joseph W. Kennedy of Washington University, Allen Latham, Jr., of Arthur D. Little, Inc., Edward M. Purcell of Harvard, and John W. Tukey of Princeton.

in its infancy, however, but the big boosters on which the satellites would have to ride to orbit were themselves only in the beginning of the blueprint stage.*

But, Killian and Land explained to Eisenhower during one of several private meetings, there was an interim solution. There was a design for a plane—for an integrated reconnaissance system, actually—that would be able to fly so high over the Soviet Union that it would be out of reach of the most advanced fighters and SAMs the Russians were known to have. In essence, the system would consist of a remarkable camera developed mostly by Baker, special film for it that Eastman Kodak was to perfect in strict secrecy in Rochester, a small but powerful ELINT system for intercepting communication signals, a radar capable of picking up threats at considerable distance, and an airplane to carry it all.

The plane would be relatively slow and unarmed, Killian and Land told the president. But it would also be light and would have very high aspect ratio wings—long, narrow, gently tapered wings like a sailplane's—that would be able to find enough air to float on so it could climb past sixty-five thousand feet. The high-flier had been conceived by Kelly Johnson, the aeronautical genius who ran Lockheed's Advanced Development Projects office in Burbank, California. The office was, and remains, a closely guarded engineering incubator known affectionately to its inhabitants and a few outsiders as the Skunk Works.† Ike knew of Johnson and he certainly knew about P-38s. What he wanted to know from Killian and Land, though, was whether Johnson's plane would really perform as advertised, especially given the consequences should it go down over Soviet territory. Eisenhower, duly reassured, approved development of the plane as a black program with some apprehension. The project's initial code name was Aquatone.

Had the Air Force gotten its way, however, there would have been no Aquatone. In March 1953 the Air Force had issued a design requirement for a one-man "special reconnaissance aircraft weapon

---

*Work on the Atlas ICBM, the first of the big missiles, had begun only the month before, in January 1955. It became a crash program the following September and was first launched successfully on December 17, 1957. The Thor IRBM, which was to carry the first U.S. reconnaissance satellite to orbit in the summer of 1960, also had begun development in 1955; like Atlas, it too would be launched successfully for the first time in the autumn of 1957.
†The name originated in 1943, when the P-80 Shooting Star was being designed in circus tents next to a plastics factory in Burbank. The pungent odor that wafted into the tents from the factory brought to mind the foul-smelling "Skunk Works" factory in Al Capp's Li'l Abner comic strip, and the name stuck.

system" that was to be unarmed and capable of reaching seventy thousand feet. Only Bell Aircraft and Fairchild were asked to submit proposals, however, as it was felt that the big manufacturers—North American, Douglas, Lockheed, Hughes, Republic, Boeing, and Convair, for example—would not take the project seriously enough because the eventual reconnaissance planes would be ordered in relatively small numbers. And so pressing had the need for long-range reconnaissance become by 1953 that the Air Force had also asked the Glenn L. Martin Aircraft Company to modify the Canberras it was building for the USAF under license from the English Electric Company as a stopgap measure. The American version of the RAF bomber which that same year made the daring reconnaissance run to Kapustin Yar was called the B-57. What the Air Force had had in mind was an RB-57 with substantially elongated wings so that it too could reach very high altitudes.* The Air Force had named its new reconnaissance project Bald Eagle.

The Bell and Fairchild proposals, called Model 67 and the M-195, respectively, had been submitted to the Air Force in January 1954. Then, on May 18—even as the Air Force neared a decision on the competing entries and Killian, up at Cambridge, was shaping his Technological Capabilities Panel—another, unsolicited proposal had come in. This one, from Kelly Johnson, amounted to a stretch-wing version of his brand-new XF-104 Starfighter (the prototype of which had flown for the first time only that January) and carried the company designation CL-282. The need for a high-altitude reconnaissance plane had been "obvious" to Johnson for some time, so with the encouragement and close support of Trevor Gardner, the assistant secretary of the Air Force for research and development, he had taken it upon himself to submit CL-282 to the Air Force. But the plane had been rejected almost immediately for several reasons, the most notable of which had to do with the fact that the Air Force had not believed that the engine Johnson had in mind for the plane was powerful enough to accomplish the mission requirement. Fairchild's M-195 had also been eliminated, leaving Bell's Model 67 the winner. The Niagara Falls firm had been notified accordingly that same month—May—and a contract had been signed in September. Bell had immediately begun building the first plane, now renamed

---

*The twenty RB-57Ds that were eventually built had wingspans of 106 feet, or 43 feet longer than those of standard B-57s. Since the original single spar running the length of the wings was maintained, the elongated wings weakened over time because of the additional stress and tended to collapse on landing.

X-16, with the expectation that it would be completed in a year and a half. But that was not to be.

Undaunted, Johnson and Gardner had lobbied Edwin Land's technical intelligence group as soon as it was formed and had won it over, not only with the CL-282's design but with Johnson's pledge to have the spy plane in the air within eight months of signing a contract. There had been two other factors, however, which even more decisively affected not only Kelly Johnson's airplane but the future of the entire overhead reconnaissance program.

First, Eisenhower had not wanted the Air Force to play a primary role in the collection of technical intelligence. Allowing any military service, but particularly the Air Force, to compose its shopping list for weapons based on a threat assessment that came from intelligence it alone collected, processed, and interpreted was absolutely untenable where Eisenhower was concerned. Second (and no doubt related to the first factor), Allen Dulles and his colleagues in the CIA had decided to fling their cloak, if not their dagger, into the air. Dulles had become convinced that aerial reconnaissance "could collect information with more speed, accuracy and dependability than could any agent on the ground," and he therefore resolved to get the agency into the reconnaissance business.

By November 1954, Killian and Land had first convinced Eisenhower that CL-282 was viable and then Ike, meeting with Killian, Secretary of Defense Donald Quarles, Allen Dulles, and some others, had made it known that he was adamant in not wanting the Air Force to control the program he had just approved or aerial reconnaissance in general. As Killian was to note many years afterward, Eisenhower was at that moment feeling the effects of the bomber gap, which the Air Force was using to pry more funding out of Congress. And the gap had only been created in the first place, Eisenhower was convinced, because of faulty Air Force intelligence. There was another reason, too. He also believed that the political blow that would come in the event one of the planes went down over the U.S.S.R. would be less severe if it was flown by a civilian rather than a military pilot. "So he said this should go ahead," Killian recalled Eisenhower stating in reference to Aquatone, "but you must find a way to do it that does not give primary responsibility to the Air Force." They did. Primary responsibility was given to the CIA, and Dulles, in turn, made it the direct responsibility of Richard M. Bissell, Jr., whom he had brought into the agency that year as his troubleshooting special assistant. Bald Eagle was dead, the Air Force had been flanked, and the CIA was into aerial reconnaissance.

Bissell was the quintessential CIA type: a tall, distinguished-looking Ivy Leaguer (Dulles was a Princetonian) partial to three-piece suits, modulated conversation, manners, and an outward modesty bordering on self-effacement. He came from Hartford, Connecticut, had attended Groton and Yale, then did postgraduate work at the London School of Economics before earning a doctorate in economics back at Yale. He had taught there (McGeorge Bundy was one of his students) and at MIT, and had gone on to assorted government jobs during and immediately after the war before being recruited by Dulles.

Sitting in his small office in Framingham, Connecticut, on a sunny spring afternoon in 1984, Richard Bissell thought back almost exactly thirty years, to the birth of the U-2. The former head of the CIA's black operations division—the architect of the most successful aerial espionage program in history up to that time, and the planner of the equally disastrous Bay of Pigs invasion—was still well over six feet tall, had clear blue eyes, and looked for all the world like the president of a small Presbyterian college in New England as he sipped sherry and rummaged through memories of events whose consequences were to be of the most profound importance to the United States.

He had been informed by Dulles "out of the blue" one morning at the very end of November 1954 that he was to head the Aquatone program, Bissell recalled. At four o'clock that afternoon, he was sitting in an office in the Pentagon with Herbert Miller, a CIA specialist on atomic intelligence; Trevor Gardner; Lieutenant General Donald Putt, the Air Force's deputy chief of staff for development; and some other Air Force officers. The purpose of the meeting was to set organizational priorities and divide responsibilities for the new black program.

"When we got into the full meeting," Bissell explained while methodically applying his penknife to an apple, "it became readily apparent that although a top-level decision had been made on the program, nothing had been worked out about who was going to do what, where the money was going to come from, or anything else. When the question of money arose, everyone looked in my direction." Bissell responded by assuring his colleagues that he would recommend to Dulles that money be drawn from the CIA's special reserve fund, which required informing the director of the budget and getting Eisenhower's approval. Although the number of U-2s to be ordered initially did not come up at that first meeting, Bissell recalled, it was hastily calculated that about $30 million ought to do the job. (The first batch of U-2s would number thirty.)

"It was decided that Kelly Johnson would be called forthwith, and I think Gardner actually called him from the meeting to say that we had a go-ahead. Johnson then told Gardner that he would begin clearing a hangar that afternoon so that work on the spy plane could begin immediately." CL-282 would shortly be rechristened the U (for the suitably ambiguous Utility) No. 2. And its code name would change to Idealist.

Within a week or so of the first meeting, Bissell added, "it was agreed that the CIA would contract with Lockheed for the airframe. It was agreed that we would go to work immediately on payloads, mainly cameras. It was agreed that the Air Force would furnish J-57 engines which they would in effect smuggle out of ongoing Air Force programs," including those for the new B-52 bombers that had begun to loom so important because of the supposed gap with the Russians, as well as those for the F-100 Super Sabre and F-102 Delta Dagger (the latter being a fighter-interceptor that was supposed to defend the country against all the bombers the Air Force insisted the Russians possessed).

Even as Johnson and his engineers at the Skunk Works began finalizing their blueprints and supervising the cutting of some metal that December and January so the U-2 could fly within the promised eight months, work was progressing on the plane's remarkable camera system. The U-2's main camera, which was to set the standard for the reconnaissance cameras that followed, represented a quantum leap from its World War II ancestors.

The Model 73B, or simply the Type B camera, was built by the Hycon Corp. of Southern California based on joint design work by Land and Baker. As amateur photographers know, moving the hands while taking a picture causes the image on the film to blur because of vibration. That problem had vexed the designers of reconnaissance cameras as far back as World War I because all airplanes (and, to a far lesser extent, satellites) vibrate. Cushioning or otherwise insulating cameras helped, but it was insufficient for operation at the kind of extreme altitudes the U-2 was to inhabit. The difficulty was overcome by inventing a system of precise image-movement compensation that allowed not only for the motion of the plane and the vibration from its engine, but for the movement of

Kodak's new, fast, highly sensitive film, which was wound on twin spools, each of which held about six thousand feet and produced four thousand pairs of stereoscopic photographs.

Baker's lens had a focal length of three feet. Using the thin low-grain film, it could produce photographs with a resolution of sixty lines per millimeter. This meant that sixty separate lines could be distinguished in every millimeter of a photograph taken "at alti-tude" (about seventy thousand feet). Put another way, the vibration-compensating camera, Baker's lens, and Kodak's film produced photographs that, blown up, could differentiate between objects the size of a basketball taken at a distance of more than thirteen miles.* In addition, there was automatic lens focusing at all altitudes and an automatic exposure control apparatus—a very sophisticated light meter—that improved tonality by exposing the film for the darker targets while reducing the washout from such light ones as snow and clouds. The photographs could cover terrain up to 125 miles wide over the course of a 2,600-mile-long flight.

But Johnson had not designed the U-2 as a platform for only one type of sensor, however good it was. The plane was a model of simplicity and adaptability. It could and did carry several different kinds of specialized cameras and a wide variety of SIGINT equip-ment, including many specialized antennas that were to sprout on some U-2s in arrays known as "antenna farms." It could also carry air-sampling filters for nuclear detonation reconnaissance, side-look-ing radar that could image ground features at night and in cloudy skies, and its own defensive system, consisting of an air-to-air radar, a "fuzz-buster" that warned when it was being tracked by enemy radar, and metallic chaff that could be released to obscure the plane from that radar.

The U-2 was designed to carry all of the snooping gear in several places, the largest of which was a temperature-controlled "Q-bay" immediately behind the pilot. There were several other bays in the fuselage, and eventually U-2s would sprout large sensor pods mid-way along their wings and special handmade blisters or domes. Most ingenious of all, Kelly Johnson and his colleagues provided their spy plane with the capacity to use several different nose sections the way

---

*At a news conference following the shooting down of Francis Gary Powers on May 1, 1960, Eisenhower made public a U-2 photograph in which white parking-lot stripes were clearly distinguishable. This did not mean that all U-2 photographs had such resolution, however. Atmospheric conditions involving dust, haze, smog, or heat thermals frequently degraded resolution, which, of course, compounded the interpreters' problems. They still do.

cameras use interchangeable lenses. This meant that rather than wasting time taking cameras out of a U-2 and replacing them with side-looking radar, for example, the nose with the cameras could simply be detached from the bulkhead immediately in front of the cockpit and replaced with another holding the radar. Changing noses took about an hour.

The first U-2, which had been given the oblique name "Article 341" by the CIA, left the Skunk Works in crates early in July 1955 and was flown in an Air Force C-124 to Groom Lake, Nevada, a remote dry lake bed some one hundred miles northwest of Las Vegas, which adjoined the Yucca Flat nuclear test site. Article 341, whose long, drooping wings, slightly rounded nose, and outsized vertical tail bore no resemblance whatever to its bullet-shaped cousin, the stub-winged Starfighter, first got off the ground by accident on July 29, 1955. Its test pilot, Lockheed's Tony LeVier, took it down the runway at sixty-five miles an hour to see how its control surfaces responded on the ground, a common practice. As it turned out, however, the U-2 wanted to fly at that speed, and before LeVier knew it, he was several feet into the air. It was the soaring quality of the U-2 that was its greatest asset, since the aircraft would be able to fly great distances at extremely high altitude on relatively little power, much like a migrating bird whose long wings keep it buoyed on a cushion of air. By the same token, however, the outsized wings could make landing tricky because the U-2 tended to cling to the air even after its engine had been throttled way back. Every pilot who flew the U-2 agreed that it took quite a bit of getting used to.

Bissell was to credit the U-2's innovative design and record-breaking delivery time not only to Johnson's ingenuity but to the close working relationship that existed between the agency and the Skunk Works. It was a relationship, he maintained, that made full use of the telephone, not voluminous pro forma letters and memoranda. Each month during the winter and spring of 1955, Bissell recalled, Johnson would send a "five- or six-page double-spaced progress report" that would briefly mention pertinent activities and any problems that had arisen, together with a statement of accumulated expenditures against budget. (Bissell added that the CIA's special reserve fund, which did not require the usual budgetary restraints and congressional oversight, also helped keep the program greased; it was tapped quickly and quietly when needed.)

Ben R. Rich, who succeeded Johnson as head of the Skunk

Works, echoed Bissell. The U-2 and its successor, the SR-71, owe their existence to the fact that the Air Force's labyrinthine specifications, regulations, and horde of "blue light specialists and red light specialists" could be bypassed in favor of a small group working informally "in a black, skunky way."

Meanwhile, LeMay, now head of SAC at Offutt Air Force Base, outside Omaha, decided that his command ought to control the U-2 program. Throughout the late spring and summer of 1955, LeMay exerted pressure to bring Idealist under SAC's wing, even as a joint working relationship was being hammered out in Washington between the CIA and the Air Force over the logistics of the program. The cigar-chomping SAC commander finally, begrudgingly, conceded the plane to the CIA, according to Bissell, but not before insisting that SAC play a major role in training U-2 pilots. "This," said Bissell, "we were only too pleased to have done." In any event, SAC was to receive its own U-2s in 1957.

Then, in January 1956, with the first two U-2s poised for deployment to England in April in preparation for the blackest, most daring aerial espionage operation in history—and one that depended in considerable measure on catching the Russians off guard, at least initially—Bissell and his colleagues were horrified to learn that yet another balloon armada had been launched at the Soviet Union from Western Europe and Turkey, this time by the Air Force.

The new balloon reconnaissance program, successively codenamed Gopher, Grandson, Grayback, and ultimately Genetrix, had as its aim the gathering of intelligence "of the highest priority" relating to Soviet bomber and fighter bases, missile launching sites, nuclear weapons stockpiles, other military installations, transportation systems, aspects of economic development, and antiaircraft batteries and radar sites. Data in this ambitious enterprise were to be collected by more than five hundred high-altitude balloons that were to float across the Soviet Union in the course of about a week under the guise of observing meteorological phenomena. When they reached the Pacific, the plan went, the cameras would be released on signal from the balloons and parachute to earth, where they would be picked up. Of the total launched, 243 of the balloons were never heard from again and only 44 were eventually recovered. Many of the balloons did not stay up for as long as had been anticipated and came down on Soviet territory; many others were apparently shot out of the sky.

The "balloon crusade," as *The New York Times* called it, exploded on page one on February 6. That edition and two subsequent ones provided rich details about how the balloons had been launched so that the prevailing winds would carry them across the U.S.S.R. (just like the Navy's Moby Dick) and how many of them had been triumphantly displayed in Moscow after having been shot down by MiGs. Each balloon was about fifty feet in diameter when inflated, and each carried a plastic container the size of a refrigerator that weighed 1,430 pounds and carried radio beacon equipment and aerial cameras. Instructions in English, French, Japanese, Arabic, and Urdu were attached to the outside of each container: "This box came from the sky. It is harmless. It has weather information in it. Notify the authorities. You will receive a valuable reward when you turn it in as is." Not to leave anything to chance, the writing was accompanied by a picture showing peasants recovering a balloon, bringing it to town, and then being presented with a bagful of money by grateful officials.

The Kremlin accused the United States of transparently attempting to unilaterally carry out the same Open Skies inspection program that had been summarily rejected the previous July. They were making that up, of course, but they were a lot closer to the truth than they had any reason to know. On February 7 the U.S. embassy in Moscow delivered a note to the Foreign Ministry claiming that the balloons were engaged in weather research and even explaining rather lamely that the cameras were carried "to provide pictures of cloud formations which bear on air movements at various velocities." But at the public display and press conference in Moscow, a Soviet colonel had exhibited exposed film allegedly taken from one of the downed cameras that showed not clouds but mountains and an air base. Soviet photo interpreters, he said, had identified the base as being in Turkey.

No sooner had the SAC-trained pilots and their pair of U-2s been formed as the 1st Weather Reconnaissance Squadron (Provisional) at RAF Lakenheath than Anthony Eden, the British prime minister, abruptly withdrew permission for the black spy planes to operate from Great Britain. Eden's decision followed the widely reported and politically embarrassing death of Lieutenant-Commander Lionel Crabb, a British frogman who evidently had been sent to snoop under a Soviet cruiser docked in the Thames on a goodwill visit, and who had been found floating, decapitated, near the vessel. The prime minister did not seem to want to risk further embarrassment by having the American spy planes operate from British soil while making forays over the U.S.S.R. But Konrad Adenauer had no such qualms. The U-2s were therefore moved to Wiesbaden, north of Frankfurt, and eventually to a smaller former World War II Luftwaffe base near the East German frontier. The forward base not only was more secure than the heavily populated environs around Frankfurt, but was closer to the target area, which helped conserve fuel.

The first operational mission went up even before the move from Wiesbaden, however. A U-2 that had been called Article 347 took off on July 4, 1956, and flew a route that took it over Moscow, Leningrad, and the Baltic coast before it returned home. The photographs were superb and proved the validity of the concept beyond any doubt. A second U-2 mission penetrated the Ukraine. Meanwhile, the 2nd Weather Reconnaissance Squadron (Provisional) went to Incirlik air base outside Adana, Turkey, that August. A third unit was subsequently deployed at Atsugi naval air station near Tokyo.

In the nearly four years from that first overflight to the day in May 1960 when Francis Gary Powers was shot down, U-2s from the three "weather squadrons" made some twenty deep penetrations, ranging over Eastern Europe, the western Soviet Union, the Ukraine, Siberia, and the Kamchatka Peninsula. Detachment 10-10, as Incirlik's unit was also called, sometimes staged out of a remote strip at Peshawar, Pakistan, always taking off at dusk. Typically, the Peshawar missions would take the planes over the nuclear testing facility at Semipalatinsk and the missile test complex at Tyuratam before they swung south for a landing in eastern Iran. One of the U-2s took off from Bodø, Norway, and flew down the entire length of the western U.S.S.R. one night, collecting reams of ELINT before it landed back at Incirlik.

While the Kremlin, frustrated by the airplanes it could track on radar but not catch, issued a stream of quiet protests defending the sanctity of its airspace, the Black Lady of Espionage, as the U-2 came to be called, provided a bonanza of data on the Soviet nuclear weapons and ballistic missile test programs (a U-2 is reputed to have spotted the first Russian ICBM in 1960) and in the process put an end to both the bomber and missile gaps by showing that the Kremlin had far fewer bombers or missiles than the Air Force supposed. They also returned with thousands of photographs of Soviet naval facilities, industrial complexes, railroad networks, military bases, details of military aircraft, and the kind of precise mapping information that SAC's targeteers were desperate to have.

The downing of Francis Gary Powers, an event virtually everyone connected with the program surmised would happen sooner or later,* forced Eisenhower to end the flights over the Soviet Union. But the scrapping of the overflight program, though it came suddenly, had really been foreshadowed three years earlier, not in a Soviet weapons laboratory but in an American think tank.

---

*In his memoir, Killian refers to John Foster Dulles, Eisenhower's secretary of state and Allen's brother, as recalling that Ike feared the consequences of such an incident even as he approved the program. "Well, boys," Foster Dulles quoted Ike as having said in the former's Princeton oral history, "I believe the country needs this information, and I'm going to approve it. But I'll tell you one thing. Someday one of these machines is going to be caught, and we're going to have a storm." No one doubted that.

4

Threats, Real and Imagined

However capable the U-2s were, no one involved in the Soviet overflights seriously doubted that someday one of the spy planes would be successfully challenged. Some calculated that a U-2 would be brought down within a year of the start of the operation. Some said two years. A very few gave it as long as four. But no one disputed the fact that air-breathing reconnaissance platforms, no matter how high they flew, were captives of the atmosphere and would therefore always be vulnerable to attack by fighters or SAMs. Awareness of the danger predated the U-2s and so did the apparent solution: Go still higher. Space was as high as cameras could go, and that is precisely where overhead reconnaissance was headed.

The Air Force had been the first to become interested in satellite reconnaissance and that interest paralleled a growing awareness in the late forties and early fifties that long-range ballistic missiles propelled by powerful boosters were theoretically possible. Notwithstanding Dr. Vannevar Bush's widely quoted testimony at a Senate committee hearing in 1945 that such weapons would not be feasible "for a very long period of time to come," German successes with the V-2 had prompted all three armed services to take long-range missiles seriously (the Army preferred to think of them as being extremely long-range artillery rounds, and therefore within its just domain, which is why the Army Ballistic Missile Agency was created at Huntsville, Alabama, to produce IRBMs like Redstone and Jupiter. The ABMA was Wernher von Braun's home roost).

During that period, even as thought centered on the development of long-range missiles, the Air Force asked RAND for a series of studies, first directed at earth satellites in general, and then at reconnaissance platforms in particular. The first report, "Preliminary Design of an Experimental World-Circling Spaceship," came out in May 1946. Others followed in rapid succession between 1947 and 1952: "Aerodynamics, Gas Dynamics and Heat Transfer Problems of a Satellite Rocket," "Study of Launching Sites for a Satellite Projectile," "Utility of a Satellite Vehicle for Reconnaissance," and "Inquiry into the Feasibility of Weather Reconnaissance from a Satellite Vehicle."

In March 1954 RAND issued another study, cosponsored by the CIA, which was code-named Feedback. This one was so long that its summary alone, titled "An Analysis of the Potential of an Unconventional Reconnaissance Method," spanned two volumes. The RAND engineers concluded that the Air Force ought to undertake "at the earliest possible date completion and use of an efficient satellite reconnaissance vehicle as a matter of vital strategic interest to the United States." (James Killian's Technological Capabilities Panel would make the same recommendation eleven months later.) The RAND report suggested two possible reconnaissance techniques.

The first involved the use of television cameras that would photograph ground targets and then store the imagery on tape until the satellite passed over a receiving station. It would then "dump" its intelligence catch by radio link to the station. Since the spacecraft would circle the planet about once every hour and a half, they could be expected to pass near a receiving station on some piece of friendly territory at close intervals. They might therefore be able to transmit their imagery so quickly that it would almost be in real time—as the event being photographed was taking place.

The second method depended upon a conventional camera taking photographs that would then be processed into negatives on board the spacecraft. As the satellite flew over a ground station the processed film would be line-scanned by a device roughly similar to an electric eye that would convert what it saw into electrical signals for quick transmission to earth. The notion of being able to collect intelligence from the other side of the world even as an event occurred was a captivating one.

The Air Force used the RAND study to shape General Operational Requirement No. 80, which was issued on March 16, 1955. It called for proposals from industry for the development of a photographic reconnaissance satellite roughly along the lines suggested by RAND, but with considerable leeway. The requirement stipulated that the USAF expected a "strategic satellite system" whose spacecraft could achieve a predicted orbit with precisely planned parameters, be stabilized on all three axes, have a high pointing accuracy for its cameras, be able to receive and execute commands from ground controllers, and send collected intelligence to appropriate ground stations.

Proposals came in from RCA, Martin, and Lockheed's Missile Systems Division at Sunnyvale, California, near Palo Alto (a sister group, the Skunk Works, was at the moment assembling Article 341 some three hundred miles to the south in a secure building adjacent to Burbank's airport). Lockheed's submission not only detailed ideas for the kind of "nonrecoverable" radio-relay reconnaissance systems covered in RAND's 1954 study, but also suggested work on a "recoverable" system in which capsules would return to earth with exposed film instead of transmitting them by radio. The idea also happened to be the subject of a RAND study that was under way at the time Lockheed made its proposal. The company was notified at the end of October 1956 that it had been awarded a contract to develop Weapons System 117L, also called the Advanced Reconnaissance System, which was to include both recoverable and nonrecoverable spacecraft. WS-117L was code-named Pied Piper.

The project was to evolve over the course of the next five years into two distinct reconnaissance systems and one surveillance system. Together, they constituted the nation's first space program; individually, they set the basis for the three fundamental types of earth observation system that remained in use for the next thirty years. The first would transmit reconnaissance imagery by radio. The second would carry the pictures out of orbit in the reconnaissance capsules, which would then float down under parachutes. The third, an early warning system to be named MIDAS (Missile Alarm Defense System), was to become the progenitor of a series of very high orbiting satellites that would stand vigil, watching for the multiple blasts of fire indicating that a Soviet ballistic missile attack was under way and then sound the alarm.

As prime contractor, Lockheed's Missile Systems Division would design all three systems. It would do so in a way reminiscent of the conceptual flexibility that had gone into the design of the U-2, with its mission-specific multiple noses. Lockheed was to develop a satellite that was in fact an extremely reliable second-stage rocket package that would fit on top of a powerful first-stage booster. The booster would carry the second stage, and the second stage would carry the payload, which would vary according to the mission. The second stage and its payload would together be the satellite where low-orbit reconnaissance missions were concerned.

The payloads would in turn be built by subcontractors such as General Electric, which was to manufacture the recoverable capsules in Pennsylvania and ship them to California for mating with the second stages built by Lockheed. The engineers in Sunnyvale were also looking at two likely boosters for their satellite: modified versions of the Douglas Thor IRBM and Convair's Atlas ICBM, both of which were in the early stages of development when the contract for WS-117L was awarded.

Lockheed's satellite was initially a nineteen-foot-long (it was soon to be stretched to twenty-five feet), five-foot-in-diameter cylinder weighing eighty-five hundred pounds at the instant its booster lifted it off the launch pad. It, in turn, consisted of three subsections. There was a conical nose that held the payload, guidance and control systems, telemetry equipment for radioing flight-performance data back to earth, and related hardware, including a battery that would power its equipment and the payload. The middle section held about seven thousand pounds of liquid fuel and oxydizer. The rear section was a Bell Aerosystems rocket engine that developed fifteen thousand pounds of thrust with a high degree of reliability. The idea was for the booster to carry the satellite to near-orbital altitude and then burn out, separate, and fall away. The satellite and its payload would then continue moving toward final orbit under the power of the Bell engine until its navigation system had aligned it with the horizon and it was parallel to the earth. Nearly all of the seven thousand pounds of fuel and liquid oxygen would be burned while the satellite maneuvered into its final mission orbit, leaving it weighing only about three quarters of a ton, including its payload.

The shiny white bullet-nosed cylinder, which was to be christened Agena, was destined to become the workhorse of the U.S. space fleet—an all-purpose truck that would carry both civilian and military sensing systems on a wide variety of missions. The versatile spacecraft would also be used on several scientific expeditions, including the Ranger moon probes, the Nimbus weather satellite series, the Echo passive radio relay project, the Orbiting Solar Observatory, and the Orbiting Geophysical Observatory. Its major early triumph in a civilian program was to come on December 14, 1962, when the Mariner 2 it shot at Venus passed within 21,598 miles of the planet to become mankind's first successful planetary probe. All of these missions lent credibility to a space program that was widely seen as being second to the Soviet Union's in the wake of the Sputnik and Lunik extravaganzas. Agena, used in combination with the Thor and Atlas boosters, would carry the bulk of America's "white" satellites as an astronautical delivery vehicle for many years.

Meanwhile, space reconnaissance remained central among the black programs, and Agena figured prominently in these, too. Even as work progressed on the two Air Force projects involving television transmission and on-board film processing for relay by radio link, RAND engineers continued to press on with the concept of getting a capsule out of orbit and returning it to earth with its film pack intact. This was necessary because television and radio transmission of pictures had a disadvantage as well as the obvious advantage of speed. The problem was that neither transmission method produced pictures with the kind of resolution that was required for effective reconnaissance. The difference in picture quality between TV and radio-transmitted imagery and that of a standard photograph was roughly similar to the difference between a televised picture of, say, someone's face and a photograph of the same face. The fuzziness, or relatively poor resolution on the television screen, occurs because the image of the face has been broken down electronically and then reassembled after transmission. The standard photograph, on the other hand, is imaged directly onto film without having been rearranged; it is therefore "sharper," though it takes longer to come by.

RAND understood the problem and therefore set about to find a way of using standard cameras on reconnaissance satellites without having to transmit their pictures. In June 1956—a month before Article 347 rose gently off the runway at Wiesbaden for the first Moscow-Leningrad-Baltic penetration—RAND issued a highly classified report entitled "Physical Recovery of Satellite Payload: A Preliminary Investigation." The study suggested the possibility of returning film to earth from a photographic reconnaissance satellite by firing it down in a capsule. Such a scheme would have seemed preposterous even a couple of years earlier because the searing heat from air friction during reentry would have burned the capsule to charcoal. But ablative nose cones that were supposed to shed layers of plastic while protecting ballistic missile warheads as they reentered the atmosphere were under development. What could protect a warhead on the way down, RAND's engineers felt, could also protect a capsule. It was on the basis of such a scheme that Lockheed pushed ahead with the recoverable capsule segment of WS-117L.

Research in this area soon produced a second, more comprehensive RAND report put together by an engineering team led by Merton E. Davies and Amrom H. Katz called "A Family of Recoverable Satellites." The 129-page study, also highly classified, was issued on November 12, 1957.* It concluded that it was indeed possible to place a three-hundred-pound photoreconnaissance satellite into a 142-mile-high orbit by using a Thor booster and a Vanguard second stage.† This was to be accomplished, the engineers calculated, by slowing the second-stage satellite's forward momentum, turning it around, and ordering it to fire its camera-carrying payload down and out of orbit:

Descent from orbit is achieved by the command firing of a braking rocket in the satellite. Assume that the satellite is coming over the [North] Pole, that it is picked up by trackers in the north, and that an impact point in the Pacific is desired. The braking rocket is then fired forward and upward, imparting a downward and backward velocity impulse superimposed on the orbital velocity. The resulting velocity vector points downward, so that the vehicle is effectively in a ballistic trajectory. . . .

Tracking of the vehicle immediately after the beginning of descent establishes a predicted vacuum path. This, together with predicted atmospheric effects, makes it possible to predict the approximate impact area. The vehicle is protected against re-

*A version of the report, severely censored by the Defense Department, was made public in March 1984. In addition to being extensively rewritten, five of the report's original eight chapters were deleted altogether (including their titles), as were four of the ten sections in the appendix. Even the word "reconnaissance" was expunged.
†Vanguard was an early satellite-booster project developed by the Naval Research Laboratory to get a three-pound payload in orbit as a response to Sputnik. Its development, like that of the early Atlases, was plagued by a series of spectacular failures. Unlike Atlas, however, Vanguard was soon quietly abandoned.

entry heating by a coating of suitable vaporizing material: 80 lb [cq] of fiberglass-reinforced plastic, such as is used on advanced designs of the ICBM nose cone and on the Jupiter nose cone, is suggested. Impact survival of the casing, payload, batteries, and beacon is made feasible by the proper selection and arrangement of structural components. Search aircraft are used to find and recover the payload. This means that the radio beacon must operate after water impact, and possibly that some type of dye marker should be released upon impact.

As it was to turn out, the photoreconnaissance capsules would be carried to orbit not by the Vanguard but by Lockheed's Agena, and they would be plucked from midair by specially rigged Air Force planes as they descended at the ends of their parachutes. That was essentially the recoverable system that Lockheed labored on in what was initially the Pied Piper project. It was soon to have its own code names, however. The Eisenhower administration, always concerned that the United States appear to be pursuing a strictly peaceful space program, would announce that the satellite's sole mission was to carry scientific experiments to orbit. They were therefore to be given the plausible, but suitably ambiguous, cover name Discoverer. While a few token biological experiments were to be undertaken, however, the system's true purpose would be to collect intelligence from space while in the process acting as a test bed for other reconnaissance systems. That overall program, which was to be a black one, would be called Corona.

Meanwhile, work progressed on the design of the capsule itself at RAND, at Lockheed, and at General Electric, where it was to be built. The government has to this day maintained secrecy about the engineering details of the capsules that, plugged into the noses of successive Agenas, were to become the nation's first functioning spy satellites. Yet there is no doubt that in many respects the capsule was similar in form and function to a "photographic apparatus" designed at the time by the same Merton E. Davies who led the group at RAND that produced the November 1957 reconnaissance capsule feasibility analysis. Davies's apparatus was conceived to photograph what he called "inaccessible areas," such as the moon, by orbiting spacecraft around them with standard format cameras and film and then returning them to earth in the manner already worked out by RAND. Designing two entirely different reconnaissance systems in the same place and at the same time to perform what was essentially the same task would have been utterly senseless.*

Davies's capsule was a marvel of compactness, efficiency, and mechanical ingenuity. It was a paraboloid measuring only three feet by two feet and weighing three hundred pounds at launch (the same as the published dimensions and weight of the Discoverers). One end was reinforced with the ablative material; the other contained the exhaust nozzle of a small solid-fuel retro-rocket that ran through most of the capsule's length like a thick spinal cord and would be fired to push the capsule down and out of orbit, just as Davies's and Katz's reconnaissance study required. In an apparent attempt to get more equipment into the Discoverer capsule, however, its retro-rocket would be attached externally and would fall away during reentry.

The camera in Davies's capsule was to be mounted in its bulging midsection, behind a heat-resistant quartz window, and opposite radio equipment and the spacecraft's control system. Twin spools of film would take up a considerable amount of space because many hundreds of photographs of "inaccessible areas" would be necessary in order to justify the expense involved in each launch. The inventor noted in his patent application that a camera with a twelve-inch focal length and a highly corrected F 3.5 lens would perform adequately on the kind of mission he envisioned. The camera that was to be fitted in the Discoverer capsules would necessarily be of that general type because it would combine high resolution with minimal weight; it would have to derive from the type Baker and Land had devised for Idealist. There was at least one important difference between the cameras carried in the U-2 program and those used in Corona. The U-2's main camera did not move, while its spaceborne counterpart was to swing back and forth like a pendulum.

In common with other satellites, the Agenas and their camera-toting capsules would have to either spin themselves or contain spinning wheels inside of them if they were to remain stable in orbit

*The "housing," or shell of the capsule, depicted in Davies's patent appears to be the same as the empty front halves of Discoverers 13 and 14, which are on display, respectively, at the National Air and Space Museum and at the Air Force Museum near Dayton, Ohio. Discoverer 13, which was photographed in Eisenhower's presence after it had been successfully retrieved from the Pacific, also bears a striking resemblance to Davies's design. Finally, a pamphlet issued by General Electric published in 1960, "Summary: U.S. Air Force Discoverer Satellite Recovery Vehicle Program," which dealt only with white aspects of the program, contains photographs and diagrams of the capsule that resemble Davies's.

and not tumble erratically out of control. Davies's solution for his moon orbiter was to have the whole satellite revolve around its longitudinal axis. A photoelectric cell, roughly the same as a photographic light meter, was to point out of the side of the capsule in the same direction as the camera. It would register the differing light values as the capsule barreled along at about seventeen thousand miles an hour, noting each time the horizon came into view and disappeared again. The changing light level striking the photocell would cause a pulse of electricity to be sent to a conductor that would engage a clutch that would start the film moving. Conversely, the light would diminish as the terrain disappeared and gave way to the blackness of space, causing the clutch to disengage and stop the film's movement. This may well have been the way Discoverer itself operated. It is also possible, however, that the capsules themselves were kept stationary relative to the horizon and that internal flywheels, spinning like gyroscopes or a child's top, were used inside the Agena to keep it and its payload stable on all three axes while the camera in the small capsule clicked its pictures. The photographic system itself was to be adjusted so that pictures would be taken at specific intervals for coverage of particular targets, rather than imaging a continuous ribbon of territory, most of it inconsequential.

Sputnik was to beat Discoverer into space by more than two years, but when the first U.S. reconnaissance satellite finally got up there—a masterpiece of applied science and miniaturization that was three years ahead of its Soviet counterpart—it would do quite a bit more than go beep in the night.

In the meantime, RCA reported to the Air Force that one of WS-117L's two nonrecoverable reconnaissance systems, the one using television transmission for near-real-time operations, was infeasible. The picture resolution would be so poor, RCA's study found, that the system did not warrant development at that time. The Air Force accepted the news and abandoned that option in August 1957. By the same token, however, it had become convinced that the then current levels of technical development made the prospect of snatching little capsules out of the air, or even finding them and fishing them out of the sea, too implausible to pursue. Further, even if such a technique could be mastered, the airmen felt that it would take an unreasonable amount of time to get the data relative to the other nonrecoverable system, the line-scanning radio relay technique. Not only was the television transmission system abandoned, then, but the Air Force at the same time officially turned away from the recoverable capsule idea, just as it had done with the U-2. And as was the case with the U-2, the decision to ignore the Discoverer capsule recovery program was to have fateful consequences that also involved the Central Intelligence Agency.

With one potential system deemed unworkable by RCA and the other relegated to the same status by the Air Force itself, Pied Piper's de facto program became the one using on-board film processing in which the picture was line-scanned by a light beam and then relayed to the ground through radio downlink. The technique, it was felt, would easily make up in quick transmission time what it might at first lack in image resolution. Radio-link imagery transmission was fully embraced by the Air Force as the reconnaissance technique of the future. And it was essentially right, too, though it was about twenty years premature. What remained of WS-117L/Pied Piper so far as the Air Force was concerned, then, was renamed Sentry and, eventually, SAMOS (Satellite and Missile Observation System).

Bruce H. Billings, head of Special Projects in the Defense Department's Defense Research and Engineering Office, was to explain SAMOS's possibilities to George Kistiakowsky in a way that conjured up Flash Gordon but which accurately reflected Air Force thinking on the subject of space reconnaissance. The president's science adviser, evidently incredulous, made this notation in his diary after the conversation with Billings: ". . . he noted that in the satellite project SAMOS, there would be ten television channels to the ground and a library of information so complete that a general (LeMay?), sitting in his easy chair in the Pentagon, just by pressing a button will be able to see on a screen the complete display of current military activities in televised form from anywhere in the world."

Reality was not to live up to science fiction, however. The first SAMOS launch, on October 11, 1960, was to abort when the power cable linking the launch tower to the Agena failed to separate, ripping off a piece of the satellite. SAMOS 2 would reach orbit on January 31, 1961, while its two immediate successors also would fail to make it into space. There were to be only two similar failures during the next twenty-six launches, however, with SAMOS 30 ending the program on a successful note on November 27, 1963.

Resolution was another matter, though. Some observers have
noted that resolution progressed from twenty feet to about five as
the program advanced. Others, including the CIA's Herbert Scoville, Jr., have asserted that SAMOS never really yielded useful
pictures.

The thunder that spilled over the reinforced concrete at Tyuratam
and across the desolate steppes of the Kazakh Soviet Socialist Republic on October 4, 1957, pounded the people of the United States
almost as palpably as the shock wave from the launch itself. At 9:36
P.M. an SS-6 ICBM (which had recently been given the contemptu-
ous-sounding code name Sapwood by NATO) lifted Sputnik 1 off
the earth and into orbit, making the U.S.S.R. the first nation to send
an object into space, demonstrating in the most blatant way the
seeming robustness of the Marxist-Leninist scientific regimen, and
in the process dealing the United States yet another blow of the first
magnitude. The ascension of Sputnik 1, followed within the month
by Sputnik 2 and its canine passenger, were broadly taken to be the
technological equivalent of Pearl Harbor.

Sputnik 1 was a 184-pound ball whose skin had been polished
so that it would be more readily visible to everyone on the planet
who searched the heavens for it; its radio signals had been set so
that they would be as easy as possible for hams the world over to
pick up. Even as the little satellite, whose name translated to "companion" or "fellow traveler," obediently beeped its way around the
earth, the reaction of surprise and general bewilderment from the
news media and a cadre of politicians of all stripes was swift in
coming.

Within five days Lyndon Johnson's Preparedness Investigating
Subcommittee of the Senate Armed Services Committee had begun
inquiries on the matter: on how such a thing could have happened
and on what, specifically, the Eisenhower administration planned to
do to even the score. The clamor soon rose to a crescendo, some of
it humorous, but most of it fueled by the exigencies of politics or
the simple response to damaged pride. MIT's humor magazine,
Voodoo, ran a cartoon showing a cutaway Sputnik, inside which
huddled a bearded cossack saying, "Beep . . . beep . . . beep . . ."
Missouri's Democratic Senator Stuart Symington warned that "unless our defense policies are promptly changed, the Soviets will
move from superiority to supremacy." Clare Boothe Luce, the out-

spoken former Republican congresswoman and conservative stal-
wart, grumbled that Sputnik amounted to "an intercontinental out-
er-space raspberry to a decade of American pretensions that the
American way of life was a gilt-edged guarantee of our national
superiority."

George E. Reedy, Jr., a staff aide close to Lyndon Johnson, probably best summed up the national feeling about the situation in
a memorandum to his boss that said, in part: "The simple fact is
that we can no longer consider the Russians to be behind us in
technology. It took them four years to catch up to our atomic
bomb and nine months to catch up to our hydrogen bomb. Now
we are trying to catch up to their satellite. We can no longer consider ourselves as having a lead in anything other than industrial
production."

For his part, Johnson lost no time in taking up the cudgel. "The
Roman Empire controlled the world because it could build roads.
Later—when moved to sea—the British Empire was dominant because it had ships. In the air age, we were more powerful because
we had airplanes. Now the Communists have established a foothold
in outer space. It is not very reassuring to be told that next year we
will put a better satellite into the air [sic]. Perhaps it will even have
chrome trim and automatic windshield wipers," the Senate majority
leader sneered.

Sputnik was unquestionably the most pernicious problem of the
Eisenhower presidency. However they sought to ease public apprehension and minimize the implications of the Russian space shots,
Dwight Eisenhower, his Cabinet, and their top advisers were increasingly being taken as frugal to the point of being foolhardy and,
worse, vexatiously naïve where Soviet intentions and capabilities
were concerned. Even the president himself came to be ridiculed as
a benevolent grandfather type who had lost touch with reality and
slipped into a dotage that caused him to bring more attention to bear
on his beloved golf game than on the demands of national security
and its requisite tough-mindedness. An exasperated Governor G.
Mennen Williams of Michigan even turned his misgivings to light
verse:

> Oh Little Sputnik, flying high
> With made-in-Moscow beep,
> You tell the world it's a Commie sky
> And Uncle Sam's asleep

You say on fairway and on rough
The Kremlin knows it all,
We hope our golfer knows enough
To get us on the ball.

The golfer actually knew a great deal more than he was letting on. Whatever the effect of Sputnik as a public relations gimmick—and that was undeniably extraordinary—the satellite and its immediate successors were in and of themselves crude and technically unimpressive to anyone acquainted with the embryonic but highly imaginative American satellite program. Ike understood that what was really important about the Sputnik launches was not the Sputniks but their launchers: the big SS-6s.

Contrary to those who had until recently charged that the Kremlin was amassing a huge bomber fleet that would soon leave its SAC counterpart weak by comparison, the Soviet leadership had decided years earlier to counter what it saw as the decided and probably unmatchable American lead in bombers with strategic missiles. If the Russians could not keep abreast of U.S. bomber production, much less surpass it, they would leapfrog it with long-range ballistic missiles. What's more, they would not wait for their heavy nuclear warheads to be miniaturized before building the rockets to carry them, but would instead construct whatever size missile was necessary to get the thermonuclear payloads to their targets. That was the reason for the SS-6: not to lift Sputniks to orbit but to lob heavy warheads at targets in the West. Sputnik 1's weighing 184 pounds was disconcerting enough (especially as compared with the relatively puny 3-pound Vanguard, which had yet to get off the ground), but Sputnik 2 weighed a hefty 1,119 pounds, which was easily warhead weight in 1956. Sapwood, which was a central "sustainer" rocket surrounded by four separate boosters, measured thirty-four feet across its base diameter, had a five-thousand-mile range, and was more than twice as powerful as Atlas: the kerosene and liquid oxygen that was mixed and ignited inside the giant missile developed 1.1 million pounds of thrust. And as if that weren't enough, Atlas had yet to break its bonds to the earth for the first time.

Whatever else they were, however, Sputnik and its booster were not surprises to Eisenhower and the intelligence specialists who reported to the National Security Council. On July 30, 1955, the Russians had announced that they would launch a satellite during the International Geophysical Year, which had begun on July 1, 1957, and they had continued to make no secret of those plans. Academician Leonid I. Sedov, chairman of an ad hoc Commission for Interplanetary Communications, and other Russian scientists attended the First International Conference on Rockets and Guided Missiles in 1956 and regaled other participants with descriptions of high-altitude experiments involving dogs. Closer to home, Killian's Technological Capabilities Panel had noted that the Russians were working on an artificial earth satellite (and suggested that the United States do the same for intelligence-collection purposes), while RAND actually predicted that some kind of satellite launch was going to take place six months before it did.

In June 1957, while the first SS-6 stood locked to its erector on a launch pad at Tyuratam, the multifaceted collection system that was to become the hallmark of U.S. strategic intelligence was already working to learn what the missile was and what it could do. That month, even as technicians prepared the monster rocket for its first flight, a U-2 flying so high above that it could neither be heard nor seen took a series of paired stereoscopic photographs of it,* which were quickly sent back to Washington for analysis by U.S. ballistic missile experts. Its size and probable performance characteristics were therefore known before its first test flight, which came on August 3, and was limited in range. A second, full-range firing occurred three weeks later. On both occasions the missile's telemetry—the performance data, such as fuel consumption, engine thrust, burn time, heading, speed, warhead separation point, altitude, and range, which the missile radioed to tracking stations on the ground —was picked out of the air by large antennas and taped at Karamursel, a U.S. listening post thirty-seven miles southeast of Istanbul. The facility, which sprawled over 697 barbed-wire-enclosed acres, was jointly manned by the U.S. Air Force Security Service and the Naval Security Group and had Tyuratam as its primary target. By the summer of 1957, other intercept stations had sprung up at Trabzon, only seventy miles from the Soviet frontier in Turkey's Kuzey Anadolu Daglari mountains and, two hundred miles to the east, at Samsun, where Air Force SIGINT specialists carefully listened to activity at Kapustin Yar and elsewhere in the southwestern Soviet Union.

*All twenty or so U-2 overflights of the U.S.S.R. between 1956 and 1960 were tracked by Soviet radar.

Thus, by the time Sputnik went into orbit on October 4, the United States knew quite a bit about the missile that carried it there. But performance capability was only part of the puzzle. The other part involved questions that ran closer to the heart of national security—with trying to assess the SS-6's initial operating capability (IOC), the number of missiles that were to be produced, and the dates of deployment. Ballistic missiles obviously must be reliable and they are therefore tested extensively to correct design flaws in their propulsion and guidance systems and to ascertain their precise capabilities before assembly lines are started up. Although the number of tests varies according to the particular missile, in no case are there fewer than twenty, and rarely more than thirty. Beginning in the mid-1950s and continuing to this day, each ballistic missile test is closely monitored, not only to learn about the weapon's capabilities but also to analyze the tests' progression for clues relating to production and deployment schedules. But in making such projections the analyses tended to take on a political edge, with the Air Force predicting the worst possible situation and the Navy and the CIA weighing in with more conservative estimates.

CIA Director Dulles gave a thorough briefing on the progress of the Soviet ballistic missile program to the National Security Council on January 18, 1958. He reported that there had been no test firings of ICBMs in 1955 or 1956, and that there had been two tests and two Sputnik launchings in 1957. (Intelligence professionals always consider some military value to derive from even supposedly peaceful space shots like those in the Sputnik series because of the immense amount of interrelated technology.) The next ICBM test was to take place in April at Tyuratam, followed on May 15 by the launching of Sputnik 3, a two-and-a-half-ton cone. There were to be no more successful ICBM tests until 1959, though delays and failures were to be observed.

Despite the fact that the Soviet ICBM test program was judged to be only one-third to halfway complete and riddled with problems, a National Intelligence Estimate (NIE) ordered by the National Security Council in May 1958 and presented the following month predicted a massive Soviet missile buildup. The NIE, which was prepared under the jurisdiction of the director of Central Intelligence,* concluded that the Russians would have one hundred

*National intelligence estimates are drawn up under the jurisdiction of the director of Central Intelligence (DCI) and with the participation of the Defense Intelligence Agency (DIA), which came into existence in 1961; the National Security Agency (NSA); the State Depart-

ICBMs in 1959, five hundred in 1960, and one thousand by 1961. Given the fact that the SS-6 testing program had sputtered in 1957 and into 1958, Eisenhower wondered why the projected figures were so high so soon. If he got an answer it has not been made public.

The high numbers, however, reflected Air Force thinking and apparent dominance in the preparation of that particular NIE. Beginning in fiscal year 1958, the Air Force's A-2, a staff section devoted to intelligence, was officially upgraded to the office of the Assistant Chief of Staff for Intelligence (ACSI). In preparation for this, Major General James H. Walsh was brought back from Great Britain in July to take command of the expanded unit. Walsh had commanded SAC's 7th Air Division and, before that, the Strategic Air Command's own intelligence operation. It had been Walsh, a "bomber man," who had been in charge of SAC's intelligence during the bomber gap. He returned from Europe that summer of 1958 convinced, and rightly so, that the reason the Russians were not building as many bombers as had been predicted was that they had decided instead to switch emphasis to long-range ballistic missiles. Now SAC thought it saw colossal numbers of Soviet missiles just over the horizon, and the men who dominated ACSI, certainly including Walsh, fully shared the view of their comrades-in-arms. SAC wanted B-52s and ICBMs, and it understood that there were two basic ways of getting them: by demonstrating to the White House and Congress that the opposition was arming to the teeth, and by relaying that message to the public through the news media. For their part, SAC's analysts, aware of the mood of their service's leadership, began to see missiles in the U-2 pictures that the civilians in the CIA did not see. "To the Air Force," one CIA officer later quipped, "every flyspeck on film was a missile." Dulles, who shared his president's suspiciousness of all military-originated intelligence figures, preferred to rely upon his own analysts and challenged two thirds of the Air Force's estimates.

The influence of political predisposition on the analysis of data— of, in effect, seeing what one wants to see—is a persistent, and often

ment's Bureau of Intelligence and Research (INR); and any other organization with pertinent expertise in a given area. As DCI, the director of the CIA not only heads his own agency but is the legal head of the whole foreign intelligence collection establishment. Any number of DCIs have admitted, however, that the role can be more apparent than real because of the traditional squabbling over turf. NIEs are supposed to reflect a general consensus within the intelligence community. Dissenting opinions are footnoted.

deplored, component in the process of sifting evidence and using it
to determine what the opposition is going to do. This is probably
unavoidable when the collected data are ambiguous (and often even
when they are not), given the fact that those who weigh them at the
upper reaches of the intelligence hierarchy tend to have deep political convictions and feel that they must be responsive to one constituency or another.* The estimates of SS-6 production that were made
in 1958 are a case in point. In that instance the raw intelligence was
unambiguous: it showed that testing was minimal the previous year
and that only one firing (plus the launching of Sputnik 3) occurred
that year. The CIA interpreted this to mean that the SS-6 program
had run into serious problems that would delay deployment. The
Air Force used the same data to conclude that testing was petering
out because the Russians had enough confidence in the weapon to
start large-scale production.

Its heavily classified nature notwithstanding, the National Intelligence Estimate predicting that one thousand Soviet ICBMs would
be in place by 1961 was promptly leaked to the press. Joseph and
Stewart Alsop were among the first to get word of the estimate and
wasted no time in getting it into print. "At the Pentagon they
shudder when they speak of the 'gap,' which means the years 1960,
1961, 1962, and 1963," the Alsops' nationally syndicated column
warned on August 1, 1958. "They shudder because in those years,
the American government will flaccidly permit the Kremlin to gain
an almost unchallenged superiority in the nuclear striking power
that was once our specialty." The second of the gaps, this one
having to do with strategic missiles, exploded amid another outcry
that the Eisenhower administration was embarked on a course that
would leave the United States at a sharp disadvantage in striking
power relative to the Soviet Union.

The following May, George Kistiakowsky recalled many years
later, Joseph Alsop invited him to breakfast at his home in George-
town. "There he emotionally told me that the Soviet Union had 150
ICBMs targeted at the United States and that they would probably
launch them that summer. We knew there were no missiles to speak
of because of the U-2s, but that was negative evidence. We couldn't

---

*William E. Colby maintains that differences of opinion benefit the decision-making process
because a variety of possibilities, rather than only one, come under serious consideration.
While there is undeniable merit to that point of view, bitter and protracted differences of
opinion can also confuse policymakers, inhibit quick and appropriate responses, and undermine confidence in the technical collection system itself.

find any deployed. The [SS-6] missiles were so big and unwieldy that only five or six of them were deployed by 1960."

Like Eisenhower, Killian, Dulles, and several others, Kistiakowsky knew that the ninety-five-foot-long ballistic missiles were not transported in pieces on the backs of yaks and assembled in randomly chosen fields. It didn't work that way. They were built horizontally in a manufacturing plant and then shipped with considerable difficulty, still on their sides, by rail to Tyuratam, where they were raised to the vertical position by erectors before being test-fired or shot into orbit. Any SS-6 in an attack mode would have to go through the identical process. The U-2 pilots who were sent looking for them therefore followed railroad tracks throughout the south of Russia on the assumption that their aboveground erectors (the SS-6's girth made the digging of silos prohibitive) would be clustered near railroad spurs, as is so much else that is of value in large nations without modern highway networks. The U-2s scoured the Trans-Siberian Railroad and returned with a staggering amount of information relating to military deployments and manufacturing activities of many kinds. But there was nothing on the film to indicate SS-6 launch complexes. Kistiakowsky could not tell this to the columnist, however, for fear of compromising the U-2 operation.

Although no nuclear-tipped SS-6s had been discovered by the end of 1959, other activity relating to the missiles had picked up sharply. Testing resumed in April and continued at a rapid pace throughout the remainder of the year; there was even a first full-range 5,000-mile test. On September 12, Luna 2, boosted by an SS-6, scored a near-perfect 230,000-mile bull's-eye by hitting the surface of the moon only 270 miles from its visible center. Three weeks later, on the second anniversary of Sputnik 1, Luna 3 circled the moon and returned with photographs of its far side. It too was boosted by an SS-6. Such navigational accuracy, let alone boosting capability, left no doubt in Washington that the Kremlin was committed to a space race and a related missile buildup that would have the most profound consequences. And as if to underscore the seriousness of the situation, the Russians laid plans for the establishment of a separate Strategic Rocket Force in 1960 so that an operational structure would be in place to accommodate the ballistic missiles that would be coming into the inventory.

The Soviet accomplishments, now no longer being laid at the door of the Peenemünde engineers, stunned Congress. After allegedly having been briefed four times by the CIA and spoken with other knowledgeable sources, Senator Symington, who had presidential ambitions of his own, lashed out at the Eisenhower administration for its shameful unpreparedness. Symington warned in a closed joint congressional hearing that the Soviet Union would possess three thousand ICBMs by the end of 1961, thereby even upping the Air Force's estimate by a factor of three. In making such a dire prediction (which he went out of his way to insist be put "on the record"), the Missouri Democrat joined ranks with several of his fellow Democrats, politicians and journalists on the far right, the Air Force, and Nikita S. Khrushchev.

The men in the Kremlin knew by the end of 1959 that very few of their SS-6s would be operational by 1961. This was because the liquid-fueled missile, while suitable for launching satellites, took too long to prepare for flight and was too vulnerable to attack on the ground to be taken seriously as an ICBM. Ballistic missiles could not be kept at the ready for long with kerosene and vaporizing liquid oxygen loaded in their tanks. Nor was it feasible to begin pumping the propellant and oxidizer into them while under attack. Rocket men on both sides of the Iron Curtain understood by 1959 that liquid-fueled missiles, such as the SS-6 and the Atlas, were therefore unsuitable for use as ICBMs and would have to be replaced either with missiles that used storable liquid fuel or solid propellant, both of which were relatively quick-starting. Solid fuel, which was compressed combustible powder, was understood to be particularly dependable and would send a ballistic missile up like a Roman candle. For this reason, as well as the SS-6's vulnerability to blast effect from nuclear explosions some distance away—it stood on its pad like a circus elephant balanced on a stool—the Russians decided not to produce the first-generation missile in quantity but to concentrate instead on more dependable types that used storable liquid fuel and could be hidden in silos. The CIA was therefore right.

Khrushchev, needing time for his SS-7s, SS-8s, and SS-9s to come on line, remembered that the Americans had taken the bait when inflated bomber figures were tossed out, so he decided to try the trick again while the factories geared up for the second-generation ICBMs. In Kistiakowsky's words, Khrushchev tried to "defend his country with his mouth."

"A few years ago I said in a speech that an intercontinental ballistic missile had been developed in our country," Khrushchev recalled at a reception at the All-Union Congress of Soviet Journalists in November 1959 with Deputy Premier Anastas Mikoyan in attendance. "Then many public leaders in capitalist countries stated that Khrushchev was probably just boasting. When we started production of these rockets, I said that in our country intercontinental rockets were on the assembly line. Again they began to say that this could not be, that Khrushchev was boasting again."

"Let *them* make such a boast themselves," Mikoyan interrupted.

"You can boast," Khrushchev continued, clearly jubilant over the SS-6's long-range test and the two successful moon missions, "but you must boast in such a way that all the world should see what you are boasting about. . . . I think, dear comrades and members of the Presidium, that I will reveal secrets, and at the same time I want to be understood correctly: we do not want to frighten anyone, but we can tell the truth. Now we have such a stock of rockets, such an amount of atomic and hydrogen weapons, that if they attack us, we could wipe our potential enemies off the face of the earth. . . ." Then the bombastic Ukrainian added, almost as an afterthought: "By the way, I shall reveal—and let the people know about it; I am making no secret of this—that in one year, 250 rockets with hydrogen warheads came off the assembly line in the factory we visited. This represents millions of tons in terms of conventional explosives. You can well imagine that if this lethal weapon is exploded over some country, there will be nothing left there at all."

Eisenhower was certain that Khrushchev was bluffing once again, but, like Kistiakowsky, his science adviser, he could not offer details in public for fear of unmasking the U-2 flights. Instead, he steadfastly insisted that there was no missile gap while again being forced to increase weapons production—this time by authorizing additional Atlas squadrons—and place renewed emphasis on overhead reconnaissance. However much he tried, Eisenhower seemed powerless to break the momentum of the upwardly spiraling arms race and the risky, but crucial, aerial reconnaissance that went with it.

The intelligence yield, or "take," brought back by Kelly Johnson's long-winged camera platforms left little doubt that Khrushchev was lying about his ICBMs, but it did a great deal more than that. It is no exaggeration to say that the amount of information recorded by U-2s during their four years of deep penetration over the Soviet Union was extraordinary.

Five main groups of targets had been established early in the

Idealist program: the Soviet bomber force, missile program, atomic energy program, submarine force, and air defense system. U-2 photographs revealed in detail activities at the nuclear test ranges at Semipalatinsk and Novaya Zemlya, and the warhead production facility not far from Alma-Ata; the missile test centers at Tyuratam and Kapustin Yar, and the anti-ballistic missile test site at Sary Shagan. The planes returned to Incirlik, Atsugi, and elsewhere with high-resolution imagery of Soviet bomber bases and adjacent nuclear bomb storage facilities, submarine pens and production areas, and enough data on the U.S.S.R's IRBM and ICBM test programs so that its ballistic missile program—the types of missiles that were being built, together with the siting of their launch complexes and the types of payloads they carried—was exposed.

But the data went to even earlier stages of the weapons-development process than the manufacturing and siting of missiles. Photographs were taken of the areas in the Soviet Union where uranium ore was mined, of the trains that carried it to the processing plants, and of the plants themselves. Analysts studying the number of types of heavy equipment at the mines, the number and capacity of the railroad cars that carried the ore, and the size, shape, and power and water requirements of the processing facilities could gauge the level of production with considerable accuracy.

"The project has shown that despite Mr. Khrushchev's boast that the Soviets will soon be able to curtail the production of fissionable material for war purposes, the Soviets are continuing to expand their fissionable material capacity," Allen Dulles would be able to tell the Senate Foreign Relations Committee in secret session in 1960, following the loss of Powers's U-2. "The Soviet nuclear testing ground has been photographed with extremely interesting results more than once," Dulles confided, adding that national and regional nuclear weapons storage sites, as well as "forward" storage depots (presumably in Eastern Europe and along the Chinese frontier), also had been pinpointed.

The flood of information helped to convince Eisenhower that Soviet bomber and ballistic missile levels posed no serious threat to the United States, Khrushchev's bellicose raving notwithstanding. The vulnerability of the U-2s themselves, however, was another matter. While the spy planes looked down, those they photographed looked back up at them with increasing frustration and anger. The Kremlin, still feeling the effects of the devastation of World War II and ever sensitive about protecting secrets and maintaining the

sanctity of its airspace, sent Washington a firmly worded, unpubli-
cized diplomatic protest concerning the U-2 flights in July 1956,
immediately after they started. It went unanswered.

The following year a new surface-to-air missile (SAM), code-
named the SA-2 Guideline, was publicly unveiled in Moscow as an
apparent replacement for the SA-1 Guilds that guarded Moscow
and other large cities, as well as some military installations. SA-1s
were fired at U-2s, but they invariably floundered in the thin air far
short of their targets and fell back to earth. Then the U-2s began
coming back with pictures of the SA-2s positioned to protect not
only the cities but also bomber bases and IRBM installations. The
weapon looked to be about thirty-six feet long, radio-controlled, and
powered by a combination of solid fuel booster and ramjet-propelled
upper stage, giving it a probable range of some twenty-five to thirty
miles and a ceiling in excess of sixty thousand feet. Starting in
mid-1959, U-2 flights were therefore planned to skirt SA-2 batteries
whenever possible. Apprehension about the planes' safety grew, but
their yield was so important that no one gave serious consideration
to cutting it off.

Nor was the U-2's increasing vulnerability its only drawback.
Whatever the extent of its coverage, it could not photograph the
entire Soviet Union, and it could not even return to high-priority
targets as often as was thought necessary for fear of establishing a
pattern that would lead to a successful attack. However logical it
was to assume that all important targets were connected by major
road, rail, or even water systems to their supply points or outlets,
there was always the nagging fear that something important had
gone undetected because it was out of U-2 range or had simply been
missed for lack of repeated coverage. There was unanimous agreement that taking cameras and SIGINT equipment to space would
rectify the problem, at least for the foreseeable future. There was a
sharp difference of opinion, however, as to whether it was to be the
Air Force or the CIA that would control space reconnaissance.

At the time Sputnik 1 went up, the Air Force was proceeding with
SAMOS as its reconnaissance satellite program and with another
planned spacecraft named MIDAS, which was supposed to use
infrared scanners at geosynchronous orbit to watch for the blasts
coming out of ballistic missiles and sound an alarm in case of attack.
MIDAS, which was to be a surveillance rather than a reconnaissance

system, became the first U.S. early warning satellite and was to be followed by the long-lived DSP (Defense Support Program)-647 platforms of the seventies and eighties.

The CIA had meanwhile become convinced that as the nation's preeminent intelligence organization and the manager of the U-2s that were successfully flying over the U.S.S.R., it too belonged in the space reconnaissance business. For its satellite it chose the design rejected by the Air Force as being too complicated: the capsule that was supposed to be fired out of orbit and return with exposed film. This was the project that would shortly be known to the world as Discoverer and to the highest echelons of the technical collection establishment as Corona.

On January 22, 1958, the National Security Council issued its Action Memorandum 1846, which set the development of an operational reconnaissance satellite as the highest technical intelligence priority. Dulles and Killian had meanwhile convinced Eisenhower that control of the reconnaissance program ought to rest primarily with the CIA, not with a military service, and Ike readily agreed. Accordingly, Richard Bissell was called into Allen Dulles's office one day in February 1958 and, in the presence of Edwin Land, told that he was from that moment on in charge of Corona, as well as of the U-2 overflight program. As Dulles explained it, Corona was technically to be co-managed by Bissell and an Air Force general, while in reality it would be funded by the CIA and run by it, just the way the Soviet overflights were. The nominal participation of the Air Force, it was hoped, would help smooth ruffled feathers. But there could be no question that the CIA would control the program. The Air Force was to be relegated to the role of getting the satellites into orbit on its boosters, maneuvering them and operating their camera and other systems in close cooperation with Lockheed employees, and then snaring the descending film pods. In a manner of speaking, the CIA was going to design, build, and have a primary influence on the uses to which the cargo was put, while the Air Force would merely drive the truck that carried it. That, Dulles and Bissell undoubtedly reflected, was what air forces were supposed to do, anyway.

At the same time, Eisenhower ordered the National Security Council to come up with a full-blown national strategy for space as a way of plotting a response to Sputnik. The resulting document, NSC 5814/1, "Preliminary U.S. Policy in Outer Space," was completed in the summer of 1958 and approved by the president.

NSC 5814/1 was one of the seminal reports in the history of the U.S. presence in space. It noted that Soviet feats in space had "captured the imagination and admiration of the world," and went on to predict that if the Russians' lead continued, it might undermine the prestige and national security of the nation. It also explained that while the distinction between ballistic missiles and space boosters was technically nebulous, weapons and the vehicles used to get satellites into space would have to be different. This was to have the effect of separating the weapons from the space program, which would concentrate only on spacecraft. And that, in turn, meant that were there ever to be a peaceful-uses-of-space treaty, it would have nothing to do with ballistic missiles, at least in the documented view of the United States.

The drafters of NSC 5814/1 dealt with both the military and civilian aspects of spaceflight, noting that communications, weather, and navigation systems would have a place in space, as well as the sort of manned orbiting bombardment satellites, lunar stations, and maintenance-and-supply space ferries that comics readers across the country were simultaneously absorbing in Buck Rogers and Flash Gordon strips. And while satellites could serve as target-spotters for a ballistic missile attack, the report continued, they could as easily be used to verify the provisions of arms control agreements with Open Skies–type operations. In regard to observation of the earth, the National Security Council was emphatic in pointing out that "Reconnaissance satellites are of critical importance to U.S. national security" and urged their development "at the earliest technologically practicable date" in order to "enhance to the maximum extent the U.S. intelligence effort." NSC 5814/1 even described in some detail the SAMOS, MIDAS, and Corona programs.

What the National Security Council did not come to grips with, however, was a definition of "space" and a judgment concerning whom, if anyone, it belonged to. The question was far from esoteric, since if a nation's sovereignty extended upward to infinity, then any foreign satellite passing over it would be violating borders and would be liable to be shot down. This was unacceptable where any U.S. spacecraft was concerned, but it was particularly worrisome in regard to the reconnaissance types, which by the summer of 1958 were taken to be of paramount importance even though none had as yet been orbited. NSC 5814/1 anticipated the problem by recommending that Washington "seek urgently a political framework which will place the uses of U.S. reconnaissance satellites in a political and psychological context more favorable to the U.S. intelligence effort." The Itek Corp., a Massachusetts firm specializing in optics, remote sensing systems, and other high-altitude hardware, and which was in the early stages of developing the status of a space consultant, noted in a report called "Political Action and Satellite Reconnaissance" that neither technical difficulties nor Soviet military countermeasures were the worst of the problems; rather, it was "political vulnerability." Reconnaissance satellites "are our last chance. Should recon sats be 'politically shot down,' no scientific or technological opportunity can be foreseen to obtain this security information during the forthcoming critical years. What is needed is a program to put recon sats 'in the white' through early and vigorous political action. . . ."

Khrushchev's feelings on the matter of U-2 and other overflights were well known at the time and were to become even more pronounced. One of the most memorable incidents at the summit meeting that convened in Paris on May 16, 1960—barely two weeks after Gary Powers had been shot down—concerned an interchange between the Soviet premier and Charles de Gaulle, who hosted the conference. After reading a long diatribe denouncing the U-2 flights, Khrushchev pointed to the ceiling and shouted, "I have been overflown." De Gaulle answered that France, too, had been overflown—by Soviet satellites. Khrushchev, startled, responded by trying to assure de Gaulle that the Soviet spacecraft were not on spy missions. The Frenchman responded by asking how the Russians had gotten the Lunik 2 shots of the far side of the moon if they did not carry cameras. "In *that* satellite we had cameras," Khrushchev explained. "Ah," de Gaulle said softly, "in *that* one you had cameras! Pray continue."

The basis for the solution to the problem of Soviet suspicion and belligerence had been approached from several directions, all at virtually the same time: in 1958. The National Advisory Committee for Aeronautics (NACA), a listless organization that sputtered through various research programs of varying importance, was transformed into the National Aeronautics and Space Administration (NASA), a purportedly civilian body that was supposed to advance the peaceful uses of space while championing freedom of travel in it. NASA's ties to the U.S. military, particularly the Air Force, were to be strong, however, at least partly because of the ambiguous nature of many of the technical systems and operations themselves. Was a photograph of Tyuratam taken by a NASA satellite not to be used for intelligence-gathering purposes, for example, because the satellite was technically under civilian jurisdiction (as was to occur on June 25, 1984, when Landsat 5 made a thematic map of the launch complex)? The other part of the sometimes intimate relationship would have to do with funds, something the Air Force had in considerable quantity, but which NASA was often hard-pressed to come by. The relationship between NASA and the Air Force was to be fairly close, but very low-keyed.

Pied Piper was publicly canceled. An article about the program had appeared in *Aviation Week* the previous October, causing concern that its security might be endangered and, more likely, that such accounts could provide Khrushchev with ammunition to attack the overhead reconnaissance program politically. It was therefore decided to announce the program's end. "Of course, there were lots of wailings and gnashings of teeth and complaints that this was Republican Party economizing where we could least afford it," Richard Bissell has said. "We of course couldn't tell anyone that the Air Force program was being replaced by a bigger one." Actually, SAMOS and MIDAS were not being replaced at all, but were merely stashed in a dark corner, where they could be worked on in secret.

Conversely, the Discoverer program, as Corona was called in public, was bleached white. Considerable emphasis was placed on the biomedical and other experiments the Discoverer satellites were supposed to carry to orbit, among them a chimpanzee named Pale Face, who was to be the first "astrosimian" and precursor of the chimps that were expected to precede astronauts into space in the Mercury program. Officially, the Discoverer series was first managed by the Defense Department's newly created Advanced Research Projects Agency (ARPA) and then by the Air Force's Space Systems Division as an "open-end" research project that could be continued indefinitely, possibly even to the benefit of NASA's Ranger moon-landing project, its Nimbus meteorological satellite program, and other ostensibly peaceful endeavors. The General Electric Company, which built the camera capsule, even published a nine-page pamphlet entitled "Summary, U.S. Air Force Discoverer Satellite Recovery Vehicle Program," complete with diagrams showing how the Agena was sent into orbit, how the capsule came down, and what the capsule looked like in a variety of configurations.

As originally presented in the November 1957 RAND study

masterminded by Davies and Katz, and then modified, this is what was supposed to happen: The Thor Agena would lift off from Cooke Air Force Base at Point Arguello,* which protrudes into the Pacific about one hundred fifty miles northwest of Los Angeles, and head south toward orbital altitude. Once the Thor booster had burned out and fallen away, the Agena's own Bell rocket engine would thrust it to orbital speed as it aligned with the horizon. Once in orbit, the Agena was supposed to turn laterally 180 degrees until its nose section, carrying the GE capsule, pointed backward. It would then take timed photographs over preselected targets during sixteen or more successive orbits around the earth, each lasting about ninety minutes.

As the Agena passed over northern Siberia and approached the North Pole on its last pass a timing mechanism would trigger tiny gas jets that would tilt the spacecraft 60 degrees downward and stabilize it in that position. Meanwhile, tracking stations in Kodiak and on Annette Island, Alaska, Point Mugu, California, and Point Kaena, Hawaii, would send data on the satellite's precise whereabouts to its operators at the new Satellite Test Center at Sunnyvale, California. Still more tracking data were to be sent from a telemetry ship named the *Joe E. Mann* and from one or more four-engine RC-121 aircraft patrolling north of the Hawaiian Islands.

As Discoverer sailed over Alaska, another timer would fire explosive bolts and release springs, separating the camera capsule with its bowl-shaped ablative nose and orbit-ejection system. At that moment, the Discoverer capsule would weigh three hundred pounds. Immediately after the explosive bolts had been discharged, separating the capsule from the Agena, the orbit-ejection system—a retro-rocket—was to fire, sending the capsule downward so that it arced gently back into the atmosphere. During its descent the Discoverer would shed its ablative protective coating and release its retro-rocket and parachute cover. At about fifty thousand feet, its deceleration would trip a switch that was supposed to pop open its exposed parachute while its radio beacon sent out a continuous signal pin-

---

*Cooke (later renamed Vandenberg) was used instead of Canaveral because imaging satellites follow roughly polar orbits and must therefore be launched to either the north or the south. Such launches from Canaveral would put populated areas under the takeoff path, risking their being hit by falling boosters and other debris. In addition, no one wanted a reconnaissance satellite that failed to orbit to turn up in the Amazon or somewhere else that would expose it to foreign hands.

pointing its location. The capsule at that point was supposed to weigh eighty-five pounds.

As it came down, a C-119 Flying Boxcar belonging to the specially created 6593rd "Test Squadron," trailing a trapeze bar at the end of long nylon cables, would snatch it in midair. The plan called for the plane's crew to winch in the capsule, put it in a canister, and take it to Hickam Air Force Base outside Honolulu, where its film would be processed before being rushed to Washington for analysis. The first of the Discoverers were not supposed to carry cameras and film but, rather, were intended to prove out the system. And a very complex system it was, too. Barely a year after the launching of Sputnik 1, the United States was preparing to orbit an extraordinarily sophisticated space reconnaissance satellite whose success would depend not only on the workings of its complicated imaging system but on the meticulously orchestrated performance of the Thor booster, the Agena satellite, and the camera payload so as to achieve a perfect launch into a precise orbit, extremely close control of the spacecraft and its imaging apparatus once orbit had been attained, and a precise ejection from orbit, reentry, and recovery. Far more was at stake in accomplishing this than its relation even to the Corona program itself; the satellites were to be proving vehicles for important elements of the SAMOS and MIDAS operations, as well as for more advanced "bucket-droppers." At any rate, that was the way things were supposed to happen.

This, however, is what *did* happen: Discoverer 1, slated for launch on January 21, 1959, was aborted on the pad because of a procedural error. The satellite did make it into orbit thirty-eight days later, only to tumble out of control when its stabilizing system went haywire. Discoverer 2 also made it to orbit. After its seventeenth revolution around the earth, however, it was sent a premature ejection signal; it followed its orders to the letter, coming down over the northern tip of Norway, not far from the Soviet frontier, and was apparently never found. Discoverers 3 and 4, launched on June 3 and 25, respectively, did not make it to orbit (number three carried four black mice, which would have lent credence to the program's cover had they been retrieved). The flight of Discoverer 5, which was launched on August 13, 1959, was excruciating for the CIA, the Air Force, and the contractors. It made it to orbit, circled the earth the correct number of times, and fired the explosive bolts separating the capsule from the Agena at precisely the right moment. Then, on cue, the retro-rocket kicked in. Unfortunately, it fired the wrong way, sending the capsule into a higher orbit and in the process precluding any chance for recovery. Number six, which went up within a week of its predecessor, orbited and released its capsule. The radio beacon didn't work, though, so the C-119s couldn't find it. Number seven, like number one, developed a stabilization problem and tumbled out of control. Number eight, launched on November 20, went into an orbit that was higher than expected and therefore sent its capsule so far from the target area that it was never located. Discoverer 9's Thor booster stopped burning prematurely, which prevented the satellite from going into orbit. It at least went higher than its immediate successor, which slanted abruptly off course at twenty thousand feet, forcing the range safety officer to hit the button that blew it up. Bissell and his colleagues pressed on. Discoverer 11, which Bissell recalled was probably carrying a camera, went up on April 15, 1960, and slid into a perfect orbit. Its capsule disappeared soon after it was ejected, however, and was never found. Number twelve, launched on June 29, nearly made it to orbit when an electrical malfunction knocked out the Agena's attitude control system; it broke up on reentry.

"It was a most heartbreaking business," Bissell was to recall. "If an airplane goes on a test flight and something malfunctions, and it gets back, the pilot can tell you about the malfunction, and you can look it over and find out. But in the case of a recce satellite, you fire the damned thing off and you've got some telemetry, and you never get it back. There is no pilot, of course, and you've got no hardware. You never see it again. So you have to infer from telemetry what went wrong. Then you make a fix, and if it fails again, you know you've inferred wrong. In the case of Corona, it went on and on."

Discoverer 13, however, was the lucky one. It was sent up on August 10, 1960, and came out of a 165- by 436-mile orbit the following day, splashing down 330 miles northwest of Honolulu. Although the C-119s missed the spacecraft, helicopters carrying Navy frogmen from the satellite recovery ship *Haiti Victory* jumped into the water, attached a line to it, and saw it winched up into one of the choppers. Eight days later Discoverer 14 was actually snared in the air by one of the 6593rd's Flying Boxcars on a third, and final, pass. Discoverers 17 and 18 brought back photographs of excellent quality, and although there were still to be occasional problems in the following months, the Corona operation soon amounted to a "milk run," in Bissell's words. The Agena A gave way to the B model, which was six feet longer and could carry nearly a half-ton payload in its nose, thereby increasing photographic capability.

The quality of even the early photographs sent down by the Agenas was "very, very good," according to Bissell, who recalled that resolution was on the order of twelve inches. "The photogrammetrists were now so good that they were able to identify the make of almost every car in Red Square from the photography," he added. If they could spot Zises, Zims, Pobedas, Moskviches, and other kinds of automobiles, they certainly could find SS-6s. But the Corona photographs, which were taken of areas well away from the railroad tracks followed by the U-2s, only bore out what the aircraft imagery so strongly indicated: there was no missile gap. Pictures from Discoverer 29, launched on August 30, 1961, provided sufficient detail of the northern ballistic missile test site at Plesetsk to confirm that it also was the first Soviet ICBM offensive launch complex. In the process of establishing what the first of the Russian ICBM launch sites actually looked like, those who analyzed Corona's imagery were able to eliminate several other suspect sites and finally reduce the number of SS-6s to between ten and fourteen.

Neither the true nature of the Discoverer program (which had been reported in *The New York Times, Aviation Week,* and elsewhere) nor its efficacy was lost on the Kremlin, which correctly saw target mapping as one of its fundamental goals. Within a week of the launching of Discoverer 17 on November 12, 1960, the authoritative Soviet journal *International Affairs* issued two warnings that were to be repeated on a number of occasions during the following three years: no matter what the spy satellites' altitude (it mentioned Discoverer, SAMOS, and MIDAS by name and outlined their missions), their flying over Soviet territory was strictly illegal, and the U.S.S.R. had the means to bring down the orbiting intruders just as it had brought down Powers seven months before. Although the article did not mention which weapons would be used against the American spacecraft, it warned darkly that the Soviet Union would "protect its security against any encroachments from outer space just as successfully as it has done with respect to airspace."

The article amounted to the opening round of a vitriolic campaign to outlaw reconnaissance from space until the Russians' own satellites were ready to perform that task. It is highly unlikely that the U.S.S.R. could have done anything to shoot down U.S. spacecraft in 1960 or in the years immediately following. Nevertheless, the Kennedy administration that moved into the White House in

January 1961 saw no reason to needlessly provoke Khrushchev and his colleagues in the Politburo by proclaiming to the world that many of their innermost secrets were now exposed to American eyes and ears in space. Within a matter of weeks after the inauguration, steps would be taken to turn the fledgling space reconnaissance program from medium gray to deep black. But whatever the color of the program, the United States was in space reconnaissance, and it was there to stay.

5

The Cuban Missile Crisis: Pictures at an Exhibition

Photo interpretation has to do with making assumptions based on association and orders of probability. Those who do it are highly skilled at deducing change and interpreting its significance based on multiple relationships that can range from the obvious to the staggeringly complex. The process, in grossly simplified form, is roughly similar to the elimination sequence used in some standard achievement tests.

The successful interpretation of imagery—analyzing what a photograph or other imagery shows and trying to predict the consequences of that event—is dependent upon the fact that all command organizations, foremost among them the military, follow sets of narrowly defined, carefully established procedures without appreciable variation. That is to say, all military organizations follow rigid patterns in the type and numbers of equipment used, training, support, and operational practices. In other words, all armies and navies "go by the book." Without such a book, there would be chaos, a situation dreaded by generals and admirals. But when the "book" is learned by the other side, it can be used to interpret the meaning of what is taking place. This is not to say that deception is not practiced on occasion, but to note only that the overwhelming majority of military operations follow established procedures for the sake of efficiency and that these can be analyzed to calculate an opponent's intentions.

In addition, intelligence data about the nature of a weapon or about its use by one unit are almost always applicable to all of its versions and to how they are used by other, similar units. Once an armed service has gone to the trouble of designing and producing a missile to shoot down enemy aircraft, for example, it does not assign it to other, less practical functions. And it follows from this that an interpreter who spots such a missile makes an immediate association between it and the purpose for which it was built. Here is the way the association might appear on an achievement test:

In 1962, Soviet SA-2 surface-to-air missiles were associated with:

(a) high-altitude weather sampling
(b) rocket astronomy
(c) orbiting small earth satellites
(d) protecting important installations from attack or observation by hostile aircraft
(e) cloud seeding to produce rain

The answer is (d). Francis Gary Powers had been shot down two years earlier by an SA-2 and many of the installations had been photographed around major Soviet cities and important military targets. They had in fact been photographed at air bases, IRBM complexes, and other strategically important locations, and the resulting information had been put in the first computerized data banks, which were then coming into use. The photo interpreters in Washington, Omaha, and elsewhere who scrutinized the photographs showing SA-2 sites took it as an article of faith that their deployment patterns had been worked out by the Soviet military in ways that were thought to be logical and efficient and that they therefore would not be changed arbitrarily.

Here is a follow-up question:

As shown by U-2 photographs from the four years of Soviet overflights, SA-2 sites in the shape of a trapezoid were used to protect:

(a) nuclear weapons storage bunkers
(b) medium and intermediate range ballistic missile complexes
(c) shipyards
(d) bomber bases
(e) none of the above

"Missiles," thought Colonel John R. Wright, Jr., one day in late September 1962 as he studied photographs taken by a U-2 high over the San Cristóbal area of Cuba a few weeks earlier. Photographs taken on August 29 had revealed the presence of the antiaircraft weapons, and President Kennedy had been advised accordingly. So the fact that the SAMs were on Cuban soil was not news. But Wright, who was in the Defense Intelligence Agency (DIA), was the first to establish a connection between the pattern in which the SAMs were arranged and the fact that similar patterns in the U.S.S.R. were always used to protect long-range ballistic missiles. That *was* news. Wright told his boss, General Joseph Carroll, what he had discovered and suggested that a closer look at the San Cristóbal area by U-2s was warranted. The Cuban missile crisis had begun to smolder.

The Soviet plan for Cuba, as subsequently outlined by Arthur M. Schlesinger, Jr., John Kennedy's special assistant, consisted of a two-part operation. The first thing the Russians had to do was set up batteries of SA-2s and MiG-21 fighter squadrons to keep Cuban skies clear of the prying U-2s. In that way phase two, which entailed the clandestine introduction of Ilyushin-28 jet bombers and medium-range ballistic missiles (MRBMs), both of which could carry nuclear weapons, could be undertaken without fear of exposure and possible attack. The first phase, involving only defensive weapons, required no special concealment. SAMs had been designed to protect Soviet ground targets, after all, not to attack American ones; the MiGs were designed for air superiority—for dogfighting with other fighters—and therefore also would not be taken to be a threat to ground facilities on the mainland.

The second stage, the introduction of the offensive weapons, called for a careful and complex program of deception, according to Schlesinger. "One can only imagine the provisions made in Moscow and Havana through the summer to ship the weapons, to receive them, unload them, assemble them, erect bases for them, install them on launching pads—all with a stealth and speed designed to confront the United States one day in November or December with a fully operational Soviet nuclear arsenal across the water in Cuba."

Although it was not aerial reconnaissance that provided the first clues that large-scale heavy-weapons deliveries were going to Cuba, or even that ballistic missiles were involved (a Havana accountant, among several others, had reported seeing what appeared to be large missiles under shrouds before he fled the country), the photographs produced what word-of-mouth never could: incontrovertible proof.

HUMINT—the use of agents to gather intelligence—is necessary, its advocates claim, because cameras cannot read minds, guess intentions, or even see through the roofs of buildings (though keeping close tabs on what goes into the buildings and comes out again is often good enough). This is true. On the other hand, no reconnaissance camera has ever lied for purposes of expediency or because it worked for the opposition, had a lapse of memory, or became confused. Eyewitness accounts of the Soviet weapons and personnel buildup in Cuba prior to the missile crisis were so disparate during the late summer and early autumn of 1962 that they fostered confusion within the United States intelligence community. But the reconnaissance photographs did the opposite. For a trained analyst like Colonel Wright to have dismissed what was in the U-2 pictures would have been to ignore what his own eyes saw. The first photographs of the SAMs had indicated that something new and possibly important was going on in Cuba; the antiaircraft missiles' very presence told him that much. But it was the trapezoid pattern in which they were arranged in the subsequent imagery that took matters a step further. The trapezoids provided the key to predicting the Kremlin's intentions and in so doing signaled a direction for further investigation. Colonel Wright's use of the early Cuban SA-2 pictures therefore amounted to a model of the way overhead reconnaissance is supposed to function as part of the total process— high-resolution imagery, unambiguously interpreted, which can be used for counteraction.

In the spring of 1962 the organization that provided the National Security Council with intelligence estimates was called the United States Intelligence Board, or USIB. Its members represented all of the services concerned with foreign intelligence collection, including the Defense Intelligence Agency (DIA), which represented the armed services, the NSA, and the CIA. The USIB was in turn the uppermost portion of a pyramid built on subcommittees that specialized in analyzing guided missiles, atomic energy, SIGINT, and many other areas. By that spring—barely a year after the Bay of Pigs invasion—Moscow had begun to bolster the Cuban armed forces. A National Intelligence Estimate in March said that the Kremlin might soon give Havana IL-28 bombers, code-named Beagles. Although the twin-engine planes were virtually obsolete by the then current standards, they were nonetheless offensive weapons and therefore were considered to pose a potential threat. At about the same time analysts in the CIA, using HUMINT and COMINT more than overhead reconnaissance, began to notice a change in the pattern of Soviet shipping. Vessels that ordinarily had gone to Indonesia loaded with military equipment were being routed to Cuba with cargo holds full. Because of this, and despite Khrushchev's assurances that his country had no bases in Cuba and did not intend to establish any, Kennedy ordered the United States Intelligence Board to make Cuba a high-priority national intelligence target, and events followed from that order throughout the summer and early autumn.

Hundreds of defectors were screened that summer, reports from spies were analyzed, and, more important, technical collection operations were stepped up considerably. Both the Air Force and the Navy began scouring the approaches to Cuba during July, searching for and following all Soviet ships headed for the Caribbean island. In addition, communication traffic aboard the Soviet vessels was tapped, as were messages on the island itself; the International Telephone and Telegraph Company, which had run the communication network during the Batista regime, knew the intricacies of the telephone and telegraph systems and played a key role in eavesdropping on them.

U-2 missions, meanwhile, were increasingly flown over Cuba in an effort to photograph much of the 730-mile-long island. The manned flights were particularly important because, it was discovered, satellite coverage was impractical owing to Cuba's shape and position. Both Corona and SAMOS were operational by the summer of 1962 (the former was returning excellent imagery, while the latter's effectiveness remained questionable), but they orbited in a north–south polar direction. Cuba, which is long and narrow and angled in a roughly east–west direction, therefore passed under the satellites at a right angle and quite quickly, reducing the opportunity to get good photographs. Imagery collection from high altitude would therefore fall to the U-2s.

In any case, the art of "crate-ology" had been learned by the CIA's photo interpreters by that summer, according to Victor Marchetti, a former executive assistant to the agency's deputy director. Crate-ology, Marchetti explained, is "a unique method of determining the contents of the large crates carried on the decks of the Soviet ships delivering arms. With a high degree of accuracy, the specialists could look at the photographs of these boxes, factor in information about the ship's embarkation point and Soviet military production schedules, and deduce whether the crates contained transport aircraft or jet fighters. While the system was viewed with caution by many in the intelligence community, CIA Director John McCone accepted its findings, and his confidence in the technique proved justified."

Based on the various technical intelligence operations and on the tales told by the Cuban expatriates themselves, there was no reasonable doubt by early September that a large-scale Soviet arms buildup was under way in Cuba. But what sort of arms? The available evidence did not persuade the CIA's national estimates staff, which was known as the Board of National Estimates (BNE), nor the experts on the USIB, that long-range missiles were headed for Cuba.

Kennedy had made John McCone director of Central Intelligence after Allen Dulles had been cashiered in the wake of the Bay of Pigs debacle the year before. Ironically, it was the Republican businessman who first had the premonition that Khrushchev was going to try to move heavy missiles into Cuba. He had a hunch, but since it would take a great deal more than that to make a case, he decided to put his analysts to work on the problem. On September 10, while honeymooning in Europe, McCone cabled the Board of National Estimates to order a Special National Intelligence Estimate addressed to the military buildup in Cuba. The new DCI wanted the special estimate to take cognizance of the fact that Soviet MRBMs or IRBMs were most likely headed for Cuba. But the report, which was completed within a week of receipt of McCone's cable and immediately approved by the USIB for recommendation to the National Security Council, said no such thing. SNIE 85-3-62, "The Military Buildup in Cuba," noted:

> The establishment on Cuban soil of a significant strike capability with [medium- and intermediate-range ballistic] weapons* would represent a sharp departure from Soviet practice, since such weapons have so far not been installed even in Satellite territory. Serious problems of command and control would arise. There would also have to be a conspicuously larger number of Soviet

*Medium-range ballistic missiles had a range of about eleven hundred nautical miles; IRBMs had about twice that range.

personnel in Cuba, which, at least initially, would be a political liability in Latin America. The Soviets might think that the political effect of defying the U.S. by stationing Soviet nuclear striking power in so menacing a position would be worth a good deal if they could get away with it. However, they would almost certainly estimate that this could not be done without provoking a dangerous U.S. reaction.

In the absence of hard evidence, the BNE concluded that precedent indicated that Khrushchev would not risk the political and military danger, nor suffer the logistical difficulties, which attended the positioning of ballistic missiles just behind North America's back door. This was a major error, of course, but an understandable one. Senior members of the national intelligence community are not supposed to produce estimates telling the president of the United States and his National Security Council that they haven't the foggiest idea of what's happening. They are expected to report something, so in the absence of conclusive intelligence, second- or even thirdhand evidence must be massaged and behavior patterns analyzed in order to shape a best possible guess. The CIA's Board of National Estimates therefore divined that ballistic missiles were not going to Cuba even as the first of them, lashed down in canisters, were heading toward the northern Caribbean. The BNE concluded that there were no offensive missiles in evidence in Cuba and that Khrushchev would be unlikely to put any there. But John McCone wasn't having any of that.

When the director of Central Intelligence learned that his Board of National Estimates had come to a conclusion that ran counter to his instincts, and that the CIA's sister intelligence services had agreed with it, he issued instructions (still from Europe) that the document be recalled and rewritten. SNIE 85-3-62, McCone insisted grimly, failed to lend sufficient weight to the additional bargaining power the Kremlin would gain with its ballistic missiles, cocked and ready to fire, on launchers that were within striking distance of Washington. Such leverage, he reasoned, would almost certainly be used to negotiate the fate of West Berlin, the removal of American IRBMs from Italy and Turkey that were pointed at the U.S.S.R.'s underbelly, and God only knew what else.

Toward the end of September and into October, evidence of a Soviet offensive-weapons buildup began to accumulate. Colonel Wright's observation of the trapezoids, the DCI's nagging "presentiment" (as Arthur M. Schlesinger, Jr., has called it) that Nikita Khrushchev would succumb to the temptation of having his missiles poised just over the horizon from the Florida keys, and reports from Langley's crate-ologists that some of the boxes lashed to the decks of the freighters plying the ocean between the Black Sea and Havana had been made to carry disassembled IL-28 bombers, begged for closer scrutiny.

Shortly after the Corona program had been pronounced viable in the autumn of 1960, the CIA's ad hoc tasking committee, which decided what it was that the satellites were supposed to photograph, was succeeded by the more formal Committee on Overhead Reconnaissance (COMOR), which functioned under the jurisdiction of the United States Intelligence Board. The rapidly accumulating evidence persuaded COMOR to recommend to the White House that U-2 flights over western Cuba be increased. Acceding to this was no easy matter for Kennedy, however, since the target area was beginning to bristle with the same kind of surface-to-air missiles that had brought down both Powers and, more recently, a Nationalist Chinese U-2 pilot. Yet if Wright was correct, it was the very presence of the SA-2 batteries that necessitated closer inspection, especially around San Cristóbal. Kennedy finally agreed that special missions be flown but, like Eisenhower, with the caveat that each had to have presidential approval.

In the meantime, another jurisdictional battle broke out between the Air Force and the CIA, this one over which organization was going to conduct the special reconnaissance flights. Initial U-2 sorties over Cuba had been flown by Air Force pilots who, like Powers, had been "sheep-dipped," or officially transferred out of the Air Force and into the CIA so that the high-altitude flights were technically being conducted by nonmilitary personnel. (This also had kept the operations under Langley's control.)

But the discovery that increasing numbers of SAM-2 launchers were being set up, together with the fact that U-2 flights would have to be stepped up as a consequence, persuaded Secretary of Defense Robert McNamara that regular Air Force Strategic Air Command pilots ought to fly the missions. McNamara's reason for preferring SAC to CIA pilots probably had a great deal to do with the possibility that one of the U-2s would fall victim to another SAM. The flights over the U.S.S.R. had been conducted during peacetime, so the downing of a military pilot would probably have been taken by the Russians as a provocation, and that would have increased the danger of the situation. Now, however, the opposite appeared to be the case. As the White House saw the Cuban confrontation developing early in October 1962, some kind of military conflict seemed likely. Were that to happen, an Air Force pilot who was shot down would merely be a military officer doing his job; a civilian U-2 pilot in the employ of the CIA, on the other hand, would be shown to the world as a spy and possibly would even be executed as such.

Whatever McNamara's reasoning, his idea pleased the Air Force, and with good reason. Were a war to have developed, the Air Staff knew, it would have fallen to the Tactical Air Command's F-100s to bear the brunt of the action by striking targets in Cuba and perhaps even on the high seas so quickly and precisely that the enemy would be crushed before he could counterattack. In order to be able to do that, the airmen understood, they needed full control of their own intelligence-gathering apparatus. This was not a matter of taking pictures of some new radar at Archangel for eventual analysis on an otherwise slow afternoon. If TAC pilots and their bomb-laden Supersabres were suddenly ordered to take out targets in Cuba, and especially if some of those targets were heavily protected IRBM complexes, they would need up-to-the-minute photo intelligence showing what they were supposed to attack. The airmen therefore wanted to take the pictures, process and analyze them on the spot at forward bases in Florida, and be able to rush the results to the fighter pilots so they could strike decisively and with minimum losses. The thought of having those valuable, timely photographs routed all the way up to Washington, where they would be pored over by CIA and State Department "GS-16s," as George Keegan called them with undisguised contempt, was abhorrent to the men who were preparing to fight the Russians and Cubans if ordered to do so.

The CIA argued that it was mandated to control overhead reconnaissance and that it had so far accomplished that task exceedingly well, not only where the four-year Soviet overflight program was concerned, but with respect to the new stream of intelligence that was coming down in the Discoverer capsules. It therefore opposed the Defense Department. Since McCone was still in Europe, his place was taken by the agency's deputy director, General Marshall S. Carter, who made those points and added for good measure that CIA U-2s were supported by a fine reconnaissance control and operations center at Langley. Neither McNamara nor Roswell Gilpatric, the deputy secretary of defense, was moved.

The dispute over who would control the U-2 flights over Cuba, which was only among the first of many such jurisdictional conflicts, finally ended up in the office of McGeorge Bundy, Kennedy's special assistant for national security affairs. Bundy explained to Carter and Gilpatric that he didn't care who flew the missions (which had already been approved), but that they had better decide the matter quickly. The president would be displeased to learn that the two of them were incapable of settling the matter short of its landing in the Oval Office. Evidently, neither relished the prospect of the squabble going directly to Kennedy for adjudication. They therefore agreed that it was to be the Air Force that would fly the missions. Kennedy issued his approval on October 10.

Cuba was covered by clouds during much of the first two weeks of October. Then, on Sunday the fourteenth, exceptionally clear weather blew in. Majors Rudolf Anderson, Jr., and Richard S. Heyser of the Strategic Air Command's 4080th Strategic Reconnaissance Wing took off before dawn from McCoy Air Force Base in Florida and headed south in a pair of U-2Es that had been appropriated from the CIA. The E models differed from the older A types in that their more powerful engines got them up a little higher; they also carried more sophisticated electronic countermeasures (ECM) systems to help stave off an attack. While Anderson worked one sector, Heyser headed toward the Isle of Pines at seventy thousand feet.

The environment through which Richard Heyser passed as he flew thirteen miles above the Caribbean was dazzlingly beautiful but also hostile. He and Anderson had spent more than half an hour "pre-breathing" pure oxygen before they took off in order to clear as much nitrogen as possible out of their blood to prevent the bends. But the bends, or the formation of painful nitrogen bubbles in joints and elsewhere, was by no means the worst of the threats that a U-2 pilot faced. Atmospheric pressure is so low at seventy thousand feet that many liquids boil at 98 degrees Fahrenheit. Since that was Heyser's approximate body temperature, his liquids, including his blood, would have vaporized and in effect exploded had he not been wearing a custom-made altitude suit known as an MC-3, which exerted enough pressure on his body to prevent the expansion of his own gases and the water vapor in his tissues and blood. Working inside an MC-3 and the visored helmet that went on top of it while strapped securely into the U-2's ejection seat with a lap belt and shoulder harness could force six pounds of sweat out of a U-2 pilot on an average mission.

When Heyser reached the Isle of Pines, he banked his airplane to the left and headed north over the Gulf of Batabanó and straight for San Cristóbal. The flight had been planned so that the U-2 would make its run over the target area at about 7:00 A.M. At that hour the sun, which was still low in the east, would strike objects on the ground at an angle of about 20 degrees, creating nice long shadows that would help the photo interpreters define what they saw. The rays of the rising Caribbean sun bathed the U-2's right side in glaring light as it passed over landfall even as the cameras behind its Q bay windows began clicking hundreds of obliques and stereo-scopic verticals.

All the while Heyser monitored the dials and gauges that told him that the imaging system was working properly and that the single engine pushing him through the dangerously thin air was not suffo-cating. A flameout, which happened to U-2s all too frequently, would have forced him down to an altitude—say, forty thousand feet—where there was enough oxygen to restart his engine. But that would have put him within reach of the SA-2s and MiG-21s. Heyser didn't want to get caught below fifty thousand feet because he knew that the opposition would exploit his vulnerability and try to kill him. A flameout could have turned the U-2 into Antoine de Saint-Exupéry's walnut.

But the mission went flawlessly. Heyser crossed the width of Cuba in about seven minutes and then swung toward Patrick Air Force Base near Cape Canaveral with damning evidence on his exposed film.

The pictures were exhibited in the Cabinet Room in the White House at eleven-forty-five on the morning of October 16, a little more than forty-eight hours after they had been taken. The film spools had been removed from the U-2 at Patrick and flown directly to Washington, where they were hastily processed downtown at the National Photographic Interpretation Center, and then scrutinized frame by frame by the same analysts who had gone over the Soviet "take" between 1956 and 1960. They did not doubt what they saw. Dr. Ray S. Cline, whose Directorate of Intelligence was responsible for the CIA's foreign intelligence analysis, was the first to get the word on the evening of the fifteenth. He immediately alerted his boss, General Carter (McCone had gone from the honeymoon in Europe to a funeral in California almost without changing clothes), and Roger Hilsman, head of the State Department's Bureau of Intelligence and Research.

Calls were made between eight and ten that Monday night to McNamara, Bundy, and Secretary of State Dean Rusk. Reasoning that meaningful, display-size blowups of the Cuban pictures would not be ready until morning, that pulling Cabinet members away from dinner parties might arouse suspicion, and that Kennedy would need all the rest he could get in the days ahead, Bundy decided to wait until morning before confronting his president with the evidence collected over San Cristóbal.

At nine o'clock the following morning, Cline and two of his photo interpreters showed Bundy the enlarged prints in his cramped office in the basement of the White House. Bundy then carried them up to Kennedy, who was reading the newspaper in his bedroom. The president studied Richard Heyser's pictures with a magnifying glass while his special assistant for national security affairs narrated.

The members of the Executive Committee (EXCOM) of the National Security Council who sat around the oval table under George Washington's vapid gaze at a quarter of twelve that Tuesday morning constituted the nucleus of the nation's command authority. There was the president and Vice President Lyndon Johnson, Rusk and McNamara, Gilpatric, General Maxwell Taylor (the chairman of the Joint Chiefs of Staff), Under Secretary of State George Ball, Attorney General Robert Kennedy, Assistant Secretary of Defense Paul Nitze, Assistant Secretary of State for Latin American Affairs Edwin Martin, Soviet expert Llewellyn Thompson, presidential special counsel Theodore Sorensen, Bundy, and a few others. Kennedy, fully appreciating the historic significance of that first EXCOM meeting, had given permission to Cecil Stoughton, the White House photographer, to take pictures. He had also ordered that the deliberation, and all those that followed in the Cabinet Room, be tape-recorded.

Now the president's inner circle looked intently at a black-and-white aerial photograph measuring perhaps sixteen by twenty-four inches that rested on an artist's easel in front of the fireplace over which Washington's portrait hung. It is fair to say that had it not been for General Carter and his photo interpreters, not one of the men sitting around the long oval table would have known what he was looking at, and some probably weren't at all certain they were seeing what they were told they were seeing anyway.

The upper third of the photograph showed an area thick with trees whose tops glistened white in the early-morning sunshine. The trees continued down the length of the picture in a series of long, ragged stands—roughly similar in appearance to bulging, twisted fingers—that enclosed several clearings. The clearing to the far left seemed to contain three rows of haystacks. The center one might have been seen to hold a short row of nondescript structures, while the one on the right enclosed what might easily have been taken to be large pipes. But even observations of that sort would have required the ability to interpret. Had the average viewer not been told that there were noteworthy things in that photograph, he or she would almost undoubtedly have dismissed it as a wasted aerial landscape shot made by an incompetent who lacked enough sense to find a subject more interesting than thickets of ordinary trees and their long, almost grotesque shadows.

But, the members of EXCOM were told by the CIA photo interpreter who wielded the pointer, the "haystacks" were temporary field tents. What looked like nondescript structures were carefully parked army trucks. And the large "pipes," EXCOM was informed, were in fact trailers used to transport heavy missiles. There were seven trailers to be seen, all of them parked next to two missile shelter tents in which the IRBMs and MRBMs would be prepared for placement on their launchers. And, the Executive Committee was told, four of the erector-launchers were already in place, as could be seen when each was touched by the pointer. None of these had been in the August photographs.

Further, the CIA's analyst explained, the trailers, shelter tents, and erector-launchers had been tagged years before: they were types that had been photographed by other U-2s over Soviet territory, always—*always*—in the immediate vicinity of medium-range ballistic missiles.* The trailers in the photographs that followed had unquestionably been designed to pull MRBMs; the erector-launchers had been designed to fire MRBMs; the SA-2s were positioned to protect MRBMs. General Carter added that the range of the MRBMs at San Cristóbal put them within striking distance of every

---

*The interpreters were also aided by having access to a manual on the deployment and use of Soviet MRBMs that had been smuggled to the West by Colonel Oleg Penkovskiy only months before and given to the CIA's Directorate of Plans.

American target within eleven hundred miles of their launch point. That meant they might be able to reach Washington. Other MRBMs at Sagua la Grande could do the same. IRBMs destined for Guanajay, due north of San Cristóbal and barely fifty miles down the main highway from Havana, would cover all targets in an arc stretching from Phoenix to Halifax.

The photographs, supplemented with charts showing missile capabilities, kept coming. They showed control bunkers, vehicle revetments, security fences, oxidizer and propellant trucks, missile-ready tents, prefabricated housing and other tents for soldiers, and, perhaps most worrisome of all, nuclear warhead storage sites, which were seen to be mounds of earth measuring 60 by 114 feet. Each launch complex spread over hundreds of acres.

The CIA photo interpreters' careful explanations notwithstanding, the men who sat around the table in the Cabinet Room that morning still had trouble believing their own eyes, at least at first. Kennedy's initial reaction was to closely question the CIA people on how they knew that the specks were what they said they were. The president, a football fan who reportedly enjoyed an occasional game of "touch" despite an injured back, later likened the objects in the pictures to "little footballs on a football field." Sorensen called the trucks, trailers, and launchers "barely discernible scratches." Bobby Kennedy, echoing the others, later wrote: "Experts . . . told us that if we looked carefully, we could see that there was a missile base being constructed near San Cristóbal, Cuba. I, for one, had to take their word for it. I examined the pictures carefully, and what I saw appeared to be no more than the clearing of a field for a farm or the basement of a house. I was relieved to hear later that this was the same reaction of virtually everyone at the meeting."

McGeorge Bundy, recalling the photo exhibition that took place that mid-October morning, has also maintained that they were meaningless to the uninitiated but that they had quickly become "absolutely decisive," in large part because Kennedy trusted the photo interpreters. "When you look at them, if you haven't been in the business, you have no reason to suppose that they are what they are. But the photo interpreters were people the President had met before, and he trusted them, as all the rest of us did. They had a very good record. I've always thought that it was very important that he had sufficient direct exposure to the way in which these fellows would take blowups and read them, and measure them, against other pictures of Russian sites," Bundy has explained. "The identifying characteristics were then absolutely as plain as day. And they [the interpreters] made them persuasive to him."

Kennedy was in fact so persuaded of the imminent danger posed by the missiles during the inaugural EXCOM meeting that for a while he seriously considered attacking their launch sites. McNamara, who was the dominant Cabinet member at that meeting, outlined three possible responses after the CIA concluded its presentation: warn Khrushchev and Castro that Washington would not tolerate the weapons on Cuban soil; blockade the island even if it meant searching every ship approaching it; attack the missile sites. Kennedy, picking up on the last, in turn divided it into three possibilities. "One would be just taking out these missiles," the president said. "Number two would be to take out all the airplanes," he added, referring to the MiGs and probably to the IL-28s as well. "Number three is invade."

Of his own three options, Kennedy leaned heavily toward the first. "I don't think we got much time on these missiles," he mused. "We're certainly going to do number one; we're going to take out these missiles." Both Taylor and McNamara then weighed in, each saying that he favored a surprise attack against both the planes and the missiles (ultimately, of course, a naval blockade, or "quarantine," was chosen as the most appropriate response).

At another point in the meeting, Kennedy wondered aloud why the Kremlin had chosen to send MRBMs and IRBMs to Cuba in the first place after making public assurances that it would do no such thing. There "must be some major reason for the Russians to set this up. Must be that they're not satisfied with their ICBMs," he said. That was in large measure true. Rusk recalled that McCone had warned that Khrushchev might put offensive missiles in Cuba precisely because "he knows that we have a substantial nuclear superiority," and that included the number and quality of delivery vehicles, as the Discoverer flights, tracking stations, and telemetry monitoring had made abundantly clear. But whatever the reason, it was understood that day that a massive reconnaissance effort was needed to keep close track of the missiles of October so that EXCOM could be continuously informed about the exact nature and timing of the threat.

Cuba and its Atlantic approaches were intensively monitored by both Air Force and Navy aircraft during the thirteen days of the official "crisis" and in the weeks immediately following. Navy P2Vs and camera-carrying F8U Crusader fighters were assigned the task of scouring the shipping lanes in search of the missile-laden freighters and photographing them, often skimming just above the waves to do so. This had the intended effect not only of producing hard intelligence for the analysts to pore over but of showing the skippers of the ships under surveillance that they were being closely watched, undoubtedly in the hope that they would transmit that information back to Moscow.

The brunt of the low-level photo missions over the island itself fell to the Air Force's 363rd Tactical Reconnaissance Wing, whose home was, and remains, Shaw Air Force Base near Columbia, South Carolina. The unit, whose motto is *Voir c'est savoir*—To see is to know—flew RF-101 Voodoo fighters. Although designed by the McDonnell Aircraft Corp. soon after World War II as a penetration fighter able to get past enemy lines to strike at rear areas, it was instead adapted as an interceptor for the North American Air Defense Command and then as a camera-carrying recce aircraft for the Tactical Air Command (TAC). Voodoos had short swept wings that supported a long, heavy fuselage containing two turbojet engines. They therefore maneuvered sluggishly at medium and high altitudes, handling "like a cow," in the words of one of their pilots, and would have come off badly in a scrap with the MiG-21s.

What the Voodoos could do, however, was dash from point to point very quickly at low altitude. The 363rd's pilots would therefore approach the target areas "on the deck"—often at treetop level —while twisting and turning in a series of violent maneuvers known as "jinking." This was supposed to have the effect of throwing off the aim of antiaircraft gunners on the ground by catching them by surprise and offering a more difficult target for them to shoot at. An RF-101 approaching a target area would customarily come in at under a hundred feet, all the while making sudden changes in direction, first banking into a tight turn, then rolling into a turn in a different direction, and then back again. The gravitational force, or G-force, exerted on the pilots who jinked at close to five hundred miles an hour was often six or more times their body weight, meaning that a pilot weighing 180 pounds would be pinned to his ejection seat by more than a thousand pounds of pressure. Blood would drain out of his head and upper body during such maneuvers, and arm movement would become extremely difficult; the pilot would feel as though he had turned to stone. Then just before the target area was reached, the RF-101s would straighten out so that their forward-looking nose cameras and the verticals and obliques behind them could click away from a stable, level platform.

None of the RF-101s were armed (neither are the RF-4Cs that replaced them later in the decade). Aside from the fact that weapons would have made the Voodoos even heavier and less maneuverable than they were to begin with, they also could have been counterproductive.

"Give a reconnaissance pilot guns or missiles and he's going to be tempted to turn on whoever is chasing him and start shooting back," according to Brigadier General Cecil W. Powell, a former commander of the 363rd who flew 104 combat missions in Southeast Asia. "But it's not his job to fight. His job is to get the pictures and bring them back so they can be used, and bring them back just as fast as he can. He isn't doing that if he's mixing it up with somebody, and his whole mission therefore becomes pointless."

By the middle of the third week in October, about halfway through the crisis, the RF-101 pilots began coming back with clear photographs that showed quickening activity, not only at San Cristóbal, Guanajay, and Sagua la Grande but also at Remedios, far to the east of Havana.

Photos taken from low altitude at about midday on October 23, just nine days after Heyser's high-altitude run, revealed startling progress in the construction of the missile launch complexes and their extensive support facilities. The pace was so rapid, in fact, that it could be said to have been almost frantic. One of the clearings in Heyser's photographs had turned into a heavily used motor pool with fuel tank trailers parked in a neat row on one side and oxidizer tank trailers lined up on the other.

Another picture, taken on the deck, showed a prefabricated nuclear warhead storage bunker going up. Five workers could be seen standing on top of the rounded structure, with several others in front of it, their countenances showing the strain of work captured forever on the RF-101's film, perhaps even as they had watched the plane race past them and felt the bunker and ground rumble under the thunder coming out of the fighter's engines.

Four days later, on the twenty-seventh, imagery taken over San Julian airfield clearly showed three IL-28 bombers being put together while the uncrated fuselage and tail section of a fourth lay

nearby. Some of the photographs brought back by the 363rd's Voodoos were so clear that unit flags of particular Soviet military groups
could be discerned.

At about ten-fifteen that morning, even as Moscow Radio was
broadcasting an offer by Khrushchev to dismantle his Cuban-based
SS-4 sites as part of a quid pro quo involving the removal of U.S.
Jupiter IRBMs from Turkey—the very ploy John McCone had
foreseen—Major Rudolf Anderson's U-2 was blown out of the sky
over the naval facility at Banes. This added an ominous new dimension to the crisis. Although the U-2 pilots, who were now flying six
or seven missions a day out of McCoy, Laughlin Air Force Base in
Texas, and Barksdale Air Force Base in Louisiana, had been playing
cat and mouse with the MiGs for weeks, there had been no losses
because of the Soviet fighters' altitude limitations. It was understood
that Anderson could have been shot down only by an SA-2, just as
Powers had been. This meant that the SAMs protecting the ballistic
missile sites had become operational. And that, in turn, meant that
any U-2 venturing over the MRBM and IRBM installations to
collect intelligence stood a chance of being destroyed. Anderson's
death stunned the 4080th, as well as others far higher in the chain
of command, and forced U-2 mission planners to give priority consideration to the location of SAM batteries, as well as to improve
countermeasures on the reconnaissance planes themselves. Though
at least eighty-two missions were flown by 4080th Strategic Reconnaissance Wing U-2s between October 22 and December 6, when
the episode finally flickered out, Anderson was the only combat
casualty among the high-fliers.

Although the tactical value of the fighters, patrol aircraft, and
U-2s that brought back a torrent of intelligence relating to the
missile buildup in Cuba is indisputable, it is often forgotten that the
drama was played against the larger backdrop of information collected by satellites conducting strategic reconnaissance: not the
minute-by-minute tactical material concerning a relatively small
area that could have turned into a combat theater, but the bigger,
longer-range situation involving the U.S.S.R.'s capacity to wage
total war.

Beginning on July 18 with the launching of a SAMOS, a slew of
camera-carrying Agenas was sent into orbit to continue the task of
measuring the state of Soviet military and industrial preparedness—
including the number of ballistic missiles in its arsenal—evidently
to search for any sign that the Kremlin was preparing for all-out

war. Thor Agenas carrying Discoverers were fired into orbit on July 21 and 28, and again on August 2. Three days later another SAMOS went up on top of an Atlas Agena, followed by more Discoverers on September 1 and 29. On November 5, even as one of the SAC U-2s was photographing two Soviet freighters taking on missile transporters and erectors at the port of Mariel, yet another SAMOS went into orbit, followed by two more Discoverers on the eleventh and twenty-fourth (the last SAMOS, no. 30, was to reach orbit on November 27, 1963).

The data returned by the various reconnaissance satellites, as well as signals intercepts made by the listening stations that girdled the Soviet Union, persuaded Kennedy and his EXCOM once and for all that the missile gap was every bit the myth the earlier U-2 intelligence had indicated and that he therefore had a relatively strong hand in dealing with Khrushchev. The ability not only to inventory the Kremlin's ICBMs but to monitor troop and naval movements with a hitherto unknown degree of accuracy provided the young president with the means to deal with his adversaries on a far firmer footing than would have been the case had he not had conclusive technical intelligence at hand.

Similarly, the Soviet Union's first two reconnaissance satellites, Cosmos 10 and 11, launched from Tyuratam on October 17 and 20, respectively, would have been crude by later standards but would nevertheless have left no doubt that Kennedy was not bluffing. Cosmos 10, which had a perigee of only 122 miles, was de-orbited after only four days, indicating that military planners in Moscow were extremely anxious to see the photographs it had taken. If Cosmos 10's resolution was even reasonably good, it returned with pictures of hundreds of fighter-bombers lined up at Homestead and MacDill air force bases and at Jacksonville Naval Air Station in Florida, and at other bases in Texas, Louisiana, and Puerto Rico, all within easy striking range of Cuba and its approaches. At the same time, Omaha placed its bomber force on a high level of alert, and went so far as to keep many of its B-52s in the air and close enough to Soviet borders so that the Russians would be able to pick them up easily on radar and therefore see that the United States was girding for a major military conflict if it was thought to be necessary.

The missile crisis thereby introduced a new element to strategic reconnaissance, and one that was to come into regular use in the years to come. Not only did Washington make use of its own reconnaissance systems to gather information about its opponent, but at the same time it in effect used the opponent's system to its own end. Although the stream of weapons that poured into Florida and elsewhere in October 1962 was hardly paraded there as part of a show of force staged for Soviet space cameras, the presence of the Cosmos satellites provided Kennedy with a perfect medium for sending an unambiguous warning to Khrushchev and the Politburo: he was in dead earnest about the removal of the missiles. In this way the United States was able to use Soviet spaceborne intelligence-gathering systems to further its own desiderata. Nor would it be the last time. As both sides quickly came to understand, a deterrent is useless unless the opponent knows that it exists, and the best way to prove to that opponent that credible strategic weapons do exist is to allow him to photograph them. To a certain extent each side would therefore come to depend upon the other's strategic recon-naissance apparatus, and especially the satellites, to validate its retaliatory capability.

By the time of the Cuban missile crisis, U.S. overhead reconnais-sance, both air- and spaceborne, was in place and shaped essentially as it was to develop during the next quarter century.

Within weeks of coming to power, the Kennedy administration had concluded that Eisenhower's relatively open attitude regarding overhead reconnaissance was misguided and potentially dangerous. It therefore resolved to cloak the system in utmost secrecy. Al-though no public justification has ever been put forward for the blackening of virtually every aspect of space reconnaissance and of most of the aerial systems as well, at least six reasons can be sug-gested.

First, there was a need to maintain the integrity of the system. If the purpose of conducting reconnaissance and surveillance is the gathering of intelligence, most of which the opposition wants to keep secret, then divulging the methods by which the intelligence is collected invites more effective concealment and ends up making the whole exercise rather pointless.

Second, the blackening would avoid exposing the Russians (and others, some of them allies) to ridicule and in the process inviting a response that might include an attack on a U.S. spacecraft. Anger at having their borders violated by Washington's various overhead reconnaissance systems had begun with the penetrations after World War II and had continued unabated through the U-2 years and into the early 1960s, when the United States enjoyed an early (and short-lived) monopoly on space reconnaissance. Given the importance of the American program, "rubbing the Russians' noses in it" by publicizing such activities was taken to be an indulgence whose risks outweighed its benefits.

Third, there was an effort to conceal the reconnaissance budget, which was enormous and growing, and prevent the Air Force–CIA rivalry for control of the spacecraft, their tasking, and analysis of the product—which was often venomous—from spilling into the public limelight. Reconnaissance and surveillance technology did not so much represent the state of the art as it did the creation of the art in the first place. That necessarily entailed large expenditures, not only because of the sophistication of the equipment and the huge support base upon which it rested, but because many blind alleys are invariably followed in such enterprises before the technology comes together as needed. Although reconnaissance budgets are customarily camouflaged in lines ostensibly devoted to "strategic programs," "intelligence and communications," "test and support programs," "basic research," "exploratory development," and "advanced technology demonstration," it is certain that a sizable portion of the $35 billion to $40 billion that Lyndon Johnson claimed had gone into the nation's overall space program was earmarked for space reconnaissance and surveillance.

Fourth, there was a desire to protect arms control negotiations. Efforts at hammering out a limited test ban treaty had run a rocky course since the subject had first been proposed in May 1955. The major sticking point throughout the Eisenhower years and into John Kennedy's had been verification, with each side trying to construct monitoring and verification systems that were as foolproof as possible. Although the limited test ban, which went into effect in October 1963, depended upon national technical means (NTM) of verification that included systems having no direct relation to space reconnaissance (seismic monitoring devices and high-orbiting Vela Hotel satellites measuring neutron, gamma ray, and X-ray emissions being but two), low-flying imaging satellites did play an important part in the process. It is likely that the Kennedy administration, which wanted the treaty, did not want the question of the adequacy of national technical means of verification debated—with accompanying photographs taken from space—on the front page of every newspaper in the country. It was well understood by the early 1960s that releasing satellite photographs in such circumstances was problematical; a picture considered adequate for treaty verification by one person could just as well be interpreted as being inadequate by another, depending upon the political attitude of the viewer. It was thought best to avoid the debate altogether.

Fifth, the Kennedy administration (and those that succeeded it) wanted to avoid the appearance of being able to use its highly advanced technology, which was already a source of bitter frustration among many less developed nations, to spy on them from the safety of space. The spacecraft designed in the sixties for NASA's Earth Resources Technology Satellite program (now called Landsat), which were intended in part to help Third World countries manage their land and water resources more efficiently, were deliberately given sensors with relatively poor imaging resolution (one hundred feet or so) specifically to avoid the charge that they were orbited to collect military intelligence.

Finally, it was no doubt felt that publicizing the capabilities of strategic reconnaissance systems and the data they produce could severely restrict a president's political options. The sharing of such information beyond the confines of the highest levels of the intelligence community invites second-guessing by other governments, the political opposition at home, disgruntled special interest groups, and the press and could therefore limit the response available to a chief of state. No president wants his foreign policy agenda made vulnerable to opponents who have the same intelligence he has, and particularly when that intelligence is splashed across page one of the morning newspaper or appears on the evening news.

The genesis of the blackening of space reconnaissance and the organizational changes that remain in effect to this day actually goes back to Eisenhower's last two years. The hostility that existed between the military services, notably the Air Force, and the CIA over control of the system and the widely disparate estimates of Soviet military strength predated the missile gap. But it was that debacle that left a lasting suspicion concerning military estimates in the minds of Ike and some of his top aides.

In March 1960, less than a year from the expiration of Eisenhower's second term, Secretary of Defense Thomas Gates suggested to the president that a study of the entire defense intelligence apparatus be undertaken. He described the national strategic intelligence establishment as being a huge conglomerate that spent up to $2 billion annually with far less efficiency than should be the case. Eisenhower favored such a study, but nothing came of Gates's proposal until Powers was shot down and the NASA cover story was bungled so horrendously. At that point—on the eve of the successful flights of Discoverers 13 and 14—the Bureau of the Budget, the President's Board of Consultants on Foreign Intelligence Activities, the CIA, and the secretaries of state and defense agreed that an interagency study was warranted and that it ought to be conducted under the supervision of the director of Central Intelligence.

The Joint Study Group (JSG), as it was called, had convened in July and met ninety times during the summer and fall of 1960, interviewing 320 individuals from fifty-one organizations that had to do with intelligence in one form or another. Among other recommendations, it had concluded in a report submitted on December 15 that military intelligence played too dominant a role in the overall process, that a central intelligence requirements organization be instituted to reduce duplication and more keenly focus on intelligence objectives, that military intelligence estimates be coordinated, that a common National Photographic Interpretation Center be started for interagency use, and that the armed services be limited to observer status on the United States Intelligence Board.

Several of the JSG's recommendations were contained in National Security Council directives that were approved only days before Eisenhower left the White House. McNamara, the incoming secretary of defense, had been so impressed by the JSG report that he acted on several of its recommendations. Its finding that military intelligence estimates needed coordination resulted, for example, in the creation early in 1961 of the Defense Intelligence Agency (DIA), which is supposed to mesh intelligence requirements and some operations of the three armed services.

The most important bureaucratic innovation to come out of the Eisenhower administration where overhead reconnaissance is concerned is unquestionably the National Reconnaissance Office (NRO), which officially came into existence on August 25, 1960, amid great secrecy and after several months of debate within the White House, the CIA, the Air Force, and the Defense Department.

As had been the case with the JSG itself, the NRO was born out of the Eisenhower administration's exasperation with the feuding, self-indulgence, and concomitant waste of time and resources that went hand in hand with every effort at space reconnaissance. In addition to the Joint Study Group, the loss of Powers's U-2 and its immediate aftermath served as the catalyst for the creation of a three-man group that was specifically empowered to come up with an efficient means of operating the SAMOS and Corona systems and their follow-ons. The three—Under Secretary of the Air Force Joseph Charyk, John H. Rubel (the deputy director of the Defense Directorate of Research and Engineering), and Dr. George Kistiakowsky—suggested in a briefing to the National Security Council on August 25, 1960, that the NRO be formed to manage space reconnaissance.

And "National" was the operative word. Kistiakowsky was to state emphatically in his memoir that the NRO was intended to be "of a national character, including OSD [Office of the Secretary of Defense] and the CIA and not the Air Force alone." It was taken to be imperative, Kistiakowsky would note, that utilization of the product of space reconnaissance not be left solely in the hands of the Air Force. As a consequence, the head of the National Reconnaissance Office was to be the under secretary of the Air Force—a civilian—and his deputy was to be from the CIA, another civilian. Charyk became the first director of the NRO and, according to both Richard Bissell and Herbert Scoville, Jr., quickly established a smooth working relationship with the agency. That, however, was not to last.

At any rate, the NRO, which was so black that it was never referred to by name (it functioned in 1960, as it was to continue to function, under cover of the under secretary of the Air Force and the Office of Space Systems), itself became instrumental in carrying out the Kennedy administration's wish that space reconnaissance in its several forms be assigned the highest possible level of classification. As Arthur Sylvester, the assistant secretary of defense for public affairs, was shortly to tell his president in a memorandum, information newly made available to the media regarding a SAMOS launch "represents a severe reduction from what had previously been issued," and he added, "Dr. Charyk has reviewed those changes and is satisfied that they meet all his security requirements and those of the SAMOS Project Director, Brigadier General Greer."

The blackout affected MIDAS and Corona, as well as SAMOS. MIDAS became program 239A. Officially at least, the last Discoverer to go into space was no. 38, launched on February 27, 1962. What would have been no. 39, however, went up on March 7 with two new designators. One was program 622-A. In addition, the March 7 launch was a historic one in that it marked the beginning of a program designation that was to encompass all photographic intelligence satellites from that point on: Keyhole. Keyhole spacecraft would henceforth carry a Byeman code name, such as Corona; a four-digit numerical designation, such as 5500 series; and a KH, or Keyhole, number. Thus, SAMOS satellites were retroactively designated KH-1s. Discoverers were renamed KH-4s (there is no record of KH-2s or KH-3s if, indeed, either ever existed).

The Cuban missile crisis marked a rite of passage for U.S. space reconnaissance. It came through its formative period and emerged as a strategic system that had already had a profound effect on international relations and was clearly destined to play an even greater role in the years to come.

Khrushchev feared and threatened American reconnaissance and surveillance spacecraft because he worried that they would sooner or later expose the Soviet long-range ballistic missile program for what it was despite his blustering hyperboles: essentially impotent. And they did just that. In addition, the pictures that came floating down from the sky provided Kennedy with the wherewithal to call Khrushchev's bluff during the crisis itself—to make him back down in the enduring tradition of the American frontier.

By the end of 1962, even as Soviet freighters steamed back to their ports carrying the exposed MRBMs and IRBMs, the technical collection systems that had done the damage quietly receded into the murky darkness of the tightest security procedure the national intelligence establishment could devise, all but disappearing from public view. But within the darkness, an infrastructure was taking root and beginning to grow: a new generation of reconnaissance satellites and their support equipment was materializing, and the U-2's successor was being readied for flight.

6.

Arms Control and the Acceptance of "Spies" in the Sky

• ─────────────────────────────

The gravest concern in the realm of space policy in four successive administrations, beginning with Eisenhower's and ending with Richard M. Nixon's, was not getting astronauts safely to the moon and back, however important those voyages were taken to be, but protecting U.S. "spy" satellites from attack, both politically and militarily. And their safety remains of such paramount importance that an attack on one would send a spasmodic shudder right through the national defense system. An attack on a U.S. reconnaissance satellite would be taken as an act of war.

Sputnik forced two space agendas on the United States, one public, the other top secret. The open agenda, involving NASA, began in 1958 and had as its aim a series of space feats designed to demonstrate to the world the supremacy of American science and technology (not to mention capitalist managerial efficiency and, by implication, the overall vitality of the Western system) and in the process demonstrate in the most explicit way the bankruptcy of Marxist technology despite the thin public relations advantage the Kremlin had gained by pelting America with a hail of Sputniks, Luniks, and Vostoks.

The Mercury, Gemini, and Apollo programs, culminating in the six moon landings, were far and away the most important and spectacular elements in Washington's own meticulously staged space extravaganza. Meanwhile, the unmanned probes, such as the

Pioneer and Surveyor missions to the moon and the Mariner expedition to Venus, plus a host of technology applications satellites, such as the Landsat earth resources platforms, were relegated to a distant secondary role irrespective of their conceptual and technical elegance. The lunar and planetary probes, which were designed and crafted by faceless savants at the Jet Propulsion Laboratory and elsewhere, could not carry men and would therefore not yield authentic heroes, however superior they were to the manned spacecraft in all other respects.

The secret agenda, which had begun with the shallow penetration flights right after World War II, called for nothing less than the encapsulation of the Soviet Union, Communist China, and their proxies inside a vast shell of electronic sensors so that information that was taken to be crucial to the survival of the West could be drawn out in an uninterrupted flow. There would be giant radar and signals-monitoring arrays ringing the enemy bloc, airplanes that snooped along its borders almost continuously, ships festooned with high-powered bugging apparatus parked off its coastlines, and even submarines to spy on its naval operations. (Submarine reconnaissance operations would include tapping into Soviet communication cables laid on the ocean floor, observing ballistic missile launches from Soviet submarines, and even photographing the undersides of some Soviet subs in port. The programs were variously code-named Holystone, Barnacle, and Ivy Bells, among others.)

But the ubiquitous satellites were to evolve as the centerpiece of U.S. strategic reconnaissance and surveillance. The dome of the shell was to be studded with speeding machines that would peer down, eavesdrop, and take measurements in an unrelenting and increasingly sophisticated effort to peel away the mask that concealed the enemy's most important military and industrial secrets.

For their part, the Russians took the fledgling U.S. space reconnaissance program to be the intrusive, potentially dangerous threat that it was. Even as early as 1952, Soviet journals had sharply criticized suggestions by von Braun and Forrestal to the effect that observation of strategic targets from space was quite feasible and most desirable.

The Russian academicians' central thesis, often reiterated, was that overhead intelligence-gathering amounted to an illegal violation of national sovereignty in that it occurred within Soviet airspace (however high that extended). The opinions of twentieth-century jurists regarding ownership of the sky, which had usually come out in favor of whatever nation sprawled under it, were frequently dusted off to make the point; so were any number of conventions on the subject, including one that took place in Chicago in 1944 that outlawed aerial reconnaissance (and which, of course, had been roundly ignored by most of the major signatories).

Barely two months after Discoverer 13 was plucked out of the Pacific by Navy frogmen in August 1960, an event soon followed by the air-snatching of its immediate successor, Dr. G. P. Zhukov, academic secretary of the Space Law Scientific Research Committee of the Soviet Academy of Sciences, published a paper in the weighty journal *International Affairs* that was a good deal less theoretical than those written by his colleagues and which came considerably closer to the mark. "The main purpose of space espionage is to increase the efficiency of surprise attack, making it possible to knock out enemy missile bases at the very start and thereby avoid a retaliatory blow," academician Zhukov noted during his condemnation of not only Discoverer, SAMOS, and MIDAS, but of the Tiros weather satellites as well.

Nor was the notion that spaceborne imaging and ferreting systems would make ideal target locaters for SAC's bombers and missiles wasted on Khrushchev. "Information about the location of such bases can be of importance not for a country concerned with its defense requirements, but solely for a state which contemplates aggression and intends to strike the first blow and therefore wants to destroy the missile bases so as to avoid retaliation after attack," the Soviet leader pointed out in a cynical, though accurate, appraisal of the dark side of space reconnaissance: the locating and mapping of targets.

Then after SA-2s had been widely deployed following the downing of Francis Gary Powers, Khrushchev took matters a step further by adding ominously that "the Soviet Union has everything necessary to paralyze U.S. military espionage, both in the air and outer space. If other espionage methods [besides U-2s] are used, they also will be paralyzed and rebuffed."

"In case of need, the Soviet Union will be able to protect its security against any encroachments from outer space as successfully as it has done with respect to airspace," Zhukov noted in yet another reference, which he could not resist making, to the downing of the U-2 at Sverdlovsk.

. . .

The threats made against U.S. reconnaissance satellites throughout the late fifties and into the early sixties were explicit, and although they were presumed to be idle at the time because the Russians had no known satellite attack capability, they were nonetheless taken with the utmost seriousness, since they clearly boded things to come. The rumblings from Moscow therefore prompted three responses.

The first, championed by Eisenhower during his tenure as president and by the State Department well beyond Ike's departure, took its direction from the old Open Skies approach and sought loosely defined cooperation with the U.S.S.R. in the realm of space while simultaneously continuing to protect the reconnaissance program's integrity.

The main vehicle for this approach was supposed to be the United Nations. In September 1958 Secretary of State John Foster Dulles had challenged the world body to start a space committee with the purpose of engendering international cooperation in areas that did not impinge directly on national security. "As we reach beyond the planet," Dulles had said, "we should move as truly united nations." His unusual obsequiousness was probably meant in large part to knock the edges off the Russians' incessant demands that all military uses of space, and most of all for reconnaissance, be banned and that foreign bases (which practically surrounded them with electronic ears and camera-carrying planes) be abandoned. Dulles's exhortation and pressure from Washington were to a great extent responsible for the creation of the UN's ad hoc Committee on Peaceful Uses of Outer Space (COPUOS), which was to write space law for years to come. As manipulated by the Eisenhower and succeeding administrations, COPUOS was also to make certain that a laissez-faire attitude toward activities in space, which favored the United States because of its technological advantage there, prevailed.

The Eisenhower administration had also gone outside the UN to carry out the same basic plan. Participants in the International Geophysical Year, which had begun on July 1, 1957, at the urging of the United States, were asked to share the knowledge gained in the many experiments that were performed on the earth and above it. A decade later, NASA's Earth Resources Technology Satellites, or ERTS, were to serve the same general purpose as they photographed the planet in copious detail for resource management and other purportedly peaceful purposes. Quite aside from the IGY's and ERTS's bountiful scientific accomplishments, both also got the peoples of the earth used to having their pictures taken from space, a gradual development that bore on the legitimization of satellite reconnaissance, however indirectly.

The second response, already noted, was the low-profile approach favored by John Kennedy and the Central Intelligence Agency. The Russians would be less likely to go after U.S. space assets, the theory had it, if they were not embarrassed by them and in the process held up to ridicule before the rest of the world. No sovereign state would want its bareness under another nation's satellite cameras ballyhooed in public—least of all the Soviet Union, where secretiveness amounted to paranoia. The blackout, which was mostly successful at the outset and became more so as it took hold, was therefore imposed by the Kennedy administration within weeks of its coming to power. Official references to strategic reconnaissance, and particularly to that relating to overhead systems, were promptly prohibited. The ostensible reason for this, of course, was that it was counterproductive, if not self-defeating, to provide those who were being watched and listened to with the wherewithal to evade detection. But at the same time there was a pervasive feeling among the technical intelligence collectors, the National Security Council, and the White House that sticking one's chin out too far and too flamboyantly would invite a punch.

The third response, strongly favored by the three armed services and such sympathetic congressmen as New York's Republican Senator Kenneth B. Keating (who was among the first and certainly the most vociferous of those carrying the Stars and Stripes to the ramparts during the Cuban missile crisis), called for a military, not a political, solution to the problem of protecting U.S. space assets, and especially the reconnaissance platforms: the development of a means of responding in kind to an attack. Those who advocated a so-called hunter-killer satellite system wanted to be able to clear the heavens of Soviet spacecraft should it ever become necessary to do so. In the process, those who wanted a U.S. anti-satellite (ASAT) capability at the dawn of the space age hoped (as they still do) that owning the weapons would discourage a Soviet attack on American spacecraft because the Kremlin would understand that such action would trigger swift reprisal against their own satellites.

The perceived requirement for ASATs in the United States began to evolve in the 1950s even before the first satellite was launched. And it is worth noting that the impetus for producing them, at least initially, was not restricted to the desire to be able to "kill" reconnaissance satellites.

The temptation to possess a satellite-killing capability was also fueled by the fear that the Kremlin would eventually be able to launch orbiting bombs that could be kept circling the earth until someone decided to push a button, sending them down to rain devastation on a defenseless foe. Indeed, von Braun's rocket team had designed an "antipodal bomber" for the Third Reich that was in essence a winged super-V-2 whose pilot could skim over the atmosphere and drop explosives on New York, Washington, and Pittsburgh (the steel capital of the country). Given the fact that the Russians had captured some of the German engineers, besides having the satellite capability they displayed beginning in 1957, the orbiting bomb theory did not seem farfetched to some defense planners. And the ability to protect the United States against such terror weapons seemed to be warranted in 1966, when it was discovered that the U.S.S.R. appeared to be testing just such a delivery system. Named the Fractional Orbital Bombardment System (FOBS) by Washington, the project was believed to involve the placing of SS-9-boosted warheads into low orbit, from where they would be able to act as "pathfinders" for a regular ballistic missile attack, knocking out U.S. ABM radars immediately before the full onslaught began.

There were eighteen FOBS tests in all, the last one taking place on August 8, 1971. It has been speculated that the program ended because the weapons were judged too inaccurate to use. Others have suggested that the ABM portion of the SALT I treaty, then under negotiation, limited each side to only two anti-ballistic missile launch sites (later reduced to one) and that arrangement did not justify so expensive an undertaking.

But it was the protection of U.S. reconnaissance satellites by instilling the fear of reprisal, as well as the intimately related but separate goal of being able to knock out their Soviet counterparts for its own sake, that acted as the true driving force behind the ASAT endeavor. The generals certainly had more on their minds than mere retaliation. There was an abhorrence of being spied upon from above that the men of the Pentagon fully shared with their opposite numbers in Moscow. The generals and admirals felt naked without a means of poking out the eyes that peered down at them if poking was thought to be necessary.

"It is inconceivable to me that we would indefinitely tolerate Soviet reconnaissance of the United States without protection, for clearly such reconnaissance has an association with an ICBM program," General James M. Gavin warned, much in the manner of Khrushchev and academician Zhukov, in a book published in 1959. And his remedy was the same as theirs. "It is necessary, therefore, and I believe urgently necessary, that we acquire at least a capability of denying Soviet overflight—that we develop a satellite interceptor."

And Air Force General Thomas White, testifying earlier that year before a congressional appropriations committee, was even more explicit. "The Soviets could be expected to respond to our reconnaissance satellites as we would respond to theirs, and if the enemy develops a reconnaissance space vehicle we probably would want to take him out of space if we could," he explained more than a year before the first successful Discoverer launch. With the development of functioning reconnaissance satellites, General White added, "there immediately becomes a requirement to intercept it and to nullify it."

There was not just one ASAT but a spate of them, and they merit brief attention because their existence was (and remains) inexorably entwined with their intended prey—low-orbiting satellites, including reconnaissance types.

The Air Force came in first, in the autumn of 1959, even as the earliest U.S. reconnaissance satellites—the CIA's Discoverers—were in the throes of the worst of their birth pains. America's first ASAT was called Bold Orion, or USAF 7795. The program had actually started in 1958 as a feasibility test series to see whether it was practical to drop-launch ballistic missiles from B-47 Stratojet bombers. It wasn't. Testing was then adapted to the ASAT mission on an experimental basis.

On October 13, 1959, a two-stage missile was launched from one of the four-engine bombers and sent after Explorer 4, which at that moment was passing several hundred miles over Cape Canaveral.

The ASAT came within four miles of its target, according to Air Force reports, and was therefore deemed a success. But in the meantime the Air Force had become interested in a ground-launched, or direct ascent, system, so Bold Orion was quietly discontinued. The abortive program had two enduring consequences, however. It turned out to be the prototype of the ASAT system that was finally reborn in the 1980s, in which another two-stage missile is launched from a climbing F-15 Eagle fighter. USAF 7795 also gave the United States the distinction of being the first nation to test an anti-satellite weapons system.

Another Air Force program, known as SAINT (for Satellite Inspector) was even more imaginative. Unlike Bold Orion, though, it never got off the ground. The plan called for installing a television camera and a radar in the nose of an Agena B—the same highly adaptable platform that carried Air Force and CIA reconnaissance sensors—and boosting it to orbit atop an Atlas. SAINT was then supposed to sail past its quarry and then gradually drop back until they were about fifty feet apart. At that point, the Agena B was to look over the other satellite, picking out such details as its communication antennas, power system, and sensors, and relay what it saw to NORAD for analysis.

Although SAINT was conceived as an inspection system only, the Air Force made it known early on that it wanted the spacecraft to have a kill capability as well, undoubtedly reasoning that discovering that an enemy satellite had to be nullified (as General White put it) wouldn't matter very much unless it could be done. Neither the Eisenhower nor the Kennedy administrations relished the prospect of armed SAINTs, however, so sticking weapons on the design was never attempted.

At some point before SAINT was canceled in December 1962 for lack of funding and for technical and conceptual shortcomings that were considered excessive, someone apparently came up with a compromise that might have pleased both the peace-in-space advocates and those who insisted that Soviet reconnaissance satellites would have to be prevented from doing their job. The idea, a fleeting one, was to have an American ASAT (most likely SAINT because maneuvering would be necessary) pull alongside a Soviet reconnaissance satellite and spray paint over its window so that the camera inside would be blinded. This, of course, would have put the Soviet satellite out of operation without actually harming it, thereby striking a neat balance between military necessity and political nicety. Nothing ever came of the mischievous scheme, though it certainly represented one of the space age's first dirty tricks, at least theoretically.*

Since SAINT was supposed to go into orbit with its target and fly in formation with it at close quarters, it was a so-called co-orbital system. With a single exception, the United States was to abandon the co-orbital technique with SAINT's demise, opting instead for direct ascent ASATs and eventually for an air-launched missile. As will be seen, however, the U.S.S.R. began testing its own ASATs in 1968, and co-orbital attacks were to be its preferred technique. That remains the case.

The Navy, always concerned that Soviet ocean reconnaissance satellites would be able to track its ships and pinpoint their location for an attack, weighed into the ASAT competition with several projects, most of them researched between 1960 and 1964 under the rubric of a program code-named Early Spring. Most of the Navy's thinking about ASATs had to do with using Polaris SLBMs for direct ascent attacks. Raytheon, which manufactured the Sparrow air-to-air radar homing missile used on Navy and Air Force fighters, funded a study in which its weapon was to be used as the upper stage on a Polaris booster. Nothing came of that plan, however, because the Polaris ballistic missiles and the submarines from which they were launched were in short supply during the early 1960s and priority had to be given to their deployment against cities and other terrestrial targets.

Hi-Ho, another Navy ASAT project, did make it off the ground. Similar to Bold Orion, it involved the use of a McDonnell F-4B Phantom fighter carrying a missile to high altitude and then launching it upward at a target satellite. Hi-Ho was tested in the spring of 1962 and then abandoned when the Navy temporarily lost interest in ASATs (it was to be revived in the 1970s when Soviet ocean reconnaissance satellites made their initial appearance).

The Army's ASAT entry, first known as Mudflap, was eventually given only a number: Program 505. It involved the adaptation of the forty-eight-foot-long Western Electric Nike Zeus ballistic missile defense (BMD) rocket as a satellite killer. The metamorphosis was

*In the same vein, the Air Force proposed a Blue Gemini program after the cancellation of SAINT that would have used a military version of NASA's manned Gemini capsule to "approach, capture, and disable an uncooperative satellite." It is unclear what Blue Gemini's planners meant by "uncooperative," but the scheme, which was worthy of Ian Fleming, was also short-lived.

logical, since both kinds of weapons must hit or otherwise incapaci-
tate a small object moving very quickly at high altitude. The Army
reasoned that with a maximum range of 150 miles and a burnout
velocity, or top speed, eleven times that of sound (both of which
were required to stop incoming warheads during a nuclear attack),
the three-stage rocket would make a fine satellite killer. And since
Nike Zeus had been designed to carry a nuclear charge in the
megaton range, giving it an explosive yield equivalent to a million
tons of TNT, a near miss would have been as good as a direct hit,
especially where something as fragile as a reconnaissance satellite
was concerned.

Following a series of tests at the White Sands Missile Range in
New Mexico and on Kwajalein Atoll in the Pacific in 1962 and 1963
—most of which were judged successful by the Army—Program
505 was pronounced operational on August 1, 1963. This meant that
one of the nuclear-tipped Nike Zeuses was technically ready to be
shot at a passing satellite at any given moment. But one would not
suffice. A horrible complication soon became apparent. Since the
number of inclination-altitude combinations that could be used by
Soviet satellites was virtually infinite, the Nike Zeus's 150-mile
range would be wholly inadequate to reach any Soviet spacecraft
programmed to stay clear of it. One obvious way to overcome that
problem would have been to dot the United States and its overseas
possessions with scores of Nike Zeus ASAT installations, perhaps
250 miles apart, so there would be some overlapping coverage. But
not only would that solution have been inordinately expensive,
given the extremely remote possibility that the sites would actually
have to be used, it still would have left most Soviet satellites, including communication, navigation, weather, and data-relay types, well
out of range anyway because they inhabited the higher altitudes.
Program 505, in its turn, was therefore abandoned for still another
system.

Program 437 was an Air Force project that started as a requirement issued in February 1962 calling for the development "in an
early time period" of a nonorbital "collision course satellite interceptor." The booster chosen for this direct ascent attack system was the
venerable Thor. It had three advantages: it was reliable, it had a
relatively long range (it could travel seventeen hundred miles as an
IRBM, though its reach as an ASAT would have been quite a bit
short of that), and it was readily available because IRBMs were
being withdrawn from Western Europe at that time. After the

completion of a series of tests that the Air Force claimed was successful, a pair of the missiles were put on alert on Johnson Island in the Pacific on June 10, 1964. Testing continued sporadically, with mixed results, through 1970. A decline in interest in killer satellites that began in the mid-sixties eventually caught up with Program 437, too, and it was quietly ended.

If the allure of killer satellites began to fade in the mid-sixties and continued throughout the rest of that decade, the possibility of using one satellite to inspect another continued to intrigue some members of the U.S. aerospace community. A spin-off of Program 437, called 437 AP (Alternate Payload) therefore came under consideration in 1963 as a kind of resurrected super-SAINT. Brockway McMillan, a Bell Telephone Laboratories executive who had been on the defense committee of James Killian's Technological Capabilities Panel, and who was under secretary of the Air Force at the time, was particularly enthusiastic about the possibility of being able to scrutinize low-orbiting Soviet satellites and therefore pushed the idea of doing so.

Program 437 AP was supposed to work in roughly the same way as Corona, except, of course, that the reconnoitering satellites were to photograph their orbiting neighbors, not ground targets. The inspector satellites would then be brought down from orbit and their intelligence yield examined. The system was tested four times during 1964 and 1965; the results remain classified. But one participant in Program 437 AP was later quoted as saying that Defense Secretary McNamara issued emphatic instructions that the satellites were in no circumstance to be used to carry out the mission for which they had been designed. That seems to have put an end to the idea of orbital inspection, at least until the advent a little more than a decade later of a reconnaissance satellite called the KH-11. And although sporadic testing in Program 437 was to continue through 1970, as has been noted, 1963 really marked the effective end of U.S. ASAT activity for the next two decades. The notion took hold that the proliferating satellites circling the globe on a variety of missions had to be allowed to follow their orbits and perform their tasks unmolested.

What had happened to make ASATs less attractive to the United States? There appears to have been several reasons why satellite-killers were effectively shelved, starting in 1963.

From a military standpoint, the burgeoning number of satellites, and therefore of potential targets, created logistical problems (and, in the process, financial ones as well). The number of satellites related to the military and engaged in reconnaissance, surveillance, meteorology, data relay, navigation, and communication that were on station by the mid-sixties confounded a potential attacker with a multiplicity of targets. Attempting to destroy another nation's satellite was hardly a whimsical matter. It would be undertaken, in fact, only in the most dire of circumstances: as, for example, the prelude to war. That being the case, selectively picking off one or two enemy spacecraft was out of the question, since doing so would simultaneously tip the attacker's hand while leaving most of the enemy satellites to continue functioning. Instead, all enemy satellites engaged in military activity would have to be cleared out of the sky at the same time, and to the extent that a war might be protracted, new satellites would need to be attacked as soon as they were sent up. In the case of Soviet reconnaissance satellites, this task was particularly daunting, since the Russians produced them on assembly lines; judging by the frequency of their launches (four went up between March 21 and May 24, 1963), at least one backup platform was on hand at all times, ready for quick launch.

That being so, the United States would have had to keep at the ready a virtual fleet of ASATs at several points around the United States and beyond its borders, all primed for immediate attack. Given the extremely low probability of war, particularly during the period of détente following the Cuban missile crisis in the autumn of 1962, the considerable expenditure of funds and personnel to maintain such a large and complex system seemed to be unwarranted.

Politically, the Cuban missile crisis had demonstrated that overhead reconnaissance, and satellite reconnaissance in particular, was a stabilizing factor because it greatly reduced the element of surprise and in the process lessened the chance of a dangerous, all-out, preemptive attack for fear that the enemy was getting ready to do the same thing. There was no serious question by 1963 that space reconnaissance platforms then in use by Washington and Moscow had helped avert a military clash that could have resulted in catastrophe because they allowed either side to keep track of what the other was doing. The satellites substituted imagery for imagination and provided a realistic look at what the opposition had and did not have.

Even targeting had begun to play a stabilizing role in the system of mutual assured destruction (MAD) that was beginning to take shape during the early years of Robert McNamara's time in the Pentagon. Khrushchev had been quite right in pointing out that U.S. overhead reconnaissance systems, both aerial and spaceborne, had among their several tasks the precise targeting of Soviet missile complexes, port facilities, uranium-processing plants, industrial centers, and other places that would need to be demolished in the event of war. But as General Gavin indicated, however obliquely, the national command authority in Washington and even the targeteers in Omaha who used satellite photographs to choreograph the obliteration of the U.S.S.R. understood that their Russian counterparts were doing the same thing. The effect was sobering.

To the extent that reconnaissance satellites helped the adversaries to keep tabs on each other and were therefore stabilizing, machines designed to kill them were seen to be destabilizing. And where targeting was concerned, ASATs wouldn't matter anyway, since all targets would have long since been marked for destruction the day the war began.

Finally, in international relations there was a new element, nuclear arms control, which had as its very keystone the use of sensors, including those in orbit.

Although Moscow had first proposed a ban on the testing of nuclear weapons in May 1955, it did so as part of a larger, comprehensive plan that also called for reducing conventional forces and eliminating nuclear weapons altogether, two caveats that were rejected by Washington. In October 1956, Soviet Premier Nikolai Bulganin had written to Eisenhower urging that the United States agree to such a ban and making the point that nuclear test explosions were so powerful that they could easily be picked up by ordinary seismic monitoring equipment and other measuring devices placed around the world. By virtue of their sheer explosive power, Bulganin asserted, nuclear detonations simply could not be hidden. But American seismologists and intelligence experts disagreed. Basically, Eisenhower was told, the Kremlin was asking him to enter into an agreement to stop all nuclear testing without any system of international control or adequate verification procedure. Eisenhower would have none of that.

A so-called Conference of Experts was held in Geneva during the summer of 1958 at which representatives of the United States, the Soviet Union, Great Britain, France, Canada, Poland, Czechoslovakia, and Romania managed to hammer out mutually acceptable verification techniques that included the use of up to 180 seismic monitoring stations, ten shipborne posts, and air sampling flights that would be able to pick up particulates in the air after an aboveground nuclear explosion.

Although it was to take five more years before the Limited Test Ban Treaty was ratified (during which an unofficial moratorium on testing was first established and then broken), the basis for the system of verification for the limited test ban, as well as for others that followed, had been established. The LTBT prohibited nuclear testing in the atmosphere, under water, and in outer space, leaving underground explosions as the only acceptable type. By the time the LTBT was signed in Moscow in August 1963, both the United States and the Soviet Union had satisfied themselves that its provisions could be monitored with enough precision so that cheating would not be a serious factor.

And the monitoring depended not only on seismic arrays and air sampling but on space reconnaissance and surveillance. Specifically, the United States would rely on its space reconnaissance capability to spot preparations for aboveground nuclear testing and upon a space-based surveillance system code-named Vela Hotel, which used sets of satellites equipped with infrared heat detecting sensors to watch for nuclear detonations on earth, in the atmosphere, and in space from some seventy thousand miles out. And the LTBT contained an ironic footnote where ASATs were concerned. Programs such as 437 and 505, which depended upon nuclear explosions to knock out their targets, no longer could be thoroughly tested without violating the terms of the treaty. That, too, helped drive another nail into ASAT's coffin.

By the end of 1963, both the United States and the Soviet Union had become heavily dependent upon space reconnaissance and surveillance for a variety of functions relating to preparations for war and the preservation of peace. For their part, the Russians could hardly operate their own space reconnaissance system while criticizing the United States for doing the same thing, especially since the satellites played an important role in an arms control agreement that had long been sought by the Russians themselves. Accordingly, Soviet denunciations of U.S. "spy" satellites and spaceborne espionage petered out in 1963, both at home and on the floor of the UN's General Assembly, and was replaced by a tacit acceptance of the increasingly pervasive space sentinels.

The interim agreement on the limitation of strategic offensive arms, popularly known as SALT I, would not have been concluded nine years later had there not been shared confidence that space reconnaissance was up to the task of monitoring the agreement. The role of reconnaissance satellites in the verification process was to become so important by 1972, in fact, that interfering with them— with national technical means (NTM) of verification—was specifically prohibited by the treaty itself.

But the systems doing the treaty monitoring were the same as those collecting military intelligence and updating each side's target data. The irony of overhead reconnaissance as it began to mature, then, was the fact that it played a decisive role in controlling arms and refining them at the same time.

7.

The Air Breathers:
Blackbirds and Cobras

There was a rush to send electronic eyes and ears to the relative safety of earth orbit following the successes of the CIA's Discoverers and the beginning of the Air Force's problem-plagued but promising SAMOS program in the early 1960s. Yet this in no way meant that aerial reconnaissance—using jet aircraft—was at an end. It had been taken for granted during the four years in which U-2s operated over the Soviet Union that planes would supplement satellites, and nothing happened to alter that plan during the spacecraft's formative years, including the shooting down of Powers and several Nationalist Chinese U-2 pilots as well.*

Strategic reconnaissance aircraft have many advantages, even in the space age. Unlike satellites, which are the prisoners of orbits that cannot vary a great deal without as yet untried orbital refueling (and which are therefore predictable to those who want to avoid being spied upon), airplanes can change speed abruptly, fly in any direction, drop under clouds with their cameras, return to a target area

---

*U-2 operations using Nationalist Chinese pilots were begun from Taiwan early in 1960 and concentrated in particular on the Lop Nor nuclear test site in Sinkiang Province and on the Chiu-chuan IRBM test range in Kansu. The first U-2 lost by the Kuomintang went down over Nanching in September 1962, followed by the loss of a second over Shanghai fourteen months later. Other U-2s were reported lost over mainland China, including three in 1964 alone and another in 1965. China claims to have shot down a total of nine Taiwanese U-2s in the 1960s. In August 1965 the black carcasses of four U-2s were put on permanent display at the Peking People's Museum.

as often as necessary, and even loiter until an intelligence-gathering opportunity ripens. The airplane's relative slowness can be particularly useful for signals interception, radar ferreting, and telemetry collection because a plane can stay in place long enough to pick up significant amounts of data.

Planes are also more mission-adaptable than satellites because they can be loaded with specialized equipment as often as necessary, unlike spacecraft, which become irrevocably committed to a particular task or a series of them the instant they leave their launch pads. And until the advent of the space shuttle, which can be used to repair dysfunctional satellites in orbit, those suffering from point failure (as a serious malfunction in orbit is called by those who operate U.S. space reconnaissance systems) had to be written off at a dollar figure that was numbing even by Pentagon standards. An airplane with an impaired or dead sensor, on the other hand, returns to base for a replacement.

Finally, there is the cost of the missions themselves. It takes $60 million just to launch a photoreconnaissance satellite into a nominally low orbit, while sending one of its SIGINT counterparts all the way out to geosynchronous orbit, which is more complicated and requires extra boosting capability, costs a minimum of $125 million.* Combined with the cost of the satellites themselves, which starts at upward of $100 million and often reaches at least three times that amount, the launching of a space reconnaissance mission is staggeringly expensive. Seen in that light, the loss of a Titan 34D carrying a KH-11 photoreconnaissance satellite on August 28, 1985, amounted to a loss of about $250 million, as did a similar accident on April 18, 1986, involving a Titan and a KH-9.

The U-2's intended successor was a 164-foot-long, bullet-shaped, liquid-hydrogen-fueled engineering marvel called the CL-400, which was supposed to reach speeds two and a half times that of sound at nearly a hundred thousand feet, thereby being able to photograph strategically important targets with near impunity. It

*The $60 million figure is based on the use of a Martin Marietta Titan 34D booster to place a 27,600-pound satellite, such as a KH-11, into a polar orbit with a mean altitude of 115 miles. The same booster used to place a 4,000-pound SIGINT satellite of the Rhyolite or Chalet type in geosynchronous orbit would cost $125 million. These figures, in 1981 dollars, are based on the procurement of six Titan 34Ds a year; the purchase of only one a year would raise the launch cost to $181 million and $251 million, respectively.

was supposed to be able to do all that and more. It was supposed to, but it never did. It never even made it off the drawing board.

The immediate impetus for Project Suntan, as the CL-400 was also called, was the rehabilitation after Joseph Stalin's death of Pyotr Leonidovich Kapitsa, a brilliant nuclear physicist whom the Soviet dictator had placed under house arrest in 1946, possibly for having refused to work on the atom bomb. Kapitsa's relationship to the CL-400 amounts to a cautionary tale about what can happen when unbridled paranoia drives the weapons acquisition process.

Late in 1955 or early in 1956, as the first of the U-2s was taking shape at Lockheed's Advanced Development Projects facility at Burbank, the CIA notified the company that Kapitsa not only had been released from confinement, but had been made director of the U.S.S.R.'s prestigious Institute for Physical Problems. The physicist was known to have extensive knowledge about liquid hydrogen, whose properties as a light, efficient jet or rocket fuel were by then well understood. The leaders of the Skunk Works somehow concluded from this confluence of circumstances that Kapitsa was at work on a very high performance, liquid-hydrogen-fueled fighter— an airplane, they contemplated ruefully, that would be able to fly high enough to get at their U-2s.

The answer, it seemed, was to develop a successor to the U-2 that was also propelled by liquid hydrogen and would therefore be able to stay out of the clutches of Kapitsa's superfighter. Kelly Johnson went to Washington in January 1956 with a proposal for such a plane and convinced the Air Force that he could have two prototypes of the advanced reconnaissance aircraft in the air within eighteen months of start-up. Having only recently lost the U-2 to the CIA, the Air Force evidently became determined that it was not going to be flanked again. Johnson was given tentative approval to proceed.

With its long, round, needle-nosed fuselage, stubby wings and matching T-shaped tail, the CL-400 bore a striking family resemblance to Lockheed's F-104 (as had the U-2 in its initial configuration). Unlike the Starfighter, which had a single engine mounted inside its slender fuselage, however, the CL-400 carried an engine at the end of either wing. It was also quite a bit larger than the F-104, not only because reconnaissance sensors can be bulky, but because liquid hydrogen, though considerably lighter than the hydrocarbon fuels used to propel conventional jets, takes up more space. The CL-400 was going to have to be made big enough to carry 21,400 pounds of cooled liquid hydrogen, in fact, in order to be able to send it on 2,500-mile-long missions at the planned speed and altitude.

But as Johnson and his engineers worked and reworked the numbers, it became increasingly clear that Suntan's range was going to fall short of what the Air Force wanted. There was no apparent way to increase that range without making the plane so big that it would be impractical. And the CL-400's limited range exacerbated another problem as well. While JP-4, the standard kerosene-based jet fuel, was in abundant supply around the world, liquid hydrogen was another matter entirely; it would have to be manufactured in huge quantities and kept in constant supply at whatever overseas bases the CL-400 was to use, creating a daunting logistical problem. Finally, Eisenhower's austerity was compelling the Air Force to weigh its advanced projects with the utmost care. As it did so, the CL-400, with its apparently insurmountable fuel problems, began to look increasingly like an unaffordable risk (particularly in relation to competing fighter and bomber designs, which traditionally took precedence over reconnaissance systems). The project finally turned sour in the summer of 1957 and was abandoned that October after an expenditure of between $100 million and $250 million.

Ironically, it was later learned that Pyotr Kapitsa hadn't been given his freedom to develop a liquid-hydrogen-fueled fighter at all. He had been put to work applying his knowledge of hydrogen to the design of the rocket engine that would be used in five clusters on the bottom of a giant booster version of the SS-6 ICBM in order to toss Sputnik 1 into orbit. The first artificial earth satellite was to go up in October 1957, in fact—the same month in which Suntan faded.

Whatever the fate of the CL-400, it was plain that given its increasing vulnerability, the U-2 had to have a successor. Johnson knew that he had to create another high-flier. Low-level strategic reconnaissance missions were out of the question for several reasons. Coming in low precluded the kind of wide-angle photographic and radar coverage that would take in great chunks of territory. As everyone in overhead reconnaissance understood, stepping back and looking at the big picture often produced better intelligence data than could be gotten by being too close. Close scrutiny yielded fine detail, to be sure, but the big picture would show patterns and spacing: information that provides clues regarding what a particular group of objects is intended to do (as was the case with the SA-2 antiaircraft missile patterns in Cuba). High-flying planes could carry telescopic lenses to get close-up imagery when that was needed, but low-fliers could never obtain the equally important wide perspective. In addition, high-altitude aerial reconnaissance meant that the platform could be kept well away from the heavily defended targets on which it spied. Finally, a low-flier would guzzle fuel in such prodigious quantities that even moderately long-range operations would be impossible. The U-2's replacement would have to get up to a hundred thousand feet, and maybe higher. And the only way to do that would be to make it fly very fast. It would have to move so quickly that the extremely thin air passing around its wings at operational altitude would build up, or become sufficiently dense, to support its weight. And its fuel, suffice it to say, would be a hydrocarbon.

Lockheed submitted an even dozen design proposals to Richard Bissell and to the Air Force between April 21, 1958, and September 1, 1959. (The Skunk Works engineers, seemingly unmindful of the usually meaningless code names and arbitrary numbers that are picked by those in covert programs to protect their secret projects, somewhat naïvely picked *A*, because it was the first letter of the alphabet, and numbered successive design changes in sequential order, starting with 1.)

The Skunk Works submissions were not the only ones, however. Convair (later General Dynamics) proposed a Mach 4 ramjet-powered aircraft it called the Kingfisher that was supposed to be carried aloft beneath the company's delta-wing B-58 Hustler supersonic bomber and then be released after the "mother" plane had passed the speed of sound. But the sleek bomber, one of the most aesthetically pleasing airplanes ever built, could not handle the mother role; it couldn't get up to speed with a Kingfisher strapped under it. For that reason, as well as some others, Convair's entry was eliminated.

The Navy came in with yet another balloon project. This time, a balloon was to carry a ramjet-powered, inflatable rubber reconnaissance platform high and fast enough so the engine would kick in and propel it over the target area. In order to get the cameras and other sensors to the target, it was calculated, the balloon would have had to be a mile in diameter. The Navy's concept also was eliminated.

On August 29, 1959, Lockheed's final entry, the A-12, was declared the winner and the company was given a tentative go-ahead to build a full-scale mock-up of its design during the following four months. On January 30, 1960, Bissell, who was working in conjunction with the Air Force at that point, since it was clear that the CIA would not be able to operate the U-2's successor because of its extensive logistical requirements and complexity, issued approval for the construction of a dozen A-12s. The project was given the code name Oxcart.

The A-12, which first flew on April 26, 1962, was designed from the outset as a reconnaissance aircraft and was the first of three high-performance planes whose dimensions were to vary slightly but whose appearance and flight characteristics were essentially the same. Lockheed, in keeping with common industry practice, had taken pains to design a fast, high-flying, truly innovative airplane and then tried to multiply its production order by making modifications that would enable it to perform more than just the reconnaissance mission. This is what automobile companies do when they manufacture sedan and station-wagon versions of the same basic vehicle. In Lockheed's case, the A-12 reconnaissance design was altered so that it could also carry air-to-air missiles or an anti-satellite missile as a long-range, very high altitude interceptor for the North American Air Defense Command (NORAD). The interceptor version of the A-12 was called the YF-12A, and although a handful of the mutants were actually built (and broke speed records), the airplane did not find favor in the Office of the Secretary of Defense and was soon relegated to limbo.

Robert McNamara had in the meantime become fixated on the notion that a single airplane could be built for both the Air Force and the Navy to handle several assignments, including fighting, bombing, and tactical—short-range—reconnaissance. The result was General Dynamics' swing-wing F-111, which turned out to be too heavy for use on carriers, too unmaneuverable for use as an air superiority fighter, and too short-range for use as a strategic bomber without a good deal of air-to-air refueling.* McNamara, resorting to an uncharacteristic use of hyperbole, pronounced the F-111 "the greatest single step forward in combat aircraft in several decades" (a period of time that encompassed the invention of jet- and rocket-propelled planes, precision all-weather and night navigation and radar fire control systems, and standoff missiles, hung from the

*The attack on Libya in mid-April 1986 was a case in point. The eighteen F-111Fs that carried the bombs and the three EF-111A radar-jamming aircraft that escorted them were accompanied from England by a fleet of twenty-eight KC-10 and KC-135 tanker planes so they could be refueled four times during the 2,500-mile flight to the target area.

wings of bombers, which were the precursors of the cruise missile). The F-111's large, but nearly muted, chorus of critics called it McNamara's Folly. Whatever it was, however, it figured in the demise of the YF-12A. There wasn't enough money to go around.

The third and final version of Johnson's reconnaissance plane was an improved A-12 called the SR-71.* It was destined to leave an enduring mark on aviation history as well as to play a major role in U.S. strategic reconnaissance for decades.

The SR-71, in the words of its designer, looks like a 107-foot-long, 56-foot-wide manta ray. Partly because of its overall, mantalike appearance, partly because of its flat black radar-resistant epoxy finish and sparse markings, and partly because of a flattened, protruding fuselage, which ends in a point and whose forward edges taper outward in a way that is vaguely reminiscent of a cobra's hood, the SR-71 appears to be deadly (though, of course, it is not). Its sinister appearance, in fact, has been likened by Okinawans to that of habu, a venomous black snake that lives on their island. SR-71s have operated out of Kadena air base on Okinawa since the Vietnam war; the plane and the snake are so closely associated that crew members who have completed their first operational mission are awarded a HABU patch showing the plane's scant, frontal silhouette. Lockheed and Air Force public relations people refer to the SR-71 as the Blackbird, but those who fly it simply call it the "SR."

A Pratt & Whitney afterburning J-58 turbo-ramjet, a huge corncob of an engine that generates 32,500 pounds of thrust, is built midway into either of the SR-71's sharply swept delta wings. But it is not the engine's power alone that accounts for the plane's terrific speed. Rather, it is the unique engine inlet, which encircles a long cone, or "spike," that moves in and out during flight, continuously regulating the exact amount of air going into the engines, that accounts for the SR's performance. The shape of the inlet and use of the movable cones set up a high-pressure airflow pattern in front of the engines that in effect transforms them from turbofans pushing the SR-71 through the atmosphere to ramjets that pull it along by

*It was supposed to be named the RS-71A, for Reconnaissance/Strike, with the number 71 having been the next available after the naming of North American's B-70 Valkyrie bomber. When Lyndon Johnson announced the plane's existence, however, he mistakenly referred to it as the SR-71. Someone in the system apparently decided that it was easier to rename the plane, making SR stand for Strategic Reconnaissance, than to inform Johnson that he had committed a gaffe in public. Similarly, a press release went out of the Johnson White House on February 29, 1964, referring to the A-12 as the A-11, an error that has probably confounded any number of journalists and aviation historians.

sucking in an enormous amount of the tightly packed air in front of them. The ingested air is then compressed, mixed with special fuel, and ignited, causing a kind of controlled explosion that propels the plane at speeds that are unexcelled in operational aircraft. The faster the SR-71's engines go, the faster they want to go. Opened up and left unchecked, the J-58s reportedly would continue to gain speed until they began to overheat and disintegrate, devouring themselves in the process. The corncobs must therefore be kept reined in.

In July 1976 an SR-71 set an absolute and class world speed record of 2,193.6 miles an hour at an altitude record for level flight of 85,069 feet. Another dashed from New York to London in less than two hours. This has allowed the Strategic Air Command, which operates the SR-71s, to gain public relations points while at the same time sticking, straight-faced, to its tenaciously held, though ambiguous, line which claims that its prize reconnaissance aircraft has a ceiling "in excess" of 85,000 feet and a top speed of Mach 3 +, or more than three times the speed of sound. In fact, the excess altitude amounts to an additional 20,000 or so feet, depending upon how much fuel is on board, giving the plane a true ceiling of more than 100,000 feet.* And the plus sign after Mach 3 really stands for Mach 4, or even a bit better than that, which translates to a top speed of some 2,600 miles an hour.

Due to atmospheric friction the heat buildup at such speed is extraordinary. Because of that, 93 percent of the SR-71's frame is made of titanium, a heat-resistant alloy that is difficult to shape with precision. At operational speed (which is not necessarily top speed), the skin midway along the plane's back heats to 511 degrees Fahrenheit, while the temperature along its engine nacelles rises to 1,050 degrees and, around the engine exhausts, to 1,200 degrees. The front canopy's Plexiglas windscreen, behind which the pilot sits in an orange space suit, heats to 622 degrees. Lieutenant Colonel Jerry Glasser, an SR-71 pilot, has said that the windscreen through which he looks becomes so hot during a mission that he is unable to keep his hand on it longer than twenty seconds even though he wears insulated, flame-retardant gloves. SR-71s get so hot that they must use a fuel called JP-7, which has a higher flash point than the standard JP-4, to keep them from exploding into fireballs on speed

*By 1976 even U-2s, with wings that had grown from 80 feet to 103 feet, were making it up to ninety thousand feet.

runs. High temperatures even had to be factored into the design of the SR's landing gear. The tires are rated at 22 ply, their rubber contains aluminum particles to help dampen heat radiating inward from the plane's skin, and they are filled with nitrogen, which is less combustible than plain air. And since even all of that may not be enough to prevent a tire's bursting during a mission, the main tires retract into explosion shields so that should one blow out, hot rubber and aluminum shrapnel would not rip into delicate hydraulic lines inside the wheel well.

SR-71s carry fuel, an array of interchangeable sensors, and two crewmen: a pilot and a reconnaissance systems officer (RSO), who sits directly behind the pilot and monitors the airplane's sensors, in addition to doing navigation and backing up the pilot in making sure that the various systems are functioning properly. There is no armament. SRs protect themselves by using a mix of stealth, speed, altitude, sophisticated electronic countermeasures, and surprise.

Stealth, a popular term for what aeronautical engineers call a "low-observable" configuration, is the quality that makes an airplane or a satellite difficult to track and therefore to attack. A key way to accomplish this is to design a platform that has a low radar cross section—one that is difficult to pick up on radar. The SR-71 is such an airplane. Seen from the front, its thin wings, thin twin vertical stabilizers, round engine nacelles, and flattened fuselage offer a poor radar target because they cover a minimal area and have many rounded edges, which, unlike angular ones, deflect rather than reflect radar signals. The plane's flat black finish, which absorbs some radar pulses, also helps to give it a low radar cross section. Electromagnetic fields that blunt, deflect, or absorb radar emissions and several other techniques are also used to give the aircraft an extremely low visibility on radar. And radar that cannot be evaded can be countered. As is the case with the U-2 and some other aircraft (notably bombers), one of the SR-71's primary electronic countermeasures is a radar detector, or "fuzz-buster," that not only warns its crew that they are being tracked on radar, but also tells them the location from which the radar is coming and its intensity. And the radar detector is linked to an infrared-detecting sensor that can pick up and track a SAM fired in its direction from as much as one hundred miles away by registering the heat coming out of the missile's exhaust. Using this system, an SR-71 pilot is able to follow closely an enemy missile's heat trail as it moves along its radar track toward his plane. He may then maneuver to avoid the weapon, jam the radar that is guiding it, turn on his "missile sucker" (as Ben Rich of the Skunk Works calls it), which can electronically deflect it away from the SR, or do all three at the same time. The technique seems to work. Following North Korea's firing a SAM at an SR-71 prowling along its frontier in August 1981, Kelly Johnson noted that about a thousand such attacks had been made, most of them during the war in Vietnam, but that none had been successful. Several SR-71s have been lost in accidents since they started in service early in 1966, but none have gone down because of enemy fire.

SR-71 operational missions are always flown by lone aircraft and are kept unpredictable, since the element of surprise helps to protect them by limiting the amount of time the opposition has to prepare an attack against them. Here the SR's great speed is essential.

Lieutenant Viktor I. Belenko, the Russian pilot who defected to Japan with a MiG-25 interceptor in 1976, has described the frustration of chasing SR-71s streaking along the Siberian coast and never being able to close within firing range because of the reconnaissance craft's extreme speed and altitude (with a maximum speed of Mach 2.8 and a ceiling of nearly 80,000 feet, the MiG-25 is not exactly a slouch, either). Belenko has been quoted as claiming that the maximum effective altitude of the air-to-air missiles carried by MiG-25s is 88,500 feet. But that does not appear to be good enough to bag an SR. Not by a long shot. "Even if we could reach it, our missiles lack the velocity to overtake the SR-71 if they are fired in a tail chase. And if they are fired head-on," the MiG pilot complained, "their guidance systems cannot adjust quickly enough to the high closing speed."

Belenko went on to assert that the SR-71s "taunted and toyed with the MiG-25s sent up to intercept them, scooting up to altitudes the Soviet planes could not reach, and circling leisurely above them or dashing off at speeds the Russians could not match." This description, perhaps meant to ingratiate him with his new countrymen, is romantic but unlikely to be accurate.

SR-71 flight doctrine has at its core the proposition that the aircraft is a reconnaissance platform that is supposed to get to its target area and back out again as quickly and safely as possible. Pilots and RSOs are aeronautical conservatives and appear to be unshakable believers in the virtues of the straight line, which remains the shortest and therefore the safest distance between the initial approach point to the target area and its exit point, when the sensors turn off. In order for the airplane's cameras, radar, and other sensors to function optimally, the craft must be flown to precisely the right place and then be held on an absolutely straight course throughout the duration of the reconnaissance run. That completed, the crew's sole task is to get home with what it has collected as quickly as possible. The requirement has remained unchanged since World War I. Circling leisurely above those who want to prevent the mission, most likely killing the crew in the process, is therefore unthinkable to those who fly SR-71s.

A straight, fast, stable reconnaissance run requires the monitoring of several systems at the same time, the most important of which are the autopilot that keeps the SR steady and the astro-tracking system that keeps it on course. Even a tiny navigational error at such high speed could have catastrophic results, particularly because the SRs often fly extremely close to heavily protected denied territory (the Russians have repeatedly charged that they have been overflown by SR-71s, and the Cubans have made the same allegation; the Pentagon has denied the former and admitted the latter). Whatever the truth, venturing close enough to SAM sites to draw fire is extremely dangerous, which makes navigation critically important.

"When the astro-tracker burps, you're doing thirty-three miles a minute," Lieutenant Colonel Glasser said, referring to an operational speed of about two thousand miles an hour. "And every minute you don't know where you are, you're thirty-three miles *farther* from where you don't know where you are. You're basically thinking about four hundred miles ahead of the airplane—twelve to thirteen minutes ahead—and while you don't have to be fast, you have to be right the first time."

"The aircraft is a very mental, cerebral, one to fly when you're at speed and altitude," added Major Robert Behler, another SR-71 pilot, who drew a distinction between subsonic training missions in which the planes are "hand-flown" and triple-supersonic-plus operations against real targets. "You're not hand-flying it, but, instead, you transition to monitoring all of the systems and making sure that the aircraft is performing the way it should be. There are hundreds of things that you're monitoring every minute: engines, inlets, stability augmentation, Mach number, altitude, dynamic pressure keys. . . . Sometimes we have control problems with one inlet. Then the airplane develops a lot of yaw [turning horizontally on its axis]. But at the speeds we fly, you know, any kind of sideslip could be catastrophic."

SRs are never hand-flown during real reconnaissance operations, Major Behler continued, because "a pilot at those altitudes can't maintain a stable enough platform for the sensors to operate properly. On an operational sortie you want to maintain a very, very stable platform, so I'm not going to put any perturbations into the aircraft—pitch input or anything like that—but I'm going to maintain as smooth a platform as possible and let the RSO in the backseat do his thing."

The reconnaissance systems officer does his "thing" with a variety of sensors—all of them state-of-the-art and interchangeable—which are mounted in the tapered chines that form the rim of the forward fuselage, and in several different noses, which, as on the U-2Rs, attach to four bolts that extend from the bulkhead just in front of the windscreen. Changing an SR-71's nose takes about an hour, though preparing one for attachment can take as long as eight hours, depending upon what's in it (infrared sensors, for example, have to be cryogenically cooled to make them more sensitive to heat; conversely, some lenses have to be preheated so they will not expand when the plane's temperature rises and create distortions in the process).

The SR-71's main sensors include:

· A pair of 48-inch focal-length technical objective cameras, which produce narrow-field, overlapping photographs of terrain immediately below and to either side of the plane's flight path over a distance of between 833 and 1,619 nautical miles, depending upon how the cameras are set and the altitude of the SR-71. The cameras produce a 1,500-foot strip of black-and-white, color, or infrared thin base film that yields 1,820 images, either mono- or stereoscopic, each in a nine- by nine-inch format and having a nine-inch resolution. The cameras are normally operated automatically, responding to commands from the aircraft's navigation system to specific geographic coordinates that are chosen and programmed into the system before the mission. They are turned on and off, in other words, by the astrotracker, which is preset for image-specific targets by punching their longitudes and latitudes into it. This is the main system used for overflights of nations in the Middle East, Africa, most of Asia, and Latin America (notably Cuba and Nicaragua) that lack the capability to shoot down SR-71s flying directly over them.

· A nose-mounted optical bar camera specifically designed to take long-range panoramic oblique pictures beyond the frontiers of nations whose borders generally (but not always) must be respected because of their significant air defense system. The U.S.S.R. and its Eastern European allies, as well as the People's Republic of China, are in this group. The OBC has a 30-inch focal length and can produce a 10,500-foot-long, 1,600-frame strip of film in black and white, color, or infrared, in mono or stereo, with a ground resolution of 12 inches. Each frame, which measures 73.3 inches by 4.5 inches, shows a separate horizon-to-horizon panorama 72 nautical miles wide. Using its OBC, an SR-71 can take such photographs along a ribbon of land between 1,478 and 2,930 nautical miles long, depending upon the mode of coverage and, again, the plane's altitude.

· A high-resolution side-looking airborne radar (SLAR) system that is able to collect imagery in any weather, day or night, of targets between 10 and 80 nautical miles on either side of the SR-71 in swaths 10 to 20 miles wide and up to 4,000 nautical miles long. Resolution is ten feet. The SLAR is of a type known as synthetic aperture. In this system the aircraft sends out an electromagnetic signal that bounces off the target and then returns to the plane, making it the antenna. The SR-71's synthetic aperture radar, a marvel of miniaturization, is a rectangular box measuring some four feet by one foot and weighing on the order of four hundred pounds. It is stored in a section of one of the plane's chines. SLAR on SR-71s has been used extensively to image Soviet submarine facilities.

The number of specialized optical systems that can be crammed into an SR-71 is considerable, with selection depending upon mission requirements. At speed and altitude, one of the planes can photograph a hundred thousand square miles of territory in an hour using more than one of its PHOTINT systems at the same time. And the pictures, which are imaged on the ultrathin, fine-grained Kodak film, can be breathtakingly clear. The cameras and radar are ordinarily used with electronic intelligence equipment that ferrets radar and collects data on other noncommunication electromagnetic signals, such as navigation transmissions. The SR-71's ELINT receivers can collect signals in a 390-nautical-mile radius.

An SR-71 tearing along the coast of Sakhalin Island, then, can photograph air bases, missile sites, and port facilities (including berthed submarines) while simultaneously eavesdropping on Soviet communication traffic and ferreting radar. The intelligence take from a single mission can therefore be considerable. After two decades of flying such sorties, the SR-71s have become dependable reconnaissance platforms, and the missions are down to a routine, though flights made to update intelligence on Soviet and other nations' military capabilities are conducted at unpredictable times.

Soon after SR-71s went into operation, Lockheed began experimenting with a novel method of extending their effective intelligence-gathering range. The idea was to build a 43-foot-long pilotless reconnaissance drone, called a D-21, and mount it between the SR's two vertical stabilizers so that it could be carried piggyback and launched toward denied territory from the safe side of the frontier. It would then make a Mach 4 reconnaissance run using cameras and SIGINT receivers in a ventral sensor bay, streak back to free airspace, and then release its reconnaissance package on a parachute before ditching at sea. The package was to be air-snatched exactly the way the Discoverer capsules and their successors were.

A total of thirty-eight D-21s were built by the Skunk Works as part of the Senior Bowl program, as the project was called ("Senior" identifying it as an Air Force operation). A pair of A-12s were modified to carry D-21s and space was converted inside each of the test aircraft to accommodate a launch control officer who was supposed to monitor the drone before it was launched. On July 3, 1966, one of the D-21s developed an engine inlet malfunction just as it was rising off the A-12's back while flying off the California coast. The drone pitched forward, into the A-12's midsection, killing the launch control officer and sending both craft into the sea (the A-12's pilot evidently ejected safely).

The incident apparently signaled the end of the relationship between Blackbirds and D-21s, since the supply of A-12s and SR-7s was not only limited but fixed.* It was decided, however, to hang a D-21 under either of the massive wings of B-52H bombers and use them against Communist China. More than a dozen such flights

---

*Both Kelly Johnson and Ben Rich have maintained that when Robert McNamara was secretary of defense, he ordered the SR-71's tooling destroyed so that no more of them could be produced and that they therefore would not be competitive with the McDonnell-Douglas F-15 and the North American Rockwell B-1 bomber for congressional funding. "We would be competitive for money," Johnson remarked bitterly in an interview, "and he [McNamara] didn't want it that way."

U-2R of the Air Force's 9th Strategic Reconnaissance Wing takes off from Beale Air Force Base, California. The U-2R, the latest and probably the last in the series of special reconnaissance planes that began coming out of the Skunk Works in 1956, is still used on operational missions, though never near Soviet-produced SAM missiles, to which it is vulnerable. The aircraft uses interchangeable noses that carry various sensors.   WILLIAM E. BURROWS

A launch complex for heavy boosters at Tyuratam was taken in 1959 by a Type B camera in a CIA U-2 at about 70,000 feet. A rail line for transporting rockets runs vertically to the square pad in the center of the photograph. The large triangular flame pit on the other side of the pad is used to draw hot exhaust gases away from the booster. Some of the pit is in sunlight, though most is in shadow, indicating that the overflight was probably made in the early morning. The shadows are useful for calculating the pit's depth and gradient, and also the size of objects such as the nearby blockhouses.   CENTRAL INTELLIGENCE AGENCY

This high-altitude vertical photograph of the Medium Range Ballistic Missile site at San Cristóbal, Cuba, was taken by a 4080th Strategic Reconnaissance Squadron U-2 on October 14, 1962, at an altitude of about 70,000 feet. Photo interpreters could make out that the missile trailers held MRBMs and were clustered near shelter tents. Oxidizer tank trailers and other support vehicles are in a nearby open field.   USAF PHOTO

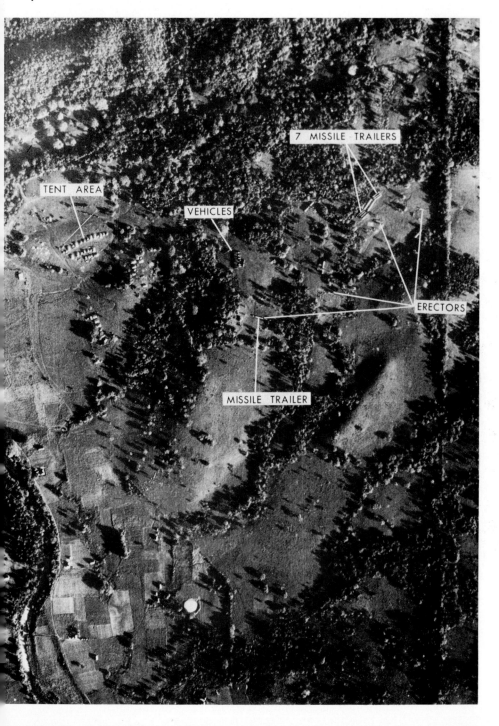

Above: Lockheed D-21 Reconnaissance Drones are shown being carried piggyback by an A-12 and beneath the wings of a B-52. The ramjet-power craft was used in limited numbers, and with mixed results, during the war in Vietnam. Engine failure at liftoff, resulting in the loss of an A-12, ended the piggyback program.   LOCKHEED-CALIFORNIA

Opposite page: The SR-71A Blackbird remains the world's fastest and highest-flying operational aircraft more than two decades after its debut. It can fly at four times the speed of sound at altitudes in the range of 125,000 feet and is used where satellite coverage is impractical. Sensors are carried in any of several interchangeable noses and in the tapered chines that run along both sides of the forward fuselage back to the wings' leading edges. The upper rear part of the fuselage glistens in this photograph because JP-7 has been sprayed over it during air-to-air refueling.   WILLIAM E. BURROWS

A Hercules snatches a satellite capsule in the same way that was used to snare the CIA's Discoverer capsules in the early 1960s. The JC-130Bs, which belonged to the 6594th Recovery Control Group at Hickam Air Force Base, Hawaii, carried heavy-duty winches that were used to pull the parachutes and capsules inside. Such missions were always flown at low speeds of about 150 miles an hour and at altitudes under 15,000 feet. The reconnaissance capsules were flown from Hawaii to Washington for analysis.   LOCKHEED-GEORGIA

(inset) The end of Cosmos 1402 is shown on this computer display terminal in the Space Surveillance Center inside Cheyenne Mountain, Colorado. The track of the radar ocean reconnaissance satellite, which was powered by a nuclear reactor, can be seen ending over the Indian Ocean, where it impacted on January 23, 1983.
USAF PHOTO

An Air Force Titan 34D booster lifts off during a night launch. Two solid rocket motors developing a total of 2.8 million pounds of thrust are igniting. Less than two minutes later the liquid propellant motors in the main (larger) booster were turned on to produce an additional million pounds of thrust to get a satellite into orbit. A Titan 34D carrying a KH-11 exploded shortly after lift-off at Vandenberg Air Force Base on August 28, 1985, followed on April 18, 1986, by a second, similar accident involving the last KH-9. The losses, combined with the suspension of shuttle operations following the destruction of the Challenger, temporarily crippled the U.S. imaging reconnaissance program in space.   MARTIN MARIETTA

A U.S. ASAT is launched by an Air Force F-15 during an early test. The missile is eighteen feet long, one foot in diameter, and carries a nonexplosive warhead, called a miniature homing vehicle, that is supposed to impact with its target at 30,000 miles an hour.   USAF PHOTO

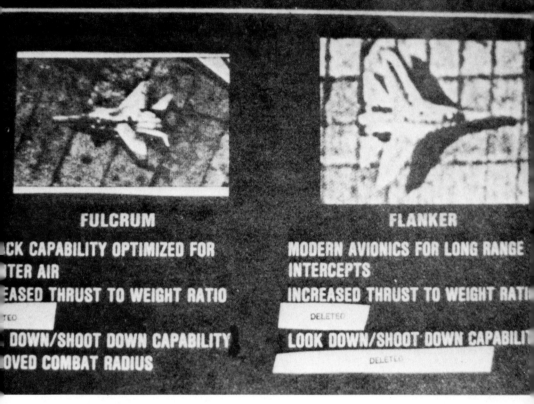

NEW AIR SUPERIORITY THREAT

FULCRUM

CK CAPABILITY OPTIMIZED FOR
TER AIR

EASED THRUST TO WEIGHT RATIO

TED

DOWN/SHOOT DOWN CAPABILITY
OVED COMBAT RADIUS

FLANKER

MODERN AVIONICS FOR LONG RANGE
INTERCEPTS

INCREASED THRUST TO WEIGHT RATI

DELETED

LOOK DOWN/SHOOT DOWN CAPABILI

DELETED

These satellite reconnaissance photos showing a MiG-29 *(left)* and an SU-27 were used during House hearings on the fiscal 1984 defense appropriations bill and were then published in volume 3 of the 8-volume record of the proceedings, apparently by mistake.   WILLIAM E. BURROWS

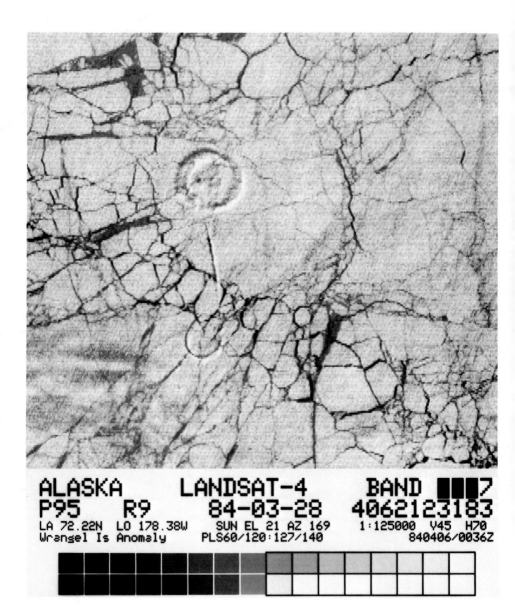

ALASKA   LANDSAT-4   BAND ■■■7
P95   R9   84-03-28   4062123183
LA 72.22N LO 178.38W   SUN EL 21 AZ 169   1:125000 V45 H70
Wrangel Is Anomaly   PLS60/120:127/140   840406/0036Z

The Wrangel Island anomaly. This picture, taken by the National Oceanic and Atmospheric Administration's Landsat 4 earth resources satellite in March 1984, was interpreted by Defense Department analysts as showing a Soviet ballistic-missile-firing submarine testing equipment designed to smash through Arctic ice prior to an underwater missile launch. The darkened area in the center of the circle was said to be broken ice beneath which the submarine floated. The circle is a contrail made by an observation aircraft and measures two miles in diameter. The line below the circle is said to be another contrail made by another airplane leaving the test area. The imagery was made just north of Wrangel Island in the East Siberian Sea. This is an excellent example of how even civilian scientific space surveillance can be used for intelligence purposes.

GEOPHYSICAL INSTITUTE, UNIVERSITY OF ALASKA, FAIRBANKS

This radar picture of Mount Shasta in Northern California was taken through cloud cover by the
Shuttle Imaging Radar-B aboard the Challenger in October 1984. The device can also reveal details of
objects underground. The ability to obtain high-resolution radar imagery through clouds will soon
add a new dimension to spaceborne technical intelligence collection.   JET PROPULSION LABORATORY

These drawings, which appeared in the Defense Department's *Soviet Military Power, 1986*, are based on satellite photographs and depict mobile SA-X-12 air defense missiles *(top photo)* and base support facilities for SS-25 ballistic missiles, which are transportable on trailers. The pictures were made clear enough to show accurately the nature of the weapons but are almost undoubtedly less clear than the photographs from which they were made.   DEFENSE DEPARTMENT

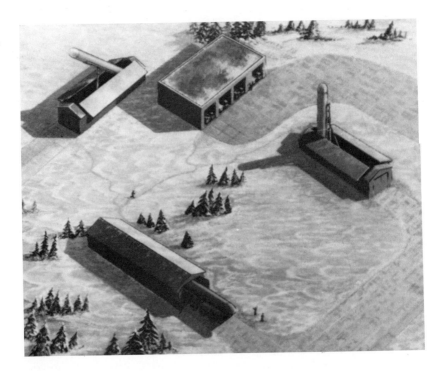

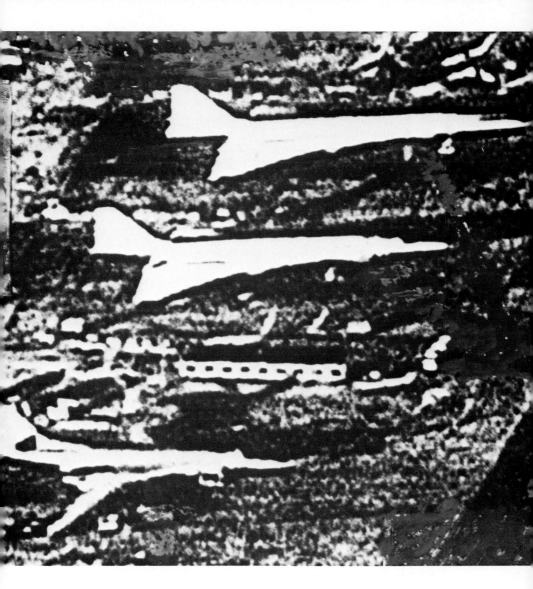

This deliberately distorted satellite photograph was taken at the Ramenskoye flight test center in the U.S.S.R. on November 25, 1981. It shows a then new bomber code-named Blackjack parked to the right of two TU-144 supersonic transports. The photograph was given to *Aviation Week & Space Technology* with the evident intention of publicizing U.S. technical intelligence prowess while protecting the true resolving capabilities of the satellite's imaging system.   *Aviation Week & Space Technology*

KH-11 real-time imagery shows two views of the U.S.S.R.'s first full-size nuclear-powered aircraft carrier under construction at Nikolaiev shipyard 444 on the Black Sea in the summer of 1984. The pictures were taken on successive days but at the same time and from a sun-synchronous orbital inclination, which is why the direction and length of the shadows are the same in both. The oblique was taken at a distance of 504 miles. The carrier is being built in two parts, with the front half under the gantry cranes and the rear half just beyond it at the adjacent dock. U.S. Navy analysts were able to determine from this computer-enhanced imagery that the ship was to have vertical silo-launched SAM missiles, two aircraft elevators, three steam catapults, phased-array radar, and hold up to seventy-five airplanes. The tall smokestack in the lower right indicates a foundry, with assembly buildings behind it. The pictures also show many railroad cars carrying heavy material to dockside. Resolution is about one foot.

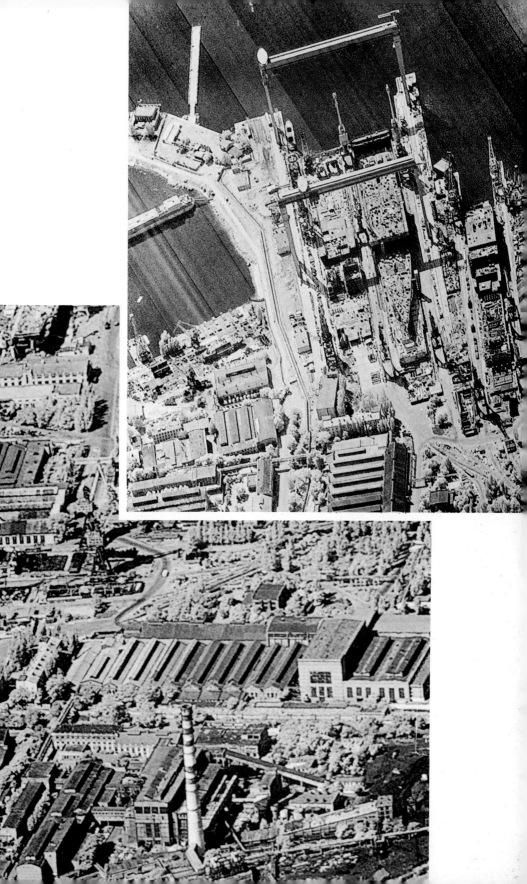

An eagle's eye view of forbidden territory. This photograph, taken by the SPOT imaging satellite in June 1986 from 516 miles, shows the U.S.S.R.'s nuclear test site near Semipalatinsk with a resolution of about thirty feet. Small white craters are made by underground explosions, all of which are connected by an intricate network of roads. Analysts concluded that the three spots circled are tunnels signaling preparations for additional tests. Imagery such as this, now accessible to the public, will profoundly affect not only international relations but arms control in particular. © 1986 CNES took place. Kelly Johnson has claimed that his drones were effective intelligence collectors; others knowledgeable in the field have called the results decidedly mixed.

The cameras, radars, SIGINT packages, countermeasures equipment, avionics, and monster engines that are the heart of the SR-71s are periodically upgraded when the planes are returned to Lockheed's manufacturing plant at Palmdale, a parched flat locality on the western rim of the Mojave Desert about an hour's drive from Los Angeles. There, in dry air and beneath skies that are so clear they offer perhaps the best flying weather in the world, SRs are thoroughly overhauled and refurbished. Corrosion left in the metal fuel cells by the JP-7 is scraped off by hand. Even the SR-71s' epoxy finish, which gradually lightens because of scorching from the air moving over it at high speed, is routinely taken off down to the polished, light gray titanium skin, and then sprayed on once again.

The SR-71s that are meticulously cleaned and thoroughly updated at Palmdale are babied by ground crewmen at Beale Air Force Base, near Marysville, California. All of the aircraft are operated by SAC's 9th Strategic Reconnaissance Wing, headquartered at Beale. (Ironically, the home of the world's fastest operational airplane was named for Brigadier General Edward F. Beale, who was instrumental in starting the Army Camel Corps before the Civil War). Beale is the preeminent strategic reconnaissance air base in the country. Besides having the SR-71s, it possesses a contingent of U-2Rs and TR-1s (Tactical Reconnaissance—the U2-R's identical descendant) and a fleet of KC-135Q tanker aircraft that are required to refuel the thirsty SRs in midair on nearly all operational missions. Imagery brought back by the SR-71s, U-2Rs, and TR-1s is processed in a windowless three-story concrete building about a half mile from the twelve hangars where the planes are kept. Access is severely restricted.

The SRs stage from Beale to Kadena and to RAF Mildenhall in England, from where they fly operations throughout much of Asia, the Middle East, and along the Soviet Arctic (especially around the Kola Peninsula and the Barents Sea, the home waters of the Northern Fleet, the largest of the U.S.S.R.'s four deepwater fleets). Mildenhall-based SRs often operate out of Akrotiri air base on Cyprus for Middle East missions. Aircrews rotate to the overseas installations on an average of three times a year for six weeks at a stretch, usually ferrying over their SR-71s from Beale, but occasionally using aircraft that are kept at the two bases. Operational missions are also flown from Beale itself, particularly for the relatively short hops to Central America.

The number of SR-71s built remains a closely guarded secret, though it was most likely between thirty and thirty-five. The last of them cost $19.6 million each, including the Pratt & Whitney engines, but not the sensors. They would therefore be quite a bargain today, since McDonnell-Douglas's smaller, less sophisticated F-15 Eagle runs to $25 million or more, depending upon such options as a second seat, bombing capability, or a tactical reconnaissance pod. There are between fifteen and nineteen remaining, since, as has been noted, several have been lost in accidents.* They are therefore treated with consummate care.

The aesthetics of flying an SR-71 can be almost palpable, at least for Lieutenant Colonel Glasser. During a night flight from Beale to Kadena, somewhere over the Pacific, he caught up with the sun, which, after all, moves across the face of the earth at only about a thousand miles an hour. Glasser saw the sun rise twice in the west on that flight as his SR streaked toward Okinawa on a heading of two-seven-zero. He and Captain Ted Ross, his Idaho-born RSO who was monitoring the plane's vital signs in the cramped darkness behind him, overtook the sun just after it had set. Then the SR turned south for a while, allowing the sun to disappear once again under the horizon. Several minutes later, Jerry Glasser swung his SR back onto the two-seven-zero heading. Slowly, the sun returned.

"Indigo." He remembered watching a widening indigo arc in ethereal silence from behind the plastic visor in the helmet that was locked tightly into the round collar of his bright orange life-support system: his full-pressure "spacesuit."

"It was incredible. Aside from going around in the space shuttle, I don't think there's anybody who's seen two sunrises in the west. I looked at that and said, 'I may be the first person to experience a

---

*The author saw seven SR-71s on a visit to Beale in June 1984. Four of the base's twelve SR-71 hangars remained closed during the visit, so there could have been as many as eleven there at the time. A tour of the Lockheed plant at Palmdale a few days later turned up four more: two had been stripped and gutted for refurbishing, one had been renovated and was awaiting a return to Beale, and the fourth was kept on hand to test new avionics and sensors. In addition, two SR-71s are reportedly kept at Kadena and another pair at Mildenhall. This would make a total of fifteen to nineteen, depending upon the contents of those buttoned-up hangars at Beale. A Joint Chiefs of Staff posture statement once put the total at nine. In addition, there are nine mothballed A-12s at Palmdale that could be spruced up in the unlikely event that the need arose.

double indigo, green, blue. . . .' " said Glasser, his voice trailing off
as the vision of flying right at the black curved horizon with its
lengthening mantle of blue fire came back to him.

"You sometimes get wrapped up in that. You get wrapped up in
the colors. In terms of air-breathing machines, we probably see more
spectacular colors than anybody flying," he added with wonder as
he considered the haunting shapes and colors that can appear so
unexpectedly beyond the windscreens of airplanes that fly very high
and well beyond Mach 3. There was in Lieutenant Colonel Jerry
Glasser the barest echo of Antoine de Saint-Exupéry as he went on
about the SR-71. "You never lose your sense of boyhood when you
look at it," he explained in evident awe of Kelly Johnson's oxcart.

If the SR-71s are the thoroughbred racers of U.S. aerial reconnaissance, the four-engine RC-135s that range around the earth day and
night on their various long, monotonous snooping missions are its
plow horses.

RC-135s have been turned out in at least a dozen specialized
versions since 1965 and are the intelligence-gathering sisters of Boeing's 707 commercial airliners. As a single entity the RCs constitute
a reconnaissance system larger than that of the SR-71s and U-2Rs.
Though unspectacular compared with a speedster like the SR-71, or
even with a high-flying powered glider like the U-2R, the RC-135
delivers a continuous stream of data on foreign communications
activity, electrical power generation, missile tests, radar capability,
naval and aircraft deployments, and much more. This multibillion-
dollar collection program, extending around the world, is the true
backbone of U.S. aerial reconnaissance: the "bread and butter" operation.

If any aircraft can be said to be a reconnaissance "platform," with
the steady, solid, even plodding existence that the word brings to
mind, it is the RC-135. Whatever its mission, each of the eighteen
RC-135s in SAC's fleet is literally crammed with electronic eavesdropping or monitoring devices, radars, and antennas of assorted
shapes that often function under bulging radomes and specially
crafted blisters running along the planes' backs and bellies like steel
warts and jowls. Crew members can number up to twenty-one and
include not only four or more electronics specialists, who work at
consoles lining the inside of the aircraft and a maintenance technician to keep the equipment in repair, but also a relief pilot and

backup specialists to operate the receivers, recorders, and radars because RC-135 sorties typically last from ten to eighteen hours. There are no space suits here—only ordinary olive one-piece standard-issue flight suits. It is the military equivalent of working in shirt sleeves.

The average RC-135 can cruise at 560 miles an hour, even with the bulges that tend to slow it down, though most missions are ordinarily flown at the lowest practical speed in order to keep the airplane in the vicinity of the target for as long as possible. That maximizes the intelligence take. Operational altitude is generally thirty-five thousand feet.

And while the SRs are used primarily for high-speed, close-up collection near (and occasionally over) many target countries, the RC's job is to stay on a slow course close enough to its quarry to get what it is after while keeping well away from air defenses. The RC-135s that seek information from the U.S.S.R., either in the Arctic or over the northwest Pacific, are relatively vulnerable to interceptors because they are slow and easily tracked on Soviet radar. Following an unofficial but well-understood agreement, the lumbering intelligence collectors are allowed to go about their business unmolested, provided they do not come too close to the Soviet frontier.*

For their part, U.S. Air Force and Navy fighters often escort the RC-135s' Soviet counterparts—four-engine TU-95D Bear reconnaissance aircraft—away from air defense identification zones 150 to 250 miles off the East Coast and even closer off Alaska. There were twenty-two such intercepts in 1982 and eleven the following year as the TU-95Ds have ranged up and down the Atlantic coast, often flying out of Cuba, to ferret U.S. radar and tap communications traffic. A typical episode occurred on July 18, 1984, when a pair of Bears headed toward Cuba was first picked up by Air National Guard F-106A Darts off the Massachusetts coast and were then progressively escorted south by Tactical Air Command F-4 Phantoms, F-15 Eagles, and Navy F-14 Tomcats operating from the carrier *Dwight D. Eisenhower* off the Florida coast. The Soviet air-

*An RC-135V that landed at Mildenhall on its way from Athens to Offutt Air Force Base on January 16, 1982, was seen to have five small red silhouettes of the Su-15 interceptor—the kind of fighter that shot down the Korean Air Lines 747 the following year—painted on its side. This very likely indicates that the aircraft had made five successful penetrations of the Soviet frontier, evading the interceptors each time while "tickling," or ferreting, radar in an effort to get it turned on.

craft had come from their own country and had not filed flight plans. No Soviet reconnaissance plane has ever penetrated U.S. airspace, which indicates that Moscow doesn't think the risk is worth the benefit, either.

The RC-135s' home is Offutt Air Force Base, headquarters of SAC's 55th Strategic Reconnaissance Wing. Like the SR-71s and U-2Rs, however, Offutt's RC-135s regularly rotate overseas. They operate out of Kadena, Mildenhall, and Hellenikon in Greece, as well as from Shemya Island in the Aleutians and Eielson Air Force Base in Alaska.

Fourteen of the RC-135s are "V" models—RC-135Vs—operating in a program called Rivet Joint. Flying out of England, Alaska, Okinawa, and Greece, Rivet Joint aircraft locate and tap foreign countries' communication and noncommunication signals and radar sites. RC-135Vs operating from Mildenhall patrol the Baltic and the Barents Sea (the latter being the site of three major Soviet naval bases and a submarine construction facility). Alaskan-based RC-135Vs scour the Kamchatka and Chukotski peninsulas, while those based on Okinawa cover Sakhalin. Rivet Joint operations from Hellenikon in Greece are ordinarily targeted against the southwestern U.S.S.R., the Near East, and the Maghreb. Two other RC-135s are configured as "U" models and are tasked to patrol the periphery of the Soviet Union and Eastern European countries collecting intelligence on an ad hoc basis as part of a program called Combat Sent.

Soviet ground-based radars, as only one example among scores of targets that are hunted by the big reconnaissance jets, are known as Back Net, Barlock, Big Bar, Big Mesh, Dog House, the Fan Song series, Fire Can, Fire Wheel, Flap Wheel, Flat Face, Gage, Gecko, Gun Dish, Hen Egg, Hen Roost, Hen Nest, Hen House, Knife Rest A, Knife Rest B/C, Long Track, Score Board, Spoon Rest, Squint Eye, Straight Flush, Token, Whiff, and Yo Yo. Each represents a particular type of ground-based radar (naval and airborne systems have separate code names). Hen House, for example, is an anti-ballistic (ABM) radar that operates on the 150 megahertz frequency band, while Spoon Rest is a 147-161-megahertz-band early warning radar used in conjunction with the Fan Song series, which are in turn at SAM command centers. These radars would have to be jammed in the event of war, and it falls in large measure to the RC-135Vs to collect the data necessary to do that. And the collecting goes on without end because radar operating modes can, and often are, changed to outsmart the ferrets.

Both a code name's prefix and suffix refer to something. Taken together, they stand for a specific piece of equipment or a program. Cobra, a U.S. system, has to do with anything regarding technical intelligence about the testing of Soviet and Chinese long-range ballistic missiles. The giant phased array radar on Shemya Island that tracks Soviet ICBM warheads as they approach their impact points on the Kamchatka Peninsula or in the Pacific, for example, is called Cobra Dane; the *Observation Island,* a ship stationed near Kamchatka that does the same thing, but from close by, is known as Cobra Judy. Similarly, two RC-135Ss that fly out of Eielson or sometimes Shemya to monitor the tests from thirty-five thousand feet over the Bering Sea are called Cobra Ball.

The Cobra Ball aircraft that collect intelligence on ballistic missile testing, including telemetry, are outwardly characterized by a sliding hatch a few feet behind and on either side of the cabins where their pilots, copilots, and navigators sit. As the Soviet reentry vehicles arc out from Tyuratam or Plesetsk over eastern Siberia and head for their targets, the hatch on whichever side of the RC-135S is facing them slides back, exposing a battery of cameras that record the event in several ways (including infrared and multispectral), so that the weapons' size, performance, and capabilities can be analyzed.

One of the cameras is a ballistic missile framing type designed especially to photograph everything having to do with the warheads as they reenter the atmosphere. Another, having medium resolution, picks out individual reentry vehicles so that their size can be determined. Meanwhile, Cobra Ball's ELINT equipment, known as an Advanced Telemetry System, automatically searches the .050 to 4.0 gigahertz bands to make a digital record of all signals coming from the warheads, which are recorded on one-inch magnetic tape. Cobra Ball thereby not only collects important military technical intelligence, but at the same time monitors the provisions of arms control treaties. There is an average of ten Cobra Ball flights a month, some of which involve air-to-air refueling and last up to eighteen hours. Although the operation is mostly routine once an RC-135S is airborne, missions are often flown on extremely short notice after SIGINT intercepts made by planes, satellites, or ground stations indicate that a missile test is imminent. With a single exception, every flight has taken place in obscurity.

The exception occurred early in September 1983, when the world learned that a Cobra Ball aircraft had been in the immediate vicinity of the Korean Air Lines 747 that was shot down off Sakhalin Island soon after it had passed through forbidden airspace near the Soviet naval base at Petropavlovsk, resulting in the death of 269 people.

The RC-135S, with its thimble-shaped nose, sliding hatches, and brace of antennas sticking out of its sides and belly, had been waiting in the night for the fiery warheads to come its way, just as they always did. Had it not been for the attack on the airliner, which the Russians may have mistaken for an RC-135S on a penetration attempt, its solitary vigil there in the darkness far above the Bering Sea would have gone unnoticed, as usual.

8

Foreign Bases:
A Net Spread Wide

The U.S. strategic reconnaissance and surveillance program as it currently exists was set in place throughout the 1960s to blanket the globe. The system was extended from the murky depths of the sea to the vacuous blackness of space for the purpose of gathering an unparalleled amount of intelligence about other nations, friend and foe alike. And the spread of collection systems was accompanied by a swelling bureaucracy whose chains of command and areas of specific responsibility were forged in occasionally fierce battles over control of the systems and just what it was they were supposed to do.

By the end of the decade American non-space-based systems—ships, planes, radar and communication interception sites, and seismic detection stations—literally ringed the Communist bloc from Berlin to the Bering Strait. U.S. and Allied technical intelligence specialists, both military and civilian, were operating at clandestine facilities, invariably fenced off and guarded, in Great Britain, Norway, Spain, West Germany, Italy, Morocco, East Africa, Turkey, Iran, Pakistan, South Korea, Japan, and Australia, in addition to scores of places in remote areas of Alaska, Hawaii, New Hampshire, California, and other states. The sites, which were otherwise unassuming and usually meaningless to the untrained eye, almost always sprouted large round white domes, radar dishes, or massive antenna farms, all of which either pulled in intelligence signals the way a vacuum cleaner ingests dust, relayed intelligence data to Washington through several different, highly specific routes, or uplinked instructions to the aircraft and satellites.

The Soviet Union's growing fleet of deepwater, missile-carrying submarines were monitored by long arrays of large hydrophones strung along cables buried on the ocean floor at several strategic choke points, by others towed in the wake of civilian-operated surface ships, and by still others that were dropped out of carrier-based helicopters and land-based maritime patrol planes.

Specially outfitted floating listening posts like the ill-fated *Liberty*, which was shot up and torpedoed by Israeli fighters in the 1967 war, and the *Pueblo*, which was captured by North Koreans off their coast the following year, plied the seven seas listening for clues that would help Washington monitor revolutionaries in Asia, Africa, and Latin America, military activity in the Middle East and East Asia, and diplomatic and commercial traffic almost everywhere. The days right after World War II, when make-do antennas and receivers were bolted onto surplus Liberty Ships, were over. The new *Liberty* was a 455-foot-long spy ship crammed with listening equipment and specialists to operate it. The vessel's most distinctive piece of hardware was a sixteen-foot-wide dish antenna that could bounce intercepted intelligence off the moon to a receiving station in Maryland in a ten-thousand-watt microwave signal that enabled it to transmit large quantities of information without giving away the *Liberty*'s location.*

In addition, submarines were performing regular naval reconnaissance in the Holystone program, as has been mentioned, and various other types of vessels were pressed into service as requirements arose. The best-known incident involving such activity occurred in the Gulf of Tonkin on August 4, 1964, when two U.S. destroyers gathering SIGINT were reportedly attacked by North Vietnamese patrol boats. The incident, which was publicly denounced by President Lyndon Johnson, led to the congressional resolution that opened the way for overt U.S. involvement in the war in Vietnam.

Special reconnaissance aircraft, such as the U-2s, SR-71s, and RC-135s, were supplemented with a variety of other planes, most of them modified to carry eavesdropping and photographic gear,

*The system, known as TRSSCOMM, for Technical Research Ship Special Communications, had to be pointed at a particular spot on the moon while a computer compensated for the ship's rolling and pitching. The computers and the antenna's hydraulic steering mechanism did not work well together, creating frequent problems.

which flew shorter range but on the whole more frequent missions
that nibbled tenaciously at communications traffic, radar transmissions, and imaging targets along the periphery of the Communist
bloc and often directly over the Soviet Union's client countries in
the Third World. The planes that flew for the Navy were called
P 2V Neptunes and later P-3 Orions, both of which also were submarine hunter-killer aircraft, and RA-5C Vigilantes. The RA-5C
was a reconnaissance adaptation of a remarkable twin-engine,
sweptwing, carrier-based bomber built by North American Aviation that was flying at twice the speed of sound in 1958 (the reconnaissance version went into service six years later).* The Air Force
used RB-57s and RB-66s—both adaptations of twin-jet bombers—
as well as EC-121 Constellations (a lumbering version of the Lockheed airliner that bulged with huge dorsal and ventral radomes),
EC-130 Herculeses, and even the ubiquitous, infinitely adaptable
C-47, the Air Force version of the Douglas DC-3. EC-47s were
widely used in Europe during the fifties and sixties and in Vietnam
to fly electronic surveillance missions along South Vietnam's western frontier and around its coastal waters near North Vietnam.

Not counting bases in Vietnam, foreign airfields supporting U.S.
Air Force, Navy, Army, and CIA reconnaissance operations by the
end of the sixties included RAF Alconbury and Mildenhall in the
United Kingdom, Rota air base in Spain, Hellenikon Airport in
Greece, RAF Akrotiri on Cyprus, Incirlik air base in Turkey,
Kadena air base on Okinawa, Atsugi air base in Japan, Osan air base
in South Korea, and other air bases in Iceland, West Germany,
Norway, Iran, and Pakistan.

In addition, listening posts, telemetry interception facilities, nuclear explosion detection equipment, submarine surveillance operations, and satellite uplink and downlink centers had proliferated in
most of the countries listed above, as well as in some others, including Australia, Ethiopia, Italy, and Morocco, where either the CIA

---

*The Vigilante, which was unheralded and remains so, was in its way the Navy's equivalent
of the SR-71, though its performance fell considerably short of the Blackbird's. It was the
largest bomber ever built for carrier operations and the only one to reach Mach 2. The
reconnaissance version, or RA-5C, was produced after the plane's bombing role was dropped.
Though keeping an attack capability, the RA-5C carried vertical, oblique, and horizon-to-
horizon cameras, side-looking radar, infrared sensors, and low-light-level television. The
Vigilante was the airborne component of the Integrated Operational Intelligence System
(IOIS) that fed immediately usable tactical intelligence data to ground-based military units
in Vietnam after one of the planes returned to its carrier. The RA-5C was almost 76 feet long
and had a 53-foot wingspan. It had a maximum speed of 1,380 miles an hour at 40,000 feet
and could cruise at that altitude at 560 miles an hour with a range of 2,650 miles.

or the NSA operated facilities or shared them with the host government. A detailed account of such operations worldwide is beyond the scope of this work, but two nations can be said to represent the multifaceted nature of U.S. foreign reconnaissance and surveillance operations overseas. Owing to the complex, expensive, and highly sensitive nature of the intelligence work involved, both nations apparently were chosen as much for their kindred political spirit and social stability as for geographic reasons. For their part, both have cooperated extensively with the United States military and intelligence services while going to considerable lengths to keep the lowest possible profiles, no doubt to avoid confrontations with local political factions opposed to such liaisons with Washington, as well as to prevent agents working for the opposition from penetrating the various systems. They are Norway and Australia.

Nature has not been kind to Russian sailors. Although the U.S.S.R. has the longest coastline of any nation, it is poorly situated for naval operations. Much of that coastline is landlocked, and what is not is blocked by thick ice for much of the year. There are two major submarine bases, one at Polyarnyy, just north of Murmansk on the Kola Peninsula, and the other at Petropavlovsk, on the eastern edge of the Kamchatka Peninsula bordering the Pacific.

Submarines leaving Polyarnyy bound for the Atlantic must first glide through a 225-mile-wide channel between Nordkapp, Norway, and Bear Island, south of Spitsbergen. They then must negotiate the relatively shallow water between Scotland and Iceland before ranging into the North Atlantic. Soviet boats heading for the Pacific from Petropavlovsk have quicker access to the open sea, but they must nevertheless pass between Hokkaido in northern Japan and the Aleutians.

Whichever of the two naval facilities a Soviet submarine calls home, however, it never leaves or returns without being heard by the opposition. This is because the ocean floor over which it moves is bugged by the United States Navy. And that's not all.

Even before a Soviet sub slips out of its berth and heads to sea, the communications activity that is a necessary prelude to such an operation is picked up by SIGINT satellites and by listening posts in Norway, Japan, Okinawa, the Phillippines, or any of more than a score of other locations, depending upon the port. In many instances the submarines are also photographed by reconnaissance satellites as they cruise on the surface of the shallow inlets between their moorings and deep water before they slip under the waves. As is the case with most elements relating to antisubmarine warfare (ASW), the Navy maintains steadfast silence about the use of satellite imagery for Soviet submarine reconnaissance. Yet one defense analyst who has studied the photographs of the Soviet boats quipped, "You can tell if the guys on the bridge watch have their parka hoods up." The satellite data are relayed to the Current Operations Department of the Navy Operational Intelligence Center (NOIC) outside Washington, where a large chart of worldwide submarine activity, friendly and otherwise, is kept up to the minute for relay to Navy command operations centers in Europe and Asia. The Soviet subs, many of which carry ballistic missiles, are tracked relentlessly wherever they go.

Underwater, submarines can be detected by two basic surveillance techniques, one active, the other passive. Active detection depends upon sonar, which sends sound waves through the water and records the strength and timing of the signal that bounces back from the target submarine. Sonar, which was used in World War II, is carried on most Navy surface ships and on all submarines, whether they are so-called fast-attack killers that are designed to hunt and destroy Soviet subs or fleet ballistic-missile types that form the ballistic-missile-carrying third leg of the bomber-ICBM-submarine nuclear-attack triad long used by the United States as its nuclear war-fighting system.

The second kind of underwater detection system, the passive one, depends upon acoustical devices that pick up the sounds made by the submarines as they move. Passive acoustical systems placed underwater, like those placed in the vacuum of space, emit nothing. They just listen.

Submarines moving at medium or high speed produce sounds primarily from their propellers and by the rush of water along their hulls, according to Dr. Richard L. Garwin, an IBM physicist who has long studied defense matters.* The major source of sound at low speed, he has said, comes not so much from the propellers and water but from machinery inside the boat, and especially the kind that rotates (turbines and propeller shafts, for example). But even a noisy

---

*Garwin is now known chiefly for his tenacious opposition to the Strategic Defensive Initiative, or Star Wars.

submarine radiates less than one watt of acoustical power, an extremely low level. "One can therefore imagine the problem of detecting this tiny signal at long range in the presence of noise from waves and wind, undersea life and hundreds—even thousands—of surface vessels," Garwin has noted. The problem is formidable, to be sure, but it is one that the United States has managed to stay on top of, Soviet countermeasures notwithstanding.

The bugs over which Soviet submarines pass while going to or from their ports are arrays of extremely sensitive hydrophones, which, together with others placed farther out to sea, constitute the Sound Surveillance System, or SOSUS. The first SOSUS hydrophones were made by Western Electric and laid on the continental shelf along the Atlantic and Gulf coasts of the United States in the fifties and sixties in a program code-named Caesar. This was followed by the Colossus line, which stretches along the Pacific shelf from the vicinity of Vancouver to Baja, and later by Barrier and Bronco, which extended the listening system to the waters off Polyarnyy and Petropavlovsk.

There are actually two SOSUS arrays moored across the approaches to Polyarnyy: one between Norway and Bear Island, and the other linking northern Scotland, Iceland, and Greenland. Submarines whose home port is Petropavlovsk are monitored by hydrophones strung from the southeastern tip of Hokkaido, along a line parallel to the Kuriles, and then up toward the northeast, off the Aleutian coast. Still others stretch from southern Japan to the Philippines, covering the approaches to China and Indochina. And there are also SOSUS installations on the Atlantic side of Gibraltar, others about halfway between Italy and Corsica, and still others at the mouth of the Bosporus, off Diego Garcia in the Indian Ocean, and not far from Hawaii. The Navy keeps the precise locations of its SOSUS equipment a closely guarded secret, since interfering with it would be a logical Soviet objective.

SOSUS hydrophones are sealed in clusters of two dozen or so inside large tanks that are probably linked by fiber optical cables and are definitely buried as deep as possible on the ocean floor to prevent their being severed by Soviet submarines or surface ships trailing cable cutters. Each hydrophone in one of the huge tanks (they are reportedly nearly as large as the oil storage tanks in refineries) is tuned to a specific frequency. By focusing all of the hydrophones on a particular submarine, many separate sounds can be tapped at the same time, including those made by its engine and cooling system, the water flow around its hull, the spinning of its propellers, and its own sonar system.

All of the individual noises combine to constitute a kind of submarine symphony: a unique set of sounds that, together, form a distinct SIGINT pattern for every sub, even those that are otherwise identical. The "music" from a particular Soviet Victor-class attack submarine moving over the SOSUS array between Norway and Bear Island is collected on the Norwegian coast and relayed to Navy data-processing facilities through Fleet Satellite Communications system (FLTSATCOM) spacecraft, five of which ring the earth in a 22,300-mile geosynchronous orbit.*

On shore, the sounds that have been relayed by satellite are sorted out almost instantly by powerful computers such as the Illiac 4 and are then compared with other "symphonies" in the data bank. In this way the identity of every submarine passing over the SOSUS line is established, and in the process its mission profile, capability, operational characteristics, and probable direction are determined.

An assessment of the satellite-linked SOSUS system's capability made by the Massachusetts Institute of Technology reportedly concluded that at its best it can pinpoint the location of older (and therefore noisier) Soviet subs to within ten miles of their actual position from a distance of ten thousand miles, and that a twenty-five-mile fix from "several thousand miles" is feasible in most cases. And although Soviet submarines are becoming quieter and rely on an increasing number of their own tricks to avoid detection (diving deeper and hiding between currents of varying temperatures being but two of those tricks), it is generally conceded that their whereabouts are known at all times, an indispensable requirement for attacking them should that ever become necessary.

*The FLTSATCOM system was developed to provide a near-global satellite communications network for the Navy and Air Force, and relaying SOSUS data is therefore only one of the satellites' functions. The system's basic mission is to provide an ultra-high and super-high frequency, anti-jam communications link between all Navy ships and submarines, many kinds of aircraft, and shore stations. It also connects the president and the secretary of defense —the National Command Authority—to field commanders around the world. In addition, twelve of a FLTSATCOM's twenty-three UHF and SHF channels are used by the Air Force for communication between SAC headquarters and its bomber force and ICBM installations. The satellites, which are built by TRW, weigh a little more than two thousand pounds in orbit, have eight-foot-wide hexagonal bodies, and sprout sixteen-foot wire and mesh parabolic antennas that open on station like umbrellas. There is also a helical antenna, which looks like a giant corkscrew, and a horn antenna for uplink communication. Hydrazine motors allow orbital maneuvering. The first FLTSATCOM spacecraft was launched in February 1978 as part of the national command control and communications system.

There are other ways to track submarines besides using SOSUS. Surface ships towing sonar arrays can spot them, and so can helicopters and P-3 Orion antisubmarine planes dropping sound-sensitive sonobuoys. Satellites also are natural sub-sniffers. Although submarine propellers can be made quieter, they must spin, and spinning underwater creates a churning vortex that soon comes to the surface and leaves a wake so minute that it cannot be seen from ships or even from most aircraft. From about three hundred miles high, however, even the faintest wake can be discerned when compared with the water around it. Another possibility has to do with tracking the billions of dead microorganisms a sub leaves in its wake. Still another satellite-sensing technique might involve the use of blue-green lasers that can penetrate water to certain depths and could be used to first fix a beam on the submarine and then lock onto the boat in such a way that no matter how it maneuvered, it could not shake off its space-based electronic leash. For the time being, however, SOSUS remains the principal component in the worldwide Soviet submarine surveillance system, and Norway is one of SOSUS's chief anchors.

Norway's extensive involvement in U.S. strategic reconnaissance and surveillance activity is steadfastly played down by Washington, and given that nation's proximity to the Soviet Union, the Norwegians like it that way. But their discretion notwithstanding, it is fair to say that Norway abounds with a variety of operations that in one way or another have been designed and positioned to either monitor events inside the U.S.S.R. or actually pull out intelligence. And SOSUS, as important as it is, remains but one Norwegian-connected system among many.

Antennas used to eavesdrop on high-frequency radio traffic, most of which comes from the Soviet military and concerns ship-to-ship, ship-to-shore, and air-to-ground communication, are located at Vadsø, which has a huge "Pusher"-type circular antenna array, as well as at Skage, Randaberg, and Jessheim. Vadsø's antennas point over the Varanger fjord and northern Lapland's bleak hills straight at the Northern Fleet's huge base at Severomorsk, a bare hundred miles away. Skage and Randaberg most likely monitor communications from Soviet ships, submarines, and long-range naval reconnaissance planes, such as the TU-95Ds that routinely head out over the Norwegian Sea. The big turboprop Bears lumber on to Greenland, where they ferret NATO radar and communications traffic and then swing down along the Canadian and U.S. coasts to extract still more SIGINT before landing in Cuba. Jessheim, only twenty-five miles north of Oslo, intercepts the capital's diplomatic traffic.

Very high and ultrahigh radio frequencies (VHF and UHF) are mainly used for short- and medium-distance, line-of-sight communication, air-to-ground links, the transmission of telemetry from missile tests, satellite-to-ground communication and, in the case of VHF, certain kinds of Soviet radar. There are VHF and UHF intercept facilities at Vadsø, Viksjøfjell, Vardø, Randaberg, and Fauske. Vadsø's antennas would mean nothing special to a casual observer, but one knowledgeable in radio reception equipment would understand that the facility's long period arrays, vertical wire dipoles, and broad-band dipoles backed by corner reflectors, are extremely sensitive receivers. A map and compass would show that they point toward the naval and air installations around Murmansk, including the submarine base at Polyarnyy. Both Vadsø and Viksjøfjell also have sophisticated VHF antennas hidden under geodesic domes that sit on top of sixty-foot-high concrete towers. The location and design of such antennas suggest that they almost undoubtedly intercept telemetry from Soviet submarine-launched ballistic missile tests in the Barents Sea.

Vetan, a tiny, suitably remote peninsula in the far northern Skjerstad fjord not far from the air base at Bodø, which was Gary Powers's destination the day he went down over Sverdlovsk, may be the single most important element in the Norwegian connection. It is a satellite ground station linked to the U.S. Satellite Data System (SDS) spacecraft network. SDS satellites relay collected intelligence from the remaining KH-11 reconnaissance satellite, as well as several different kinds of communications traffic. What is more interesting, however, is that some satellites that appear to be SDS types (chiefly because they use the same highly elliptical orbit) are no such thing. They are actually anti-ballistic missile radar ferrets code-named Jumpseat. The impostor's orbit, like that of the real SDS, is so elliptical that it can "hang" over Siberia for some eight hours as it soaks up the microwave pulses coming from there. Thus, Vetan not only picks up SDS signals but most likely Jumpseat's as well, making it one of the most important downlink facilities in the U.S. reconnaissance and surveillance system.

If that weren't enough, Vetan's antennas also intercept transmissions from Soviet Molniya communications satellites. More important, the Norwegian antennas listen to the Russians' own ferret platforms as they pass over Murmansk's large receiving dishes and "dump" streams of the electronic nuggets they have collected high over the North Atlantic. This means that the National Security Agency knows what the Russians are ferreting over Western Europe and North America because it intercepts their interceptions.

Project Vela, which was invented to coincide with the Limited Test Ban Treaty (LTBT) of 1963, is supposed to allow Washington to make certain that Moscow is adhering to the agreement, and also to the 150-kiloton limit set by the so-called Threshold Test Ban Treaty of 1974. It evolved out of recommendations made by two special panels convened in Washington in 1959 (one on seismic improvement and the other on high-altitude detection), as well as the Conferences of Experts that met in Geneva at about the same time. Vela, which was to involve Norway, as well as Australia and other countries, provides an example of how a single surveillance program can serve two masters at the same time: arms control and military intelligence. There are, of course, many others, perhaps the foremost being Cobra Ball.

The overall project was divided into three distinct programs designed to provide assurance that Soviet nuclear explosions took place only underground. Vela Uniform was to use seismic detectors and other equipment to pick up the vibrations from underground and underwater explosions; Vela Sierra was to use earth-bound measuring instruments, such as riometers (radio receivers that measure the intensity of signals coming over great distances) to spot atmospheric and space-related detonations; and Vela Hotel would use satellites working in pairs to detect nuclear explosions on the surface of the earth or in space.*

Overall responsibility for developing Vela went to the Advanced Research Projects Agency, and therefore to the Defense Department. And although the Atomic Energy Commission, Army Corps of Engineers, and Office of Naval Intelligence played key roles in

---

*Considering that America's first successful satellite, Explorer 1, had gone up only in February 1958 and that boosters were still exploding on launch or flipping out of control immediately afterward with appalling regularity, the very notion of orbiting a sophisticated nuclear test surveillance satellite in those days smacked of audacity, especially since the orbit had to be synchronous. But plans for Vela at such an early stage give some indication of the optimism of the engineers and planners and the quickening momentum of research and development.

the development of several of its components, it was the Air Force that became the principal military adviser for Vela and, eventually, the entire program's operator. Uniform and Sierra—monitoring underground tests and scanning the skies from earth for explosions —were to be handled by the Air Force Technical Applications Center (AFTAC) at Patrick Air Force Base in Florida. Hotel, the satellite surveillance program, would go to the Air Force's Space Systems Division (now simply the Space Division) at El Segundo, California, which was responsible for managing the design, production, launching, and operation of Air Force satellites.

The first seismic station built in the Vela Uniform program was called the Wichita Mountains Seismological Observatory. It became operational near Lawton, Oklahoma, in October 1960 with an array of ten short-period vertical seismometers spaced at intervals of about three thousand feet, plus twenty-one seismographs.*

The Wichita Mountains detection station went into business relatively quickly given its complexity, and with good reason. "AFTAC was able to achieve this result rapidly because the station involved only a modest expansion of the existing Air Force research facility, where most of the techniques and equipment had previously been deployed," according to Dr. Carl Romney, an AFTAC geophysicist, who made the statement to the Congressional Joint Committee on Atomic Energy during hearings on Vela in 1961. Romney thus made it clear that the Defense Department had been working independently during the 1950s to develop a seismic monitoring system with which to take the pulse of every Soviet nuclear explosion irrespective of the outcome of the treaty negotiations.

More than a decade after Dr. Romney testified in Congress, ARPA Director Charles Herzfeld was asked by a congressman whether a huge seismic array in Montana called LASA had been built specifically to tell whether the Russians were cheating on the test ban treaty. "Yes," Herzfeld answered with apparent impatience, "but what I'm trying to highlight now is that this is important in the absence of any treaty whatever. In fact, this was started before any underground treaty seriously was thought about. We feel rather strongly in the Defense Department that we must know more, and more accurately, what the Russians and other countries [sic] are getting in their underground tests."

*A seismometer is a detector that can sense tiny movements in the earth. A seismograph is a seismometer with an amplifier and a recorder. The more detectors in an array, the tinier the movements it can pick up.

The military as well as the political imperative to monitor all nuclear testing, both under and above ground, led to the establishment of a string of seismic stations girdling the U.S.S.R. as part of a program originally called IONDS (Integrated Operational Nuclear Detection System) and later shortened to NDS (Nuclear Detection System).* And Norway, by political inclination and geological accident, figures prominently in the NDS.

With two exceptions, no nation in the non-Soviet camp has such an uncomplicated vibration travel path from the underground nuclear test site at Semipalatinsk as does Norway. The exceptions are Iran, whose seismic arrays and other intelligence installations were dismantled, destroyed, or confiscated during the revolution that ended the reign of the Pahlavis, and the People's Republic of China. There are two U.S. nuclear detection monitoring stations in China, both on a wedge of territory in the northernmost part of Sinkiang Province, and therefore a scant three hundred miles southeast of Semipalatinsk. One is at Qitai (or Ch'i-t'ai), a town set in the northern foothills of the rugged Tian Shan mountain range, and the other is at Korla, just on the other side of the mountains, to the south. The seismic stations are not far from the large tracking dishes, also American, that follow the warheads that come arcing out of Tyuratam and then slam down onto the test ranges on the Kamchatka Peninsula. Northern Sinkiang provides the technical intelligence collectors in Washington with a window on the Soviet Union the likes of which they haven't seen since the departure of the Shah.

Hamar, north of Oslo, is another excellent place to put a seismic station. It is built on the same continental plate as the Kazakh Soviet Socialist Republic, which is where Semipalatinsk is. Seismologically speaking, the two localities are in effect connected by a 2,500-mile-long iron pipe. Every time a nuclear weapon goes off under the crusted mantle of Semipalatinsk, it seems to those who watch the seismographs at Hamar that the pipe has been struck by a giant mallet.

The Hamar facility, which is unguarded and operated by Norwegian civilians, is a dual-purpose monitoring operation. Its overt assignment is to gather and accumulate seismic data that can be used for the development of ever better verification techniques for a comprehensive ban on nuclear weapons testing. In that regard,

---

*IONDS, and then NDS, is an outgrowth of the Vela system, not a part of it.

scientific results are freely shared with researchers from other nations, including the Soviet Union.

But Hamar is also equipped to make instant transmissions of what
it picks up to passing satellites at a rate of twenty-four hundred bits
a second—near instantaneously. The satellites in turn relay the data
to the Seismic Data Analysis Center in Alexandria, Virginia, where
they are analyzed in an effort to pinpoint the location of the "event"
and determine whether it was natural or man-made. The SDAC
works in close conjunction with the Air Force Technical Applications Center, which keeps track of nuclear weapon test signatures
—their distinctive pattern—as part of its role in the NDS program.
But why would it be so important to get seismic data on a Soviet
nuclear weapon test so quickly that they have to be relayed by
satellite? Even underground nuclear tests can leak residual radiation
through cracks in the soil surface or out of partial cave-ins. The only
apparent reason for sending news of an explosion in real time would
be that a reconnaissance satellite carrying appropriate sensors to
measure radiation and other effects can be maneuvered into position
before the dust settles, both figuratively and literally.

Given the extent of Norwegian involvement in the NDS program and all of the other technical intelligence operations, it can be
assumed that the Russians have worked out a variety of electronic
countermeasures to thwart Norwegian-based NATO activity both
in peace and war. But they seem to have done more than that.

It has been reported that elite Soviet *spetsnaz* commando teams
specializing in reconnaissance, sabotage, and assassination, and operating out of the island fortress of Kronshtadt, have made more than
one hundred fifty clandestine landings along the Swedish coast
since 1962. According to the reports, the practice landings seem to
be part of a larger Soviet plan to outflank NATO forces around the
western Baltic in time of war and neutralize Swedish and Norwegian defenses, including surveillance facilities. These landing operations are said to be in part rehearsals for invading and crossing
Sweden in order to reach targets in Norway that are marked for
destruction. This could partly explain the heavy Soviet submarine
traffic off the Swedish coast. In October 1981, for example, a Soviet
Whiskey-class submarine ran aground off Karlskrona, a naval base
in the south of Sweden. The incident, one of several involving
Soviet subs at the time, was ignominious. But the Russians, following the practice of their U.S. Air Force counterparts, hastily explained that their boat had trespassed because of a navigational error.

. . .

Dr. Desmond Ball, who is head of the Strategic & Defence Studies Centre of the Australian National University at Canberra, has noted that geography alone makes his country a natural site for the kind of electronic intelligence and other facilities that are used in conjunction with U.S. strategic operations, and particularly with those relating to space reconnaissance and surveillance.

Ball has pointed out in a book that is widely read by those interested in technical intelligence that Australia not only is a large continent whose desolate center is about five hundred miles from the nearest coast, but also has the advantages of being relatively close to Southeast Asia and virtually on the other side of the globe from the United States.

The remoteness of the continent's center makes it an ideal place for the building of installations that must be kept away from the prying eyes of those who inhabit population centers. Where people are concerned, central Australia is easily "secured" (to use the government argot). Proximity to the Asian landmass means that Australia is especially well suited to eavesdropping on some kinds of communication and electronic signals coming from there, helping U.S. submarines, surface ships, and aircraft navigate and communicate throughout the western Pacific, monitoring the nuclear blasts going off above ground at Lop Nor in China and under it in the hills of Soviet Kazakhstan, and listening to Soviet, Chinese, and other nations' submarines on tapes connected to SOSUS amplifiers.

Australia's location nearly opposite the United States is especially important where space reconnaissance and surveillance are concerned. The geostationary spacecraft engaged in SIGINT reconnaissance and ballistic missile early warning (BMEW) surveillance of the Soviet Union, China, and elsewhere in the Eastern Hemisphere can be fully monitored because the positions high above the equator from where they look and listen are in unimpeded communication range of Australia.

The island-continent is so fundamentally involved in U.S. space reconnaissance and surveillance programs, as well as a wide variety of other intelligence-gathering, monitoring, and communication operations, that it amounts to the Southern Hemisphere's equivalent of the Norwegian connection. Indeed, if there is a difference in the degree of participation between the two countries, it is that the Australians probably have an even more intimate and extensive

188   DEEP BLACK

relationship with the U.S. intelligence establishment than the
Norwegians do.

Unlike Norway, Australia was not occupied during World War II,
and it therefore quickly developed into an extremely important
forward base for American and British forces in the Pacific. Its size
made it a daunting prospect for invasion by Japan, while its location
made it a natural staging area for Allied soldiers, sailors, and airmen.
Douglas MacArthur made his celebrated return to the Philippines
from Australia in October 1944.

At the same time, Australia was turned into an intelligence-gathering mecca by a number of secret services that ran spy networks
or, more usually, pulled information out of thin air with directional
antennas and powerful receivers. Ball has claimed that more than
twenty separate intelligence organizations operated in Australia
during World War II under British, Australian, or American auspices (with the last dominating) and that some of them were so black
—so structured on a need-to-know basis—that to this day exactly
what it was that they did remains unclear and untangling their
relationship with one another is all but impossible.

What emerges quite clearly, however, is that SIGINT, and especially its communications aspect, had become so refined by 1943 that
it was already playing a significant role in the outcome of the war.
Using the Japanese naval codes that had been cracked in Washington before the attack on Pearl Harbor, intercepts of encoded radio
transmissions led to the ferocious and highly successful attacks by
U.S. submarines against Japanese shipping, the naval disasters inflicted at the battles of Midway and the Coral Sea, and even to the
death of Admiral Isoroku Yamamoto, the commander in chief of the
Japanese Navy, who was killed on his way to inspect fortifications
on Bougainville when his bomber was jumped by P-38s that were
waiting for it.

Australian experience in technical collection and the sharing with
the country's allies of the take and the facilities necessary to get it
were well established by the end of the war. And although some
Australian combat units were disbanded outright or thinned by the
armistice, the nation's essential SIGINT apparatus, human and mechanical, was kept intact for the day it might have to be pointed in
another direction. Many who followed events in 1947 behind the
Iron Curtain and in China (where Mao Tse-tung's spreading War

of Liberation had already claimed more than a million of Chiang Kai-shek's troops and was threatening all of Manchuria) knew that that day was swiftly approaching.

The close working relationship that existed between the Allied secret services during the war was formalized and codified in 1947 with the signing of the UKUSA Agreement, or Secret Treaty, as it was also called. The principal parties—the United States, United Kingdom, Canada, Australia, and New Zealand—agreed to cooperate in the collection of several kinds of SIGINT, to share what was collected, and to jointly operate some of the relevant installations that are on Australian soil.

Communication and assorted electronic signals are routinely intercepted at Australia's Defence Signals Directorate (DSD) headquarters in Melbourne, as well as at listening posts in Watsonia, Darwin, Shoal Bay, Harman (outside Canberra), Pearce (near Perth), Cabarlah, not far from Toowoomba in Queensland, and North West Cape. Pearce, to take one example of listening-post coverage, is responsible for monitoring naval and air communication around the Indian Ocean. Cabarlah, to take another, taps radio traffic—COMINT—throughout the southwest Pacific. DSD personnel at both facilities use Plessey-built CDAA antenna arrays: the same type, code-named Pusher, that is used by the Norwegians at Vadsø.

Australia also hosts the U.S. Air Force's Detachment 421, which operates a seismic station at Alice Springs as part of the Nuclear Detection System. The unit operates nineteen seismometers, most of which are buried more than one hundred fifty feet underground, and all of which are arranged in a circle several miles wide to enhance overall receptivity. The station records an average of twenty-one hundred "events" a week, occasionally including an underground nuclear explosion, and, like Norway, relays the data to AFTAC at Patrick Air Force Base in Florida by satellite. Three similar stations due north—one on Okinawa and two in the Philippines—perform the same monitoring mission.

Most SIGINT collection is technically a joint endeavor involving the National Security Agency (NSA), Australia's DSD, and Great Britain's Government Communications Headquarters (GCHQ). Ball has written that "NSA and GCHQ operations in Australia are so closely interlocked with those of DSD that it is impossible to consider them separately." While that is true, only one of the three intelligence organizations represents a country that has a space reconnaissance and surveillance program, and that agency—the NSA—therefore plays a dominant role in space-related activity.

U.S. space reconnaissance and surveillance operations in Australia are focused at two locations, each of which possesses several capabilities, though each also has a distinct primary mission. The installations, both of which are as black as such things get, are at Pine Gap, a valley near Alice Springs (and therefore smack in the center of the country's barren outback), and Nurrungar, which is hard by the old rocket-firing range at Woomera, about two hundred fifty miles north of Adelaide. Pine Gap's primary mission is to serve as the downlink—the intelligence receptacle—for a series of multipurpose geosynchronous SIGINT satellites whose first version was named Rhyolite. Similarly, Nurrungar is the terminus for data coming from a platform known as DSP-647 (for Defense Support Program), which images the heat coming from ballistic missile tests and is supposed to sound an alarm in case of a ballistic missile attack.

Rhyolite and its several modified namesakes, all synchronous orbiters, are in many ways the most remarkable reconnaissance satellites ever developed. They were also intended to be among the most secret. But that was before the espionage trial of Andrew Daulton Lee and Christopher John Boyce, which took place in Los Angeles in 1977.

Having abandoned three colleges short of graduation and meanwhile holding jobs as a janitor, pizza cook, waiter, and liquor-store delivery boy, Christopher Boyce finally decided to use family connections to land a clerk's job at TRW's Redondo Beach headquarters, just south of Los Angeles, in July 1974. After making it through successive CIA security checks with apparent ease, Boyce, who was twenty-one, was put to work in the company's supersecret Black Vault. He soon learned of the existence of a spy satellite that was referred to as RH, for Rhyolite, which sent great quantities of intelligence data to Australia. The information in turn was transmitted from there to the Black Vault, which relayed it in code to CIA headquarters in Langley, Virginia. Boyce was therefore in a position to monitor whatever kind of intelligence Rhyolite collected.

During a subsequent twenty-one-month period Boyce and Lee, his childhood pal, sold thousands of documents relating to Rhyolite operations to KGB agents in Mexico City and Vienna. They did this, according to testimony at their subsequent espionage trial, to finance drug purchases, improve their life-styles and, in Boyce's case, almost as a "whim" because of vague feelings of enmity he had for the CIA and for his country in general. It was the time of Vietnam. Boyce was given forty years in prison and Lee got life.

The spacecraft whose secrets Lee and Boyce sold to the Russians was described to Boyce at an early TRW briefing as "a multipurpose covert electronic surveillance system," according to Robert Lindsey, whose book *The Falcon and the Snowman* chronicles the spies' exploits. "Project Rhyolite . . . had been developed by TRW to eavesdrop electronically on foreign countries, especially the eastern Soviet Union, China and Soviet test ranges in the Pacific. It was a 'bug'—much like the listening devices detectives plant on telephones to eavesdrop on private conversations—except that it was a listening device on the missile-launching tests of the two countries and on their telecommunications system—and on several other nations whose communications traffic the United States might want to monitor," Lindsey wrote. "Chris was to learn that each satellite carried a brace of antennas capable of sucking up foreign microwave signals from out of space like a vacuum cleaner picking up specks of dust from a carpet. American intelligence agents could monitor Communist microwave radio and long-distance telephone traffic over much of the European landmass, eavesdropping on a Soviet commissar in Moscow talking to his mistress in Yalta or on a general talking to his lieutenants across the great continent. . . ."

But Langley and the National Security Agency, which shared the intelligence that came down in a steady stream from far above the equator, had bigger fish to fry than commissars exchanging endearments with their paramours or generals giving orders to junior officers. As good as Rhyolite's intercept capability was against Soviet and Chinese radio and telephone communication links in the VHF, UHF, and microwave broadcast bands, COMINT was not the satellite's primary target, and neither was RADINT—radar intelligence—although it did a little of that, too. Rhyolite's main task was to collect TELINT, or the telemetry from Soviet and Chinese ballistic missile tests, and to relay what it heard in coded form to the CIA and the NSA through Pine Gap and Redondo Beach. And it did that very well indeed.

The first fully operational Rhyolite went up on top of an Atlas Agena-D on March 6, 1973, though at least one experimental operational version was orbited as early as 1970 (the year the U.S.-Australian "Joint Defence Space Research Facility" at Pine Gap began functioning). The spacecraft, a squat cylinder about five feet long and weighing three quarters of a ton, was positioned 22,175 miles over Borneo. Once on station, its main dish antenna, measuring more than seventy feet across, was unfolded and extended forward as though on the end of an accordion. Other, smaller antennas received instructions from Pine Gap (whose code name was Merino), and answered with a bonanza of telemetry intercepted from the ballistic missiles that roared off the pads at Tyuratam and Plesetsk and separated from their warheads, which then arced far over Siberia and impacted on Kamchatka or the north Pacific.

Subsequent Rhyolites were launched on May 23 and December 11, 1977, and on April 7, 1978. Of the initial batch of four operationally capable satellites, two are understood to have been put to work on telemetry collection, communication intercepts and some radar mapping, while the other two were kept in reserve for the day when point failure or attack crippled one or both of their sisters. So sensitive were the satellites' listening equipment that they could pick up walkie-talkie chatter during Red Army field exercises from more than twenty-two thousand miles over the equator. They also collected signals from the People's Republic of China, Vietnam, Indonesia, Pakistan, Lebanon, and elsewhere.

The NRO reacted to Lee's and Boyce's having compromised Rhyolite, as well as to the subsequent public trial, in traditional fashion: its name was changed. Though still essentially the same satellite, Rhyolite was rechristened Aquacade in an effort to get the Soviet Union to believe that its TELINT and other intercept activities were mostly, or even totally, being taken over by a newer system. Meanwhile, the Rhyolites continued tapping the approximately fifty channels, most of them UHF and microwave, that the Russians use for telemetry transmission.

Nor is Rhyolite the only heavy SIGINT spacecraft to have been put in geosynchronous orbit by the United States. Even as Lee's and Boyce's trial was taking place, finishing touches were being put on a second major signals intelligence platform, this one code-named Chalet. The first Chalet launch apparently took place on June 10, 1978, followed by others on October 1, 1979, and October 31, 1981. After an article in *The New York Times* mentioned Chalet by name, it too was assigned a new designator: Vortex.

Yet another large signals collector, this one code-named Magnum, was launched amid glaring (and unwanted) publicity when the space shuttle Discovery went into orbit on January 24, 1985. A month before, Brigadier General Richard Abel warned reporters at a crowded press conference that coverage of the mission—51-C— was to be severely restricted because of the nature of the heavily classified cargo. Abel, who was the Air Force's director of public affairs, added that subsequent similar launches would also come under the new rules, which were intended to "deny our adversaries" as much information as possible. And, Abel went on, any press "speculation" about the nature of Discovery's mission and the cargo it was to carry to orbit would set off a federal investigation for breach of national security.

Although some news organizations withheld details of Mission 51-C, Abel's threat, combined with a fear that the shroud of secrecy covering the NASA launch would become a precedent, proved too much for *The Washington Post*. Two days after Abel issued his warning, the *Post* ran a page-one story saying that the shuttle would be carrying a "new military intelligence satellite that is to collect electronic signals and retransmit them to a U.S. receiving station on Earth." The article went on to report that the collected data would include missile telemetry that could be used to verify arms control treaty compliance and that the SIGINT satellite's cost was $300 million. Caspar Weinberger promptly denounced the newspaper, saying that the article might have given "aid and comfort to the enemy." General Abel was reassigned.

But there was at least one more attempt to deceive the press and, therefore, it was hoped, the Soviet Union regarding Magnum's mission. By international agreement, the initial orbits of all satellites are filed with the United Nations. In the case of U.S. military launches, procedure calls for the Air Force to supply the State Department with a satellite's initial orbital characteristics within several weeks after it has gone up. The State Department then passes the information to the UN. In the case of Magnum, someone seems to have tipped *The New York Times* that the satellite had gone into a most unusual orbit for a reconnaissance platform. A *Times* reporter then requested details. He was told that the secret spacecraft had been put into a highly elliptical orbit with an apogee of 21,543 miles, a perigee of only 212 miles, and an inclination of 28.4 degrees. The reporter noted in his lead paragraph that it was a "radically different orbit from many spy satellites" and quoted an expert at MIT as saying, "It's a very funny trajectory." It *was* a funny trajectory for a reconnaissance satellite, but it did not remain so for long. Magnum's initial orbit was just that: a temporary so-called parking

orbit where it was stabilized before being rerouted to geosynchronous. Although the Air Force had been absolutely truthful in describing Magnum's initial orbit, it had neglected to add that the orbit
was subsequently changed, thereby attempting to undo what it saw
as the damage that had been done by the earlier disclosures. This was
a neat bit of what was later to be officially called a deliberate policy
of disinformation by the Defense Department.

Nurrungar, located five hundred miles south of Pine Gap along the
arterial highway that runs up the middle of the Australian continent,
occupies only about eight acres in a valley that is a quarter of a mile
by half a mile, forming an oblong bowl whose rim of hills is several
hundred feet high. The hills help to maintain privacy and shut out
electrical interference.

Nurrungar was built specifically to service TRW's Defense Support Program Code 647 satellites, or DSP-647s, as spacecraft in the
long-lived series are commonly called. Construction of the isolated
facility began in the autumn of 1969. It was pronounced operational
on November 6, 1970, when the first nonexperimental DSP-647 was
launched under whole or partial control of Nurrungar (four experimental predecessors, called Code 949, had been launched with
mixed results while under control of Pine Gap). Although that first
Nurrungar-controlled DSP-647 did make it off the ground, it did
not achieve geostationary orbit. It nevertheless marked the opening
of the facility. The first DSP-647 to make it to its assigned station
went up on a Titan 3C on May 5, 1971.

There were 396 persons working at Nurrungar by the summer
of 1978: 189 Australian military officers and 207 Americans, who
were probably employed by the military, the contractors, and perhaps by one or more of the intelligence services. The facility, which
is quite a bit smaller than Pine Gap, consists mainly of two large
buildings and two of the same sort of whitish-silver radomes that are
at Pine Gap. As is the case at Vadsø, Viksjøfjell, Pine Gap, and all
of the other similar installations around the world, the radomes at
Nurrungar are there to keep out dust, dirt, weather, and Soviet
spaceborne telescopic cameras (though one of Nurrungar's radomes
conceals a Hughes AN/MSC-46 Defense Satellite Communication
System [DSCS] antenna having a forty-foot Cassegrain dish with a
four-horn monopulse feed, the design for which dates from the
1960s and is generally available). The only other facility similar to

Nurrungar is at Buckley Air National Guard Base, not far from the large granite bunker in Cheyenne Mountain, just outside and above Colorado Springs, belonging to the North American Aerospace Defense Command (NORAD).

It is the mission of the aged DSP-647s that ring the earth around its equator to sound the alarm when they see enemy ballistic missiles heading toward the United States from land or sea. The warning would flash from the sentinels in space to Nurrungar and Buckley to NORAD to the National Command Authority in Washington. Provided the entire system works as it should (it is vulnerable to attack and glitches at several points), the alarm would reach Washington in from three to five minutes after the start of the attack (depending upon weather conditions, since DSP-647 does not see well through clouds). This would in no sense give the people of the United States time to seek shelter, but it would probably give the Air Force and Navy time to strike back. DSP-647 and its fragile support system are therefore an integral part of the nation's deterrent capability, as are the intelligence-gatherers—the reconnaissance platforms—that provide targeting data for the counterattack itself.

DSP-647 replaced MIDAS as the nation's ballistic missile early warning space program. As originally intended when the Defense Department issued requests for proposals in 1966, the satellite system was supposed to combine spaceborne missile launch detection, nuclear test detection, and a meteorological capability for use exclusively by the military. Following a design philosophy that called for cramming as many different mission capabilities as possible into one satellite system, Daniel J. Fink, the Defense Department's deputy director of strategic and space systems in the Directorate of Defense Research and Engineering, explained in late April of that year: "We have concluded that these functions are compatible and could be married into a single, newly proposed satellite. Consequently, during the past year we have reoriented each of these programs toward such a common goal." Superior sensors had been developed for the ballistic missile early warning system, Fink added, and "by incorporation of additional sensors other functions could also be performed simultaneously." He did not elaborate beyond mentioning nuclear test detection and weather observation.

By the end of 1966 the Air Force Space Systems Division, which had the responsibility of developing the MIDAS follow-on program, picked TRW and Aerojet-General to handle the project, which was variously known as Program 949, or Integrated Satellite, or Research Test Series 2. The Lockheed Missiles and Space Co., which had lost the competition for the contract, was in the meantime designing advanced versions of the CIA's Corona and the Air Force's SAMOS photo intelligence satellites as part of the Keyhole program. Initial total funding for Program 949 was $105 million for the first three satellites, though it was estimated that the program's cost would run as high as $600 million through the following five to seven years. As conceived in 1966, Program 949 satellites were to use five-hundred-mile-high polar orbits. This was soon changed to geosynchronous, however.

By March 1969 the Integrated Satellite (shortly to be renamed DSP-647) was unveiled by the Pentagon. It stood about twenty-three feet high and was nine feet wide. Its weight was understood to vary between 1,700 and 2,600 pounds, depending upon the contents of its sensor package. The top of the satellite was a squat cylinder covered with solar panels that would provide power to the sensors; extra power was to come from four small solar paddles that came out of the top of the cylinder. There was a monopropellant hydrazine thruster system with which the satellite would be kept where it was supposed to be and a separate hot gas-propelled motor system to keep it stabilized on all three of its axes and prevent tumbling. The spacecraft was also seen to have antennas for uplinked command and control signals and downlinked transmission of data to Nurrungar and Buckley. The sensors included a Vela-type nuclear radiation package, an attitude control mechanism, a sun sensor so the satellite could orient itself, ultraviolet sensors, and a television camera. The last was put on as a kind of double check against the spacecraft's main sensor, its large infrared telescope. Since sunlight bouncing off high-altitude clouds and other natural occurrences could be seen by the telescope and interpreted as an individual or multiple missile launch, a nuclear explosion, or even an attempt to blind it by laser, the simultaneous transmission of a television picture with the infrared imagery theoretically acts to prevent the sending of a potentially dangerous false alarm to NORAD.

The heart of DSP-647 is its infrared telescope, a hydrogen-cooled Schmidt-Cassegrain type measuring twelve feet in length and having an aperture of thirty-nine inches. The telescope, which is protected by a small sunshade, protrudes out of the bottom of the main

cylinder and points downward. Infrared radiation strikes the telescope's main mirror and reflects onto a detector array composed of
twenty-three hundred wafer-thin lead-sulfide cells that are kept cold
by the hydrogen. The pattern of infrared energy striking this mosaic
is registered in reasonable (but not fine) detail and transmitted to
earth.

The system's engineers also devised a clever way of extending the
telescope's field of view without changing its dimensions. They set
the telescope 7.5 degrees off the center of the satellite's vertical axis,
which means that it doesn't really point straight down, but is off at
a slight angle. Since DSP-647 rotates at between five and seven
revolutions a minute, its telescope's field of view is extended outward well beyond where it would be were it only pointed down.
Seven and a half degrees may not seem like much of an angle, but
it adds many thousands of square miles of coverage from an altitude
of 22,300 miles.

Three DSP-647s are in orbit at all times: one, called DSP East by
NORAD, is parked over the Indian Ocean; the other two, known
collectively as DSP West, are positioned over the Atlantic and the
Pacific. DSP East's primary job is to scan the Eurasian landmass, and
specifically the twenty-six Soviet ballistic missile complexes that are
strung out along a swath that roughly parallels the Trans-Siberian
Railroad. In addition, the spacecraft's nuclear detection sensors,
including particle detectors, electromagnetic pulse sensors, and
gamma-ray and X-ray measuring equipment, gather specific data on
Soviet underground tests and on French and Chinese detonations
above ground. Successive satellites on the DSP East station have also
detected ballistic missile multiple test launches, space launches, and
rocket research launches, according to Senate testimony. Meanwhile, both DSP West satellites watch for heat plumes coming from
the Atlantic, Pacific, and Gulf of Mexico that would indicate a
submarine-launched ballistic missile attack. Warning time would be
between five and fifteen minutes.

It is also very likely that some launches that are said to involve
DSP-647s have in fact been masks to cover Rhyolite and Chalet
operations. Desmond Ball, who has done extensive studies of U.S.
military satellite activity as it relates to his own country, Australia,
has suggested this as a real possibility after doing a little arithmetic.
". . . given that only three early warning satellites are in operation
at any given time, and that these have operational lifetimes of five
years, then no more than about a dozen satellites would have been

needed for this mission since the 647 program began, even allowing for several launch failures," Ball has noted. "The launch rate of just on two satellites per year is certainly excessive for the early warning mission alone. This suggests that perhaps half of the DSP satellites are dedicated to SIGINT and other 'special intelligence' missions."

In fact there were ten DSP-647 launches between 1971 and 1982, leaving somewhat more than twice that number in synchronous orbit and unaccounted for, at least officially. Three of the black launches—on June 10, 1978, October 1, 1979, and October 31, 1981 —were Chalets, while another was probably an Argus (the code name derives from AR, for Advanced Rhyolite). The remainder were Rhyolites, including spares—redundant platforms—that were supposed to perch near their operational sisters, waiting for the day when point failure or war would require their being brought to life.

9

Through the Keyhole

The National Reconnaissance Office, which officially does not exist, is headquartered in a guarded sanctum—4C-956—inside the Pentagon. The NRO's cover, according to a small sign on the outermost of its several doors, is that of the Office of Space Systems, which, in turn, reports to the under secretary of the Air Force for Space Systems.

The NRO's cover may be suitably ambiguous, but its mandate is explicit. It is responsible for the design, development, and procurement of all U.S. reconnaissance satellites and for their management once in orbit. The NRO does this with the largest budget of any intelligence organization—close to $5 billion in 1985—and from under a cloak of secrecy so pervasively tight that it is the blackest of all of the nation's covert intelligence-related operations.

Besides its headquarters in the Pentagon, the NRO maintains small offices elsewhere in the country from which its employees, mainly engineers trained in the astronautical sciences who also possess security clearances that are among the most stringent obtainable, work with reconnaissance systems' manufacturers, the NSA, the Navy, and the Air Force to develop new spy satellites, modify existing ones, and make certain that those already in orbit are doing what they are supposed to do.

There is an NRO presence at the Air Force's Satellite Control Facility at Sunnyvale, California, about an hour's drive south from

San Francisco. The SCF, or the Big Blue Cube, as it is sometimes called, is the place from which all U.S. military satellites are controlled. Some of those who do the controlling belong to the Air Force, and a few to the Navy. Most, however, are shirt-sleeved employees of the contractors that design and build the various and far-flung navigation, communication, meteorological, data-relay, and mapping satellites, as well as the whole family of reconnaissance and surveillance types, that maintain U.S. military presence in space. The civilians who operate and closely monitor the reconnaissance and surveillance spacecraft come from the chief systems contractors, mainly Lockheed and TRW, as well as from the various subcontractors that provide the satellites' propulsion and maneuvering engines, imaging and SIGINT hardware, antennas and other communication equipment, and the all-important navigation and attitude control systems.*

The Air Force's Special Projects Office at El Segundo, California, is technically subsidiary to that service's Space Division, also located at El Segundo. In fact Special Projects is an NRO field office whose engineers work closely with the satellites' contractors and subcontractors on the design level, as well as with the Aerospace Corporation, which is located nearby and serves as a think tank for military space projects, including reconnaissance and surveillance. The Special Projects Office may come under the USAF Space Division on organization charts, but it reports directly to 4C-956. The people in the NRO tell El Segundo what is required by way of new reconnaissance systems and the updating of existing ones; it is El Segundo's job to make certain that the requirements are met by the contractors and to report back.

When the Air Force Space Command's Consolidated Space Operations Center (CSOC, pronounced See-sock), near Colorado Springs, becomes fully operational around 1992 as expected, the NRO will be there, if only as an occasional visitor. Since Sunnyvale's Big Blue Cube not only stands above a fault that is considered to be ripe for a major earthquake, but is also within bazooka

---

*The operation of attitude control systems, which keep satellites stabilized and pointing where they are supposed to point, is often critically important. As one engineer has said, "Satellites are dumb. If you don't keep telling them exactly where to be and what to do, they soon tend to wander off, or begin to tumble, or point where you don't want them to point." In this regard, those who control low-flying reconnaissance satellites occasionally become almost frantic because of the number of precise and highly integrated maneuvers and other operations that must be done quickly and with consummate care during a photographic pass, computers notwithstanding.

and other weapons' range of a busy thoroughfare, CSOC has been designed as a second satellite control facility. It will take over the operation of several military satellites that are unrelated to reconnaissance but have the capability of controlling the TECHINT assets as well, should that suddenly become necessary.

Finally, the NRO has direct ties to the CIA's Directorate of Science and Technology (DS&T), its Office of SIGINT Operations (OSO), the Navy Space Project office, and the National Security Agency, all of which either send it reconnaissance satellite technical requirements—what is needed to get particular kinds of intelligence, as is the case with the NSA—or contribute ideas for improving technical collection systems, which is part of what the DS&T does, for example.

The NRO's budget, which is for the most part buried in Air Force expenditures and to a lesser extent into Navy and CIA programs, is immense even by Pentagon standards. Of a total national intelligence budget estimated to be about $200 billion for the decade of the 1980s, upward of 15 percent, or $30.8 billion, has been spent or is earmarked for the NRO/Air Force alone. And that does not include another $2.9 billion spent exclusively by the CIA for research, development, testing, and evaluation of new reconnaissance systems as part of its contribution to the NRO, and another $1.8 billion that will have been spent by the Navy Space Project on its White Cloud ocean reconnaissance satellite system, another National Reconnaissance Office enterprise. And the NRO's budget fails to include some $1.5 billion that will have been spent by the National Security Agency on its own space-related SIGINT operations, which, while also hidden in the Pentagon's budget, are not part of NRO expenditures.

A close reading of federal government budgetary items bearing the program element number 34111, which relates to NRO research, development, testing, evaluation, procurement, operations, and management, plus careful scrutiny of closely associated activities, shows that between 1980 and 1989 the NRO/Air Force alone will have spent about $14.8 billion on procurement (mostly on satellites and the boosters on which they ride to orbit), and close to $11 billion more on research and development. The total tab for technical intelligence collection in the decade of the 1980s is impossible to come by with accuracy, but most informed observers put the figure at close to $50 billion. Allowing for inflation, that is almost twice what it cost to land men on the moon.

It is that last item, research and development, that draws the most criticism from those who are acquainted with NRO operations and are able to discuss it. They contend for the most part that the office's secret budget amounts to a carte blanche for wild engineering schemes that not only are expensive in their own right but also drive up the cost of the finished hardware because many development costs are passed along when the spacecraft and their boosters come off the block. They charge that the NRO's excessive secrecy prevents proper monitoring and encourages some dubious projects that can be pursued at almost any cost with the knowledge that mistakes will be concealed from Congress by the large black security blanket. The NRO is "mission-oriented," according to one source, which means that "results are all that count, not the cost." The critics charge that systems contractors have a habit, not unknown elsewhere in the defense industry, of bidding low and then slapping add-ons to the cost of a given program because of unforeseen problems. They have a tendency, in the words of one insider, "to promise technology that is not available" so that after a contract has been awarded, "crash programs" can be started that raise costs considerably. John Pike, a defense analyst with the Federation of American Scientists in Washington, has called the space reconnaissance research and development program a "playpen for engineers."

Those who take a more charitable view of the enterprise maintain that, as is the case in other areas of science and technology, it is nearly impossible to predict with accuracy how much it is going to cost to probe into unknown environs. "We were operating at the frontiers of technology," said one former high-ranking NRO official as he looked back on the development of some extraordinarily advanced systems, "and no one really knew how much things would cost when we started."

The NRO itself started on August 25, 1960. It was created in an effort to focus what until then was a technologically fragmented and administratively muddled collection system that was evolving erratically and against a background of internecine warfare not only inside the Air Force over appropriations that were also wanted by the fighter and bomber generals but also, far more important, between the Air Force and the Central Intelligence Agency.

It is easy to blame the competition for funding as the cause of the battle for control of space reconnaissance between the Air Force's "blue-suiters" and their tweedy rivals in the CIA, but that misses the point. The money was only a means to an end.

The end itself was to be found not on federal accountants' methodically constructed balance sheets but in the vast, unfathomable reaches of the human psyche. The contest was over that part-physical, part-psychological wellspring of power that the heavy-hitters who came to the fray from important positions in the Air Force and the CIA, or who were recruited from the pinnacles of industry and the legal profession, called "turf." The players in that game—and to a significant extent that is exactly what it was—competed for control of the nation's sensory system because that was where the power lay. And as any number of participants and close observers have explained in interviews, not only did the drive to capture and hold the reconnaissance turf have to do with the acquisition of power as an instrument to affect decision-making on the highest levels of government or at best, to serve the targeting, technical intelligence or arms control constituencies, but it also seems to have been pursued in some instances simply because it was there. A few of the combatants seem to have defined themselves according to whether they could wrest and hold power for its own sake, irrespective of any goal to which it could be addressed.

Throughout 1959 and well into 1960, the Corona and SAMOS programs, championed by the CIA and the Air Force, respectively, had competed not only for funding but for the honor of becoming America's preeminent reconnaissance system in the new, wide-open realm of space. It was by then widely accepted that earth satellites were to be the glamorous centerpiece of the national technical collection system.

But having been forced to share space with NASA when the purportedly civilian space agency was formed in 1958, the Air Force then faced the specter of yet another civilian agency trying to muscle into what it took to be its just domain. The airmen, who had been bruised by the CIA in the acquisition of the first U-2s, remained "contemptuous" of the agency (according to Dr. James R. Killian, whose chairmanship of the TCP and role as Eisenhower's science adviser had provided him with a front-row seat) and were loath to see that happen. The generals therefore prepared during the spring of 1960 to protect SAMOS, whatever its faults, from the CIA at all costs. And as if the feud over space reconnaissance had not created

enough turbulence, the pathetically bungled response to the downing of Powers's U-2 on May 1 further dramatized the need for a
tightly coordinated strategic reconnaissance program.

Eisenhower had been mindful of this. And he also recalled quite
clearly that it was the Air Force that had invented the bomber gap
and, following that, a missile gap that he was convinced did not exist
but which at the moment was causing him serious political problems
and in the process contributing to his growing angst where the
Pentagon was concerned. The missile gap was another problem, he
doubtless reflected ruefully, that would not have happened were it
not for the exuberant imagination of senior officers in Air Force
intelligence and a seemingly insatiable craving for funding and
power by their superiors in SAC and on the Air Staff.

Exasperated, Eisenhower had ordered Thomas S. Gates, Jr., his
secretary of defense, to have the SAMOS program evaluated and to
report the results to the National Security Council. Gates in turn
had appointed a panel consisting of Dr. Joseph Charyk, the under
secretary of the Air Force; John H. Rubel, the deputy director of
the Defense Department's Directorate of Research and Engineering; and Dr. George B. Kistiakowsky, the Harvard chemist and Los
Alamos veteran who had succeeded Killian as Eisenhower's science
adviser. The most obvious target for the SAMOS panel's scrutiny
was the Air Force's Directorate for Advanced Technology, which
coordinated satellite development for the chief of staff of the Air
Force. What quickly became clear to the panel, however, was that
the tangled space reconnaissance situation was a managerial, not a
hardware, problem. And the remedy was just as apparent: Create an
organization that would oversee the development of space reconnaissance systems after independently identifying whatever tasks
needed to be accomplished and matching them with technologically
feasible solutions. This was to amount to a thorough administrative
shake-up. The airmen had understood that. They had also understood that the president didn't seem to trust them very much. They
therefore had reacted to the SAMOS panel's ruminations with a
degree of alarm that even transcended the immediate threat to their
pet satellite.

"The notable event of the day," Kistiakowsky penned in his diary
on August 3, 1960, "was a series of phone calls from such as Charyk
and [Ivan] Getting [president of the Aerospace Corporation], the
result of a rumor spreading in the Pentagon concerning the supposed recommendation of our SAMOS panel to transfer its manage-

ment to the CIA. I assured everybody of my innocence," Kistiakowsky added, "but urged Charyk that the organization *should have a clear line of authority and that on the top level the direction be of national character* [italics added], including OSD [Office of the Secretary of Defense] and CIA and not the Air Force alone. Quite obviously the Air Force is trying to freeze the organization so as to make a change more difficult by the time the NSC is briefed."

The National Security Council, with Eisenhower in attendance, was duly briefed between eight-thirty and nine-thirty on the morning of August 25, 1960, just six days after the CIA's Discoverer 14 became the first satellite to have its film capsule snatched in midair. The SAMOS panel's recommendations, as amended by Allen Dulles and perhaps a few others, formed the basis for the creation of the National Reconnaissance Office. For his part, Eisenhower approved the panel's suggestions on the spot. Although the minutes of that meeting are still classified, the essence of the recommendations provided for civilian leadership of the new organization, as well as a set of carefully delineated responsibilities.

Under the system that was put in place during that summer of 1960, the Air Force was given responsibility for launching and controlling the satellites and for recovering capsules ejected out of orbit by the Discoverers and their descendants. This seemed entirely appropriate because the Air Force owned the rockets and associated hardware necessary to perform such tasks and no one dreamed of changing that. But the CIA was theoretically the nation's paramount intelligence-gathering organization (and its leader was nominally in charge of all foreign intelligence collection), so it was given responsibility to develop the satellites themselves, including the various sensors that were to go into them. As would soon become apparent, however, the Air Force was to continue doggedly pursuing its own ideas for reconnaissance satellites, presidential directives notwithstanding.

The composition of the NRO's leadership had been another knotty problem. The distrust that Ike felt toward some of his former comrades-in-arms and the SAMOS panel members' suspicion of them led to a recommendation that the director of the NRO come from the CIA. That having been decided, it quickly became apparent that there was no one better qualified for the job than Richard Bissell, whose management of the recently terminated U-2 operation over the Soviet Union had earned him a reputation at Langley that bordered on the heroic. But the former economics professor from Yale was not convinced that the NRO would prove to be what its adherents hoped. "It seemed like one of those bureaucratic solutions that look awfully tidy and nice on paper, but in fact can easily confuse things," he recalled years later. Nonetheless, when Charyk, acting in his capacity as a member of the SAMOS panel, suggested to Bissell that he become the first director of the National Reconnaissance Office, the CIA's deputy director for plans agreed to take on the job.

But Allen Dulles's political instincts told him that such an arrangement would be a dangerous one and he therefore would have none of it. "Allen did not approve of the sort of situation in which a CIA individual is in line of command over people that work in the Pentagon," Bissell explained. This was because it was clear to Dulles that any CIA man who directed the NRO would be a potential scapegoat for the Defense Department in the event of some serious foul-up. And given the U-2 calamity four months earlier, such a notion was hardly farfetched. It is not difficult to imagine Dulles looking ahead to the day when some secretary of defense would explain to the president and the assembled members of the National Security Council that such and such a space reconnaissance mishap had occurred because his people had been following the orders of a CIA administrator.

As a result of Dulles's decision, which apparently was implacable, it was decided that the head of the NRO should be the under secretary of the Air Force and that the organization's second in command would come from the agency. Since the under secretary is an appointed civilian, this meant that there would be no military officer in the NRO's top echelon. There was no way, however, to ensure that the under secretary would not be just as vociferous an exponent of the imperatives of Air Force domination as a blue-suiter. And that was to prove to be the case in at least one instance.

Charyk himself became the first director of the NRO. Both Bissell and the late Herbert ("Pete") Scoville, Jr., have praised Charyk for the cooperative and congenial way in which he ran the organization. They have independently cited Charyk's tenure as proving that a harmonious working relationship can exist between the CIA and the Air Force, at least at the NRO level. But it was not to last.

Charyk was replaced as under secretary of the Air Force by Brockway McMillan, a Bell Telephone Laboratories executive who had served with Scoville on the defense committee of Killian's Technological Capabilities Panel back in 1955. At about the time

McMillan was appointed to his new position, John McCone, who had succeeded Dulles, decided to enhance the agency's space reconnaissance research and development program relative to Air Force activity in that area. In order to do this, McCone created a Directorate of Science and Technology and hired a young scientist named Albert ("Bud") Wheelon to head it. McMillan had meanwhile become determined to break the agency's hold on the design and procurement of reconnaissance systems through the NRO and, apparently, to wrest management of strategic reconnaissance away from the CIA in the process. This put McMillan and Wheelon on a collision course that soon developed into a series of battles over turf that were so vituperative that they are still talked about by old hands who were involved in the agency's technical collection operations.

"Bud Wheelon, essentially, was battling to maintain the agency's influence in the reconnaissance programs," said Bissell, who had departed well before McMillan's and Wheelon's arrival, but who had kept abreast of all the dirt, "and also to have the agency designated by the NRO as the procurement agency for a lot of the payloads. The Air Force was battling for the exact opposite. They wanted to do as much as possible of the procurement and have as much influence as possible on the technical decisions and operational matters. And that was really the essence of Bud's continuing battles. What kind of programs will receive what kind of funding? Who will be the procurement agency for this or that?" Bissell recalled, edging each word with mock weariness to emphasize how bitter and protracted the conflict was. "And they went on, and on, and on. . . ."

At bottom, the political dimension of space reconnaissance as it began to evolve at the outset had to do with a finite system that had to serve many masters. The sort of clashes described by George Keegan, Richard Bissell, Herbert Scoville, Jr., and others resulted from competition for control of a precious resource by several voracious constituencies, all of which depended upon it not only to take the measure of their foreign opponents, but to help grease the budget wheels at home at the same time. The way technical intelligence is collected—which satellites are built and in what numbers, for instance—and which targets are covered to the exclusion of others, can have profound effects on a military service or a civilian agency, not to mention national security as a whole.

The Navy, to take one example, is acutely interested in what its Soviet counterparts are doing. The State Department, to take another, must know whether arms control agreements are being violated. The intelligence requirements of both can overlap, as would happen in the event that the Soviet Union tested a nuclear weapon underwater. The Navy would want the data in order to be able to find ways to protect its ships from similar weapons or to be able to build its own so that it could respond to an attack in kind. The State Department would be more concerned about knowing whether the Limited Test Ban Treaty had been contravened. The same piece of technical intelligence, assembled in adequate detail, could therefore benefit both constituencies; intelligence is shared for precisely that reason. But the Navy's primary responsibility lies in controlling the seas, not in policing arms control agreements, while Foggy Bottom is charged with maintaining the nation's international political integrity, not with ensuring military supremacy on the high seas (or under them).

Differing responsibilities often require different kinds of technical intelligence. And that, particularly during times when the budget has been trimmed, can stimulate competition, especially over tasking: which targets are given priority for coverage by the snooping spacecraft.

For its part, the Air Force's reconnaissance requirement had to do mainly with targeting for its Strategic Air Command: with finding targets to attack, assessing how best to destroy them, and finding ways to overcome enemy air defenses, including the radars that were supposed to guide defending fighters and missiles to SAC's bombers. By 1963, when "Brock" McMillan became under secretary of the Air Force, SAC's mission planners and targeteers were beginning to experience an intelligence bonanza. Satellites were returning imagery and radar intelligence that no U-2 could have gotten. The Strategic Library Bombing Index grew thick and target folders began to bulge with nice, clear photographs of fighter and bomber bases, port facilities, ballistic missile complexes, railroad hubs, important bridges, dams, generating stations, nuclear fuel reprocessing plants, weapons factories, SAM batteries, vehicle and aircraft assembly plants, and every population center deemed to be worth attacking.

"The early thrust [by the Strategic Air Command] was for mass coverage," according to one highly knowledgeable former technical intelligence official. "The targeteers drove it [satellite reconnaissance]. They wanted to map all of the Soviet Union to use as potential targets. Their greatest interest was also in revisiting [reconnaissance targets] to look for changes and for the totality of what could be covered." "Revisiting" was always a problem. Nothing remained static where intelligence was concerned, so taking the pictures and ferreting the radar once were seldom considered to be enough. It was the search for change, not merely discovering new points of interest, that fueled strategic reconnaissance, since what was photographed last month could have changed last week and what was photographed last week might have changed overnight. Old intelligence was useless, but you never knew whether it was old or not until you rephotographed it. SAC never had enough photographs. The targeteers always wanted more.

The CIA, however, had its own agenda. It saw as its main mission the collection of technical intelligence: the relatively arcane stuff that, measured precisely and fitted into a large mosaic, would little by little cause a picture to materialize that represented the portrait of the opposition as depicted in the National Intelligence Estimate. The agency wanted to know, for example, how much uranium the Russians were refining and how much more they could refine if they cared to do so. Such information was hardly so dramatic as the imagery SAC used to draw a bead on an entire Soviet ballistic missile complex or on Kiev, but it and supplementary intelligence served the useful purpose of helping the analysts at Langley make educated guesses at how many nuclear weapons the Kremlin was ordering turned out each year.

Tasking, then, was immensely important and was a continuing source of conflict because of all the demands placed on a relatively small and fragile space reconnaissance program. "Everyone had to wait in line with his request," as General Keegan has put it, so it was only natural that people grew increasingly testy as the line lengthened or, worse, when they were sent back to the end of it because a competitor had been given a higher priority. Who, exactly, was to say that calculating Soviet nuclear warhead production was more important than updating the target data on the SS-11 complex southwest of Komsomolsk? Such questions have been taken with the utmost seriousness since the U.S. space reconnaissance program began in 1960 because it was understood at the start that if left unresolved, they would fuel a level of animosity that could be dangerously disruptive, and probably even counterproductive, in terms of the objectives of technical intelligence collection.

. . .

While the NRO was invented to manage the development of space reconnaissance systems and control them while in use (including, but not exclusively, the satellites themselves),* it became clear at the outset that a separate bureaucracy would have to be created to resolve these questions, among others: What installations or areas ought to be covered by space reconnaissance? Which systems should be used for such tasking? What should the frequency of coverage be? Who should process the imagery or SIGINT and who should have access to it? (Regarding the last, General Keegan has pointed out, correctly, that however good the technical collection may be, it has to be seen or heard to be of use; control of access to the material is therefore also a source of considerable power.)

The bureaucracy that has evolved over a quarter of a century to try to resolve these questions is a formidably complicated affair having a number of interrelated organizational "boxes" that are inhabited by the intelligence establishment's true decision-makers, in addition to several dark corners that are so remote or ambiguously named that it is difficult to understand exactly what happens in them or how whatever happens helps anything. What follows, however, is a simplified description of the core apparatus.

All basic decisions having to do with satellite reconnaissance are made by four bodies: the National Foreign Intelligence Board (NFIB), two of its thirteen committees, and the National Reconnaissance Executive Committee (NREC).

The NFIB, which succeeded the United States Intelligence Board (USIB) in 1976, is the nation's top interagency intelligence organization. Like the USIB (which itself was formed in 1958), the National Foreign Intelligence Board meets once a week so that representatives of its component agencies can exchange information, set a common course for specific intelligence priorities, and pass on the national intelligence estimates that are sent to the National Security Council and, therefore, to the president.

The director of Central Intelligence chairs the NFIB. Its members are the directors of the National Reconnaissance Office, the National Security Agency, the State Department's Bureau of Intel-

*Satellite systems include not only the spacecraft but the worldwide tracking, guidance, communications, and data-acquisition networks that are necessary to keep the satellites functioning and productive. NRO representatives therefore are present at operational ground facilities in the United States as well as at sites such as Pine Gap.

ligence and Research (INR), and representatives of the CIA (the director of the CIA chairs the group in his capacity as director of Central Intelligence, so his deputy represents the agency), the FBI, and the departments of energy and the treasury. In addition, the assistant chiefs of staff for the intelligence branches of the Army, Navy, and Air Force sit in.

Like the old USIB, the NFIB works through its committees to list targets for U.S. intelligence and prioritize them, coordinate estimates of enemy strength and coming military and political events, control the classification and security system for most of the U.S. government, decide what classified information will be passed on to allies, and direct research in the various fields of technical intelligence (which is one of the main reasons for NRO representation on the board).

The listing of targets for space reconnaissance and their prioritization is handled by two of the NFIB's committees: COMIREX and the SIGINT Committee.

COMIREX, the Committee on Imagery Requirements and Exploitation, succeeded the Committee on Overhead Reconnaissance (COMOR) in July 1967. To it (and specifically to its Imagery Collection Requirements Subcommittee) falls the job of drawing together the general imagery collection requirements and the tasking of specific systems to accomplish the objectives. COMIREX, in other words, decides on the order of tasking and on the most appropriate (and most readily available) reconnaissance satellite to carry out the mission. Its members represent the same organizations that sit on the NFIB and, in addition, include the Army's assistant chief of staff for intelligence, the director of naval intelligence, and the Air Force's assistant chief of staff, intelligence. It is here, among these people, that the competing imagery requirements of the respective agencies and intelligence organizations are thrashed out. Having decided that it wants photographs of a Soviet aircraft carrier being built on the Black Sea, for example, the Office of Naval Intelligence instructs its representative on COMIREX to put forward a request for the necessary satellite coverage. It is then collectively decided by negotiation, and based for the most part on urgency, as to when the pictures will be taken relative to a request by, say, the Air Force for imagery of a new Soviet fighter. The "exploitation" part of COMIREX's name means that it is also responsible for the processing and distribution of the collected product, which also is decided by the full committee, just to keep things as honest as possible. Signals intelligence is handled in much the same way by the SIGINT Committee. Recommendations are sent to the NFIB for approval and, that done, on to the NRO for execution.

The fourth and final organization is one that exercises executive control over the NRO itself. The National Reconnaissance Executive Committee (NREC) was created in 1965 as the direct result of five years of almost incessant feuding between the Air Force and the CIA over control of the National Reconnaissance Office (irrespective of the Eisenhower administration's effort to make peace between them while establishing a line of responsibility favoring the CIA). The Air Force, ever in pursuit of the kind of tactical intelligence that would provide targeting data and information on its opponent's fighters, bombers, and missiles, simply could not reconcile itself to abandoning satellite research and development to the CIA, which had other priorities and which, the airmen feared, would therefore place its own interests first. As mentioned, John McCone took a keen interest in overhead reconnaissance (most likely because he had been impressed with it during the Cuban missile crisis), and therefore decided to reinforce his agency's capability in that area. This led to all-out tribal warfare from 1963 to 1965.

The NREC, like the National Foreign Intelligence Board, is chaired by the director of Central Intelligence, who reports directly to the secretary of defense. In addition to a representative of the Defense Department, the president's national security adviser also sits on the committee, thereby adding a modicum of impartiality to the group. If the DCI objects to a decision by the secretary of defense, he may take his argument directly to the White House, as apparently happened in 1975, when James Schlesinger overruled CIA Director William Colby's request for the advanced Rhyolite SIGINT satellite (Argus). Colby appealed to President Gerald Ford, who in turn asked the National Security Council to look into the matter. Ford eventually sided with Colby.

Given the highly secret nature of these organizations—all of them require SCI clearances on an extremely high order—it is nearly impossible to judge from the record how effectively they are managing the national overhead reconnaissance program. One highly knowledgeable source has said that the wars have subsided in recent years, partly because the competing factions have grown more used to working with each other, and partly because their ranks have increasingly been filled with a kind of professional reconnaissance specialist who is better able to understand his counterparts in the other intelligence organizations than did his more parochial predecessors. In addition, the highest echelons of the National Reconnaissance Office itself have come to be staffed more and more by professionals who have made their careers in it and who therefore tend to be loyal to the organization, rather than to either the CIA or the military intelligence services.

Meanwhile, increasing numbers of the NRO's satellites began lifting off Lockheed and TRW drawing boards and heading for space in the mid-sixties. The second generation of imaging satellites—the lineal successors to Discoverer and SAMOS—had first orbited in 1963 under the then new code name Keyhole, or simply KH, a catchall covering all spaceborne image collectors (aircraft such as U-2s and SR-71s bear the generic code name Talent; Talent-Keyhole therefore covers all overhead imaging platforms).

After two failures (on February 28 and March 18, 1963), the first super-SAMOS, designated KH-5, had successfully orbited on May 18. Its first stage had been a Thor IRBM with three solid-propellant rockets, each developing fifty thousand pounds of thrust, strapped to its sides. The booster therefore was called a Thrust-Augmented Thor, or TAT, in the new missile jargon. The combination of liquid-powered main stage and three thrust-augmenters allowed the Thor to lift a little more than a ton of payload into orbit, or about twice that of the old, unaugmented Thor-Agena. And the Agena had changed, too. The Agena-D, unveiled by Lockheed in the summer of 1962, had had an engine that itself featured three important improvements: it burned longer than its predecessor, it was more powerful, and it could be turned off and restarted in orbit. The extra power meant that the payload's weight could be increased and that a maximum amount of fuel for maneuvering could be carried. The restart capability was important because it would help to extend the satellite's life a bit by allowing it to be lowered for enhanced resolution during an imaging pass, then raised to reduce atmospheric friction as it headed toward its apogee.*

The KH-5, the super-SAMOS, thereby became the first maneuverable reconnaissance spacecraft and the second in a series of so-

---

*Maneuvering in orbit was not, and still is not, done routinely, however, since such changes risk malfunction. Maneuvering a KH-11 to increase coverage of the Iran-Iraq war in 1980 reportedly caused partial point failure.

called area-surveillance types that were supposed to use their low-resolution videcon cameras and radio-link transmitters to send back broad panoramas of denied territory. The data bank, which at the time was growing by the month, would then reveal changes that might warrant more careful scrutiny by the so-called close-look successors to Discoverer. It is important to note, however, that the KH-5 was an Air Force satellite program. Its very existence as such provides the clearest possible indication that during the early 1960s the Air Force had indeed decided that it was not about to be relegated to a bus-driver role for CIA-developed satellites, NRO or no NRO.

A total of forty-six KH-5s were orbited between that first failure in February 1963 and March 30, 1967 (four of fifty attempts were failures). The mean lifetime of the KH-5s was twenty-three days, though some never came close to that, suggesting that they suffered point failure soon after going into orbit. Occasionally one KH-5 was sent up while a predecessor was still in orbit, indicating that the first had developed an imaging or other kind of problem and had to be backed up because of the importance of the intelligence that was being collected. The average inclination of the KH-5 series was 78.7 degrees, while the average perigee and apogee were 114 and 243 miles, respectively. Operations at Vandenberg and Sunnyvale had become so smooth by 1964 that the radio-transmitting KH-5s were being fired into orbit on area-surveillance missions at a rate averaging one a month.

The successors to the Discoverers in the CIA's Corona program were called KH-6s. They too were basically Lockheed Agena-Ds with specialized noses. Unlike the KH-5s, however, they were launched on top of unaugmented Atlas boosters. This was possible because, being close-look platforms like their progenitors, they required lower orbits and therefore less rocket thrust than the higher-flying KH-5s. The average perigee for the KH-6 series, in fact, was only 93.2 miles; in one notable instance, the launch of July 6, 1964, the KH-6's lowest orbital point was but 76 miles. Although such low orbits got them nice and close to their targets and produced photographs of excellent quality, the laws of atmospheric physics extracted a price: the average lifetime of a KH-6 was only 5.3 days because of the searing heat they encountered at such low altitudes. There were thirty-eight KH-6 launches between July 12, 1963, and June 4, 1967, resulting in thirty-six successful attempts to reach orbit. The KH-6s' ground tracks ranged from 90 degrees, or right over the poles, to 110 degrees.

That second generation of imaging satellites, the Air Force's KH-5s and the Central Intelligence Agency's KH-6s, proved the compatibility of using area-surveillance techniques in conjunction with close-look operations in the absence of a single satellite that could handle both missions. The KH-5s would customarily survey vast stretches of the U.S.S.R., Communist China, and elsewhere, and return low-resolution imagery that was put to use for the mapping of SAC's target routes, establishing the targets themselves, and for counting aircraft, ships, tanks, and other pieces of military hardware that would go into the preparation of the United States Intelligence Board's national intelligence estimates.

But KH-5 imagery would frequently reveal something that was considered important enough to warrant sending up a KH-6 for a closer look. The KH-6s used long focal-length lenses in combination with low-level passes to produce standard stereoscopic photographs of such resolution that objects measuring a foot, or the size of a carton of cigarettes, could be discerned. The KH-6s, like the Discoverers before them, ejected their film capsules northwest of Hawaii, where they were routinely snatched in midair by JC-130Bs for return to Honolulu and then to the National Photographic Interpretation Center in Washington for processing and distribution. By the end of 1963, KH-6s had provided the first clear evidence that the Russians were building silos for their SS-7 and SS-8 ICBMs and were starting construction of ballistic-missile-firing submarines. The tracking stations in Turkey, Iran, and Pakistan, the telemetry interception from land, in the air, and in space, and the imagery returned by the Keyhole satellites told the National Command Authority that the new SS-7s and SS-8s could carry five-megaton warheads more than sixty-five hundred miles. The warheads were not very accurate, but their great size and weight meant they could make a hell of an explosion. And the missile-packing subs would add a new dimension to the threat faced by the United States in the 1970s and beyond because they would be able to position their lethal cargoes off American coasts, thereby increasing the number of targets, improving accuracy in some instances, and cutting warning time by more than 50 percent. This was intelligence of the most profound kind, and it was unobtainable any other way.

. . .

The imagery coming out of the Keyhole program went to the National Photographic Interpretation Center (NPIC), which looked then, as it does today, like a bricked-in warehouse that stands at the corner of M and First streets in the southeast quadrant of the District of Columbia. Federal Building 213, as it is also called, is just eight blocks down New Jersey Avenue from the Capitol. But the neighborhood, which is adjacent to the old Washington Navy Yard on the banks of the Anacostia River, was so dilapidated and forlorn that few tourists ever ventured near it. That, of course, was precisely the idea.

NPIC had come into existence in 1961, partly to reduce the confusion, duplication, and attendant waste that resulted from totally independent imagery analysis during the reconnaissance wars, and partly because it was considered unhealthy, if not dangerous, for the military (or the CIA) to provide sole analysis of the intelligence it collected. In another context, Ray Cline, the CIA's deputy director for intelligence in 1962, has explained that a "cardinal rule" of sound intelligence organization prohibits the same unit from conducting intelligence operations and then having the right of exclusive evaluation of the results. Not only can errors go uncaught and even be compounded in such an incestuous relationship but, worse, the temptation to reach self-serving conclusions can become irresistible.

Until the creation of NPIC, military intelligence and the CIA had pretty much gone their own ways where film processing and interpretation were concerned. The agency started a Photographic Intelligence Division in 1953 with about twenty photo interpreters headed by Arthur Lundahl, who had been in naval intelligence during World War II and immediately afterward, and whom Cline has called "one of the authentic heroes of post–World War II intelligence technology." Lundahl built the CIA's Photographic Intelligence Division to the point where it employed twelve hundred people who worked at the continual refinement of interpretation technique even as improvements in cameras, films, planes, and satellites were being made. It was Lundahl's interpreters at NPIC who found the missiles in Cuba in 1962.

NPIC was the direct result of one of forty-eight recommendations for centralizing and refining the collection, processing, and interpretation of raw intelligence that had been made by the special

Joint Study Group in 1960, during the height of Eisenhower's unhappiness with the armed services. The group, which represented the Bureau of the Budget, the National Security Council, the State and Defense departments, and the CIA, came to the conclusion that the military exerted excessive influence in strategic intelligence. It called for, among other curatives, the creation of an organization of common concern that would be responsible for processing and interpreting imagery for the whole intelligence community. NPIC was the result. Following what was then becoming common practice, the leadership of the new organization was divided between civilians and the military; its head would come from the CIA and the second in command from the Defense Intelligence Agency (DIA). Processors and interpreters came from both agencies but did not work side by side. Sections in the six-story building, most of the windows of which were bricked in to enhance darkness and shut out unwanted observation, were divided into those used by the CIA and those where DIA interpreters worked. Each agency, in turn, had its own areas of specialization where the interpreters, most of whom were retreaded engineers, scrutinized pictures of nuclear reactors, dams, bombers, bomb shelters, and so forth in an effort to extract useful information from them.

After the imagery had been given a general analysis by an interpreter, he or she filled out a short standard form, reporting on what had been seen. "I have processed this photograph this day," the interpreter would note, briefly describing each photograph in the set. "In this photograph of Chongjin, North Korea, with a resolution of one foot and no cloud cover, I see the following. . . . I have discovered what appears to be the construction of a major road between the city and the reservoir. . . ."

The original negative, called the first-generation negative, and a second-generation duplicate would be kept by NPIC. First-generation negatives—the ones that come out of the aircraft and satellites —were meticulously treated and carefully stored at NPIC because they might eventually be needed for what Amrom Katz, one of the fathers of U.S. photoreconnaissance, has called "a high order of business." Comparing old and new photographs to see whether a mobile IRBM had been moved into a certain area would constitute such business. Negatives leaving NPIC risked being scratched or damaged in other ways, which would have unnecessarily complicated an already painstaking job; a scratch on a nine-by-nine negative made from a hundred miles away not only takes on the dimensions of a road but can totally obliterate important objects that cost a great deal of time and money to photograph.

Duplicate negatives and, later, computer-generated imagery would then be forwarded to a so-called second echelon, together with the interpreter's brief report. This would ordinarily mean routing them to a major intelligence command, such as SAC's 544th Strategic Intelligence Wing at Offutt Air Force Base, or to the CIA or DIA themselves. In the case of SAC, photographic intelligence would go from the intelligence wing to the 544th Intelligence Exploitation Squadron, which would analyze the imagery in greater detail, then to the 544th Intelligence Analysis Squadron, which would further analyze and then integrate it with previous imagery and, if it pertained to targets, update the relevant target file. The pictures would then most likely end up at the 544th Trajectory Division, which was (and remains) responsible for calculating the routes that SAC's long-range missiles would have to take to reach their targets.

The third and final echelon was in the field, at Air Force reconnaissance and technical support squadrons, fleet intelligence centers, and major Army command headquarters around the world, where the photos would be checked and filed for use if that became necessary.

Today, Federal Building 213 is painted a studiously inconspicuous shade of beige and is enclosed by a Cyclone fence topped with a double row of barbed wire. The building's two gate entrances, on M and First streets, are guarded by employees of the civilian Federal Protection Service. Except for the blue-and-white sign—National Photographic Interpretation Center—that spans the length of the main entrance and the massive air-conditioning system on the side of the solid-looking structure, Federal Building 213 might indeed look like some government warehouse. The air conditioners together are nearly eighty feet long and almost as high as the building itself. They are used to cool the supercomputers inside NPIC that continuously scan the stream of incoming imagery and store the billions of bits of information that go into the data base for comparison with fresh intelligence. The torrent of digital imagery that began coming into Building 213, starting in January 1977 with the advent of a new satellite called the KH-11, would have been unmanageable without the monster computers and their huge data banks.

The interpretation of imagery went through a revolution in the 1970s that was no less profound than that of the space-based intelligence collectors themselves. Photo interpreters who had used their eyes almost exclusively to examine the size and shape of objects, the patterns made by those objects and others near them, as well as the shadows, tones, and shades of light, were supplemented by high-speed digital computers that took the analysis of imagery—what, exactly, was in the pictures—far beyond mere "eyeballing."

By the end of the decade the computers inside Building 213 and elsewhere were routinely being used to correct for distortions made by the satellites' imaging sensors and by atmospheric effects, sharpen out-of-focus images, build multicolored single images out of several pictures taken in different spectral bands to make certain patterns more obvious, change the amount of contrast between the objects under scrutiny and their backgrounds, extract particular features while diminishing or eliminating their backgrounds altogether, enhance shadows, suppress glint from reflections of the sun, and a great deal more. Radar and infrared imaging used in conjunction with the digital computers would allow objects only partially seen through cloud cover or haze to be reconstructed, and even some targets underground could be defined and highlighted.

The computers on the other side of the wall from the giant air conditioners would be able to take several images of the same scene that had been shot from slightly different angles and build them into three-dimensional images of extraordinary depth and clarity; bridges spanning the Volga, the smokestacks of Sverdlovsk, and SS-19s being readied for tests at Tyuratam would pop out at the viewer almost as though he or she were suspended right over them. Moreover, they revealed what human eyes could not: fine details of workmanship, the chemical composition of the object itself, and, by analyzing infrared emissions, what was happening inside it. No human eye could look at smoke coming from a furnace and tell what was being burned, but the computers could analyze the smoke multispectrally and come up with the answer.

It became apparent during the 1970s that there was no hope of keeping up with the millions of images that poured into NPIC and the other processing and interpretation centers by simply looking at them the way they had been looked at in World War II. The computers therefore also had to be taught to compare new imagery of a given scene with old imagery, ignoring what had not changed and calling the interpreter's attention to what had. To further facilitate the interpretive process, the computers have been fed recognition data from a vast quantity of objects ranging from uranium ore to railroad tracks to IRBM silos and are programmed to alert the interpreters when such objects appear in new imagery. Accurate count can be kept of Soviet ICBMs and submarine-launched ballistic missiles because the computers know those weapons when they see them and will sound an alarm when new ones are spotted either coming off production lines or being placed in service. Coupled with interpreters who are themselves often highly specialized engineers,* the computers provide a range of analytical capabilities that were considered science fiction when the first reconnaissance satellites went into orbit.

Given the mutual suspicion and distrust that has plagued the interpretive process throughout most of the postwar period, it is not surprising that each intelligence service or agency maintains its own processing and analysis organization irrespective of NPIC's role as an institution of common concern (or perhaps because of it). Despite the quantity of imagery that has been coming down from the various reconnaissance platforms, NPIC does not appear to be a very busy place at all, at least judging by the relatively small number of people who work there (even allowing for the use of the supercomputers).

For its part, the CIA wasted no time in making certain that it would have its own photo interpretation capability, irrespective of the fact that it technically runs NPIC. In 1961 (the same year NPIC came into existence), the agency created an Office of Imagery Analysis as part of its National Foreign Assessment Center. Appropriately, the OIA functions with the CIA's Office of Central Reference, the Office of Scientific Intelligence, and the Office of Weapons Intelligence. Similarly, the Defense Intelligence Agency —NPIC's other tenant—handles its own interpretation at its new Analysis Center at Bolling Air Force Base in the District of Columbia, while the large Naval Intelligence Support Center at nearby Suitland, Maryland, works on technical intelligence analysis for its own service. The indications are that photo interpretation has become a secondary role at NPIC, while its primary function is that

---

*The Defense Intelligence Agency took a Help Wanted ad in *Aviation Week & Space Technology* in November 1985, for example, seeking aerospace and electronics engineers to assess "Soviet, Warsaw Pact, and PRC [People's Republic of China] ballistic missile systems and subsystems, foreign fighter aircraft and weapon systems, aerodynamic [cruise] missiles and weapon systems, advanced avionics integrated into aerodynamic weapons systems, and developments relating to foreign space systems." The word "foreign" indicates that the DIA is watching nations other than those listed in the ad. Starting salaries ranged from $26,381 to $57,759.

of a large imagery data base, or imagery library, for the intelligence community as a whole.

While imaging satellites remained the most glamorous of the spacecraft that were developed and refined during the sixties and seventies, they were outnumbered by an assortment of SIGINT platforms that were distantly related to Rhyolite and carried the brunt of technical collection. They were (and are) formally known as electronic reconnaissance platforms and less formally as radar "ferrets," after the animals whose reputation as relentless hunters of rats and other rodents has made their name synonymous with the quality of being a scrupulous and tenacious searcher.

The first U.S. ferret satellite seems to have been a Thor-boosted Agena-B that went up on May 15, 1962. It was placed in an 82.3-degree near-polar orbit, which, with a perigee of 180 miles and an apogee of 401 miles, was fairly elliptical. Those that followed, as did another on June 18, had almost circular orbits at altitudes of about three hundred miles. That would have put them close enough to the earth to pick up whatever signals were to be ferreted, yet high enough to greatly reduce drag (the spacecraft that went up on June 18 remained in orbit for 498 days, as opposed to its lower-flying PHOTINT cousins, which stayed up on the order of three weeks or less).

Philip J. Klass, a writer for *Aviation Week & Space Technology* who is a longtime observer of reconnaissance satellite activities, has said that at an altitude of three hundred miles, "a satellite would be within line-of-sight range of radar and radio stations up to 1,200 miles away. During one day in orbit, a single ferret satellite would pass within receiving range of all radars within the vast reaches of the U.S.S.R. and Red China."

Ferrets have come in a wide variety of sizes and shapes, and have been orbited at any number of altitudes, depending on the mission. Since the first ferrets were Agena-Bs (succeeded in February 1964 by Thrust-Augmented Thor Agena-Ds), they were a relatively long nineteen feet and weighed a hefty eighty-five hundred pounds. This meant that each of the satellites had to have its own booster, a fabulously expensive proposition, given the fact that SIGINT operations outnumber those for imaging by as much as four to one, according to George Keegan.

The answer, where the NRO was concerned, was evidently to

press for lighter, miniaturized, more sensitive listening equipment that could be squeezed into satellites small enough to be carried "piggyback" on boosters carrying larger satellites such as those in the Keyhole series. This became common practice by the mid-1960s. The Atlas Agena-D mentioned earlier as having boosted a KH-6 close-look imager to an orbit having a 76-mile-high perigee on July 6, 1964, for example, carried a second passenger. It was a ferret, probably octagonally shaped, which weighed about one hundred thirty pounds and measured only about a yard across. Launch records show that that particular satellite had a near-polar inclination of almost 93 degrees (the same as its imaging companion), but that its initial perigee and apogee were higher than the KH-6's: 184 and 233 miles.

Klass's "intuition" suggested that a "family" of complementary types of ferret satellites worked together throughout the 1960s in the same way that the area-surveillance and close-look imagers did. He has guessed that the small piggyback subsatellites were sent up to do simple inventories of Soviet radar installations and record the bands on which they operated. Then larger and more sophisticated spacecraft would be launched for more detailed collection. Other knowledgeable observers have found this notion credible.

The major difference between imaging satellite operations and those having to do with signals intelligence concerns time over target. A single photograph taken in a split second can yield considerable information, so imaging satellites do not need to loiter over their targets; the picture captures the intelligence almost instantly.

Not so with SIGINT. Radar emissions travel across an extremely wide band of frequencies, so fixing and measuring them takes time. Nor are RADINT analysts in the National Security Agency's giant SIGINT City complex at Fort Meade the only ones with such problems. COMINT also is difficult to collect with low-orbiters because messages often take longer to transmit than the three minutes or so during which a low-orbiter passes from horizon to horizon. Picking up perhaps three minutes or less of an important transmission that might have lasted five times that long is obviously an exercise in futility. As a consequence, both the CIA and the NSA pushed hard in the sixties and seventies for satellites that could be put in highly elliptical or geosynchronous orbits in order to maximize their time over target. With the exception of Rhyolite and its successors, the CIA showed no particular interest in SIGINT systems and left them to the code-breakers at Fort Meade while it remained locked in battle with the Air Force over control of the imaging spacecraft.

There are eight or nine American ferrets in orbit at any given time, and never more than three are alike. Although their orbits vary, they must always be high enough so that their time over target surpasses their imaging counterparts by a factor of two or three, and occasionally by a good deal more than that.

Of seventeen large SIGINT satellite launches between 1962 and 1971, plus thirty-five smaller ones sent up between 1963 and 1975, the great majority had near-circular orbits in the three-hundred-mile range (though five of the subsatellites orbited at altitudes of almost nine hundred miles). Low-orbiting ferrets have at least two advantages and three drawbacks. Their low altitudes make them relatively inexpensive to put up, which promotes more extensive coverage, and they register signals with great accuracy. On the other hand, they have a relatively short time over the target; they are easily tracked by the Russians and the Chinese, who are therefore able to stop transmitting just before they come over the horizon; and their operation is sufficiently well known so that they can be foiled by jamming and other means.

But thanks to miniaturized, extremely sensitive receivers, more powerful transmitters, and very large antennas, satellites with geosynchronous or highly elliptical orbits have been built that can pull in staggering amounts of data while remaining far enough away from their quarry so that clear identification, and such ensuing countermeasures as jamming or frequently altering transmission bands, become more difficult.

Jumpseat is a fine example. As previously noted, the satellite has orbital characteristics that are virtually identical with those of the SDS spacecraft that relay intelligence data from an imaging satellite, the KH-11. Jumpseat therefore appears to Soviet trackers like a data relay platform, while, in reality, its job is to take precise measurements of high-performance phased array ABM and space tracking radars (such as the huge one at Abalakova) by recording their microwave emissions. Jumpseat ferrets ABM radar for the dual purpose of providing verification that the terms of the anti-ballistic missile treaty are being adhered to while at the same time collecting data that would allow SAC's and the Navy's ballistic missiles to penetrate Soviet defenses in case of war. Being able to do this also allows Jumpseat to size up the Kremlin's space tracking radars, which operate in much the same way as the ABM units, so that ways can be found to make U.S. military satellites less visible to the Russians. And that's not all. The satellites (two are believed to be in orbit at all times) also collect ELINT and COMINT.

Jumpseat was first orbited in 1976. Its perigee is only about 200 miles as it passes over the Southwest Pacific Basin between Argentina and New Zealand. But as it continues south, skimming low over the Antarctic, it begins to swing increasingly farther away from the earth until it reaches its apogee, 24,200 miles, while over Siberia. And although the spacecraft's speed averages about 17,000 miles an hour, its movement relative to the terrain beneath it slows considerably because of the great distance (similarly, like all satellites in elliptical orbits, its speed relative to the earth increases as it approaches its perigee, as does its absolute speed because of the greater gravitational pull at low altitude).

Jumpseat's journey over Siberia lasts for about eight hours. During that time, the ferret takes and records the pulse of the very radars that look silently up at it, meticulously tracking its course as it sails far above them, tracing a solitary arc across the dome of the world. The adversarial machines face each other, as they always do, with one watching, the other listening. That is the nature of space reconnaissance.

10.

Real Time:
The Advent of
Instant Intelligence

Jimmy Carter's first full day as president of the United States—
January 21, 1977—was deliriously hectic and peppered with controversy, as contemporary news accounts and the handful of memoirs
written by those who were close to him indicate.

Newspapers throughout the country gave substantial space on
their front pages to the fact that, in his first major act as president,
the Navy engineer turned politician granted a pardon to almost all
of the ten thousand or so young men who had evaded service in
Vietnam. The document that accomplished this, a historically important one whose specter had fired deep emotions during the campaign the previous autumn, was signed in the early hours that
Friday and was then reported, along with attendant expressions of
praise by pro-amnesty groups and equal doses of wrath by the
veterans' lobby, on television that evening and in the morning papers the next day. The White House press corps played up the
amnesty angle, but it also laced its record of the day's events by
noting that several celebrations took place in the mansion to honor
the new president's friends and fellow Georgians, as well as members of the Democratic National Committee, state campaign manag-
ers, representatives of labor, business, and the entertainment
industry, and those who had acted as hosts and hostesses during the
inaugural festivities. The day was punctuated by the parties, the first

of which began at ten in the morning, while the last ended at five-thirty on that bitterly cold but exhilarating afternoon.

E. Henry Knoche's visit, however, went unrecorded. Enno ("Hank") Knoche was the acting director of the Central Intelligence Agency. He was a career CIA analyst who had been promoted to deputy director of Central Intelligence by George Bush in 1976 during the latter's yearlong stint as DCI following the sacrificial firing of William E. Colby in the wake of the Church Committee's rigorous (and well-publicized) investigation of CIA malfeasance.

But since Bush's directorship of the CIA had ended the moment the presidency passed from Gerald Ford to Carter, Knoche was acting as the country's chief of intelligence until the new president had time to nominate his own man.* Not only had the temporary head of the CIA come to the White House to offer his own and his agency's best wishes to Carter on his first full day on the job, but he had even brought a present of sorts that might at the same time entertain the new president, educate him, and perhaps even leave him with a good feeling about the CIA and its technical prowess. Knoche brought Carter a set of the most remarkable reconnaissance satellite photographs.

The pictures had come down early the previous morning, just before the regular 9:00 A.M. senior staff meeting at Langley and several hours before Carter recited the oath of office on Capitol Hill in blustery, subfreezing weather and then gone on to take an unprecedented mile-and-a-half walk to the White House with his wife and nine-year-old daughter. They were mundane pictures as space reconnaissance imagery went—Knoche does not remember to this day what they showed—but they were of consummate importance because they represented the fulfillment of the oldest and most cherished dream of those who ran overhead reconnaissance: that of being able to look down on events happening perhaps halfway around the world and watch them from right up close, virtually as they happened, the way an angel would.

This was called real-time imaging, and although an actual transmission could take up to ninety minutes to get from the satellite to the viewer, it was dazzlingly fast compared with the bucket-dropping technique and produced pictures with far better resolution

*It was to be Admiral Stansfield Turner, who became DCI that March. Turner promptly sacked Knoche, along with two hundred other senior CIA officers and some six hundred lower grades in a purported attempt to streamline operations.

than that made by the kind of television cameras used in area-surveillance platforms of the KH-5 type, which was patterned on SAMOS. The system, which was digital, had been tested before-hand, but the stream of pictures that had come down early that morning were the first to be considered the product of a fully operational spacecraft.

The real-time imagery had been taken by a remarkable, though not altogether loved, new satellite called the KH-11. The spacecraft was the carefully nurtured, fiercely protected, and fabulously expen-sive brainchild of the CIA, and it therefore had gestated and been born at TRW while the Air Force, claiming with justification that the craft was crippling other space reconnaissance programs, suf-fered the vapors. (George Keegan was to grumble a decade later that the KH-11 had gone $1 billion over budget to the detriment of other space imaging programs, a charge that has bubbled to the surface elsewhere.)

The imagery that came down on the day Jimmy Carter became president of the United States was sent by the first of a new breed of imaging satellites, a sixty-four-foot-long behemoth that weighed close to thirty thousand pounds and had been lofted into orbit the previous December 19 on top of a Titan 3D that blasted off from Vandenberg. The satellite's inclination, about typical for those that followed, was a near-polar 97 degrees. It was to spend most of its 770-day life describing an ellipse whose perigee was 164 miles and whose apogee was 327 miles. The first KH-11 therefore remained on station 509 days longer than its longest-lived predecessor, an-other hefty imaging platform called the KH-9, or Big Bird.

KH-11s, also known by the Byeman code name Kennan, or as satellites in the 5500 series, send their real-time imagery up to other satellites, including the high-flying SDS platforms (a relay method that complicates Soviet attempts to intercept the data), which, in turn, downlink it to the ambiguously named Defense Communica-tions, Electronics, Evaluation and Testing Activity, a large, win-dowless two-story concrete structure at Fort Belvoir, Virginia, just outside Washington. On Carter's Inauguration Day, as now, the imagery—motion pictures (or, more accurately, pictures in motion) —came down in digital code and was instantly converted into rec-ognizable high-resolution pictures on a screen. This meant that under ideal conditions a viewer could watch tanks rumbling across the Polish countryside or an ICBM being readied for a test flight virtually as those events occurred. The images then could be put on film (moving or still) or on tape, from which they could be digitally manipulated to highlight particular features or characteristics. It was therefore possible to have photographs of, say, the occupied U.S. embassy in Teheran, taken from a spot in the sky that the Ayatollah Khomeini's young militants could not even see, much less attack, on the desk of the president within an hour of their having been requested.

Since transporting the large apparatus used at Fort Belvoir to turn the KH-11's data into pictures was obviously out of the question, Knoche decided to select several images of no particular importance that were representative of the KH-11's capability, have them printed, and simply carry them to the White House. His first inclination was to try to get the pictures to Carter on the day they came in, but he quickly decided that interrupting the jubilation, or "merry-making," as he put it, might have been considered intrusive and therefore would probably not have been welcome. Accordingly, the excited CIA officer made an appointment to see the president at three-fifteen the following afternoon.

Knoche and Admiral Daniel J. Murphy, a senior CIA official who was responsible for coordinating the work of all the nation's foreign intelligence organizations, arrived at the White House the next day with what Knoche has recalled was a "handful" of photographs, each of which was black-and-white and measured about six inches square. Both men were ushered into the Map Room on the second floor, where they met Carter and Zbigniew Brzezinski, the Columbia University professor of international relations who had become his national security adviser.

Knoche spread the photographs on the map table, a large ornate one that was planted solidly in the center of the room. Although Carter had never seen KH-11 imagery, he had been told of the satellite's existence as part of the presidential transition process a few weeks earlier, when George Bush and others at Langley had spent the better part of a day briefing him on the world situation. The CIA's view of the world and how that view was to be shaped in years to come, Carter had been told, would depend to a significant extent on the new spacecraft. They had then told the president-elect about the KH-11 in some detail.

At twenty minutes past three on the afternoon of his first full day as president of the United States, Jimmy Carter looked down and studied the photographs that Knoche had just spread on the map table: detailed photographs that had been taken from space the previous morning when the first KH-11 had been pronounced operational. After scrutinizing the pictures for a few moments, Carter looked up at Knoche, grinned, and then laughed appreciatively. He congratulated the two CIA men on the apparent excellence of their system and then asked Knoche to send over some more samples for the following day's National Security Council meeting, his first as president. "Of course," Jimmy Carter said as he turned to Brzezinski, "this will also be of value in our arms control work." The KH-11 had made its White House debut, and on that hopeful note the meeting in the Map Room came to an end.

When the KH-11 came on-line that January 1977, it joined two other imaging spacecraft, the KH-8 and KH-9, which were the last in the line of distinct close-look and area-surveillance platforms. Together, the three would bear the burden of the nation's spaceborne reconnaissance for another decade.

The refinement of close-look and area-surveillance spacecraft before the advent of the KH-11 had been driven by three factors.

First, there was the persistent fear that however capable U.S. orbital reconnaissance was, it lagged behind the opposition's ability to conceal, confuse, and confound. The technical collectors, and especially those in the Air Force, tended to be less gratified by what they could see than frustrated and apprehensive by what they were convinced was eluding them. The seeming absence of something did not so much mean that it wasn't there, in the view of the men of Air Force intelligence and their superiors, as that it most likely was diabolically hidden. Someone had even claimed during the missile gap that a church tower in the Ukraine clothed an ICBM. Russia was the land of Grigori Potemkin, after all, and he had been a master of guile. Russia was a place where chess, a game of subterfuge and cunning (not to mention sacrifice) amounted to a national pastime. The Russians had even institutionalized deception, concealment and distortion, and given it a name: *maskirovka*. And this evil talent was most worrisome where ballistic missiles, or at least the ballistic missiles that could not be located, were concerned. But although the Air Force never said so, the phantom Soviet missiles had at least two salutary effects: they helped make the case in Congress for more strategic nuclear weapons, and they were used to try to convince the executive branch that more and better space reconnaissance systems were needed to improve the search process.

There was also the pressing matter of technical intelligence collection, which was vital to the three armed services as well as to the CIA. Although technical intelligence involved targeting to the extent that radars had to be measured for jamming to allow the bombers to get through, and silos and other structures had to be gauged so that appropriate kilotonnage could be used against them, there were much wider concerns. The armed services wanted to know what their counterparts had in the way of equipment so that an effective response could be mounted against them if necessary. The Army thought it imperative to know not only how many heavy tanks the Warsaw Pact had, for example, but what those tanks' operational characteristics were and what it would take to stop them. Similarly, Tactical Air Command generals needed intelligence regarding the MiG fighters and Sukhoi interceptors and fighter-bombers with which their pilots might have to tangle, and high-resolution photographs of such planes, even parked on tarmacs, would reveal a great deal about them to the aeronautical engineer–photo interpreters who studied them at the DIA, the CIA, and in Air Force intelligence.

Finally, there was the brand-new realm of arms control, which primarily concerned the State Department (with the CIA acting as its first-line intelligence-gatherer). Arms control requirements amounted to an amalgamation of counting and analyzing technical intelligence—of determining, in other words, which equipment came under the terms of the various treaties, what that equipment could do, and how much of it there was.

The most celebrated example of controversy involving interpretation in arms control had to do with the U.S.S.R.'s Tu-26 bomber, code-named Backfire by NATO, and its relation to the SALT II negotiations, which in part set a limit on the number of heavy bombers each side could have. But was the sweptwing twin-engine bomber a heavy one? The question was more than esoteric because "heavy" is military shorthand for a bomber with intercontinental range, meaning one that could carry bombs or cruise missiles to an enemy country. Before and during the SALT II debate, both the CIA and the DIA scrutinized the same satellite photographs and tried to determine whether the plane constituted a real threat to the continental United States by studying the Tu-26's shape, fuel capacity and consumption rate at various speed and altitude combinations, in-air refueling capability (or lack of it), weapons-carrying capacity, and other factors.

What sort of pictures were required to make such a determination? The analysts needed high-resolution stereo verticals and obliques so they could use photogrammetric equipment to calculate the bomber's precise size. They also needed infrared photographs that would show how much fuel was in the Backfire's wings by contrasting the cooler surfaces of the wings (inside which the cold jet fuel was stored) with the relatively warmer sections. Accurate fuel-load measurements could be made with such data.

After all of the calculations had been tossed into the respective hoppers at the DIA and the CIA, the airmen concluded that the Tu-26 could in certain circumstances make round-trip bombing missions against the United States. In order to do that, they would have to take off from bases in the Arctic, refuel in midair, and fly at high altitude to conserve fuel. "All Backfire aircraft apparently are either equipped for or actually carry air refueling probes," one Air Force general told the Senate Foreign Relations Committee at the SALT II ratification hearings in November 1979. But the CIA took a less threatened view of the Soviet bombers, apparently because its analysts were not convinced that the Tu-26s had midair refueling capability and, anyway, the tanker aircraft needed to refuel them were in extremely short supply. (It is also quite likely that the agency disputed the feasibility of Tu-26s making a high-altitude attack, which would have been suicidal in the face of the Distant Early Warning radar network spread across Canada and Greenland; bombing doctrine since the early 1960s has called for low-level attack to avoid radar detection.) In the end, the DIA recalculated and lowered its estimate, though it didn't get around to doing so until the fifth year of the Reagan presidency.

Far from being mutually exclusive, these technical collection requirements were in most cases complementary and together drove a single space reconnaissance system that became increasingly sophisticated during the sixties and seventies, particularly with regard to the specialized sensors carried on the satellites and the increasing use of Digital Image Processing (DIP) to extract information beyond the range of the human eye.

The third-generation area-surveillance and close-look satellites were called the KH-7 and KH-8, respectively. Whatever else the two satellites may have accomplished (and in the case of the KH-8, it was considerable), they were notable for being the first reconnaissance

platforms to carry infrared and multispectral scanners. Resolution
of the infrared scanners, in particular, was by most accounts poor
to terrible (and nil through cloud cover), but the effort marked the
beginning of the move toward effective night imagery for reconnaissance satellites that would only be achieved with the launch of a
spacecraft called the KH-12 some two decades later.

The infrared capability, which had been around since World War
II, allowed film or silicon receptors to register heat the way a standard camera's film registers visible light. And like a camera, an
infrared sensor is able to register even minute differences in the
temperatures of the objects it scans, thereby producing an image that
can define several objects at once according to their differing temperatures. High-altitude aircraft photos taken of air bases at night
had by then revealed planes, fuel trucks, buildings, and sometimes
even people because of the heat they radiated relative to their sur-
roundings. Infrared color film, which is also known as false color
film, records objects according to the heat they radiate and depicts
them in colors that have nothing to do with those in the visible part
of the electromagnetic spectrum. Infrared film therefore shows
healthy vegetation as red, while dying or dead vegetation shows as
pink or blue. It therefore generally does no good to paint an object
green or toss a camouflage net over it in order to make it appear like
grass or foliage from the air or from space.* Infrared imagery can
even be used to record the past by depicting shadows. Airplanes, for
example, cast shadows on the concrete aprons where they are
parked even in hazy weather. Hours after the plane has departed,
its shadow silhouette, which is cooler than the surrounding area,
remains visible to the infrared sensor. Although this capability was
realized in aerial reconnaissance, and in fact was widely used in
Vietnam, it was an unachieved goal in space reconnaissance until the
advent of the third-generation reconnaissance satellites.

Multispectral scanning (MSS), which was developed by Itek, a
Massachusetts firm that manufactures lenses and cameras for both
air- and spaceborne reconnaissance, involves the use of separate
lenses to shoot the same scene in several pictures, each in a different
part of the visible and infrared electromagnetic spectrum. This allows the wavelengths of the various substances—their characteristic

*Typically, there is an exception. The Israelis have developed a lightweight, reversible
camouflage netting that reflects light on a chlorophyll green wavelength similar to natural
vegetation.

radiation—to be screened, sorted out, and analyzed. Plywood painted green might look like grass in a standard color photograph shot from high altitude, but MSS imagery would show it to be what it was: a coat of paint. By the same token, MSS would differentiate between aluminum, steel, and titanium so that analysts could determine the composition of Soviet aircraft, which, in turn, would have a bearing on their performance.

Like infrared imaging, multispectral scanning did not produce high-resolution intelligence data, however. In the case of the KH-7, a low-resolution area surveillance craft, this was in part due to the use of radio-link transmission, but it also had to do with the inherent limits of resolution in the MSS itself. MSS was therefore supplemented on the KH-7 and KH-8 series of reconnaissance satellites by thematic mapping cameras. The thematic mappers had three times the resolving power of multispectral scanners. They used a movable mirror that could be made to drop onto the focal plane of the satellite's telescope and direct the image from the earth to a group of sensors that registered electromagnetic energy in seven bands: blue, green, red, near-infrared, first mid-infrared, second mid-infrared, and far-infrared. The resulting picture was then converted into digital numbers that quantified the intensity of the light in each band, resulting in a single picture that was made of as many as three hundred million digits, which, taken together, constituted a richly detailed portrait of the chemical elements of whatever had been imaged.

The first of twenty-nine successfully launched KH-7s lifted off at Vandenberg on August 9, 1966, on top of a Long Tank Thrust-Augmented Thor and went into an elliptical orbit of 120 by 178 miles with a near-polar inclination of slightly more than 100 degrees. Besides carrying infrared and multispectral scanners, the first KH-7 took to orbit an improved four-and-a-half-foot-wide unfurlable antenna designed to help improve the still-poor resolution of the Air Force's radio-link imaging system.

The KH-8, a direct descendant of the CIA's Discoverer and KH-6 close-look programs, was designed for use on the special occasions when extremely close examination of a target had to be made even at the cost of having the satellite decay relatively quickly. At about sixty-six hundred pounds, Keyhole 8 was so heavy that it had to be sent up on top of a two-stage liquid-fueled Titan 3B, a modified ICBM that towered a dizzying eleven stories above its launch pad and developed more than a half million pounds of thrust. And like so many of its predecessors, the satellite itself was a specially adapted version of the tried and true Agena-D.

The first KH-8 blasted off from Vandenberg on July 29, 1966, beating the first KH-7 into space by twelve days. The third-generation close-look platform had a telescopic system that could produce standard photographs with resolutions of six inches, in addition to the poorer-quality infrared imagery, MSS, and thematic mapping. That first KH-8, with the restartable Aerojet engine, was ordered into a low 98- by 155-mile orbit two days after launch. Not surprisingly, the multimillion-dollar spacecraft turned into a fireball and disintegrated a week later because of the severe atmospheric friction. The lifetime of the KH-8 series increased as their launches continued into the mid-1980s, however, apparently because their orbits were made more elliptical.

The spacecraft were typically sent up under special circumstances, either because an area-surveillance platform had spotted something that was thought to require close inspection, or because some other intelligence source had performed that job. A KH-8 was launched on January 21, 1982, for example, with orbital characteristics that took it over the frontier shared by Libya, Chad, and the Sudan at a time when Qaddafi's troops were thought to be massing for an attack on either of those countries and when Soviet Tu-22 Blinder bombers were being flown for possible air support.*

As was the case with the two previous close-look satellite series, the KH-8s were programmed to eject film pods as they sped past the Arctic so that they could be snatched over the Pacific near the Hawaiian Islands. There were at least two, and possibly four, "buckets" on each of the KH-8s. More than fifty-two of the satellites were launched through 1985 to photograph specific developments in

---

*That particular KH-8 had a most unusual life. After its first orbits, which were quite elliptical at 88 by 233 miles, it bounded to a higher and more circular orbit of 330 by 415 miles, which is well out of photographic range and more indicative of a ferret mission. Twenty-four hours after launch the Agena-D's engine was turned on twice, raising it to an orbit of 346 by 403 miles. Then, on January 29, its perigee was moved up slightly to 364 miles. It was moved yet again in the following days until it reached its final orbit of 389 by 403 miles—nearly circular. On March 21 the spacecraft released three smaller satellites into orbits similar to its own and then loosed yet another on May 3. The satellite was ordered out of orbit twenty days later and was incinerated reentering the atmosphere. The four subsatellites may have been ferrets or ocean surveillance types, which go up in fours. Whatever the mission, that sort of maneuvering gives an indication of how versatile reconnaissance satellites had become.

Libya, Poland, Nicaragua, and Afghanistan, to name only four of the low-orbiter's target countries.*

One event that was satellite-covered, almost undoubtedly by a KH-8 because of the extremely high resolution pictures that were required, was the massive series of explosions that took place in mid-May 1984 at the ammunition depot at Severomorsk. At least one in a group of tremendous detonations was so big that it was at first thought to be nuclear. The explosions blew out the roofs and walls of several ammunition-storage buildings and bunkers, strewing a variety of intact weapons, including missiles, mines, and torpedoes (and possibly cruise missiles) throughout the area. This presented an irresistible photo opportunity to the technical intelligence collectors, but one that demanded extremely high resolution imagery so that the weapons could be scrutinized in great detail. Dipping as low as 69 miles, a KH-8 can take photographs with a resolution of between three and four inches. Typical missions of the KH-8, which was Byeman code-named Gambit, had fifty- to eighty-day durations by 1980 because of extensive maneuvering into more elliptical orbits, with parameters averaging 77 by 215 miles.

However good U.S. reconnaissance satellites had become by the end of the 1960s, they had problems that irked their users. The area-surveillance platforms sent their imagery down relatively quickly, but it was not of very high quality. The close-look types, which took fine pictures, were still dropping them out of orbit on parachutes, a time-consuming and chancy operation. What was needed was a single satellite that could produce uniformly high-quality area-surveillance and close-look imagery and get it down as the event being watched was happening. But this was a dream of such technical sophistication that it could not be realized for several more years.

Meanwhile, the nation's fourth-generation area-surveillance satellite, the KH-9, appeared, representing a compromise of sorts, but definitely a step in the right direction. The new spacecraft was itself a partial substitute for another of the extremely ambitious programs conceptualized by the Air Force in the 1960s. This one was called the Manned Orbiting Laboratory, or MOL, and it was supposed to be able to accomplish a formidable variety of tasks, including in-

*Primary close-look targets as set by COMIREX almost invariably came with a list of secondary targets that would be imaged in the same mission in an effort to make each as cost-effective as possible.

specting satellites in space, testing the accuracy of an orbital bombardment system, commanding and controlling military operations
during all-out war, testing the effects of month-long missions on
astronauts, and performing both imaging and ELINT reconnaissance.

The MOL, a cylinder having about thirty-four cubic yards of
work space, was to be lifted to orbit by a thrust-augmented Titan
3C. Once in low orbit, it was to be joined by two astronauts in a
Gemini capsule who would dock, climb inside, and perform the
various experiments in addition to operating the reconnaissance
apparatus. They were then to return to earth in their capsule, leaving the laboratory to await a replacement crew.

The MOL's potential as a fine reconnaissance platform was not
wasted on Langley, which decided early that it had enormous potential as a kind of very high flying SR-71, and that in such a role
it properly belonged under the operational mantle of Central Intelligence, notwithstanding the fact that it was an Air Force project.
The Air Force reacted to the CIA's overture with customary belligerence and the rhubarb that followed was only settled by Lyndon
Johnson himself, who insisted that the MOL be a space asset of
common concern when he approved it in 1965. Whatever its other
roles, the orbiting "laboratory's" chief mission was to be reconnaissance. Having a manned platform in orbit was attractive to the
technical intelligence community because the human eye could
compensate for the motion of a spacecraft relative to the earth better
than machines could, at least at that point. A crewman would therefore take the required imagery. The MOL's main camera was to
have a lens measuring six feet across that would have a theoretical
resolution of four inches and an actual resolution, allowing for
atmospheric distortion, of nine inches. In the end, however, the
MOL succumbed to cost overruns (it was to consume $1.6 billion),
interest in other kinds of manned space projects, and political considerations (the CIA, suddenly fretting that Russians would use an
ABM to attack the manned spy platform as they had attacked Powers, finally had the MOL killed). But for their part, the KH-7s,
KH-8s, and ferrets had proved to be effective enough so that they
largely preempted the MOL's reconnaissance role anyway. The
space laboratory was scratched in 1969.

Where reconnaissance was concerned, the MOL had a backup.
Lockheed was working on a project called Program 612, which it
had contracted for with the National Reconnaissance Office at about

the time Johnson approved the MOL. Evidently, the NRO had decided to take the precaution of developing an alternate space reconnaissance system in case something happened to the manned platform. And Program 612 was in fact far enough along even in 1967 that the Air Force was able to contract with Martin Marietta for a suitably powerful new booster: the Titan 3D. The fact that the Air Force contracted for the new booster two years before the MOL was killed further suggests that the project had been going sour for some time.

By 1968, design work on the fourth-generation U.S. reconnaissance satellite had progressed substantially. That year its code number was arbitrarily changed to 467, possibly so that it would be easily confused with DSP-647, the missile early warning system. It was also given the designation KH-9 and the Byeman code name Hexagon. Unofficially, however, the new platform would come to be known as Big Bird.

It is unlikely that any reconnaissance system has ever been more aptly named than Big Bird. The NRO wanted an unprecedented array of sensors in the KH-9, which was intended to be primarily an area-surveillance spacecraft but was nonetheless to have close-look capability as well.

Big Bird's heart was a Perkin-Elmer Cassegrain telescope having a "folded" focal length of twenty feet and a concave primary mirror that was more than six feet in diameter. The primary mirror, a giant perfectly curved, highly polished version of the sort found in many bathrooms, would direct the image it picked up to a smaller, secondary mirror that faced it some eight feet away. The image reflected off the primary mirror would strike the secondary mirror and would in turn be sent through a hole in the center of the primary mirror, behind which was the focal plane, where the earth images picked up by the primary mirror would come into sharp focus. The telescope was said to be folded because use of the two large mirrors doubled the system's focal length in a relatively small space.

The sharply focused image that struck the focal plane would in turn be directed to any of the satellite's specialized sensors by the use of a series of small mirrors and prisms set around the focal plane. Big Bird's controllers at Sunnyvale would therefore be able to obtain infrared imagery, for example, by tilting the appropriate mirror in the area of the focal plane so that it directed the incoming image to the infrared sensor. The same would be true for the multispectral scanner, thematic mapper, and other sensors, such as a photomultiplier that would excite photons to make a picture taken on a clear night useful for analytical purposes. For standard photographs, the image would be split and overlapped by another mirror to give it a three-dimensional effect. It would then hit thin, highly sensitive low-grain film that wound around a series of spools leading to between four and six capsules that were to be ejected from orbit in the same way as those that had been carried by the Discoverers, KH-6s, and KH-8s. Resolution would be about a foot, and possibly a bit better than that.

And that wasn't all. Big Bird would carry a second large imaging system, this one a double-lens area-surveillance camera made by Kodak. One of the lenses would be used for relatively high (for area surveillance) resolution pictures, perhaps on the order of about three feet, while the other captured the broad, wide-field, low-resolution imagery whose collection constituted the KH-9's primary mission. The Kodak camera would have its own infrared and multispectral scanning systems. The resulting imagery was not to be dropped in buckets, however, but scanned by a television camera that would tape-record it for transmission either to a relay satellite or directly to New Boston, New Hampshire, Vandenberg, Oahu, Kodiak Island, Guam, or the Seychelles.

Not counting some SIGINT equipment and related antennas, plus the guidance system, ground control receivers, transmitters, and other standard hardware, plus provision for three or four of the small ferret subsatellites, that was the total load except for fuel. Hexagon was going to need to carry a lot of fuel in order to maneuver in orbit. Two kinds of maneuvers, horizontal and vertical, would be mission-related, while a third maneuvering "situation" would arise only in the event that one of the satellites appeared to be coming under attack by an opponent in a closing orbit. Mission-related maneuvering would be used to put the KH-9's sensors within reach of targets that might otherwise go uncovered, and also to raise it periodically to prolong its life. In addition, the satellite's engine would have to be started for a short time every seven to ten days to stave off for as long as possible the decaying effect of atmospheric drag.

The spacecraft that started as an NRO concept and basic design specification and then progressed to Lockheed's drawing boards, to the company's machine shop and fabrication facility at Sunnyvale, and to the assembly area—where the Perkin-Elmer telescope, Kodak camera, and other sensors were precisely mated to computers, radio receivers, large folding antennas, paddle-type solar collectors, the guidance system, engine, and other components for an eventual launch at Vandenberg—was nothing short of a colossus by reconnaissance satellite standards. The engineers had taken the reliable Agena and then widened and lengthened it until it was ten feet across and fifty feet long and weighed about thirty thousand pounds (twenty thousand of it being the sensors and related hardware). Big Bird was as big as the MOL itself was supposed to have been, and that was as big as a Greyhound bus.

Early on the evening of June 15, 1971, a Titan 3D spewing flame from all three exhaust nozzles and developing almost three million pounds of thrust lifted the first KH-9 to a moderately elliptical orbit of 114 by 186 miles. Its inclination was 96.4 degrees. This orbit allowed the spacecraft to circle the earth once every eighty-nine minutes, passing over every spot on its ground track once in daylight and once at night during each twenty-four hour period. During its fifty-two-day lifetime, the first of the Big Birds proved out its sensing, guidance, communication, and propulsion systems, made test transmissions, and was extensively calibrated, as is done to all reconnaissance satellites.* It also returned imagery taken over denied territory. The newest of the nation's space assets was directed out of orbit on August 6 and incinerated on its way down.

There were three launches in 1972. The first KH-9 to go up that year did so on January 20 carrying one of the 130-pound ferrets, which was then reboosted to its own 293- by 340-mile orbit. That second KH-9 had a lifetime of only forty days, but it also had the distinction of being the last of those committed mainly to operational testing.

Since the SALT I interim strategic arms treaty was signed in Moscow on May 28, the third Big Bird, which went up on July 7, was assigned the task of helping to provide national technical means of verification that the agreement's terms were being honored, in addition to its collateral intelligence-gathering chores. It had seemed prudent to continue launching KH-7s while Big Bird's wrinkles were being ironed out, so four of the older area-surveillance spacecraft were sent up while the initial two KH-9s were being tested, thereby providing overlapping, redundant coverage. With the

---

*Imaging satellites are routinely calibrated, or fine-tuned, by photographing targets in the United States or elsewhere whose dimensions and other characteristics, including energy emissions, are precisely known. This gives a clear indication of how to judge the quality of the intelligence they send back from operational missions.

July 7 launch, however, the NRO decided that the new system was
fully operational. The KH-7s were therefore phased out, with the
last of them going into orbit three days before SALT I was signed.
The third and last Big Bird to be launched in 1972 went up on
October 10 carrying yet another passenger, this one going into an
882- by 911-mile-high orbit that would keep it up for about ten
thousand years. The little hitchhiker had all the earmarks of a radar-
sniffer. It was clear at that point that Big Birds were going to carry
quite a bit of freight to orbits other than their own.

The Soviet missile test program received special attention from
KH-8s and KH-9s during 1972 and 1973. Tests of the then experimental SS-16, -17, -18, and -19 ICBMs were closely monitored.
Satellite intelligence, as well as data from the various ground stations
and tracking ships, showed that by early 1974 the SS-16 remained
in an early developmental stage, the SS-17 was encountering serious
technical problems, and the SS-18 and SS-19 programs were moving along quite smoothly. In January 1974, in fact, the SS-19 made
its long-range flight test debut before a veritable audience of Washington's intelligence-gathering platforms on land, at sea, and in
space. Preparations for the launch were undoubtedly photographed
by a KH-9 that had gone up the previous November 10. And far
above that particular Big Bird, unsuspected by the Russians, the first
of the Rhyolites listened quietly in the starry blackness to the beat
of the SS-19's pumps and the working of its gyros and other systems
as transmitted in a stream of uncoded telemetry.

Nor were ICBMs the only long-range Soviet missile that aroused
Washington's curiosity. Both the technical intelligence collectors
and NASA were keenly interested in the Russians' enigmatic G-1,
a mysterious monster booster that seemed to have been developed
to get cosmonauts on the moon. Its engines, which were thought
to date back to 1963, delivered 4.75 million pounds of thrust, or
enough to put 155 tons into low orbit, 63 tons on the moon, and
up to 27 tons on Venus. KH-7s and KH-8s had first spotted G-1
test facilities under construction at Tyuratam in the summer of
1966. By early June 1969 the massive rocket had been ready for a
series of full-blown rehearsals prior to an actual test launch or,
perhaps, even for the real thing. KH-8 imagery taken over Tyuratam on June 3 showed that the awesome booster, which towered 360
feet above its pad, was being serviced.

But pictures of the same spot taken only eleven days later revealed
evidence of a massive explosion and fire that left charred and twisted

debris scattered over a wide area. The pad itself was left unusable. As reconstructed by the interpreters, the G-1's first stage had been filled with fuel, its second stage had been nearly topped off, and its third, or uppermost, stage had just started filling when a large leak developed in the second stage. Fuel had then gushed over the side of the second stage and had flowed down the length of the booster until the entire launch pad had become a pool of propellant. Then a fire had started near the base of the seventy-seven-foot-wide first stage, enveloping it and the second stage and causing the fuel tanks in both to rupture. It was plain to those who studied the KH-8's high-resolution photographs that the ensuing explosion had blown the G-1 apart and destroyed much of its pad.

A second G-1 did make it off the ground in August 1971, but it literally shook itself to pieces at an altitude of only seven and a half miles, probably because of a first-stage malfunction. A third, and final, attempt to get the G-1 into space was made on November 24, 1972. Less than two minutes after lift-off, however, some new catastrophe struck, and the giant rocket had to be destroyed in flight by its ground controllers. Although no other G-1 launches are known to have been tried, satellite reconnaissance in the summer of 1974 showed that the G-1's test stand was being modified and the pad destroyed five years earlier was being rebuilt. This indicates that the G-1 or a successor may still be under development, perhaps for use in lifting pieces of a prefabricated space station to orbit or for sending a very heavy probe out into the galaxy.

Big Birds continued going up throughout the 1970s and well into the 1980s, initially three a year and then, beginning in 1974, on an average of two a year as their orbital lifetimes increased steadily from 52 to 275 days. And as their time in orbit increased, so did their intelligence yield.

KH-9s spotted the development of a phased array radar at the Sary Shagan ABM test center and closely monitored submarine construction under the huge canvas shrouds at Severomorsk. During the summer of 1974, a KH-9 discovered that the Russians were trying to conceal construction of what appeared to be new missile silos. That winter, another of the spacecraft recorded the first deployment of SS-18s. In the following months, KH-9s inventoried ten SS-17s, an equal number of SS-18s, and fifty SS-19s, all of them deployed. Big Birds also participated in the discovery and subsequent monitoring of an important new ballistic missile being tested: the mobile SS-20 IRBM.

In July 1976, one of the Perkin-Elmer telescopes, which could spot individuals from the KH-9's mean perigee of 103 miles, recorded the fact that the Russians were beginning to modify the six hundred IRBMs pointed at NATO countries and China with Multiple Independently Targeted Reentry Vehicles, or MIRVs. That same telescope, mounted in the twelfth KH-9, also counted forty SS-17s, more than fifty SS-18s, and one hundred forty SS-19s in their hardened silos. Such precise inventories would produce national intelligence estimates that were a far cry from those of the fifties and sixties that could only refer to "from 100 to several hundred bombers," and so forth. The KH-8s and KH-9s were replacing uncertainties about the Soviet and Chinese weapons programs with data banks and files full of hard information. Coverage by the mid-1970s had gotten to be very good.

But from the point of view of some in the intelligence community, George Keegan among them, it was by no means good enough. Jeffrey Richelson, an assistant professor of government at The American University and a leading authority on intelligence, particularly on technical collection, has calculated that 365-days-a-year PHOTINT coverage began only in 1977. There were only 158 days of coverage in 1971, when the first Big Bird went up, and although coverage climbed to the low 300s during 1973 through 1975, it dropped to only 248 days in 1976. This, of course, meant that there was no coverage for 117 days that year.

Such lapses made George Keegan's flesh crawl. It was hard enough trying to figure out what the opposition was up to when you were watching it, Keegan reflected, but it was obviously impossible when you weren't watching it at all, and he profoundly hated that. Maybe nothing important was happening during periods of noncoverage. But maybe something important *was* going on, yet remained unnoticed, because there weren't enough imaging platforms to carry the whole PHOTINT load. And the reason the number of KH-8s and KH-9s was thinning out, the chief of Air Force intelligence knew, was that fantastic sums were being diverted from production of the two existing systems to finance the CIA's pet imaging satellite project. And ironically, that project was the conceptual descendant of the Air Force's own SAMOS, a system the CIA had denigrated and tried to kill since its inception. Meanwhile, the Air Force now found itself championing the KH-8 and the KH-9, both of which were the sort of bucket-droppers that had developed from

Discoverer—a CIA project—against the better judgment of the Air Force.

Langley's hot new project had its genesis in the Six-Day War of 1967, which demonstrated a need for faster technical intelligence collection than was possible with either of the film-return satellites. Although film could go from orbit to NPIC in four or five days under ideal conditions, three or four weeks was more often the case because of the intricate logistics involved and the vagaries of weather. In the case of the Israeli attack on Egypt, this meant that a whole war could be fought and concluded before a single photograph showed up in Washington, leaving the National Command Authority virtually blind. That wouldn't do. In addition, film-return spacecraft were the prisoners of their buckets. When the last ejectable capsule and its spool of exposed film had been kicked out of orbit, a KH-8 was utterly useless, and a KH-9 nearly so.

Accordingly, study panels analyzing PHOTINT requirements for the NRO after the Six-Day War shaped specifications for a fifth-generation imaging satellite, code-named KH-X, that would have a significant advantage over other imaging satellites: it would take pictures electronically and transmit them in near-real time, or virtually as events occurred. But the money to develop KH-X would in part come out of the Gambit and Hexagon programs, thereby cutting into actual coverage of the U.S.S.R. at a time when several ballistic missile systems were being tested and deployed. In such circumstances, curtailing operations in order to pursue research and development—and particularly R and D on such a far-out, high-risk system as the KH-X—seemed to George J. Keegan to smack of a level of folly that was almost treasonous.

Early in 1972 the National Reconnaissance Office selected TRW to develop the KH-X, thereby awarding a contract for an imaging satellite to a company other than Lockheed for the first time. The project was immediately dubbed Program 1010, and later it was assigned the Keyhole number 11 and, as noted, the Byeman name Kennan.*

Those who once dreamed that SAMOS's radio-link resolution

---

*There was a satellite assigned the Keyhole number 10, though it was never built because the KH-11 made it obsolete. The MOL was the KH-10.

would someday be the equal of the standard photographs that come out of the bucket-droppers have seen their vision come true. Semi-official statements, "backgrounders," and leaks to the trade press have it that the KH-11's electro-optical resolution is inferior to that of the bucket-droppers that used standard film. While that was true at the outset of the KH-11 program, it no longer is. By 1984 the resolution of the KH-11's electro-optical system was every bit as good as that of its bucket-dropping immediate predecessor, the KH-9.

The KH-11 owes its real-time capability and high resolution to the charge-coupled device, or CCD, which was invented at the Bell Telephone Laboratories in New Jersey in 1970 and today is in widespread use in hundreds of civilian and military programs, in-cluding medical imaging, plasma physics, astronomy (both the Galileo spacecraft and the space telescope use them), and home video cameras. The CCD is a technical work of art: a simple, easily produced, extremely sensitive radiation collector whose scientific elegance and practical versatility are revolutionizing high-speed imaging. And most CCDs are smaller than a postage stamp.

Basically, a CCD collects radiated particles of energy, including those in the visible part of the light spectrum, by capturing them in an array of tiny receptors, or picture elements, called pixels, which automatically measure their intensity and then send them on their way in orderly rows until they are electronically stacked up to form a kind of mosaic. A standard CCD manufactured by Texas Instru-ments for use in the Space Telescope measures eight hundred by eight hundred pixels, for a total of 640,000, yet it is less than half an inch square.

The analogy most often used to explain the working of CCDs is that of buckets collecting rain in a field. Each of the 640,000 buckets, all arranged in neat rows to form a square, represents a pixel. The rain, heavy in some places and light in others, is the equivalent of incident radiation (photons, electrons, neutrons, or protons, for example). Since different amounts of rain are coming down on the various parts of the field, the buckets catch varying amounts of water and therefore fill to different levels. As the buckets catch the water they move in vertical rows, called channels, toward a conveyor belt —a line transport register—which in turn carries them, a line at a time, off to the side where each of the eight hundred buckets in each line is simultaneously measured for its water content. If the amount of water in each bucket represents a different color or tone—say, black, white, and several shades of gray—then the entire string of eight hundred would take on the appearance of a line that is dark in some spots and lighter in others. Eight hundred pieces of precisely quantified information, constituting a line in a picture, would have been created. No sooner has the last of the eight hundred buckets moved off the conveyor than a second line gets on, and it, too, is measured. Then a third line follows, and so on, until all eight hundred lines of eight hundred buckets have been measured for their water content, or tonality. The net effect would be a highly detailed "picture" composed of 640,000 dots of varying tone. But the process is instantaneous and continuous, so that the picture moves.

A CCD collects photons and other particles of radiated energy instead of water, but the principle is roughly the same, except that the pixels themselves do not move. The photons that strike the pixels generate charges that move along from one pixel to the next along a series of horizontal "gates." As a result, the CCD acts as a kind of tiny, extremely precise light meter that captures radiated energy emissions across the visible and invisible bands of the spectrum so that they can be amplified and turned into pictures. A charge-coupled device, then, is an electronic tabula rasa that continuously registers whichever photons strike it, automatically moving the resulting photo-generated charges along, down the channels and through the gates, in an endlessly flowing procession. Unlike the standard cameras in its predecessors, the KH-11's CCDs do not "stop the action." Rather, they keep recording it as fast as it happens, in real time. The fact that the imagery can take up to an hour and a half to reach Fort Belvoir has to do with delays in the transmission process, not with the CCDs. Like a television camera, a charge-coupled device cannot be overwhelmed by the frequency of the particles hitting it.

No reconnaissance satellite system remains static. Just as the first SR-71s and other intelligence-gathering aircraft have been steadily modified through the years with state-of-the-art electronic systems to keep them operating optimally, so, too, are spacecraft like the KH-11. Two satellites in the same series may have different modifications, depending upon varying operational needs.

The KH-11's imaging system consists of four essential parts: a powerful mirror telescope, an infrared scanner, a separate sensor electronics package containing a photomultiplier tube, thematic mapper, multispectral scanner and appropriate mirrors and prisms, and an array of CCDs linked to each other to form a mosaic. As usual, the telescope brings in all the radiated energy within its field of view at great magnification. That energy can then be directed to any of the sensors, depending upon tasking requirements, so that it is broken down according to whichever part of the electromagnetic spectral band is wanted for analysis. Night preparations for a missile launch at Plesetsk, for example, might call for the use of the infrared scanner. The telescope would draw in all the radiated energy coming from the scene, but routing the image to the infrared scanner would automatically filter out energy on all wavelengths but infrared. The infrared imagery would pass through the scanner and register on the CCD array to form a moving infrared picture, which would then be amplified, digitized, encrypted, and transmitted up to one of the SDS spacecraft or another type for downlinking to Fort Belvoir.

But infrared imaging is not the only way the KH-11 "sees" at night. It can also use its photomultiplier to take advantage of existing light, even at night, for clear imaging. Photomultipliers used in combination with CCDs are employed all the time in astronomy to count photons, even at levels so low that they come in at a rate of only about one a minute (by comparison, an automobile's headlight generates many trillions of photons a second). Given the fact that KH-11s pass over or near their targets in a matter of a minute or so, such pervasive darkness would make it impossible to pick up imagery with a photomultiplier. But near total darkness is not a problem on earth.

"It's never going to be pitch-black because there's sky glow, which is significant," James R. Janesick, an authority on CCDs at the Jet Propulsion Laboratory, has noted. "There's got to be some sort of energy out there. If you don't have energy, you're not going to see anything. But it's to the point now where a photomultiplier system would work at any time because there's enough light. If you've got the moon, you know, it's incredibly light. But the universe has its own light source," Janesick added. "When you go out at night [with no moon], you can still see around because there's light coming from the galaxy." A photomultiplier used with an infrared scanner can provide fine imagery of objects such as darkened buildings from the KH-11's operational altitude on even the darkest nights. And the resulting real-time pictures, like those taken in broad daylight, are three-dimensional. Similar imagery has been collected on the Viking missions to Mars when scientists wanted to use the three-dimensional effect to study the planet's canyons. The resulting imagery was "spectacular," Janesick recalled.

However efficient the KH-11's charge-coupled devices are (and they are a hundred times more efficient than standard film cameras at collecting visible light), they are only as good as the telescope in front of them. And the indications are that that is very good indeed. Since the Air Force donated six 1.8-meter (71-inch) mirrors to the University of Arizona and Harvard's Smithsonian Observatory several years ago, it can be inferred that the KH-11's primary mirror is wider than that, though not so wide as the Space Telescope's, which measures 94.5 inches across. The KH-11's primary mirror is therefore most likely on the order of two meters, or roughly six and a half feet, wide. Its secondary mirror would therefore be about a foot in diameter, a size that would narrow the image coming off the primary mirror and sharply focus it. And the telescope itself is almost undoubtedly plugged into a two-position zoom lens, giving it both area-surveillance and close-look capability.

There has also been some speculation that the KH-11's primary mirror is a so-called rubber type whose thin, highly polished surface can be continuously computer-adjusted to compensate for atmospheric distortion when the zoom lens is in its close-look mode (distortion is less important when large tracts are under surveillance). Light travels up to the satellite along wave fronts that are theoretically straight but in fact bend in many directions because of the effects of thermal currents and pollution in the lower atmosphere. Active optics, as the corrective system is called, compensates for the distortion by relying on computers to detect curved light waves hitting the mirror and then adjusting for them—flattening them out—by making extremely subtle changes in the shape of the mirror itself (which is why it is called a "rubber" mirror, even though it is metallic).

One way to do this is by using a shearing interferometer to look at the whole wave front in order to spot slope errors so that they can be automatically corrected. "If you're looking at a point source [of light], then its non-flatness is a measure of what's wrong with it, and if you can detect the non-flatness, you can correct it out," according to Dr. Jerry Nelson, a professor of astronomy at the Lawrence Berkeley Laboratory in San Francisco. Nelson designs ten-meter aperture optical and infrared telescopes.

How clearly, then, can the KH-11 see? The resolution of the satellite's main telescopic imaging system is one of Washington's most closely guarded secrets. Yet it is easily calculated by anyone with a knowledge of optical science and just as easily confirmed through the use of political science. The results in both instances are surprisingly close, and show that the popular analogy about reading license plates is in fact correct.

Nelson calculated in a matter of seconds that the theoretical limit of the resolution of the system described here (and which he thought was an entirely reasonable one for a reconnaissance satellite like the KH-11) is two inches in the visible light part of the spectrum, including night imaging with the photomultiplier, and somewhat more than that for the invisible bands.

This calculation is borne out by the terms of the SALT II agreement, which not only limits each side to the development of only one new ICBM, but stipulates that ICBMs existing at the time the treaty came into effect could not be altered in length, diameter, launch weight, or throw weight (the size of their payloads) by more than 5 percent.

As is the case with all of the other terms of the agreement, the 5 percent proviso is subject to monitoring and verification by national technical means—in this instance, by imaging satellites. Prior to signing the agreement, in other words, Arthur Lundahl or someone else from NPIC assured the State Department negotiators that U.S. spaceborne imaging platforms could produce pictures that would show whether changes of more than 5 percent were being made on Soviet ICBMs. This would have to apply to the smallest of the Kremlin's long-range missiles as well as to the largest. The smallest Soviet ICBM at the time SALT II was concluded was the SS-11, a three-stage MIRV'd missile that was sixty-four feet long and six feet in diameter. Five percent of six feet is 3.6 inches. That is how good resolution in the visible light spectrum has to be to enable the United States to spot a widening of the SS-11 by 5 percent or more. This closely matches Nelson's calculation, the more so because his theoretical limit would be unattainable much of the time owing to some atmospheric effects that even active optics might not be able to cope with. And, as noted, the KH-11's electro-optical imaging system using CCDs has caught up with the finest of the film cameras where resolution is concerned.

The second of the KH-11's—5502—went up on June 14, 1978, and functioned for 1,166 days. No. 5503, which was orbited on February

7, 1980, had a lifetime of 993 days, despite a malfunction that report-edly reduced coverage of the early stages of the Iran-Iraq war. A fourth KH-11 was sent up on September 3, 1981, and a fifth, on November 17, 1982. No. 5504 remained in orbit for a record 1,175 days. A fifth KH-11 was sent up on November 17, 1982, and func-tioned for 987 days. A sixth, sent up in 1984, was still in orbit at this writing. No. 5507, which had been intended to replace one of its aging predecessors, was lost on August 28, 1985, when its Titan 34D booster had a partial power failure just short of two minutes after lift-off.

The KH-11's real-time reconnaissance exploits appear to be for-midable. The satellite is supposed to have disproved reports that the Russians had built a new chemical and biological warfare manufac-turing facility by returning pictures that showed the place to be an arms storage depot. It was a KH-11 that was used to locate the Americans being held hostage inside the U.S. embassy in Teheran in April 1980 and also to provide data on the route that the ill-fated Delta Force rescue team was supposed to use.* A year later a KH-11 reportedly photographed the space shuttle Columbia on its inaugu-ral flight so that an accurate damage assessment could be made after several of the spacecraft's protective heat-shield tiles broke off dur-ing launch. This indicates that the satellite's imaging apparatus can be used to look in directions other than down, a handy capability for use in checking out the opposition's low-orbiting satellites, both reconnaissance and otherwise.

The single KH-11 operating in April 1986 was evidently worked overtime.† Its imagery was used to plan the air attack on Libya that took place on the fifteenth and then to provide intelligence on damage assessment following the raid. Less than two weeks later, the satellite sent down imagery showing that the explosion at the nuclear reactor at Chernobyl had blown off most of the reactor building's roof, that the large graphite moderator was burning, and

---

*Sometime after the failed rescue attempt, purported copies of KH-11 imagery of the embassy compound and a sports stadium that was supposed to be used as a landing area for the evacuation of the hostages were distributed in Teheran, together with various maps of the city and lists of code words. The documents were painstakingly pieced together from U.S. files marked "Secret" that had been shredded immediately before U.S. personnel evacuated the embassy, according to Iran. Even as photocopied several times, the overhead pictures show considerable detail.

†Standard procedure called for the use of two KH-11s at all times, one working in the morning light, the other in the afternoon for maximum shadow effect.

even that a soccer game was in progress in a field adjacent to the stricken plant after the accident.

The KH-11 has capabilities that are thought to be so good that on at least one occasion it received credit where none was due. It was widely assumed during and immediately after the Falkland Islands war between Argentina and Great Britain in the spring of 1982 that intelligence was gathered for Washington and London by one or both of the KH-11s in orbit at the time. One detailed study even went so far as to analyze KH-11 ground tracks and orbital maneuvering during the war to show that the satellites, working in conjunction with a Big Bird and with the Navy's White Cloud ocean surveillance satellites, gathered intelligence on the military activities taking place below. The analysis is compelling. But it is wrong. Weather conditions during the conflict precluded KH-11 coverage. Although the satellite's imagery through haze or partial cloud cover can be enhanced by Digital Image Processing, it does not function through the kind of thick blanket that hung over much of the South Atlantic during that conflict.

For all its accomplishments, the vast majority of which concern the relatively small day-to-day intelligence triumphs that go un-recorded, the KH-11 is not without its faults. As noted, its develop-ment and production were so expensive that other systems had to be curtailed. This resulted in the sort of lapses in coverage that angered George Keegan. "The volume of coverage began to steadily decrease" as funds were diverted to the KH-11, according to an-other highly knowledgeable source, to the point where "by the mid-seventies, it really began to pinch. For months at a time, or even up to a year or more, there were lapses in wide-area coverage, and that's how the erection of the large ABM radar [at Abalakova] in Siberia went undetected."

Jeffrey Richelson has shown that with the exception of fifteen days in 1981, there has been continuous imaging satellite coverage since 1977. But by "coverage," the American University professor meant time in orbit, not necessarily time during which the sensors were working. The indication, in fact, is that through mid-1983 imaging sensors were not turned on as much as they ought to have been as a cost-saving strategy. At about that time, however, the effects of the Reagan administration's doubling the NRO's budget began to alleviate the problem.

And there were restrictions on the ground as well, some of which remain. "A great deal of collected data is not being analyzed because of manpower shortages," a former high-ranking intelligence official has complained. "They gave up manpower in 1971 and afterward in order to buy more systems," the foremost of which was the KH-11 itself. Ironically, then, the KH-11 also forced reductions in the ranks of the very people who were supposed to cope with the enormous amount of data it was designed to produce.

But even at full strength the people on the ground are easily swamped by all the data that come down from space when the satellites are operating at full strength. This leads to what is perhaps the central paradox of the new space reconnaissance. Partly closed down, the system can miss an event that may be of considerable importance. Unbridled real-time reconnaissance, on the other hand, can bury its interpreters under more intelligence than they can assimilate.

"The information coming down from these things is just going to choke you," said Jerry Nelson, who is well acquainted with the remote sensing satellites that are the KH-11's civilian counterparts. "It gets awful real fast. You can't buy big enough computers to process it. You can't buy enough programmers to write the codes or to look at the results to interpret them. At some point you just get saturated," the physicist added, "and that defeats your whole purpose."

11 .

In the Arena: Cosmos, Spoofing, and Killer Satellites

Operation Bright Star, which opened with a plane crash on November 12, 1980, and flickered out in obscurity sixteen days later, was unspectacular as military exercises go. Except for the C-141 transport that plowed into the desert while on final approach to the Cairo West air base on the first night, killing six crewmen and seven soldiers, it was no different in a tactical sense from hundreds of other maneuvers that have been conducted by the United States Army and its allied counterparts since the end of World War II. If anything, the operation was so modest by usual standards that it prompted one senior officer in the Pentagon to note with unconcealed scorn that it was merely "cosmetic."

The idea was to get 911 paratroops of the 101st Airborne Division, some Cobra attack helicopters, and A-7 fighter-bombers to Egypt within forty-eight hours of a supposed attack somewhere in the region by an "aggressor" force. Once there, the GIs were to join elements of the Egyptian army in the desert northwest of Cairo to repel the imagined enemy. And with the exception of the plane crash on the first night, that is pretty much the way Bright Star went. The Americans and Egyptians spent the better part of ten days living in wall tents, lowering themselves down ropes that dangled from helicopters, and staging mock attacks against objectives in the desert near the Wadi el Natrun oasis and elsewhere while the A-7s strafed the phantom foe ahead of them with real bullets.

When the shooting ended, the men of the 101st Airborne took camel rides in the desert, caught the sound-and-light display at the Pyramids, bought brass trays, camel saddles, and other souvenirs to take back to their base housing, and went home. Appraising Bright Star, Drew Middleton, the military correspondent of *The New York Times*, reported with uncharacteristic evenness that it had been "so modest an effort that it is unlikely either to impress potential allies in the Middle East or cause sleepless nights in the Kremlin." Middleton was no doubt right about the effect on potential allies, but if the Russians slept through Bright Star, it was with one eye open. And that eye was in orbit.

The exercise was the first overseas test of the then new Rapid Deployment Force, an interservice command designed to get American soldiers overseas quickly. The Middle East had been selected because it was the most likely potential trouble spot in the Eastern Hemisphere. American hostages at that moment were languishing in Teheran in the wake of a miserably failed rescue mission. Iran itself was under the control of an unpredictable, anti-Western zealot who had gone to war against Iraq two months earlier and was considered easily capable of undermining other governments in the region. There was the unending tension between Israel and her neighbors, a situation always ripe for war. Finally, the Russians had invaded Afghanistan the previous December, and there was some feeling in Washington that if they had been brazen enough to do that, they might go for Iran as well, thereby threatening much of the West's oil. A Soviet invasion of Iran would have to be checked, and quickly, and that is why Operation Bright Star amounted to more than it seemed.

There is no record of how the supreme high command of the Soviet armed forces reacted to the planned exercise, though it probably took it to be exactly what it was, no more, no less. But it is in the Kremlin's interest to know how such operations work. So standard procedure in such circumstances, and there had been many over the years, called for taking a look.

In the early afternoon on Wednesday, November 12, even as the doomed Starlifter and her sister C-141s were strung out in a long line across the Atlantic heading for West Germany, where they were to refuel before pushing on to Egypt, a large rocket booster

known in the West as an A-2 blasted off from Plesetsk carrying a
modified Soyuz spacecraft named Cosmos 1221. The satellite was on
a reconnaissance mission. Unlike its American counterparts, however, the A-2 did not thrust its payload into a near-polar orbit.
Instead, the booster headed for a lower inclination of 72.9 degrees,
or some 23 degrees lower than the route taken by the Titans that
deliver Keyhole satellites to orbit.

Less than twenty-four hours after Cosmos 1221 roared off its pad
at Plesetsk—at exactly 1:15 P.M. local time on the thirteenth—it
passed 25 miles to the east of Cairo at an altitude of 140 miles. The
light was excellent, shadows were short, and it was early enough in
the afternoon so that distortion from the desert's heat thermals was
not severe. From that vantage point, Cosmos 1221's cameras were
perfectly positioned to record the beginning of Operation Bright
Star. The cameras pointing out of the satellite's spherical front
would have photographed the helicopters, jeeps, trucks, folded
tents, field kitchens, ammunition boxes and all the other equipment
being unloaded from the bellies of the cavernous transport planes.
And they would not have failed to see the wreckage of the one that
had crashed just short of the runway.* The following day Cosmos
1221 passed 25 miles to the west of Cairo, no doubt following the
whereabouts of the battalion of American soldiers as it headed toward the desert northwest of the city.

Cosmos 1221, a third-generation, medium-resolution photoreconnaissance spacecraft, was joined on the seventeenth by Cosmos
1218, a newer, high-resolution type that had been sent up from
Tyuratam on October 30. Cosmos 1218 sailed directly over Cairo
at 8:00 A.M., or about an hour and a half after dawn, at an altitude
of 115 miles. That ground track would have allowed it to take fine
obliques of the mock combat taking place in the desert.

At some point, however, the Russians became more interested in
the actual shooting that was taking place between the Iranians and
the Iraqis than in the practice going on near Wadi el Natrun.
Accordingly, on November 20, Cosmos 1218's orbit was altered so
that it passed just to the west of Khorramshahr and Ahwaz and right
over Teheran at an altitude of only between 102 and 108 miles.

Cosmos 1221 was de-orbited and retrieved with its film pack on
November 26 (the day Bright Star ended), while its companion

---

*By the sheerest coincidence, Voyager 1 was at that moment passing through Saturn's moons
on the first close "photoreconnaissance" of the solar system's second largest planet.

spacecraft floated down under its own billowing parachutes on December 12. Both missions were strictly routine but nonetheless said a great deal about Soviet space reconnaissance and how it differs from that conducted by the United States.

The most fundamental difference between U.S. and Soviet space reconnaissance operations has to do with the frequency of launches —with the number of satellites that are put into orbit. While the United States sends up relatively few reconnaissance satellites each year, the Russians launch thirty-five or more (some being civilian earth resources surveyors similar to the Landsat series used by the United States or France's SPOT spacecraft). This is possible because, unlike their Western counterparts, Soviet reconnaissance satellites are relatively simple and are produced in quantity. And although the computer technology used to run those satellites isn't as good as the kind at Sunnyvale, Colorado Springs, and elsewhere, there is no truth to the occasional assertion that Moscow uses many satellites to compensate for relatively poor imaging resolution. Rather, it is a matter of trying to keep costs down while maintaining as much flexibility as possible.

"They have a technology philosophy which they adhere to— although they have their options—of building a lot of cheap things instead of building very few, very sophisticated things," according to Nicholas L. Johnson, the Colorado-based advisory scientist for Teledyne Brown Engineering and an authority on the Soviet space program. "This gives them a lot more flexibility" than the U.S. space reconnaissance program has, Johnson explained.

Cosmos 1221, now long gone, illustrates to a significant degree how Moscow runs its space reconnaissance program. The satellite itself was not designed from scratch as a reconnaissance platform. Like many other types of Soviet spacecraft, it was in fact a modified version of the Soyuz space capsule. Soyuz was conceived as the successor to the Vostok and Voskhod spacecraft and made its debut in April 1967 as the U.S.S.R.'s primary manned space vehicle,* and one intended for a multimission role that included carrying cosmonauts around the moon (which was dropped after Apollo 8 did

---

*The event ended disastrously. Problems on the flight resulted in Soyuz 1's having to be brought down early. Then its parachute failed to open properly, causing it to slam into the ground at nearly three hundred miles an hour. Vladimir Komarov, the sole occupant, was killed on impact, thereby becoming the first flight fatality of the space age.

it first at Christmas, 1968) and serving as a space station that could dock with other manned orbiters.

Soyuz comes in three parts: a cylindrical equipment module to which solar panels are attached, a bell-shaped crew module that can hold two or three cosmonauts, and a spherical orbital module through which the cosmonauts are supposed to pass while they are attached to another spacecraft.* The Cosmos reconnaissance satellites are simply modified versions of the manned capsule. The equipment module was made to carry fuel, small maneuvering rockets, and a large chemical battery to power the sensors (the standard solar panels were left off the reconnaissance version), while the crew module in the center of the craft was converted to a compartment holding film canisters and other equipment. The round orbital module up front is where the cameras and other sensors are kept. Like its manned counterpart, the photoreconnaissance version of Soyuz is slightly more than seven feet in diameter, just over twenty-three feet long, and weighs on the order of seven tons. Also like the manned version, it goes up on top of a reliable moderate-size A-2 booster. Thus configured, the imaging satellite comes in low-, medium-, and high-resolution versions.

Even the launching of Cosmos 1221 and its sisters was planned to maximize efficiency. The booster that sent it into its 72.9-degree inclination was aimed 23 degrees lower than the path taken by the Titans that deliver Keyhole satellites to orbit. Using lower inclinations (in some cases as low as 51 degrees but more often in the high 60s through the low 80s) is standard practice for Soviet reconnaissance launches, and with good reason: it's cheaper than launching toward the poles.

Since the earth spins from west to east, launching a spacecraft as much as possible in that direction cuts down on the amount of thrust required for a given amount of payload weight, since the momentum of the planet itself helps get the booster off the ground. Conversely, launching to the north or south, and therefore at a right angle to the motion of the earth, requires extra thrust to place a given amount of weight in orbit because the booster has to overcome half of the effect of that motion. And a KH-11 launch, which is typically inclined nearly 97 degrees, actually goes against the movement of

*A red-and-pale-green Soyuz attached to a silver Apollo spacecraft hangs in the National Air and Space Museum to commemorate the Apollo-Soyuz joint mission that took place in July 1975.

the earth, which is enormously taxing.* The Russians therefore use the earth itself as a free booster of sorts. As it is, the margin between payload weight and booster thrust where Soyuz and the A-2 are concerned is not all that comfortable. The booster's lifting capacity is seven and a half tons, or only a thousand pounds more than the weight of its cargo. Sending thirty-five or more reconnaissance satellites into orbits perpendicular to the movement of the earth would mean having to go to a much more powerful booster, perhaps one even in the giant D-1 class, and that would add considerably to the cost of the program.

The real underpinnings of Soviet space reconnaissance, however, remain simple, easily adaptable designs typical of the sort of assembly-line production that is unknown at TRW and Lockheed, where large and immensely complicated satellites are literally handcrafted over many months. The CIA's penchant for exotic, fabulously expensive satellites, such as the KH-11, has one advantage and one distinct disadvantage. On the positive side, such satellites are qualitatively superior to their Soviet counterparts, and therefore yield better intelligence. On the other hand, their enormous cost limits the number that can be produced, which can create havoc when there is point failure or catastrophic accident. The loss of the KH-11 when its Titan 34D booster blew up at Vandenberg Air Force Base in August 1985, for example, left only one other in the inventory —a demonstration model at TRW that was used to test new sensor systems. Although the problem resulted from a failure of the launching system, not the satellite, it nevertheless left only one KH-11 in orbit: the middle-aged 5506, which had been orbited the previous December. Where space-based imaging reconnaissance was concerned, the accident, plus the loss of a KH-9 the following April, left the United States half blind (see Chapter 13).

Johnson has pointed out that the Soyuz series is more than two decades old and is still being used for both manned and unmanned

*Although a satellite in a 97-degree orbit technically flies over more of the earth than does one that is inclined 73 degrees, geographic coverage is not the central consideration in choosing the near-polar orbit, since there isn't much to image at the ends of the earth, anyway. Cosmos satellites in 73-degree orbits pass over everything south of Point Barrow, Alaska, and every country in the Southern Hemisphere, so they are not really at a disadvantage in that regard. But they do lose constant light conditions. U.S. imaging satellites fly near-polar orbits in order to be sun-synchronous, which means that the sun is in the same place every time they fly over a given spot. This greatly aids photo interpretation because shadows and other lighting effects remain constant.

missions. The latest in the line, the so-called T model, has also been adapted to reconnaissance. Of the basic spacecraft, whatever its mission, Johnson observed: "You're talking about assembly-line techniques. There's nothing fancy about them. We know that simply from the hard data we have on the manned spacecraft. The French have flown on it and the Soviets released a lot of data when we had the Apollo-Soyuz mission back in '75. We know a lot about it. It's very simple, and rugged, and mission-effective. It does what it needs to do." So do Soyuz's boosters, which also roll off assembly lines at frequent intervals.

Large-scale photoreconnaissance satellite production has at least two advantages. It allows the Russians to respond quickly and repeatedly to emergencies or to any situation in which imagery is useful, and it also increases the odds that they will keep at least some reconnaissance capability in the event that those of their spacecraft in orbit are attacked by anti-satellite (ASAT) weapons.

"They're very reactive," Nicholas Johnson observed. "We've seen many times that they put up a new satellite within twenty-four hours of a world crisis." A U.S. reconnaissance satellite launch, by comparison, can take weeks or even months to prepare because of the complex logistics. The Russians, on the other hand, stock both reconnaissance satellites and their boosters, and keep some of each ready to go on short notice. "When the rocket comes out," Johnson added, "the upper stage is already fueled, the payload is already on, it's already been checked out, so they erect the thing, fuel the main booster, and it goes." During the Arab-Israeli war in 1973, that kind of capability allowed the U.S.S.R. to send up seven reconnaissance satellites in one three-week period. And rather than keep them up for the then normal fourteen days, they were brought down after less than six in order to retrieve their film as quickly as possible.

During the summer of 1984 the Soviet Union operated a record six photoreconnaissance satellites at a time on a number of occasions. On June 24, for example, two earth resources satellites, one medium-resolution reconnaissance type, one high-resolution, one low-altitude short-duration, and one of the new long-duration reconnaissance spacecraft were all in orbit. "The ability to handle such an assortment of missions at the same time is indicative of the maturity of the Soviet photographic reconnaissance program," according to *The Soviet Year in Space: 1984,* one in a series of authoritative annual compendiums of Soviet space activities.

And in the event of a war that is so extensive that anti-satellite weapons are used against their reconnaissance assets, the Russians will derive yet another benefit from all the satellites they keep "in the barn" because there is safety in numbers. "If you start looking into the Star Wars–type scenarios—if you have an ASAT war— then you need to get replacements up quickly if your resident satellites have been negated," Johnson added. Since the Kremlin could theoretically get its satellites into orbit in a matter of days, not months, survivability is inherent in their system by sheer dint of numbers (presuming, of course, that SAC does not go after all those satellites while they are still in the barn, which is a plausible scenario for an all-out war). The numbers mean something else, too. Unlike the technological thoroughbreds in the U.S. inventory, the Soviet spacecraft do not require extreme measures of self-protection because they are expendable.

For all their capabilities, both sides' reconnaissance satellites not only are so "dumb" that they have to be tended almost constantly, but are for the most part easily tracked and "acquired" (military terminology for being set up) as targets. Dr. Albert Wheelon, the former CIA space expert who went to the Hughes Aircraft Company, has listed some of the more obvious means of pinpointing the location of satellites with great accuracy. Because they radiate electrical energy, they show up clearly as bright infrared sources against the cold backdrop of space. In addition, even satellites in geosynchronous orbit are easily tracked by microwave radar or laser reflections. Both PHOTINT and SIGINT spacecraft must betray their whereabouts when they downlink their collected intelligence, while radar satellites give themselves away by virtue of the electromagnetic pulses they emit. All of these factors help establish extremely predictable orbits for almost all satellites—where they will be at any given time—and that information is imperative for those who plan ways to kill them. At the same time, there are many ways to help protect satellites from attack, none of them foolproof and all relatively expensive, in terms of either performance or financial cost.

Additional fuel can be carried for emergency maneuvering when attack seems imminent, or decoys can be let loose to draw an attacking satellite off the scent of its real target. Both of these measures consume space and increase weight that might otherwise go to the sensors themselves. In addition, satellites cannot maneuver abruptly like fighter planes because of their enormous speed and the absence of air, so outmaneuvering a pursuing ASAT would be highly unlikely.

Satellites can also be provided with a measure of artificial intelligence, making them sufficiently autonomous so they can assess an attack situation, adopt a defensive mode that would include "buttoning up"—shutting doors to shield lenses and mirrors from laser attack—and even repair themselves when damaged by diagnosing the problem and finding ways to circumvent it. As will be seen, the move to make U.S. military satellites more autonomous is already under way.

"Hardening" is yet another protective technique. One of the many ways to do this is by encasing the satellite's sensors, computers, and communication and navigation systems in sheet metal. Another is to coat its lenses so they are laser-resistant and therefore less susceptible to being "blinded." Still another, currently being done, is to use gallium arsenide in place of silicon to manufacture the CCDs that go into the sensors, as well as other silicon used in the spacecraft's computers and its fiber optical system. Although gallium arsenide is extremely difficult to rid of impurities and is therefore an enormously expensive semiconductor, it carries signals much faster than silicon and is resistant to the kind of radiation bombardment that would pervade near-space in a thermonuclear war, particularly if the warheads were detonated high in the atmosphere. Such explosions would produce a radiation flux that could destroy unprotected electrical equipment both in satellites and on the ground.*

Finally, spacecraft can be provided with their own phased array radar jammers, which can be programmed to go on as soon as a positive threat assessment has been made, and they can be configured to have an extremely low radar and infrared cross section. The National Bureau of Standards, for example, has developed an "ultrablack" coating that could be electrodeposited on titanium, beryllium, composites, and other spacecraft materials which not

*Although the term "electromagnetic pulse" (EMP) is widely used in connection with satellites, it is really more of an aerial and ground effects phenomenon because it is dependent on the atmosphere. In space, radiation striking a satellite would generate electrical currents within its components, and it would be those currents, not the radiation, that would cause the damage. The more accurate term is therefore "system-generated electromagnetic pulse," or SGEMP, since the system would in effect destroy itself. Nor would SGEMP be the only radiation effect. Nuclear explosions would leave wide bands of very energetic electrons and protons in orbit, forming disruptive swaths similar to the Van Allen belt. Ariel 1, which was launched in April 1962 as Britain's first space satellite with an intended lifetime of fifteen years, was knocked out of action after it flew through such a radiation belt following one of the U.S. nuclear atmospheric tests that took place over the Pacific.

only would absorb 99 percent of most radar wavelengths, but would increase resistance to laser damage in the process.

Although great uncertainty exists regarding the effectiveness of each of these countermeasures because the actual toll of an enemy attack cannot be accurately assessed in most cases until it happens, large sums of money are nonetheless going into research that promises to at least better the odds of satellite survivability, if not assure it, in time of war.

But the Russians do not have this problem, at least in the magnitude faced by their American rivals. The advantage in turning out so many satellites, though they are less sophisticated than their American counterparts, lies in the fact that such survivability aids do not necessarily have to be engineered into them. The problem for the United States was postulated in a different context by IBM's Richard L. Garwin in a talk before the New York Academy of Sciences in 1983: "If you are driving your fancy automobile down the street you are even more desirous that people don't throw low-technology rocks at it than if you didn't have any kind of such [high-] technology vehicle."

Since Moscow is no more forthcoming than Washington with information about its black programs, the capability of its photoreconnaissance and other intelligence-gathering platforms must be deduced. No Soviet satellite has ever been seen by Western observers to eject a capsule, for example, but the fact that orbital lifetimes for high-resolution (close-look) satellites has jumped over the years from 14 to 207 days (a record set in 1985 by Cosmos 1643) suggests that dropping buckets, as opposed to bringing down the entire spacecraft, has become a fairly routine practice. Close-look satellites, after all, are supposed to be able to do many things, including the gathering of high-resolution imagery during crises or periods of unusual activity and getting it down for analysis as quickly as possible. It therefore makes no sense to go to the trouble of developing a close-look spacecraft that is capable of six-month missions unless some provision is made to get pictures down short of de-orbiting it before its operational life would otherwise be over.

There is also strong evidence that the Soviet Union, too, has developed the ability to transmit digital imagery in real time. Both U.S. and British analysts came to that conclusion after noting that

three reconnaissance satellites—Cosmos 1543, 1552, and 1608—
worked in conjunction with a relay type in geosynchronous orbit
parked off the coast of West Africa in much the same way that the
KH-11s send their imagery through the SDS and other platforms
(though SDS satellites are in highly elliptical, not stationary, orbits).
Moscow's high-flier, Cosmos 1546, was launched on March 29,
1984, and was watched as it interreacted with the lower-orbiting
reconnaissance platforms later in the year. Cosmos 1546's position
puts it in view of the reconnaissance satellites that regularly fly
south–north tracks over the United States. It is thought that transmitting imagery from them to yet another relay satellite over the
U.S.S.R. would provide Moscow with near-instantaneous pictures
of the United States, including those showing the amount of damage
done in a nuclear war.

Orbital parameters—apogees, perigees, inclinations, periods, and
so on—plus the sort of maneuvering that results in abrupt changes
in ground track can tell a great deal about photoreconnaissance
satellites and their missions, particularly when the maneuvering
coincides with important political events. An analysis of Cosmos
1548's ground track over the Persian Gulf in April 1984, coming at
a time when half a million Iranians were poised for an all-out assault
on Iraq, and when a rash of air attacks against oil tankers broke out
in the Gulf itself, leaves no doubt as to what the spacecraft was
doing. Similarly, Cosmos 1599's maneuvering into low orbit over
Chad during two lengthy periods in October and November of the
same year would have provided Soviet photo interpreters with the
wherewithal to count the number of French and Libyan soldiers
who were allegedly withdrawing from that country. Such sorties go
on routinely throughout the year and provide clear indications of
what Soviet space reconnaissance is doing. They provide no clues,
though, about the quality of imaging resolution.

If the national intelligence establishment knows how good Soviet
space imagery is (and three likely ways of finding out are through
spies like Oleg Penkovskiy, by tapping the stream of data coming
down from relay satellites like Cosmos 1546, and by undertaking
important but physically small or even minute activities to see
whether they elicit a response),* it is keeping the information as

*The third means of assessment can be unreliable, however, because both sides understand
how that game is played. It might be better not to challenge a small arms-control violation,
for example, than provide the violator with an indication that the transgression was spotted
and in the process reveal the true capability of one's imaging or SIGINT system.

secret as that relating to its own systems. Making such knowledge public would constitute a double sin in the convoluted "arena" (as intelligence people on both sides call their common domain) of international espionage, where secrecy and deception are the heads and tails of the coin of the realm. It would probably compromise the way in which the data had been collected, thereby causing a self-inflicted wound on the collection process itself, while simultaneously giving the Kremlin new insight on what the United States can get away with by masking some of its own key military activity from prying eyes and ears in space.

Still, there are indicators. There is the low-orbit weather imagery that is routinely sent down electronically by Soviet satellites, along with pictures that were returned in the late sixties and well into the seventies by their unmanned lunar and Martian probes. The weather imagery is comparable to that returned by National Oceanic and Atmospheric Administration (NOAA) Nimbus and NOAA spacecraft for use in formulating daily weather forecasts, as well as some published imagery taken by the Pentagon's Defense Meteorological Support Program (DMSP) satellites that search for holes in cloud cover so that KH-11s and other imaging satellites can be turned on when it is feasible to do so.

But lunar and planetary imagery is another matter. Beginning in 1968 with the Zond series (which also were modified Soyuzes) and continuing through 1976, the U.S.S.R. launched a series of probes that either orbited the moon or landed on it. And in 1971 two Soviet satellites named Mars 2 and Mars 3 reached the red planet and returned data for three months each during that autumn and winter.

"If you compare the quality of those pictures with the quality of the pictures that NASA was getting [from similar probes] at the same time," Nicholas Johnson has observed, "they were vastly different. They were grossly inferior. They didn't even come close to the resolution NASA had."

It is possible, though unlikely, that the Russians were giving space probes their second-best shot in deference to their higher-priority, strictly military, imaging programs. In 1968, when Zonds began reconnoitering the moon, the Apollo program was in full momentum for a manned landing there. Moscow was feeling the full heat of the competition and was therefore straining for every possible propaganda triumph. Then, having been beaten to the moon, Moscow denied that there had ever been a race in the first place and pointed its imagers toward Mars in the apparent hope that it could redress the damage caused by the Apollo program's spectacular technical and managerial coup. In such circumstances the Russians would have wanted to show the world the best possible pictures of the Martian landscape. "It's a high-priority program for them," Johnson added. "You spend six or eight months sending something to Mars, you want to make sure you get the very best pictures coming back."

Nor did the Russians fuzz the imagery or otherwise diminish its quality in an attempt to forgo a propaganda victory in favor of deceiving the West about their spacecraft's real capability. Such a tactic would have been seen through because in a couple of instances, and especially in the 1960s, the United States intercepted imaging signals directly from Soviet probes, according to Johnson. "So it's not like you're always relying on a picture released by the Soviet government," he added.

(Though it is not germane to an analysis of Soviet imaging capability, it ought to be noted in passing that the ability to plug into downlinked Soviet deep-space imagery transmissions and tap them raises intriguing possibilities that would, if accomplished, add another dimension to competition in reconnaissance. However slow bucket-dropping is, the system is for all intents and purposes impossible to penetrate. Electronic transmission, on the other hand, is much faster but potentially vulnerable to interception no matter how "secure" it is made by changes of frequency and encryption. Far from being only a remote possibility, it is difficult to believe that both sides have not been working on such intercepts for years. The advantage would go to the side having the fastest, highest-capacity computers.)

There is a point somewhere along the development "tree" at which the technology of all imaging spacecraft, whether they image Vladivostok or Venus, is indistinguishable. They are all essentially the same generic platforms and share a technology that is commonly understood by engineers in both the black programs and the white ones of whichever nation produces them. This is not to say that the white systems and the black ones share the same capabilities, for they do not, nor that the engineers who work on the respective programs are fully communicative with one another, which is also not the case. (An apocryphal story that has lingered in the aerospace industry for years has to do with "white hat" engineers and "black hat" engineers sitting at adjacent tables in the company cafeteria; when talk among the white hats turns to a particularly knotty problem that has evaded them for months, causing deep frustration, their colleagues in the black hats break out in uncontrollable giggles.) Reconnaissance systems vary according to the resources put into them and are configured differently, depending on what is required of them, so close analogies between civilian (or, more correctly, scientific) systems and their national security counterparts cannot be drawn too closely.

Yet all spaceborne imaging systems, to take one example, share a common basic technology and the study of that technology allows certain inferences to be made. Landsat 1, which was launched by NASA in July 1972, and the last of the KH-7s, which had been sent up by the NRO two months earlier, were at core the same basic satellites (though they looked different and were not similarly equipped, of course). Had Landsat 1 been provided with a different telescope and other specialized hardware, it would have in effect *been* a KH-7, since the state of the art where standard daylight imaging was concerned was essentially the same for both programs in 1972.

Mariner 10 was a case in point. The JPL-designed spacecraft, launched in November 1973, returned extraordinarily detailed photographs of Mercury. This was in sharp contrast to the pictures the Soviet engineers were able to extract from their Mars probes. There is an implicit assumption that the respective engineering teams did the best job they could in these endeavors. In the case of Mariner 10, as opposed to successive Soviet Mars probes, the best was very good indeed. The spacecraft (which also returned the first TV pictures of Venus as a by-product of the Mercury mission) carried a Cassegrainian telescope with a five-foot focal length for close-looking, a multispectral filter wheel, infrared radiometer, videcon camera, and a high-capacity tape recorder.

Mariner 10's photographs of Mercury's rugged Caloris Basin taken from a distance of 37,300 miles were enlarged to a resolution of .6 miles. Had the spacecraft taken its pictures 125 miles over the U.S.S.R., then, resolution would have been 10.6 feet (not allowing for atmospheric distortion). That number was in the KH-7's ballpark. It indicates that while the black and white space imaging programs of the time were hardly related in an official sense, the technology used by both produced roughly similar results.

If a basic commonality of technology runs through all U.S. space imaging systems, then as much must necessarily be said of their Soviet counterparts. It is unreasonable to assume that Russian astronomers and astrophysicists were content to receive and make public third-rate imagery when they could have obtained a superior type while their counterparts in strategic intelligence were pulling down imagery of excellent quality. It must therefore be deduced that the resolution obtained from Soviet space reconnaissance lagged substantially behind that of the United States throughout the 1970s, though it has probably almost closed the gap in this decade. All indicators but one point to inferior imaging: they were late in developing ejectable capsules, late in setting higher orbits and therefore in prolonging the lives of their satellites, late in establishing a real-time system, and dreadfully late in producing the kind of high-speed computers that are now and forever wedded to strategic reconnaissance in all its forms.

The only indicator pointing the other way is the fact that the Russians, too, signed SALT II, presumably in the belief that they too could verify its provisions (or at least enough of them to justify approving the terms of the agreement).

But in treaty verification, as in the collection of technical intelligence for targeting and other national security requirements, the Russians enjoy a significant advantage relative to the United States, and one that reduces much of their dependence on overhead reconnaissance. According to Dr. Hans Mark, who was under secretary of the Air Force (and therefore director of the NRO) in the Carter administration, the openness of American society allows the Russians to have a technologically inferior reconnaissance system—which he readily acknowledged—because they can purchase at nominal cost or even obtain for free what U.S. technical collectors must pay dearly to get. There is little need to image the National Photographic Interpretation Center or the Satellite Control Facility from orbit when both can be photographed in better detail from across the street, or to get Cosmos pictures of Beale Air Force Base or the Trident submarine facility at Groton, Connecticut, when clearer and certainly less expensive shots can be taken from up close. SR-71s and U-2s coming to or leaving Beale can be photographed in crisp detail from just outside the base's main gate, while anyone with a rowboat and a good camera can get close enough to the drydocked submarines under construction at the Electric Boat Company's Groton plant to photograph their seams. The same is true for many kinds of university research, open scientific meetings, and publications of all sorts (including, in Mark's view, this book).

Prohibitions on travel to most areas of the U.S.S.R. and pervasive censorship, on the other hand, force the United States to bring its technical superiority to bear for the collection of tactical and strategic data that otherwise would be unobtainable.

Where space reconnaissance is concerned, the Soviet Union appears to be better at listening and using radar than at imaging, although there have been some spectacular and embarrassing setbacks in those areas. The Kremlin's overall space signals intelligence program roughly parallels that of the United States and concentrates on ferreting radar, intercepting telemetry and communication, and conducting ocean reconnaissance.

The first Soviet SIGINT satellite, Cosmos 148, went up on March 16, 1967, or about five years after the first U.S. ferret was sent into orbit.* The spacecraft was shaped like an ellipsoid measuring about six by four feet and weighing only about nine hundred pounds. Sixty-four of these first-generation Cosmos SIGINTs were sent up during the following decade, with typical perigees of 105 miles, apogees ranging from 185 to 310 miles, and inclinations of 71 degrees. But seven months after the launching of Cosmos 148, a heavier, cylindrical platform called Cosmos 189 was put into orbit from Plesetsk. It was followed by some forty others, all operating in groups of four so as to improve their chances of fixing the exact locations of their ground targets. The first- and second-generation SIGINT satellites therefore coexisted for years.

The first of a third series of SIGINT satellites, Cosmos 895, was sent up on February 26, 1977, on top of an A-1 booster, which is a slightly smaller version of the A-2 used for Soyuz launches. Following a trend in both East and West, the satellites in this series are substantially larger and heavier than their predecessors, being about sixteen feet long and weighing between 5,500 and 8,800 pounds. These spacecraft are placed in 372-mile-high circular orbits with inclinations of 81.2 degrees. The most interesting operational characteristic of the satellites is the fact that they are deployed in constellations of six, each of which is separated from its immediate

---

*It was a Thor Agena-B launched on May 15, 1962, and put into an elliptical 82-degree orbit. It lasted 560 days.

neighbors by 60 degrees on an imaginary orbital plane. This means that all six are spaced equidistantly around the earth, providing continuous global coverage.

Then, on September 28, 1984, the Russians launched what appears to be a new type of SIGINT spacecraft, and a huge one at that. The satellite, Cosmos 1603, was probably carried on a giant Proton booster. With a low-orbit lifting capacity of twenty metric tons, the Proton is the most powerful launch vehicle in the Soviet space fleet.

Cosmos 1603 first went into a 115-mile-high circular "parking" orbit with a relatively low inclination of just under 52 degrees. Trackers in NORAD's Space Surveillance Center in Cheyenne Mountain noted that the satellite had a very large radar cross section. The next day, as Air Force personnel in the dimly lighted chamber watched with growing amazement, Cosmos 1603's own rocket shot it up to a circular orbit averaging 530 miles while changing its inclination to 66 degrees. Finally, yet another maneuver established a final inclination of 71 degrees.

Those who watched Cosmos 1603 were particularly interested in its size and maneuvering capability, both of which are related, since a good proportion of the satellite's bulk goes for fuel storage.

The Russians were less fortunate fifteen months later when Cosmos 1714, a SIGINT platform in the same series, was lost. The mission illustrates how glitches in even the most practiced procedures can cause total point failure. Cosmos 1714 was launched on December 28, 1985, for the purpose of monitoring U.S. military radio traffic. It was first put into an elliptical orbit whose parameters were 120 miles by 535 miles. But when its controllers tried to move the giant spacecraft into a circular 535-mile orbit, its engine failed, leaving it stranded in a useless orbit, from which it descended a few weeks later as a glowing blob of molten metal. But that was by no means the worst or most embarrassing accident to befall a Soviet spy satellite. Credit for that dubious distinction goes to the Kremlin's ocean reconnaissance program, and to its nuclear-powered spacecraft in particular.

The Soviet strategic reconnaissance apparatus has responded to the U.S. Navy, a far-flung enterprise that is capable of inflicting devastating damage throughout the seven seas and far inland, by laying special emphasis on ocean reconnaissance satellites designed to keep track of U.S. and Allied warships, and particularly those that would go after Warsaw Pact land and sea targets in the event of war: the huge carriers whose fighter-bombers would be laden with nuclear weapons, as well as the other large ships that carry cruise missiles.

While Soviet space reconnaissance in general has lagged behind that of the United States, its spaceborne ocean reconnaissance program got under way two years before Classic Wizard (its American counterpart), since the U.S. deepwater fleet has always constituted a graver threat to the U.S.S.R. than the other way around. Just as the American bombing force would rely on ferret satellite data to jam the radars protecting Soviet targets, so, too, would Soviet bombers, submarines, and long-range missiles be pointed to the American attack carriers by the ocean reconnaissance platforms in an attempt to knock them out before they launched their murderous swarms at the motherland. The Russians know they will have to stop the attack planes and missiles before they leave their nests if catastrophic destruction is to be avoided or reduced, and that cannot be done unless they know where those nests are at all times, no matter what the hour or how poor the weather.

The U.S.S.R. uses two types of dissimilar but complementary ocean reconnaissance satellites that work together to detect, identify, and track the warships of the Western powers: electronic ocean reconnaissance satellites (EORSAT), which intercept signals from the ships' radar and communications systems, and radar ocean reconnaissance satellites (RORSAT), which track their targets using powerful radar scanners. EORSATs are passive, since, like most ferrets, they merely listen while emitting no signal of their own. The radar satellites, on the other hand, are active because they beam radar signals downward and then register the bounce-back to define their targets.

EORSATs, which weigh close to ten thousand pounds, work in pairs along near-circular orbits with perigees of 265 miles and apogees of 280 miles. They are inclined 65 degrees north and south of the equator, a track that takes them over every important body of water on the planet. Precision is vital here because the satellites have a problem that most of their sisters do not have: their targets move a great deal. So unless the speed and direction of their quarry are transmitted with extreme accuracy, the undertaking is pointless. EORSATs therefore are equipped with ion microthrusters, which permit minute adjustments of altitude so that their periods are kept at exactly 93.3 minutes. In this way, the movement of the ships whose progress they are following can be correlated with their own positions so that the vessels' location, speed, and heading can be calculated. Using two EORSATs allows the Russians to get a more accurate fix on their targets' position—a procedure similar to the triangulation used by U.S. White Cloud ocean reconnaissance satellites.

EORSATs and RORSATs are often sent up together in precise, unvarying orbits. The combination is effective because it is both complementary and redundant. That is to say, if the vessel being tracked goes radio-silent, the passive EORSAT will not be able to pick it up but the radar satellite will still register its position. If the ship attempts to jam the radar, it must do so by sending up a very strong signal that will be picked up by the EORSAT. Using the spacecraft in combination therefore makes it extremely difficult for the ships they track to hide (though there are ways to do so).

EORSATs repeat their orbits over the same track every four days, while their radar sister satellites repeat their orbits every seven days. And although the number of minutes separating the passage of a pair of EORSATs and a RORSAT may vary according to the particular mission, the time interval within each mission is rigidly fixed. As a result, the satellites pass over the same piece of ocean within a short period of time and in a formation that is precise enough to allow them to establish the positions and headings of their targets with extreme accuracy. The radar satellites apparently can even identify particular types of ships.

However capable Soviet ocean reconnaissance satellites are, the program has not been without setbacks. Two of these involved the widely publicized falling back to earth of RORSATs, debris from which hit Canada and the Indian Ocean. Both incidents, and particularly the first, evoked negative reaction because the debris was radioactive.

Radar operations require a great deal more power than can be collected by solar panels. As a result, Soviet RORSATs have been fitted with nuclear reactors that are thought to be modified versions of their small Romashka type that use 110 pounds of enriched U-235 to develop ten kilowatts of power.

The RORSAT's designers faced a quandary when the satellite was still on the drawing board. As is the case with all reactors, those aboard the satellites were going to need thick metal shielding around them, not only to protect workers on the ground but to keep instruments on the spacecraft as free as possible from radiation interference. But this raised a problem. Whereas other satellites reentering the atmosphere would incinerate and disappear before striking the ground because of atmospheric friction, the dense shielding surrounding the RORSAT's reactor would protect it from decay during reentry in much the way ablative material on the nose of a nuclear warhead protects it by gradually peeling away while the bomb inside remains intact. Since no one wanted the reactors to fall out of the sky, possibly on populated areas, another solution had to be found.

The answer, it seemed, was to build RORSATs in such a way that they would break into three parts at the end of their missions. While two of the parts would plow into the atmosphere after separation and burn up normally, the third part, containing the hot reactor, would be fired upward by its own small thruster and placed in a storage orbit, where it was supposed to remain for more than five hundred years.

The system seems to have worked satisfactorily until the flight of Cosmos 954. The forty-five-foot-long spacecraft was launched on September 18, 1977, and apparently performed without incident until the following January 6. On that day, however, it lost pressurization and began to tumble out of control. Cosmos 954's violent gyrations evidently prevented its controllers from jettisoning the reactor, whose core at that point was extremely radioactive. On January 24, 1978, the very problem that the spacecraft's designers had foreseen came true. The satellite dropped out of orbit, and as it did so, the reactor's shielding protected it even as the rest of the craft disintegrated. The nuclear reactor and what remained of its fuel came apart after passing through most of the atmosphere, leaving a trail of radioactive debris in the vicinity of Great Slave Lake in the Canadian tundra.*

The demise of Cosmos 954 prompted Russian engineers to rethink RORSAT design throughout the next two and a half years, during which no other radar reconnaissance satellites were launched. Then the design bureau came up with a solution that

---

*Cosmos 954 was not the first satellite to spill radioactive material on earth. A U.S. Navy satellite launched by a Thor Able Star at Vandenberg broke apart on April 21, 1964, before reaching orbit, and spilled fragments of plutonium-238 into the Indian Ocean. The reactor, called SNAP-9A, was twenty inches wide, ten inches high, and weighed only twenty-seven pounds. It was superseded by SNAP-10A, the only U.S. reactor believed to have been sent up, which operated for forty-three days.

illustrates the differences between the way Russian engineers and their American counterparts resolve such problems. Faced with a satellite reactor whose booster could fail on launch, whose platform could go out of control in orbit or undergo any number of other problems, the Americans would engineer in a series of redundant systems that would be expensive and consume space and weight in an effort to prevent the accident at all cost.

The Russians, however, were fatalistic and seem to have concluded that given the complexity of such systems, there was no way to guard against all possible contingencies. They therefore redesigned the reactor itself so that when the mission is over or an accident occurs, the small fuel rods are ejected out of it. Although the reactor's empty core, with its residual radiation, remains protected by the shielding, the rods themselves are fully exposed to the atmosphere and decay as they come down.

The fuel rod ejections began in 1980 and apparently were perfected by January 1983, when a second RORSAT, Cosmos 1402, came to an ignominious end after it too went out of control. Instead of breaking into three parts, Cosmos 1402 broke into only two, neither of which was sent up to a storage orbit.

"At that point, they said, 'Okay, we've lost the bird, so we're gonna eject the fuel,'" Nicholas Johnson explained. "And that's exactly what happened. They admitted it was a nuclear reactor. They admitted it was a nuclear fuel element they kicked out. They admitted that they did it in response to 954." The crippled satellite's reactor plunged into the Indian Ocean on January 23, 1983.

Nor are radar ocean surveillance satellites the only maritime reconnaissance platforms that go awry. On January 25, 1985, an EORSAT, Cosmos 1625, broke up after failing to get into its proper orbit. Debris came down about two hundred miles northwest of Bucharest, Romania, according to the North American Aerospace Defense Command, which monitors all activity in space. It was not known whether any of the spacecraft's pieces actually hit the ground.

Almost nothing happens in the arena that goes unheard or unseen by the adversaries, though each is occasionally surprised or fooled. Space tracking was a vital element in both the Soviet and American satellite programs from their inception, since it made no sense to put a spacecraft in orbit unless those who did so knew where it was at all times. A reconnaissance satellite could return the clearest possible imagery of an ICBM silo, for example, but it would be of scant use to a targeteer who did not know where that imagery had been taken.

It was also understood even before the advent of Sputnik in 1957 that the same system used by a nation to follow the course of its own spacecraft as they streaked across the heavens could be used to track the opposition's as well. So over the years, each side has evolved increasingly refined tracking capacities in order not only to operate its own space systems with the necessary precision, but to simultaneously gather information about the other's satellites and, more important, maintain a constantly updated threat assessment.

This is a contest of orbital hide-and-seek. The hiders on each side try to reduce as much as possible the mission of its satellites by adding capabilities that might go undetected (giving the KH-11 a SIGINT system or installing COMINT equipment on Tracking Data and Relay Satellites, for example), or by sending up some satellites that are disguised by virtue of their orbital characteristics so as to pass for others (Jumpseat radar ferrets that look like SDS relay platforms, for instance, or Rhyolite-type geosynchronous SIGINT satellites that appear to function like the more beneficial DSP-647 early warning spacecraft). In the main, however, it is the seekers who have a permanent, and considerable, overall advantage because, in the manner of the interpreters of imagery at NPIC and elsewhere, they have over the years categorized everything they've seen in order to establish precise operational patterns. What does not fit the pattern causes immediate suspicion.

The launching of Cosmos 1603, the giant ELINT satellite, on September 28, 1984, was a case in point. Since there had never been a Soviet launch quite like it, the sudden appearance of the massive spacecraft prompted immediate consternation at NORAD. Its Space Defense Operations Center (SPADOC), which is responsible for monitoring and assessing the intent of all foreign spacecraft and for watching for threats to U.S. systems in particular, scrambled to get a quick fix on the newcomer and determine its intent.

"When Cosmos 1603 was launched, it did not fit anything that had happened before," Colonel William E. McGarrity, the Air Force's director of space operations inside Cheyenne Mountain, said sometime later. "We had to bring in extra analysts and do special tasking of the U.S. satellite tracking network to get every possible look at the object. We had several different people trying to analyze it and determine what it was going to do next and also build tracking element sets good enough for the sensors to continue tracking it," the colonel added. "Each maneuver and change of inclination brought us additional problems. We lost it two or three times, but then it would reappear. The thing that mystified us most about it was there is no logical reason for putting something into orbit the way they did it in this particular case." McGarrity went on to note that Cosmos 1603's extensive maneuvering at first led some of SPA-DOC's analysts to think it might be an anti-satellite spacecraft, but that notion was quickly ruled out.

In the vast majority of instances, however, other nations' space launches are pegged so routinely that the young airmen and women who peer at the consoles in SPADOC's dimly lighted interior as they trace innumerable ground tracks might as well be working as insurance claims adjusters for all the excitement in the air. Cosmos 1402, the ill-fated RORSAT, for example, was correctly seen to be a "reactor-powered radar ocean-surveillance vehicle" having a 159- by 173-mile orbit and an inclination of 65 degrees soon after it was launched on August 30, 1982. Cosmos 1405, which went up five days later, was quickly pegged as another ocean-surveillance type, though it was cataloged as conventionally powered. The data back in Cheyenne Mountain told Colonel McGarrity and his fellow officers that China's twelfth spacecraft, which was sent up on September 9 on the FB-1 launcher version of that nation's CSS-X-4 ICBM, had all the characteristics of a reconnaissance satellite. Its 107- by 244-mile orbit and 63-degree inclination would have allowed it to make its lowest run over the same general area every day. It also came back out of orbit five days after it went up. Reconnaissance. No doubt about it.

The Space Defense Operations Center receives its tracking data from the Space Surveillance Center, which uses a worldwide network of radars, telescopes, cameras, and radio receiving equipment to sort out and track everything except deep space probes. The network, which itself is called the Space Detection and Tracking System, or SPADATS, makes about thirty thousand satellite observations a day, all of them transmitted to the Space Surveillance Center's computer banks, where they are compared with the normal characteristics of similar satellites and then stored for later reference. Between four thousand five hundred and five thousand objects— ranging from Soviet and other nations' reconnaissance, navigation, and meteorological satellites to U.S. and Soviet early warning platforms in synchronous orbit, to derelict boosters, to discarded or misplaced equipment (one piece of which is an astronaut's hand-held camera)—are tracked with great precision every day by the SPADATS' round-the-world sensor network.

While most of the Space Detection and Tracking System's sensors are rather mundane radars and radio antennas, the system uses one kind of imaging apparatus that is anything but ordinary. This is the TRW-built Ground-Based Electro-Optical Deep Space Surveillance System, or GEODSS, which is a computer-linked telescopic system that uses CCD arrays to get real-time images of objects as small as a basketball at synchronous range—22,300 miles. The system uses two forty-inch aperture telescopes to spot new movement of even extremely faint objects while compensating for the movement of the earth and stars and other natural phenomena. GEODSS arrays are already in place at the White Sands Missile Test range, in New Mexico, at Taegu, in South Korea, and on Maui, in Hawaii. Others are scheduled to be built in Portugal and on Diego Garcia, the island in the Indian Ocean that serves as a major U.S. naval facility.

The Air Force maintains that GEODSS's function is to spot new objects in space and relay their precise locations to the Space Surveillance Center, and also to identify and track satellites whose existence is known but whose mission may be obscure. The telescopes are designed to be especially effective at ranges of from three thousand miles to synchronous and are calibrated to move at a rate that is exactly counter to the rotation of the earth. This technique, an old one in astronomy, in effect freezes the stars in place so that they do not appear to move. But satellites, even those in synchronous orbit, move ever so slightly against the background of stars. GEODSS's computers erase everything that does not move from one picture to the next, while objects that have moved, however slightly, are recorded in real time and relayed to to the Space Surveillance Center's computers for analysis. If the GEODSS's telescopes can acquire basketball-sized objects in high resolution from 22,300 miles, they can certainly define Soviet satellites in great detail and no doubt do.

GEODSS is supplemented by two highly classified telescopic cameras code-named Teal Amber and Teal Blue. The former is at Malabar, Florida, while the latter is on Mount Haleakala, in Maui, Hawaii. Both cameras provide NORAD, and specifically its Space Defense Operations Center, with computer-enhanced high-resolution close-up photographs of Soviet and Chinese spacecraft in real time. This, of course, means that NORAD can watch the Cosmos reconnaissance satellites as they watch the United States. Teal Amber and Teal Blue are so good that they were used to scan the space shuttle Columbia on her maiden flight in April 1981 in an effort to determine the extent of tile damage. They have also reportedly been used to watch cosmonauts doing extravehicular activity outside the Salyut 6 space laboratory.

While the Air Force will say nothing about the cameras' resolving power, data about their immediate predecessor shed some light on the matter. Starting in 1962, the Air Force Avionics Laboratory ran an Electro-Optical Observation Site at Cloudcroft, New Mexico, near Holloman Air Force Base. The installation's job was to take highly detailed photographs of anything in orbit that the Air Force wanted to see close up. To do this, two five-inch spotting telescopes, which scanned a wide area of the sky for potential targets, were "slaved" to a large, forty-eight-inch reflecting telescope by means of an IBM 1800 computer. Having located the satellite to be photographed, in other words, the spotting scopes would tell the computer exactly where it was so that the large telescope could be set to track the satellite and photograph it with pinpoint accuracy. A Leica 35-mm. camera was mounted at the end of the big telescope, giving it the equivalent of a 129-foot-long telephoto lens. Observers looking at photographs of the Pegasus 2 micrometeoroid detection satellite, launched on top of a Saturn booster in May 1965, could plainly make out discoloration around the exhaust area of the booster's upper stage (which remained attached to the satellite) from its engine having been fired. In another instance, pictures of the Manned Orbiting Laboratory test payload taken in 1966 showed how special marking stripes that had been painted on it had gradually paled because of the eroding effects of ultraviolet radiation. That sort of capability has provided NORAD with a highly detailed catalog of pictures of all manner of Soviet and other nations' spacecraft.

ASAT is a kind of netherworld in satellite operations. It means anti-satellite, and it goes right to the heart of what most concerns Colonel McGarrity and his colleagues in the Space Defense Operations Center. All of the radars, telescopic arrays, and signals intercept antennas that feed satellite data into SPADOC's computers do so to help the analysts in Cheyenne Mountain recognize a threat to

U.S. satellites should they see one, and to formulate methods for attacking Soviet spacecraft should that ever be considered necessary.

Just as nuclear bombs are referred to as "devices," warheads as "reentry vehicles," and enemy combat pilots as "players," so too has the Air Force sought to distance itself psychically from the reality of a satellite war by using a sanitized term to mean the destruction of satellites by direct attack. It is called "negation."

The bible of negation, or at least the sort that possibly awaits U.S. space assets, is a dark blue loose-leaf notebook called the *Space Threat Environment Description*. It is a highly classified compendium of hundreds of possible attack scenarios that could be carried out by the Russians against U.S. satellites, ranging from ground- or space-based laser attack to the use of space mines, killer satellites that could ram their targets, explode near them, or fire salvos of pellets at them, and to such exotic techniques as electronic jamming or reprogramming of the spacecraft to make them useless. The book is the product of many thousands of hours of gaming in which every conceivable way of attacking a satellite has been attempted in order to provide SPADOC's personnel and computers with the means of understanding that an attack is under way at the earliest possible stage. Such gaming never ends, which is why the *Space Threat Environment Description* is in loose-leaf form.

ASAT is not a single weapon but, rather, a generic term covering anything that can be used to attack or impair a satellite from earth or space. The Kremlin is considered by the Pentagon to have four distinct kinds of ASATs in various stages of development.

The first, and best-known, ASAT is the so-called co-orbital interceptor that was first tested in 1968. It is actually a satellite sent into orbit on a giant SS-9 booster. The ASAT's orbit has the same inclination as its quarry, although its altitude can be either a bit higher or lower than the spacecraft it is after (this is called a grazing orbit). The killer satellite stalks its target during the course of one or two complete earth orbits, constantly drawing closer to it while tracking with either imaging radar or infrared sensors. When the ASAT is within lethal range, it explodes, sending a fusillade of pellets or shrapnel into its prey.*

The co-orbital ASATs, which operate from two pads at Tyuratam, have been tested in two phases. The first, which started on

---

*An artist's rendering of such an attack appears in *Soviet Military Power 1983*. If accurate, the picture indicates that at least one of the ASATs has been photographed in detail, no doubt by one or both of the Teal telescopes.

October 20, 1968, and ended with a launch on December 3, 1971, involved seven of the killer satellites, all of them radar-guided. Following a moratorium, the Soviet Union resumed testing on February 16, 1976, and continued through the launch of Cosmos 1379 on June 18, 1982 (it malfunctioned because of a fusing problem, according to sources in Washington who evidently had access to some extraordinary telemetry data). Six of the thirteen ASATs tested in the second phase were guided by the more advanced optical-infrared system, while the remaining seven relied on radar to find their targets. In all, twenty co-orbital ASATs were tested during the fourteen-year period. The highest altitude reached by one of the killer satellites was fourteen hundred miles, which would have put it within striking distance of all U.S. photoreconnaissance satellites, some ferrets, White Cloud ocean reconnaissance formations, weather satellites, the space shuttle and, during the time of perigee, SDS and Jumpseat.

Although there is some difference of opinion as to what constitutes a successful co-orbital test,* it is generally conceded that five of the seven tests in the first phase were on the mark, while only four of those in the second series were successful. This means that nine of twenty tests, or 45 percent, were lethal.

The effectiveness of Soviet co-orbital ASATs (and the possibility of the Kremlin's perfecting one or more of the three other kinds: direct-ascent, laser, and electronic interference) have been the subject of heated debate for years. As is the case with the whole realm of space, perspectives tend to be shaped as much or more by political persuasion as by technical reality. This is because ASATs directly affect three highly charged areas.

To the extent that the superpowers (and particularly the United States) would be dependent on their satellites to perform the crucial command, control, communication, and intelligence functions in time of war—the so-called C^3I—those systems' being incapacitated

---

*Marcia S. Smith, a space expert in the Library of Congress's Congressional Research Service has suggested that an ASAT that has come to within one kilometer of its target ought to be judged successful, since the Russians may be testing a close-inspection system as well as kill capability, judging by the number of ASATs that have come that close to their targets only to be sent out of orbit without exploding. On that basis, she has noted, thirteen of the twenty tests have been successful. The matter is further complicated by the criteria used to determine what constitutes a test in the first place. Dr. Hans Mark believes that if the heart of a co-orbital ASAT test entails trying to get one spacecraft as close as possible to another, then every Soviet co-orbital mission, including those in which cosmonauts rendezvous and dock Soyuz spacecraft to Salyut space stations, constitutes a kind of ASAT test. The navigational requirements of such military and civilian missions are virtually indistinguishable, he said.

by enemy ASATs would be catastrophic. In addition, the introduction of dependable ASAT capability by either side would in effect introduce real weapons (as opposed to the essentially passive current systems) to space and touch off an arms race there. Finally, as has been noted, ASAT technology is intimately related to ballistic missile defense technology of the sort now being considered for the Star Wars ABM system; each places a premium on the development of weapons that could hit a rapidly moving target in space. What can hit a relatively small warhead, after all, can quite easily finish off a much larger satellite.

Accordingly, those who see little danger from the co-orbital ASATs, and who are emphatic in insisting that the United States should not test and deploy its own system, maintain that by and large the Kremlin's weapon is undependable, clunky, and useless at the middle and upper altitudes, where most U.S. satellites reside. They also point out that every successful Soviet co-orbital test involved the use of radar for tracking, and that such a target acquisition system is easily jammed and possibly even avoided altogether by maneuvering. In addition, they say, the co-orbital ASAT can be launched only from a facility able to service the huge SS-9s, which makes the weapon inflexible and able only to travel along inclinations in the mid-sixties. Finally, the ninety to two hundred minutes it would take to reach even a low-orbiting target not only would allow ample time for defensive measures to be taken, but would sound the alarm that an attack against the United States was in the offing, thereby making the exercise self-defeating.

Those who believe that the Soviet ASAT is a viable weapon insist that it has already placed arms in the heavens and that the United States should follow suit by building its own system. Proponents of a U.S. ASAT rest their case on the proposition that even a less than perfect Soviet satellite-killing capacity will do quite nicely if it is the only ASAT system around. Without the possibility of retaliation, the argument goes, the U.S.S.R. could pick off U.S. spacecraft at will whether or not its capability is perfect. Also, ASAT adherents claim, more fuel for maneuvering and perhaps an extra booster would extend the Soviet ASAT's range and provide it with the ability to change inclination on the way up, giving it a better shot at U.S. high orbiters.

Relative to Soviet co-orbital satellites, the U.S. direct-ascent system is a model of sophistication. It is an eighteen-foot-long two-stage rocket designed to be carried under the belly of a fighter (currently the McDonnell Douglas F-15) and launched toward an enemy satellite from an altitude of about fifty thousand feet. The missile, which weighs twenty-six hundred pounds, is then accelerated by its two boosters to a speed of about thirty thousand miles an hour while its nose cone separates and falls away, exposing a Miniature Homing Vehicle (MHV) twelve inches in diameter.

The MHV, nicknamed the Tomato Can because of its squat, cylindrical shape, carries no explosive charge. It is guided to its target by eight tiny heat-seeking infrared telescopes and a laser gyro while continuous directional adjustments are made by fifty-six small one-shot solid-fuel motors. The MHV is moving at a little better than eight miles a second when it rams into its target, either puncturing a hole in it or, more likely, smashing it into metallic shards.

For its first test against an actual satellite, the Air Force ASAT program selected a functioning gamma ray spectrometer satellite, named P78-1, which contained a small solar Corona observatory. P78-1 was chosen, the Air Force explained, because the craft was nearing the end of its useful life and at the same time could provide a valuable live target with which to better assess the results of the ASAT attack.

On September 13, 1985, an F-15 in a steep climb two hundred miles off the California coast fired its ASAT at P78-1, which was passing overhead. The MHV scored a direct hit, blowing P78-1 into about one hundred fifty pieces, some of which were quite small (but all of which were delineated on SPADOC's radar, and most likely the giant Pave Paws array at Beale Air Force Base as well). Caspar W. Weinberger, the secretary of defense, hailed the successful test as a "great step forward" in the race to develop a U.S. satellite killer. But the scientists who had been using P78-1 for experiments did not share his enthusiasm. "It was very sad to see it go," a disgruntled solar physicist at the University of California at Los Angeles said of the small spacecraft, which had been launched on February 24, 1979, with an expected lifetime of forty years. It "was like an old friend up there . . . not one of the more glamorous projects, but it did a particular job very well."

The F-15s that would carry ASATs belong to the Tactical Air Command, but their pilots would get navigational instructions from the same people in the Space Defense Operations Center who track all of the satellites. SPADOC's supercomputers would be expected to provide precise data on where the F-15s would have to be relative to their targets' orbits in order to ensure successful intercepts.

The U.S. ASAT has at least three advantages over its Soviet co-orbital counterpart. Since it is aircraft-launched, it can be used from anyplace airplanes operate, including carriers. This gives it considerable logistical flexibility. Second, its tiny size and terrific speed make it extremely difficult to spot, evade, or repel. Finally, it is easily hidden and is therefore difficult to locate by the very reconnaissance satellites that would constitute some of its most important targets (though it was designed primarily to kill ELINT and ocean reconnaissance satellites).

The sixty-four ABMs that guard Moscow are also thought to provide a limited so-called direct-ascent ASAT capability. The fact that the older ABMs are apparently being replaced by two new hypersonic types, one of which is exo-atmospheric (its range extends above the atmosphere), has disquieted the Air Force. Those who dismiss the ABMs as effective ASATs point out, however, that the simplest way of nullifying them is to keep low-orbiting U.S. spacecraft away from tracks that go directly over the Soviet capital (which isn't a high-priority reconnaissance or mapping target, anyway).

Both the United States and the U.S.S.R. are conducting extensive research in two other ASAT areas: lasers and what, for a better term, can be called electronic interference.

Stories of Soviet ASAT laser development have circulated for years. The Defense Department has charged that there are at least two laser test facilities at Sary Shagan, the Soviet Union's principal ABM research site, and although both appear to be dedicated mostly to ABM applications, the Pentagon has warned that they could just as easily be used against U.S. space assets.

"The Soviets could deploy antisatellite lasers to several ground sites in the next 10 years or they could deploy laser-equipped satellites, either available for launch on command or maintained in orbit, or could deploy both," according to *Soviet Military Power 1984*. The report went on to speculate that the Russians "could test a prototype laser antisatellite weapon as soon as the late 1980s," with initial operating capability coming in the early- and mid-1990s. Both U.S. and British intelligence officials have from time to time grumbled about high-altitude satellites in the vicinity of Sary Shagan suffering "temporary anomalies" that could have been caused by test lasers being directed at them. Why the Russians would want to give away secrets of their own research program by practicing on U.S. satellites, as opposed to their own, has gone unanswered, however.

For its part, Space Command is also pushing laser ASAT research. "It is a technology that looks like it could possibly fulfill our requirements better than the aircraft-launched ASAT we are developing now," according to General James V. Hartinger, the former head of Space Command. The Air Force developed a formal statement of need early in 1983 for a laser ASAT capability "to counter hostile Soviet spacecraft." Such a system would be so similar to the Star Wars laser ABM defense as to be virtually indistinguishable from it.

The most insidious (and by far the blackest and therefore least mentioned) way to make a satellite dysfunctional is not by attacking it but by interfering with it electronically so that it can be jammed, disoriented, made captive, or in effect told to shut down and take the rest of the day off. Each side has put considerable effort into analyzing the other's satellite operational patterns and procedures in order to be able to break into the opponent's up- and downlink signal stream, which would result in havoc.*

Electronic interference with satellite operations has benefits that firing hardware or pointing lasers lack. Its range is theoretically unlimited and not subject to degradation by atmospheric effects, as are lasers. It is essentially instantaneous and can be directed at every enemy satellite at the same time so that it would come as a surprise. Finally, if done only to selected spacecraft, it would cause real uncertainty as to whether an ASAT attack is actually under way or whether the target satellite or satellites are simply malfunctioning on their own.

Such "spoofing," according to a study done for the National Defense University, "is a subtle, effective means of defeating a satellite. Spoofing is either controlling an enemy satellite directly or making the satellite—or the ground controller managing the satellite systems—think that an on-board system needs to be controlled when it actually does not. For example, if you know the correct frequencies, codes, and transmission sequences to control the ma-

---

*The technique was vividly illustrated on April 27, 1986, when someone calling himself Captain Midnight overpowered the Home Box Office transmission coming from a Hughes Galaxy 1 satellite for four minutes to protest HBO's having begun scrambling its signal the previous January. "$12.95/month? No way!" the printed message read in protest against the charge that HBO made for use of its channel. Equipment used to interrupt the Galaxy 1 transmission would have been more powerful than that used to merely jam it. While "Captain Midnight's" prank was harmless, it illustrated "the ease with which commercial satellite transmissions can be interrupted and calls into question the security of satellite traffic including a large volume of government and military communications carried by commercial satellites," according to one report of the incident.

neuver engines of an enemy reconnaissance satellite, then when the satellite is over your territory, you simply send a transmission to fire the engines. The satellite will either become disoriented or lost, or it will burn all its fuel."

Similarly, a reconnaissance satellite can be ordered to wobble, tumble, de-orbit, dump its collected imagery into the waiting arms of the target country's counterintelligence specialists, or simply shut down altogether as it passes over a particularly sensitive event and then be turned on again three or four minutes later. The value of such cosmic dirty tricks, again, is that they would most likely appear to be the result of on-board glitches whose cause is ambiguous. "The advantage of spoofing an enemy satellite," the National Defense University study concluded, "is that the enemy may never know what happened."

But even in the realm of electronic interference there is, as usual, a caveat. "Although it is relatively easy, in some respects, to try and jam, it is a low-confidence system. You're not sure that you've done your job. How do you know that you've *really* jammed that signal?" Nicholas Johnson remarked as he reflected upon the uncertainty of life in the arena.

12

Reconnaissance as Politics: Nicaragua and the Missing MiGs

On March 9, 1982, a rare press briefing, reminiscent of those that had been given during the Cuban missile crisis almost exactly twenty years earlier, was held at the State Department. The subject this time was Nicaragua, not Cuba, though Havana figured prominently in the narrative, which took place in the same auditorium as had the Cuban briefings.

The reporters had been invited so that the Reagan administration, frustrated over the American public's unwillingness to be drawn into a military confrontation with the Sandinista regime, could present graphic evidence showing the dangerous degree to which the Central American country was being equipped with Soviet, East German, and Cuban weaponry and other items. Although no one was pretending that the United States was under the threat of attack by the Managuan government, there was a distinct sense of déjà vu among those reporters present who remembered the crisis of the missiles of October two decades earlier, and now watched large slide projections and dry-mounted photographs, shot straight down, that were set on the same kind of easels that had been used to brief JFK and his executive committee.

The pictures were intended to show that there was a serious large-scale Communist military buildup in Nicaragua. With two exceptions they were identical with those that might have been used in a National Security Council briefing. For one thing, they were a bit grainier than they would otherwise have been, which to some extent protected their true resolution. Also, the original photographs—those that had been shown to the National Security Council—had been taken by satellite. But following long-standing procedure, once it had been decided to make the reconnaissance imagery public, an SR-71A from Beale had been sent down to reshoot the pictures.

Retaking overhead imagery that is already perfectly usable is expensive, time-consuming, and unnecessarily dangerous from an intelligence-gathering standpoint because it risks losing two men and their irreplaceable aircraft in order to get what is in essence duplicate pictures. Yet it is always done for two reasons. First, using aerial photographs absolutely protects satellite imagery, as has been done since the Corona program in 1960. At the same time, the substitution is done to forestall one of the technical collection establishment's worst nightmares: a deluge of requests for still more pictures, and maybe even SIGINT intercepts, made under the aegis of the Freedom of Information Act. Requests for such pictures, it is felt, would pour in almost immediately following even the barest hint that the government had volitionally released reconnaissance satellite imagery, and they would probably never stop.

Admiral Bobby R. Inman, the deputy director of Central Intelligence, opened the briefing by addressing the secrecy issue head-on, and in the process indicated the frustration felt by senior intelligence officials who were prohibited from going public with what they considered to be incontrovertible evidence that Nicaragua was turning into an armed Communist camp and was therefore a threat to the region. Inman was a good choice to lead the briefing. A career intelligence officer who had headed both the Office of Naval Intelligence and the National Security Agency, he was known to be a technologically literate, clearheaded political moderate who was not given to the reflexive seizures of competitive zeal that frequently afflicted some of his Air Force counterparts at the first sight of a new enemy weapon or the mere mention of arms control.

"I'm angry because I've watched, over the past couple of weeks, public servants trying to grapple with the difficulty of conveying information while protecting critical intelligence sources and methods and finding that they're standardly greeted with, 'How can we believe you unless you show us all the detailed evidence?' " Inman said rhetorically.

"And over the weekend we were treated to the occasion of the

visit of [Agriculture] Minister Jaime Wheelock [Román] from
Nicaragua, who used the platform given him to talk at substantial
length about what wasn't happening in Nicaragua. And as you will
see from what we have to say, he lied directly and no one seemed
to challenge that process, at least not in the stories I read. . . . But
we are going to respond today with some declassified intelligence
on the nature of the buildup that we've been watching for some
time." The intelligence was to be "manned reconnaissance imagery," the admiral added before introducing John T. Hughes, who
would do the actual briefing. Hughes, whom Admiral Inman called
the best photo interpreter in the country, had conducted the press
briefings during the missile crisis.

"Let me now share with you the evidence that is available to us,"
John Hughes began. Speaking clearly and with a level of dispassion
that is one of the sure marks of his profession, Hughes explained to
the reporters in the darkened room that "comparative coverage"—
before and after pictures—had been used to make the case against
the Cubans and their Nicaraguan clients.

Then, for the better part of an hour, Hughes, grasping a pointer
that was close to five feet long, repeatedly tapped the spots on a
screen—otherwise meaningless shapes in successive blown-up slides
—that to him amounted to hard evidence that Nicaragua was turning into a bastion (in Inman's words) overrun with Warsaw Pact
arms and Cuban advisers. Although the aircraft had changed since
the Cuban days, with the U-2s having given way to the better-
protected SR-71s, the imagery remained essentially the same and so
did the analytical process. The interpreters still relied upon confluence of evidence. And, as in 1962, much of the case had been built
by tagging equipment, construction, and land-use patterns.

"Most of these garrison areas are built along Cuban design. In
fact, we have evidence of facilities in Cuba that we'll exhibit today
that are seen in Nicaragua," Hughes explained.

"This is one of the new Sandinista garrisons at Villanueva," he
said, pointing at a slide. "This garrison measures some one thousand
by one thousand seven hundred feet overall—across and down—
having a standard rectangular configuration, like we have seen in
Cuba. This configuration, or a battalion-sized unit area, is broken
into three parts. And that pattern repeats itself again and again and
again. Part one is the vehicle storage and maintenance area shown

here. These are vehicle sheds here and here. These are foundations for four more: here . . . here . . . here . . . and here," Hughes said, his face bathed in the projector's light as his pointer and its shadow converged and then parted over four small rectangles. The incomplete sheds had been resolved to nine inches and frozen forever by the pair of technical objective cameras that had peered down at them from the nose of one of Beale's Blackbirds as it sped past, more than fifteen miles high. "Here are the grease pits, where vehicles are serviced. . . .

"The second third of the area, typical again of Cuban construction, is the barracks area. These are five barracks buildings, fifty-five meters in length. And then the third segment of this battalion-sized area, ground-force fighting area, is the training area, where we see the Soviet-style obstacle course here, where we see the Soviet-style physical training area and their exercise field," Hughes noted, tracing the trouble back to the Kremlin, where the technical intelligence people thought it properly belonged. "For this unit, this is the parade field and this is the reviewing stand, situated here. And as typical of Soviet military doctrine, they have antiaircraft defenses already in place at these new garrison areas.

"This is the pattern we see time and time again in Nicaragua. It's the pattern we've already seen time and time again in Cuba. Next graphic, please."

(Slide) "Let me show you another one. Here's one dated nineteen February '82, just last month. It's just been recently completed and is now being occupied. . . . Let me show you the sequencing of photographic coverage we've had as the Sandinistas and the Cubans have built this up over time. Let's look at the next picture, please."

(Slide) "Here are two shots of that installation under construction. This is an early stage, a mid-stage, construction of the same facility near Managua. Here are the foundations, garages, and this is the vehicle storage and maintenance area," Hughes said, repeating the now familiar pattern.

More than just illustrating how all the near-identical training facilities compounded the danger, the repetition gave insight as to how John Hughes and the other interpreters came to their conclusions by comparing photographic coverage. "The point I want to make is that the United States government has detailed, recurring, repetitive coverage, over time, of these garrisons that they've been developing over the past year-and-a-half- to two-year period."

The pictures continued to flash on the large screen, progressing in stages from the relatively innocuous barracks, exercise fields, and grease pits to more dangerous stuff.

(Slide) "Let's enlarge this segment here, which is outlined in white." Hughes looked up at a photograph of a large area, near the center of which was a rectangle purported to have within its white boundaries a temporary armor storage area and an adjacent firing range. He noted that the vehicles, which were clearly visible in pictures that had been blown up from the SR-71's nine-inch- by nine-inch negatives, were Soviet-built T-54 and T-55 tanks—thirty-six-ton monsters that hefted 100-mm. guns.

"Notice the roads, all torn up here by tank treads; torn up through here and through here." The pointer skipped rapidly over the screen, landing on tanks that were supposed to be concealed but which the imagery and its interpreter were laying bare. "And here are covered revetments, or storage points, marked by these white tarpaulin covers—ten arrows—where the other tanks are hidden and covered out of view and just kept out of the sun. They have twenty-five of these in the garrison areas.

"This is an enlargement of that segment situated here, and as you can see it in the enlargement, here is a tank," Hughes continued. "And if you look closely, you can see the gun turret, tubes in the turret. Here's a tank under cover with a tube protruding. Here's a tank under cover here." The pointer came down on the motionless vehicles, one after another, like a stick touching beetles whose hibernaculum had been exposed. There seemed no place for the tanks to hide.

Hughes saved the intelligence about the worst weapons, the airplanes, for last. The airplanes were of particular concern, not only because they could be effective in attacking the so-called contras who wanted to bring down the Sandinista government, but because they would also put every square mile of Honduras, El Salvador, Guatemala, and Costa Rica (not to mention the Panama Canal) within bombing range of Nicaraguan air bases. So John Hughes next turned to the threat from the air.

(Slide) "Now, we show a MiG-17 configuration here, but there's a question mark behind it, the question mark because we believe that soon either MiG-17s or MiG-21s will be delivered to Nicaragua. Why do we say that? For two basic reasons. There are fifty Nicaraguan pilots in Bulgaria and Cuba, training on MiGs today. We expect them to return sometime this year. In addition, four major airfields are being configured in Nicaragua to accommodate heavy jet attack aircraft. Let me show you what we see at the airfields. Next graphic."

(Slide) ". . . this field is being recently expanded in capacity by addition of hardened revetments at this end of the field, just off the main taxiway. One—U-shaped revetments—one, two, three, four, five, six, seven," Hughes said as he counted the enclosures that were supposed to help protect the MiGs from strafing or attack on the ground. "These revetments are for fighter-bombers, jet-capable kinds of aircraft. They're aircraft with revetments like we see in Cuba, like we see in East Germany, like we see everywhere in the Communist bloc," Hughes added, carefully omitting any reference to reconnaissance directed specifically against the Soviet Union. "These are to house fighting aircraft, probably the MiGs that we expect to be delivered to the Sandinistas sometime this year. Next graphic."

(Slide) "Now, at the fields on the Caribbean, this is one that's being blacktopped. It was getting blacktopped at the time of photography, at Puerto Cabezas. It measures some six thousand feet in length, and that's the older runway being improved and repaired by the Sandinistas. But that's not long enough to take a MiG-21 off-loaded with bombs. You need six thousand six hundred feet; it's only six thousand. Look at this extension now under construction at the present time. . . ."

The Nicaraguan reconnaissance photographs were first-rate. They were unambiguous in showing that a large-scale military buildup was under way. But what did the weapons mean?

To Admiral Inman, John Hughes, and others in the intelligence community, they meant that an avowedly Marxist government with close ties to the Warsaw Pact and Cuba was hurriedly acquiring the wherewithal to subvert other nations in Central America by terrorism, overt military action, or both. For them, the weapons and the entire infrastructure supporting those weapons were offensive.

During a question-and-answer session after Hughes ended his briefing, one reporter noted that Managua freely acknowledged Cuban military assistance. He then pressed Inman for his own appraisal of the weapons increase.

"I may well have been around too long in this business and the historical perspectives may not all apply," the admiral answered. "But in my earliest days in the intelligence business in this country,

I remember the newspaper reports of a fine agrarian reformer in the hills of the Sierra Maestra—my Spanish is nonexistent, as you can tell from my pronunciation—we decided to withdraw our support from the dictator. We didn't decide whom else we wanted to support. When he fled the country, the agrarian reformer walked across the island, and once he established control he turned out not to be an agrarian reformer, but in fact had delivered Cuba into the Soviet bloc, and to use it, to build it, into a military bastion, and to ultimately use it as a vehicle to export revolution elsewhere in our hemisphere. I believe you're seeing exactly the same pattern being followed here."

But that same day, when informed of the press briefing that had taken place at the State Department only hours before, one of the two original members of the Sandinista junta that had overthrown Anastasio Somoza Debayle in 1979 heatedly denied that his country had offensive designs in the region. The official, Sergio Ramírez Mercado, conceded in an interview with a reporter from *The New York Times* that Nicaragua had both increased its weapons stockpile and expanded the number of its military garrisons, just as John Hughes had asserted. He did not quibble with the content of the reconnaissance pictures. He took strong exception, however, to their meaning.

"When Mr. Haig is saying every day that they are going to bomb us and attack us and blockade us," he said, referring to threats he claimed had been made by Ronald Reagan's first secretary of state, "how can they then turn around and ask us not to defend ourselves?"

And garrisons were being set up around Nicaragua only as a consequence of the deposed dictator's having gathered his soldiers around Managua, leaving the rest of the country unprotected, Ramírez maintained. "Mr. Somoza's national guard was not based on national defense but on internal repression. He didn't want to have any of his military units out of his reach in Managua because he feared that independent garrisons would revolt. He centered the military here in the bunker with his armored cars, tanks and elite forces all in one place in Managua." But the revolutionary government, not fearing an upheaval caused by its army, was merely spreading its garrisons out "the way any regular military force in the world does," Ramírez asserted.

Washington was unconvinced. The Reagan administration had become fixated on the need to cut the Sandinistas out of Central

America's body politic before their doctrine spread like a cancer throughout the region—before it metastasized, just the way the Cubans' had. By the autumn of 1984 the conflict had ripened, with overhead reconnaissance once again playing a pivotal role.

Neither the CIA nor the DIA believed Sandinista claims that their weapons buildup was purely defensive. The MiGs were the sticking point. Hughes had been right about the air bases being expanded and fortified to accommodate the fighters. He had been wrong in his prediction that they would arrive by the end of 1982, of course, but that was taken to be of minor significance, since it was only a matter of time before they showed up.

The confluence of evidence, after all, was indisputable, just as Hughes had said. If runways and taxiways were being lengthened and reinforced to handle planes like MiGs, and revetments were being built in exactly the same way as those that protected MiGs in Soviet client states, then it had to be assumed that sooner or later the opposition was going to try to get MiGs into Nicaragua.

On August 16, 1984, the hypothesis proved out. That Thursday, Sandinista officials took reporters to the airport at Punta Huete, thirteen miles outside Managua. There the press was told that a main runway more than fourteen thousand feet long was under construction and that an alternate, more than twelve thousand feet long, was in the planning stage. And the work was being done, the officials added, to accommodate combat aircraft that were due to be delivered the following year.

Less than a month later Humberto Ortega Saavedra, the Nicaraguan defense minister, said that his country was in fact going to acquire MiGs in order to stave off "flagrant violations" of its airspace and territorial waters by U.S. planes and ships. Although he refused to reveal the number of fighters he expected, Ortega explained that the long runway at Punta Huete would be completed by the end of the year, as would flight training for his country's MiG pilots. At the same time, he rejected the idea that the planes would pose a security threat to the region. "The danger would be if we put missiles or Soviet bases here, but the MiGs are another matter," he said angrily, adding that the fighters would represent Nicaragua's "legitimate right" to have its own air force. Where Managua was concerned (or at least as it was claiming in public), the MiGs were to be interceptors whose role would be to protect Nicaraguan skies and coastal waters from intruders, as was its sovereign right.

But, again, Washington saw matters differently. Where the Joint

Chiefs of Staff and the various intelligence agencies were concerned, the advent of MiGs in Nicaragua represented at least five potential problems.

They would indeed be used against planes and ships that encroached on Nicaragua's airspace and territorial waters, and that would make intelligence-gathering far more difficult. The fighters' first job would be to inhibit U.S. aerial reconnaissance and offshore SIGINT operations so that still more fortifying could take place undetected. The Navy's eavesdropping destroyers, which regularly prowled close off Nicaragua's west coast, would be in particular jeopardy with MiGs only ten minutes away.

The fighters could also be used against U.S. forces in the remote event that circumstances developed in which a direct invasion of Nicaragua became practicable. They would unquestionably be used against the U.S.-sponsored contras who were trying to topple the government, thereby complicating that situation. And armed with bombs, air-to-surface missiles and napalm, as well as with cannons,* they would be capable of flying sorties in close support of Communist insurgents in neighboring countries. As analysts in the CIA, the DIA, and the Air Force well knew, attaching bomb racks to the hardpoints under a MiG's wings to convert it from an interceptor to a bomber was only a little more difficult than changing a light bulb.

Finally, there was the psychological dimension. Possession of MiGs would simultaneously intimidate other countries in the area, enhance Nicaraguan credibility on the international level, and imbue Nicaragua with a degree of prestige that might well spark emulation elsewhere in the hemisphere.

Then, late in September—within two weeks of Ortega's having claimed that Nicaragua was to be the beneficiary of MiGs by year's end—a KH-11 returned some anomalous imagery from the port of Nikolayev on the Black Sea.† The initial imagery apparently

---

*Although intelligence reports indicated that the Nicaraguan pilots in Bulgaria and Cuba were training in MiG-23s, the most likely choice would have been a late-model MiG-21, which the Soviet Union had already exported to thirty nations. Standard armament on the MiG-21 includes a twin-barrel 23-mm. cannon and up to thirty-five hundred pounds of bombs, rockets, or napalm canisters.

†It was the same satellite that less than three months earlier had sent down pictures of the Soviet Union's first full-size carrier that was being constructed. Three of the pictures were shortly to appear in *Jane's Defence Weekly*.

showed twelve large wooden boxes on a pier beside the freighter *Bakuriani*. Crate-ologists tagged them as the kind that ordinarily contain disassembled MiG-21s, while the vessel was known to be of a type that carried them. There followed several days of cloud cover, during which no imagery was collected over Nikolayev. But a second brace of pictures, made after the weather had cleared, showed that the crates were gone and the *Bakuriani* had set sail. This caused no particular alarm because the freighter's destination was not yet known.

Suspicion was aroused during the second week in October, however, when the *Bakuriani* rounded Cape Horn and steamed up the Pacific coast of South America, past Chile and then Peru. Skirting the Panama Canal to take the long way around from Europe to the Pacific made no sense unless a vessel's captain wanted to avoid having his ship's contents inspected, which is customary at the canal. At that point, someone in technical intelligence seems to have decided that the confluence of evidence, including Ortega's word and the air-base reconnaissance imagery, indicated that the *Bakuriani* had crated MiG-21s in her hold (there were no crates on deck). This conclusion, appropriately qualified, was then leaked to the press.

On Tuesday, November 6, even as the *Bakuriani* neared Nicaragua's west-coast port of Corinto under virtual escort by U.S. Navy ships and planes, one unnamed "senior Administration official" was telling a reporter from *The New York Times* who inquired about the MiGs that "we have a strong suspicion that it is happening." Another said that a Bulgarian freighter had docked at a Nicaraguan port and that other ships might well have been on the way with "crates associated with such aircraft." Late in October a Pentagon official was quoted as saying that military equipment from a Bulgarian freighter had been unloaded under extremely tight security at Bluefields, an east-coast city that was the site of one of the Sandinistas' new air bases. "One indication of heightened Administration concern," the *Times* reported in its initial story on November 7, "was the fact that senior State Department officials of the department's Inter-American bureau were meeting into the early evening and were not taking telephone calls." Other unnamed officials confided that the situation was "very sensitive" and that emphasis was being placed on trying to determine whether there were in fact any MiGs aboard the *Bakuriani*.

That same day, while both the Nicaraguans and the Russians

were denying that there were any MiGs aboard the *Bakuriani*, the State Department pressed the initiative by issuing warnings to Soviet officials in Washington and Moscow that no MiGs outside of those in Cuba would be tolerated in the Western Hemisphere. Having apparently been surprised by the intelligence leak, the administration quickly decided to capitalize on it in order to arouse popular support for its undeclared war against Nicaragua.

While President Reagan was telling a news conference in California, "We cannot definitely identify that they have MiGs on there, or planes of any kind," and his vice president was saying for the record that he didn't think all the facts were in yet, nameless sources were keeping the fire fanned by saying on condition that they were not identified that there was sufficient suspicion about the MiGs to justify reissuing the warnings to Moscow and Managua.

"Specifically, the officials said, the aircraft would give Nicaragua the ability to attack nearby nations, including Honduras and El Salvador, that lack sophisticated air defense systems," *The New York Times* reported in the sixth paragraph of a page-one story about the warning that had gone out to the Russians. "In addition," the anonymous official was quoted as saying, "with advanced fighters, Nicaragua would be within relatively easy striking distance of the Panama Canal."

The following day, Thursday, November 8, while Secretary of State George Shultz was indicating that the Kremlin had emphatically denied that any MiGs were on the way to Nicaragua—and in the process providing the first hint that a blunder had been committed from which the administration was about to back off—other "senior Reagan Administration officials" were invoking the Monroe Doctrine as proof of the nation's determination to keep MiGs and other dangerous hardware out of Sandinista hands.* "I don't think there is any question about the United States concern in such an area very close to our own borders. We have compelling national interests in that area," a State Department spokesman explained.

In the end, no MiGs could be found, however carefully the reconnaissance people looked. Window-rattling passes by supersonic SR-71s over the docks of Corinto every day through Sunday, November 11, when the *Bakuriani* set sail, produced not a single photo-

---

*The doctrine, enunciated by James Monroe in 1823, held that the United States had special interests in the Western Hemisphere and would not accept interference with those interests by European powers. It is often forgotten, however, that the doctrine also stipulated that the United States would stay out of European spheres of influence.

graph of anything even remotely resembling a crated MiG. Nor had the missing fighters been left belowdecks. However neatly packaged, a dozen MiGs take up considerable space. But a tally of all the cargo that was unloaded from the *Bakuriani,* including four Soviet patrol boats and a couple of helicopters, left no doubt that she was empty. Bathers in the surf outside Corinto saw that much as they watched her, high in the water, while she steamed down the channel and headed for home.

The saga of the missing MiGs is a cautionary tale that applies to bigger things.

There was in the first instance an analytical failure by the interpreters, whose evidence did not converge as neatly as they seemed to think. This shows that, however good the raw intelligence, it is still subject, as it always will be, to interpretation by people who are susceptible to making erroneous conclusions. No amount of hardware can make a reconnaissance system foolproof.

The misjudgment was then compounded by making it public. Far from being an isolated event, such selective leaking by intelligence officials or those who receive their reports is commonplace. The late Herbert Scoville, Jr., told the Senate Foreign Relations Committee in March 1972 that "the history of the past twenty years is dotted with example after example of intelligence being misused to promote within the Congress the programs of individual organizations or even of the administration as a whole."*

In the case of the MiGs, the leak by design or otherwise played directly into the hands of an administration that was thirsting for an excuse to eradicate the government of another nation. Apparently caught by surprise, the Reagan White House wasted no time in trying to capitalize on the disclosure—still unproven—by using

---

*Examples abound. One of the most glaring appeared on the front page of *The New York Times* on September 18, 1986. Without so much as one reference to TELINT spacecraft such as Rhyolite or to the tracking stations in Norway, Turkey, China, and elsewhere, the article reported that a new version of the Soviet Union's SS-18 ICBM had exploded during a test flight the previous month, that an earlier SS-18 test had also run into severe problems, that there were development difficulties within the SS-24 ICBM program, and that following the SS-18 explosion a submarine-launched SS-N-8 ballistic missile had gone fifteen hundred miles off course and had landed in Manchuria. The leak, attributed to "Reagan Administration experts," warned the American public that the Soviets were pressing ahead with ballistic missile development, made an oblique but unmistakable case for congressional support for technical intelligence funding, and at the same time managed to do a little public nose-thumbing at the Kremlin.

it to whip up public support for dislodging the Sandinistas. Indeed, the ferocity with which news of the MiGs was immediately greeted —proposals to recall the U.S. ambassador, public discussion of the possibility of a naval blockade like the one that had been imposed on Cuba, and the incessant threat of air strikes to protect the sanctity of the Monroe Doctrine—suggests that the president, his closest aides, and a number of Pentagonians were actually hoping that there were fighters in the *Bakuriani*'s hold.

"What we need to do is translate concern about the military buildup in Nicaragua into support for renewed aid for the rebels," one Defense Department official explained soon after the episode. Another was even more candid. "Some of those who want us to adopt a harder line have long wished that MiGs would be delivered because they know that would tilt the policy in their direction. . . . The next best thing to the delivery of the MiGs was the possibility that they might arrive any day."

The use of strategic reconnaissance (faulty or not) for political purposes, and especially to rouse public concern over politically motivated, narrowly perceived threats to the national security, is a hazardous undertaking. Done often enough, it can end either as a self-fulfilling prophecy or, perhaps worse, as an alarm that goes unheeded because of the frequency with which it has been sounded.

13 .

Into the Future:
HALO, SPOT, Radar Farms,
and Other Exotic Assets

•─────────────────────────────

The fifth voyage of the ill-fated space shuttle Challenger, which took place during the second week in April 1984, bore no obvious relation to the national security of the United States. Neither did a subsequent Challenger flight the following October or one made by Discovery, her sister spaceship, in mid-November. Yet all three missions were watched with keen interest by the Air Force and the National Reconnaissance Office because each did, in fact, have a clear bearing on military activity in space, and specifically on reconnaissance.

The single operational thread running through all three missions, however nonmilitary they appeared, had to do with the shuttle crews' launching satellites into orbit and retrieving and repairing those already there. One of the missions even involved practicing to refuel a spaceborne satellite. Whatever else they accomplished, these NASA-run "civilian" activities had profound implications for the design of reconnaissance platforms and for their operation. And, in fact, the three missions showed that there is not, and never has been, a clear line separating "military" and "civilian" space activities, as many in the nation's space program like to pretend.

"There are no civilian programs," according to Professor Jeffrey Richelson at The American University. He did not mean that literally. What he did mean, however, is that to some degree there is a technological base from which all space systems evolve, and in the vast majority of instances it is military requirements, not civilian ones, that drive the system. This is explicit in reconnaissance.

The highlight of Challenger's April 1984 seven-day journey, called Mission 41-C, was snaring, repairing, and sending on its way the Solar Maximum Mission observation satellite. The spacecraft, better known as Solar Max, was supposed to use its telescope to monitor the sun. But a partial attitude control system failure eight months after its launch early in 1980 had prevented the telescope's being pointed in the right direction. That made it all but useless.

So Solar Max was snared by the Challenger's remote manipulator arm and berthed in the Shuttle's open cargo bay. There astronauts George D. Nelson and James D. van Hoften spent seven hours working on it as they sped along, upside down, through several sunrises and sunsets three hundred miles up (with the moon therefore appearing beside the astronauts' feet). The problem was in the Solar Max's attitude control module, a removable 550-pound "black box," that was pulled out of the crippled satellite and replaced by one that functioned properly. Solar Max was then checked out by the Goddard Space Flight Center in Maryland, which controlled it. Having been certified to be healthy by its operators, Solar Max was relaunched by the Challenger's crew so that its observations could resume. The advent of miniaturized modular components has come to mean that virtually any malfunctioning sensor, navigation or communication package, or other equipment can be changed in orbit the way road servicemen replace batteries on highways.

"This mission's significance is that it will change the way designers around the world think about satellites," noted Lieutenant General James A. Abrahamson, who at that moment was abandoning the directorship of NASA's shuttle program to head the then embryonic ballistic missile defense research and development effort known as the Strategic Defense Initiative, or Star Wars, as it is more popularly called. But Navy Captain Robert L. Crippen, the Challenger's commander, was less oblique. "Our impression from this particular mission," he explained, "is that satellite servicing is something that's here to stay."

Challenger's next flight, Mission 41-G, came in October. Once again astronauts performed feats in space that were to have direct applications to orbital reconnaissance and surveillance. Dr. Sally K.

Ride, making her second voyage around the earth,* launched an earth radiation budget satellite designed to measure the amount of solar energy reaching the earth and the amount of energy emitted from it. To be sure, sending a satellite into orbit from the shuttle, which had been done before, provided additional experience for coming reconnaissance launches. But the radiation satellite was not Challenger's most important cargo, however valuable the launching experience it provided. More important, Challenger carried the SIR-B imaging radar, together with a thirty-five- by seven-foot foldable antenna, which produced high-resolution pictures through cloud cover. The radar's purpose, according to NASA, was to provide a new geological perspective of the earth's surface features. The smaller, less powerful SIR-A that had been carried on the second shuttle flight in November 1981 had picked out individual images beneath the sands of the Sahara.

But perhaps Mission 41-G's most important contribution to space reconnaissance came when Dr. Kathryn D. Sullivan and Lieutenant Commander David C. Leestma spent three hours practicing satellite refueling at the far end of Challenger's cargo bay, turning NASA's second operational space shuttle into the prototype orbital filling station. Sullivan (who became the first American woman to do extravehicular activity during the refueling exercise) and Leestma moved hydrazine back and forth between two tanks in several practice transfers. NASA maintained that such orbital refueling could prolong the life of satellites such as Landsat 4, the remote sensing platform that monitors earth resources, by allowing them to maneuver away from the earth's atmosphere. No mention was made, however, of the fact that Landsats are not equipped for refueling, nor that such capability is not especially important for satellites having such regularized orbits as those in the Landsat series. But there is at least one satellite that was designed from scratch to have refueling capability because of its need to do extensive maneuvering: the KH-12.

Finally, on November 16, Discovery ended Mission 51-A when it landed at Cape Canaveral carrying the first two satellites ever salvaged from orbit by Americans. The spacecraft, Hughes-built communications satellites named Palapa B-2 and Westar 6, were

---

*During Dr. Ride's first venture into space the previous June, also aboard Challenger, she and her companions used the robotic arm to release and retrieve a West German satellite five times as practice for the Solar Max mission.

snatched in orbit and maneuvered to the waiting shuttle (waiting, that is, in a precisely controlled seventeen-thousand-mile-an-hour co-orbit) by astronauts scooting around in self-propelled backpacks known as manned maneuvering units, or MMUs. The derelict satellites, which had accidentally been fired into useless orbits the previous February, were brought down without incident.

"In a week of startling images of the shuttle Discovery on a salvage mission in space," William J. Broad observed on page one of *The New York Times*, "one stands out as a vision of the future: astronauts manipulating wrenches as they worked methodically in the cold void. They plucked satellites from orbit, wrestled them into the payload bay and bolted them into place."

Jesse W. Moore, who had replaced Abrahamson as chief of shuttle operations, was quick to pronounce the successful completion of Mission 51-A as "a very historic day for the American space program." Referring specifically to the April and October missions, Moore went on to call the one that had just ended "the third leg of a triangle." And that is exactly what it was.

Some fifty-five large reconnaissance satellites were sent up on the giant Titan boosters between 1970 and that November morning in 1984, when Discovery glided out of the west into a pale blue dawn, made a wide left turn over the Atlantic, and gently touched down on the Kennedy Space Center's long runway with its two salvaged satellites, thus closing the triangle.

About half of the total number of reconnaissance launches involved KH-9s and KH-11s, both of which fly long-duration missions (nearly three years in the case of the KH-11). The length of time on station for such satellites is directly governed by the amount of hydrazine they carry, since the fuel is burned not only to position them for imaging, but also to make the constant tiny but critical course adjustments that keep them under control so that they don't wobble or drift out of orbit. The hydrazine-powered thrusters also keep them high enough to reduce atmospheric drag when they aren't imaging. As matters stood before Mission 41-G, reconnaissance satellites were as good as dead when their hydrazine was depleted, since they could no longer maneuver. But Sullivan and Leestma demonstrated that orbital refueling can be done, and in doing so, they showed that there is no limit to the amount of propellant that can be carried by the new reconnaissance satellites. Access to filling pumps will allow almost constant maneuvering for target coverage, making the KH-12 and those that come after it particularly long-lived and quite unpredictable. And that, in turn, will make concealment and subterfuge—*maskirovka*—all the more difficult.

Miniaturized components—the black boxes—will also extend satellite life when used in conjunction with the shuttles. Both the Hubble Space Telescope and its military reconnaissance counterpart, the KH-12, were designed by Lockheed in such a way that they can be repaired in orbit by astronauts substituting one box for another.

"A June, 1984, Air Force study on spacecraft maintenance pointed out some areas where potential payoffs exist for repair, refueling or preventive maintenance for satellites," Air Force Under Secretary Edward C. Aldridge, Jr., wrote to Air Force Vice Chief of Staff General Lawrence D. Welch late in 1984. "The nation's growing spacecraft maintenance capability coincides with upcoming black design changes on some of our [reconnaissance] satellites, making this an opportune time to establish an appropriate policy," Aldridge added.

As adopted by the Air Force's Space Division, the new policy orders the blue-suiters to "actively examine the utility of spacecraft maintenance options, particularly preventive maintenance, refueling and repair, and avoid wherever practicable design actions that would appear to preclude on-orbit maintenance later in the spacecraft's cycle." This means that retrieval, refueling, preventive maintenance, and repair of orbiting satellites have become an inherent consideration in their design. Aldridge's order carried with it the weight of the National Reconnaissance Office, which he headed in his capacity as under secretary of the Air Force.

Finally, Mission 51-A proved that satellites that cannot be repaired in orbit or need to be refurbished can be carried back down and worked on in the factories where they were born so they can fly again another day. In the case of the Space Telescope, a malfunction in either of its major mirrors, for instance, would result in its being de-orbited for overhaul. The same will be done with the KH-12 or any of the other vastly expensive reconnaissance platforms that develop serious malfunctions or have total point failure in orbit.

All of this points up the intimate relationship between the space shuttle and the reconnaissance programs and, by extension, between NASA and the Defense Department.

The old-timers at NASA had come to cherish the agency's civilian orientation (though it had never been wholly free of military involvement, as was evident by the fact that the Mercury, Gemini, and Apollo astronauts were all military officers). But there had not been money to go around for all of the space programs everyone wanted at the end of the sixties and into the seventies, so NASA had been forced to rely on Air Force funding for part of the shuttle's development. There were some at the space agency who tended to think of their relationship with the Air Force as being roughly equivalent to that of an impoverished prodigy who is forced to live off the largess of a well-heeled but slightly unsavory cousin. But they took the money.

For their part, the generals could see great military potential in a vehicle that could lift sixty-five thousand pounds to orbit (versus a little less than half of that for the Titan 34D). On the other hand, they fretted over the shuttle's relatively low launch rate, the myriad technical glitches that could postpone any launch with people aboard, and the nagging possibility that a major accident could seriously disrupt the sending to space of reconnaissance and other important satellites. The shutdown of the Discovery's main engines four seconds before scheduled lift-off on its maiden flight in June 1984 reinforced Space Command's fear, as did the same shuttle's delay in January 1985, when it was held on its pad with the large SIGINT satellite named Magnum inside because of icing caused by a cold snap. And the grim end of Challenger on January 28, 1986, which at once demonstrated the fragility of the manned spacecraft while cutting the number of annual missions by a wide margin, drove the Air Force's point home with stunning force.

Where imaging reconnaissance in particular was concerned, the airmen's nightmare came true in 1986 because of the confluence of three low-probability mishaps whose cumulative impact was momentous.

The NRO's plan, which called for overlapping coverage leading to a phase-out of the KH-11s, was rational enough. The fifth KH-11 had been launched on November 17, 1982, followed by 5506, which achieved orbit on December 4, 1984. The schedule called for 5505 to be de-orbited in August 1985 after 987 days on station and to be replaced that same month by 5507, thereby ensuring that two of the spacecraft would be operational through the autumn of 1986. Then, according to the plan, the first of the KH-11's successors—a KH-12 —was to be orbited by a space shuttle operating from the new Space Launch Complex 6 at Vandenberg. "Slick Six," as the launch area is called, is the heart of a specially built $2.8 billion space shuttle facility that was designed to permit shuttles and their KH-12s to reach polar orbits after being launched in a southerly direction. With the orbiting of the first KH-12 (no. 5601), the sixth KH-11 could be brought down, leaving the last of the KH-11s working in conjunction with the first of its successors. That last KH-11 (no. 5507) would eventually be ordered out of orbit and replaced by a second KH-12, thereby neatly completing the transition to the sixth generation of imaging spacecraft. The space shuttle figured prominently in launching KH-12s because, due to the enormous amount of fuel they were to carry, they were too heavy to be boosted by the Titan 34Ds that were used to boost KH-11s. The phase-out, phase-in plan had been used before in the Keyhole program and had worked relatively smoothly each time. This time, however, it was different.

KH-11 no. 5505 was sent out of orbit early in August 1985, right on schedule. But then, on the twenty-eighth, its replacement was lost when one of the Titan 34D's two liquid-fuel core engines (as opposed to the solid propellant boosters attached to the core's sides) abruptly shut down a little more than a minute and a half after launch and only forty-five seconds before it was due to be turned off anyway. The power failure prevented the huge booster and its payload from reaching orbital velocity, however, and both were lost over the Pacific.

The loss of the seventh KH-11 left only two others in existence. One—5506—had been launched the previous December and was therefore almost a third of the way through its expected three-year lifetime. The other, a demonstration model used to test new sensors and other hardware at TRW's Redondo Beach plant, was not flyable at the time of the accident. It would require some modification to be so.

Although the loss of the Titan booster and its KH-11 was taken with the utmost seriousness by the Air Force and the NRO, there was at least one ray of hope. If everything else went normally, no. 5506 would remain functional until the end of 1987. By then it was to have been joined not only by the shuttle-boosted KH-12 but by the last of the Big Birds, which could also ride a Titan 34D to orbit.

Then, on January 28, 1986, another of the imaging reconnaissance program's underpinnings was knocked out with the loss of Challenger. Whatever else the calamity meant to the nation's space program, it constituted an appalling setback for the NRO because it relegated the first KH-12 launch to limbo. If there was one small consolation in the Challenger disaster where the Defense Department (and specifically the Air Force) were concerned, it was that the accident proved beyond doubt that the shuttles were not sufficiently dependable to be used as the nation's sole means of launching military satellites. The policy of using shuttles exclusively for all Defense Department launches had been urged on the Carter administration by NASA, which was desperate to get the business, and the White House had finally agreed over strenuous Air Force objections. On the morning of January 28, 1986, the folly of the plan could be seen as plainly as the rockets, wings, crew cabin, and other debris that tumbled out of the sky just to the east of Cape Caniveral.

But ten months earlier, in March 1985, the Air Force had taken the precaution of awarding Martin Marietta a $5 million contract to design a successor to its Titan 34D, to be called the Titan 4. In laying out the new booster's specifications, the Air Force was careful to stipulate that its payload capacity where size (but not weight) was concerned was to be equal to that of the shuttle's. The Air Force called the advanced booster the Complementary Expendable Launch Vehicle (CELV) and ordered ten of them at a cost of $2.09 billion with an option to order more if necessary. The CELV/Titan 4, which at 204 feet in height stands twenty feet taller than the shuttle, is expected to become operational in 1988 and will be able to carry a lightened KH-12.

Meanwhile, there remained the single KH-11 in orbit following the grounding of the shuttles. Because the inaugural launch of the KH-12 had been postponed indefinitely, it was decided by the NRO to send up the last of the KH-9 Big Bird area surveillance spacecraft in order to supplement the KH-11 in orbit, probably while the demonstration version at TRW was hurriedly made flightworthy.

The Big Bird that blasted off from Vandenberg's Space Launch Complex 4 at 10:45 A.M. on April 18, 1986—the last in a line of heavy reconnaissance platforms that had provided dependable coverage of the world for fifteen years—ended its existence ignominiously, another victim of a Titan 34D malfunction. Eight and a half seconds after lift-off and at an altitude of about seven hundred feet, one of the Titan's solid fuel boosters ruptured, sending out a twelve-foot ball of fire and then totally exploding. Within a millisecond of the initial blast, the Titan 34D's self-destruct system automatically set off explosives in the other solid rocket booster and in the larger core itself. Everything, including the reconnaissance satellite in the upper stage, was turned into an orange-and-black fireball that was described as "spectacular" by someone who saw it from eleven miles away. Although some flaming debris arced gracefully out in all directions, most of it came crashing back down in the launch area, crunching automobiles, destroying trailers, cratering sidewalks, setting multiple grass fires, and leaving the launch pad itself a charred and twisted ruin. The third major mishap in eight months left only the single KH-11 in orbit, meaning that the United States remained blind in one eye where space reconnaissance was concerned. "It's a real crisis," observed Paul B. Stares, a military space expert at the Brookings Institution. However dire the situation was as 1986 wore on, though, no one doubted that highly advanced satellites were going to replace those that were lost. So vital had they become to the national security of the United States that their total absence was literally unthinkable. The shuttle was to play an extremely important, but by no means exclusive, role in the operation of the coming generations of space reconnaissance platforms.

U.S. space reconnaissance and surveillance in the twenty-first century and beyond will have a mission that is extraordinarily complex from a technical standpoint, but rather straightforward where their mandate is concerned. They will be responsible for seeing and hearing everything of importance to the national security everywhere on earth and in space, day and night, regardless of the weather. And they will be expected to send their intelligence not only to the agencies and departments in Washington for dissemination to the National Command Authority, but directly to military units in the field as well.

Drawing upon his own experience from the 1970s, William Colby has peered into the future and concluded that such "science fiction" capabilities as "constant visual surveillance of all areas of the globe despite weather, darkness, or camouflage" and "instant translation of electrical messages and oral transmission anywhere in the world" are "well within the possibility of development." Given the extreme sensitivity of the subject, the former director of Central Intelligence's prediction is suitably nonspecific, but it is nevertheless on the mark.

American scientists and engineers are now in the process of designing various stages of a complex but highly responsive electronic shell that is to enclose and describe the sphere on which we live. The planet and the space surrounding it are becoming encapsulated by whole networks of orbital devices whose eyes, ears, and silicon brains gather information in endless streams and then route it to supercomputers for instantaneous processing and analysis—for a kind of portrait of what is happening on planet Earth painted electronically in real time.

The reconnaissance and surveillance platforms will vary considerably, yet all are to be interconnected to constitute a single, all-encompassing, intelligence collection apparatus. There are plans for advanced versions of nearly all of the current space systems, including those in the Keyhole series, Rhyolite and its various derivatives, the Jumpseat radar ferrets and their low-orbiting counterparts, the ELINT satellites that use intermediate orbits, and the White Cloud ocean-surveillance spacecraft. The imaging satellites will be far more maneuverable than those now in use, while all of the next generation of spacecraft will have more powerful sensors, real-time data-processing and transmission, and enhanced attack-hardening.

And there will be new types of satellites. One is being designed to watch for laser tests. Another will carry a nuclear-powered radar that will be able to peer through cloud cover by using a giant dish or a rectangular array the approximate size of a football field that is built of ribs and membrane having the thickness of tinfoil. The rectangular antenna would be carried to its orbital point in the shape of a cylinder and then unrolled like a giant window shade. Another spacecraft, whose heart is to be a large mosaic of infrared sensors, will stare down from its celestial perch and track individual aircraft and cruise missiles by following the heat they emit. Still others, constituting a Space-Based Surveillance System, will keep watch over other nations' satellites in order to provide early warning of an attack on the U.S. assets.

Aerial reconnaissance will have its place as well. The SR-71's eventual successor is probably going to be a so-called trans-atmospheric vehicle (TAV), or hypersonic airplane, powered by supersonic combustion ramjets ("scramjets"). It will take off and land on conventional runways, but will carry sensors, satellites, and other cargo to low orbit at blistering speeds in the range of Mach 25—seventeen thousand miles an hour—which will get it from New York to Peking in slightly more than thirty minutes. The civilian version is already being called the Orient Express.

Finally, there are plans, rarely mentioned, to place a second space station in orbit. This one, unmanned, would travel the polar route carrying a variety of sensors for meteorology, target mapping, and reconnaissance.

The KH-11's immediate successor is the KH-12. It is the military equivalent of the Space Telescope and has been called by some "the ultimate imaging platform" because of its enhanced real-time imaging and shuttle-compatible refueling capability, making it infinitely maneuverable. Not only does the ability to change its orbit over long periods allow the KH-12 to alter its ground track by substantial margins (thereby extending its coverage and making it more unpredictable), but it will add months to its mission life.

The KH-12 carries advanced versions of the KH-11's sensors. In addition, it has a greatly enhanced infrared imaging and SIGINT capability. It has been designed to operate at high orbit when not engaged in reconnaissance or when area surveillance at such altitude will suffice, and to drop to a much lower altitude when close-look scrutiny is required. The low orbit and improved telescope (with its computer-controlled "rubber" mirror) gives it a real-time electro-optical resolution of less than three inches.

KH-12s are supposed to operate four at a time. Two will probably conduct night reconnaissance while the other two observe during the day. In theory, this arrangement makes it possible to get real-time pictures of any spot on earth within twenty minutes of the transmission of the order. Like the KH-11s, the KH-12s uplink their data to SDS and other spacecraft, although, as will be seen, their receiving stations on earth have been conceived to extend well beyond the confines of Fort Belvoir in Virginia.

The KH-12 was designed from scratch by Lockheed to be fully integrated with the space shuttle. NASA's "Baseline Reference Mission Description," a limited-circulation list of the kinds of cargo-hauling missions the shuttle is supposed to perform, contains a specific flight profile for the KH-12 (the satellite is not named), which is called Mission 4:

Mission 4 is a payload delivery and retrieval mission of a modular spacecraft weighing 32,000 lb at lift-off. The mission will deploy a spacecraft weighing 29,000 pounds in a 150 n. mi. circular orbit at 98 degrees inclination within two revolutions after lift-off. A passively cooperative, stabilized spacecraft, weighing 22,500 pounds, will be retrieved from a 150 n. mi. circular orbit and

returned to VAFB [Vandenberg]. The mission length [of the
shuttle], including contingencies, will be 7 days. . . . For mission
performance and consumable analyses, a cradle weight of 2,500
lb will be assumed to be included in the ascent payload weight,
but must be added to the retrieved payload weight. . . . Contin-
gency EVA [extra-vehicular activity] capability shall be provided. . . .

The "Baseline Reference Mission Description" also describes another mission, called 4Y, which has the same payload requirement
as Mission 4 but has the shuttle in orbit for only one day. This
suggests either a refueling operation of the sort performed for practice by astronauts Sullivan and Leestma or an emergency deployment, as might happen if one or more of the four KH-12s already
in orbit suffered point failure during a crisis.

At 29,000 pounds, the satellite that is the subject of Missions 4 and
4Y was approximately the same weight as both of its immediate
predecessors, the KH-9 and the KH-11. The mission outline also
noted that when the KH-12 was collected and brought back down
to Vandenberg, it would weigh only 22,500 pounds. It was to be
lighter because it had burned 6,500 pounds of hydrazine while
maneuvering. The satellite's 150-nautical-mile orbit (or nearly 175
statute miles) would keep it well out of almost all of the earth's
atmosphere when it wasn't dipping lower for imaging, and its 98-
degree inclination, which is near-polar and sun-synchronous, would
be but one degree different from the KH-11's.

The Mission 4 and 4Y profiles, written in the early eighties, were
eventually to be modified at Air Force insistence so that the KH-12
could carry a great deal more fuel than originally intended, thereby
extending its maneuverability and prolonging its life by an estimated thirty-five to forty days. Whereas the satellite's original
launch weight had been set at 32,000 pounds, including its 2,500-
pound cradle, it was made progressively heavier—first to 34,000
pounds and then to 40,000 pounds—because of the additional fuel.
As the KH-12 now stands, waiting to be mated with either a Titan
4 booster or cradled in the space shuttle, it can carry 15,000 pounds
of hydrazine. The extra fuel will make it more maneuverable, as the
Air Force has ordered, but the benefit will not come without cost.
Since the Titan will not be able to carry 40,000 pounds to even low
earth orbit, any KH-12 launched on one will have to go up without
its tank topped off and then be replenished on station. Little consid-

eration seems to have been given this problem because, Air Force apprehension notwithstanding, there had been no Challenger accident when the decision was made to add the extra fuel. It was presumed that the shuttle would be able to handle the KH-12's additional weight. But then, it turned out, even the shuttle as currently configured would have only a marginal chance at carrying the reconnaissance platform. Accordingly, it has been decided to lighten the shuttle by replacing its problem-ridden steel-encased solid rocket boosters with new ones that are held together by filament-wound composite material. Some astronauts have reportedly expressed reluctance at riding the shuttle to orbit on the lighter solid rocket boosters, which are far from having been thoroughly tested.

Nor was weight the only problem the KH-12 had. By the summer of 1986, potentially dangerous problems had been discovered at the shuttle launch facility at Vandenberg itself. As it turned out, Space Launch Complex 6's main engine duct—the cavity under the shuttle where the flame from its engines hits before being deflected and drawn off—was thought to trap hydrogen and therefore be capable of causing an explosion even before the giant manned rocket was able to rise off the pad. That difficulty, as well as others (a high incidence of dense fog being one of them), caused the Defense Department to give serious consideration to breaking precedent and launching the first KH-12 aboard a shuttle from Cape Canaveral. Kennedy Space Center planning charts showed that the first KH-12 launch, originally scheduled for the shuttle's second launch from Vandenberg as Mission 62-B, had been changed to the second shuttle launch from the Kennedy Space Center at Canaveral after shuttle flights resumed. Aside from avoiding the hydrogen explosion problem at Vandenberg, a launch from Kennedy would be restricted to 57 degrees latitude or less in order to avoid populated areas, allowing the shuttle to take advantage of earth rotation for additional boosting capacity. The minus, however, is that such an orbit extends only as far as about one hundred miles north of Moscow, leaving uncovered the naval facilities around the Kola Peninsula, as well as the ICBM complexes at Yedrovo, Kozelsk, Kostroma, Yurya, and Derazhnya, in addition to the large ballistic missile test facility and satellite launch complex at Plesetsk. The shortcoming would no doubt be rectified by using the KH-12's large fuel supply and unlimited capacity for replenishment by the shuttle to move its orbit in a more northerly direction after launch. For its part, "Slick Six" has been relegated to limbo indefinitely.

. . .

Robert S. Cooper, the then director of the Defense Advanced Research Projects Agency, or DARPA, shared his vision of the future of space surveillance one April morning in 1985 as he gave the keynote address at the American Institute of Aeronautics and Astronautics' annual meeting in Washington. DARPA, which is physically tiny as bureaucracies in the federal government go, wields considerable power within the nation's scientific and technical community because it is responsible for stimulating and overseeing the development of advanced military technologies, including many of the exotic systems associated with the Strategic Defense Initiative. DARPA decides what is technically feasible and then uses research and development contracts and grants to pursue its vision. The audience, which sat appreciatively in the Sheraton Washington's Cotillion Room, consisted mostly of engineers. But there was also a sprinkling of Air Force and Navy officers whose crisp silver- and gold-trimmed uniforms and glistening insignia quietly but surely overwhelmed the engineers' tan and brown suits, colorfully patterned shirts, turquoise Indian rings, bolo ties, and belt buckles, and plated tie clasps and lapel pins that celebrated a wide assortment of flying contraptions ranging from the DC-3 to the Titan 3. But they all paid close attention as Cooper told them about what he saw as he peered ahead to the year 2000.

Space surveillance and Star Wars technologies are intimately related, at least theoretically, Cooper said. And no matter what fate holds for the ballistic missile defense shield, the surveillance system will be needed to see enemy missiles and bombers coming at the United States so Washington can respond (he did not say how). The early warning spacecraft now on line—the aged DSP-647s with their infrared eyes—are too inaccurate and slow to warrant having their place kept in the new order of battle. They are therefore to be switched off and left hanging in their synchronous orbits, a semicircle of retired night watchmen whose infrared eyes will be allowed to dim and then go out while their cryogenic coolant degrades to the point of uselessness.

Their replacements, Cooper told the engineers, will be two-dimensional arrays of supercooled infrared sensors that will stare down at the earth, unblinking, as they search each section of the terrestrial grid for significant levels of heat, separate the heat they feel from the ground clutter around it, and go through their computers' data banks for associated signatures.

"The system would be based on a staring sensor," Cooper explained dryly. "It would cover, essentially, one half of the earth's disc." That would amount to about a quarter of the planet, since a disc covers half of it. "The number of pixels in this satellite could be as many as fifty million in the focal plane, which would cover each square kilometer of one half of the earth's disc with a pixel, continuously, in real time."

This means that a spacecraft placed 22,300 miles from earth will scrutinize one quarter of the planet at all times, each of its pixels (CCDs, actually) concentrating on a tract of land or water measuring only about eleven hundred yards to a side. A CCD would note any important heat source within its assigned jurisdiction. If the source moved, as would a cruise missile being tested on the Kola Peninsula or an ICBM being fired from Tyuratam, it would be spotted at launch by one CCD and then passed along to successive ones like water in a bucket brigade until it impacted on its target. The missile would be identified by type, speed, and direction. The kind of platform Cooper was talking about would be able to track thousands of missiles while simultaneously separating them from such extraneous clutter as reflected sunlight, brushfires, and moving steam locomotives. It would also make distinctions between real missiles and decoys—an engineering feat that would require some damned hard design work. None of the engineers, airmen, or sailors seemed impressed or surprised by what Cooper said.

There was no murmur of amazement in the Cotillion Room as Robert Cooper described the future infrared surveillance satellite, partly because engineers are a conservative bunch who are not easily impressed, and partly because most of them were already aware of the concept, if only vaguely.

Many who listened to the head of DARPA knew that some of the basic components to which he referred had already been built by Rockwell International's Shuttle Integration and Satellite Systems Division at Seal Beach, California, which is just south of the NRO's regional office on the San Diego Freeway. Rockwell's system is called Teal Ruby, and it is sponsored by DARPA. Essentially, Teal Ruby is a preliminary proof of concept in which charge-coupled devices arranged in a large mosaic are used with a powerful telescope to track flying aircraft from space. The CCD array and telescope are used on a made-to-order boxlike Air Force satellite called AFP-888.

Teal Ruby is itself part of a larger concept that gets closer to what Cooper had in mind. It is called HALO, for High Altitude Large Optics, and it is also being aggressively researched under DARPA's auspices. HALO's objective is to test a variety of imaging sensors so that a satellite can eventually be built that will closely follow both aircraft and cruise missiles from synchronous orbit. It is the cruise missiles, in particular, that worry defense planners and arms controllers. They can be launched from the ground, from aircraft, and from the sea. They are small, which makes them relatively easy to conceal from current reconnaissance systems, and they are ground-huggers that fly low, which makes them difficult to track with ordinary earth-based radar. Cruise missiles using hermetically sealed computerized maps in boxes the size of a book can closely follow terrain over a thousand miles or more just above tree level.* Cooper's surveillance platform would be able to track hundreds of them, as well as aircraft, simultaneously.

However much attention is given by the news media to laser battle stations, pop-up mirrors, electromagnetic rail guns and other "kill" mechanisms popularly associated with the Star Wars defense, it is the surveillance systems that lie at the heart of the concept. After all, you can't hit what you can't see.

"The popular press has emphasized the exotic nature of certain technologies included in our study," James C. Fletcher, chairman of the SDI Defensive Technologies Study Team (and currently the head of NASA), told a House subcommittee in March 1984. "I feel compelled to set the record straight on this illusion. Our recommended program does not concentrate on so-called 'Star Wars' weapons. The directed energy area, which I suppose has elicited the most attention, is less than a fourth of the program. The largest portion of the recommended effort is to develop effective surveillance, acquisition, tracking, and assessment sensor systems," Fletcher added, noting that "precision sensors make unambiguous detection and discrimination of warheads from decoys and debris possible." These sensors, modified for particular missions, will also be put on many of the reconnaissance platforms.

Radar imaging is also to figure prominently in space reconnais-

---

*The digitized maps are made by the Defense Mapping Agency using data from geodesy satellites.

sance and surveillance, whether or not Star Wars comes to pass. The imaging radar that Challenger carried to orbit on Mission 41-G in October 1984 may have had a 35- by 7-foot flat antenna, but its console was about the size of a shoe box because of miniaturization. Radar imaging of Montreal, Quebec, parts of New Hampshire and southwest Maine, and Mount Shasta, California, was done on that flight. Much of the radar imaging was done under cloud cover, but it provided a batch of excellent high-resolution photographs that give a clear indication of what the system will be able to do in a few years over Eastern Europe and the U.S.S.R. during autumn and winter, when the clouds roll in. Nor is imaging at night or through clouds radar's only value as a space reconnaissance system. It is also unexcelled at defining contours, not only on the surface of the earth but beneath it. In the case of the desert, radar pulses can penetrate through several feet of sand and define objects buried in it. This can be done to objects hidden under snow and water, too. In one experiment, during Challenger's ninety-sixth orbit, the synthetic aperture radar peered well beneath the ocean surface to measure the dynamics of internal (subsurface) waves. Although the study was undertaken to gather data so that the movement of the sea's currents could be better understood, it also has clear implications where the tracking of such relatively easy to spot objects as submerged submarines is concerned.

Radar images transmitted from space can come in either analog or digital form. In either case the images may be turned into standard photographs to show what's going on at night or under clouds. But radar imagery in digital form has a significant advantage over the analog variety: it can be computer-manipulated. What appears to the unaided eye in an analog photograph, for example, can be digitally massaged so that distinct shapes appear.

"You can digitally manipulate data in such a fashion that you create very strong contrasts," according to John Ford, supervisor of the Imaging Radar Geology Group at the Jet Propulsion Laboratory, where SIR-A and SIR-B, the shuttle's radars, were built. "That allows you to see things which were completely obscured before this processing technique had been applied." In other words, bulges in the earth that might not appear in a standard photograph or an analog radar image that was made by pointing the sensor straight down would be clearly delineated by digitally manipulating the radar picture. The fallout shelters along the Moscow beltway and elsewhere that so worry George Keegan form such bulges (though they were spotted without the use of radar satellites). In addition, radar images taken from directly above an object can be digitally rearranged so as to give the viewer the perspective of seeing it from all sides. This has profound implications where the analysis of foreign weapons systems and military installations are concerned.

The space around planet Earth in 2001 will be surrounded not by the great white roulette-wheel stations that come to mind through the novels of Arthur C. Clarke, but by a series of antenna farms floating at altitudes of between one thousand and five thousand miles and pointing downward. Space-based nuclear-powered radar technology is being actively pursued by the Air Force and DARPA so that systems can be placed in orbit that will detect Soviet bombers (whether they are stealthy or not) and cruise missiles, and also will be used to watch ballistic missile tests, the whereabouts of the world's navies, and all man-made objects in space. The Pentagon earmarked $40 million in fiscal year 1984 for research leading to the development of radar satellites that will in effect "put a fence around the U.S.," as one Air Force officer described it. It is estimated that six or seven such spacecraft would be needed at the five-thousand-mile altitude, while between fourteen and sixteen would be necessary in one-thousand-mile-high orbits because they would not be able to see as far. Although the United States may have launched one phased array radar satellite in January 1982, it bore no resemblance to those currently on the drawing boards at Grumman Aerospace, which is designing the antenna, and at General Electric, Raytheon, and Texas Instruments, which are developing solid-state transmission and reception modules (which will be smaller than a twenty-five-cent piece) for the satellites.

Although the SIR-A and SIR-B radar on the shuttle had a resolution on the order of a hundred feet, the resolution of the phased array radar that the Air Force is going to place in orbit is quite a bit better than that, according to one knowledgeable official at Goodyear Aerospace, which produces aircraft radars. It will be less than seven feet, he said.

The Space Surveillance and Tracking System (SSTS) will comprise another fleet of spacecraft—at least four—that will use infrared and visible wavelength sensors to monitor Soviet satellites with a view to defining in precise terms what they do and what their capabilities are, as well as providing early warning of an attack on U.S. space systems.

. . .

The SR-71 will be replaced, but probably not by a specially constructed reconnaissance aircraft. Instead, research is now under way (with the approval of President Reagan) on a trans-atmospheric vehicle (TAV)—sometimes called a hypersonic plane, a national aerospace plane, an advanced aerospace vehicle (AAV), military aerospace vehicle (MAV), or the X-30—which is to perform several missions, one of the foremost being reconnaissance.

Although the spaceplane's specific configuration and precise role varies according to the company doing the study, its central concept centers on a manned vehicle that will take off from a standard runway, climb to the fringe of space at dazzling speed, orbit the earth if necessary, and then return to terra firma the way a standard airplane would. Some envision the craft as a second-generation space shuttle able to carry twenty-thousand-pound cargoes to low orbit, while others think of it as a multirole space bomber that will be able to attack any place on earth within ninety minutes of taking off. It is to have a ceiling of about thirty miles in one plan, and more than twice that in another. Some designers think it ought to be rocket-powered, though most would like it to be propelled by a highly advanced supersonic combustion ramjet. If it turns out that the spaceplane is ramjet-propelled, its fuel, ironically, will be liquid hydrogen, thereby providing an odd vindication for the Skunk Works engineers who conceived of Suntan in 1956.

The Skunk Works, in fact, is designing a trans-atmospheric vehicle that would be 205 feet long (or 83 feet longer than the space shuttle orbiter) and would be able to climb to a hundred miles at speeds of about seventeen thousand miles an hour. Lockheed's entry is big because the company prudently sees the vehicle as having potential civilian as well as military applications. It could fly from New York to Los Angeles in twelve minutes, reaching an altitude of three hundred thousand feet, a Lockheed-California press release claims.

But it is the military mission that drives the spaceplane, which, in the view of DARPA and the Air Force, will have at least three advantages over the shuttle: it will be launchable on immediate notice; it will be able to go up during severe weather conditions if necessary; and it will operate in both air and space, giving it greater mission flexibility.

"A TAV could react quickly from the continental U.S. to any global incident with the versatility to provide reconnaissance, force projection, strategic defense and interdiction support as desired," the deputy for development planning in the Air Force's Aeronautical Systems Division told an engineering meeting, adding that the craft's most promising role appears to be as a reconnaissance platform. An aeronautical consultant at the same meeting reported that he had gotten an enthusiastic response from the "reconnaissance community" when asked whether its members would prefer flying missions at Mach 3 and one hundred thousand feet or at Mach 29 and forty-five miles.

Although it is unlikely, high-altitude hypersonic reconnaissance may also mark the end of the sort of missions SR-71s currently fly along the periphery of Eastern Europe, the Soviet Union, and the People's Republic of China. A forty-five-mile-high mission flown at better than seventeen thousand miles an hour over denied territory would transform a spaceplane into the equivalent of a manned spy satellite—a modern MOL. Such missions might well resurrect the sort of political and legal conflict that attended the beginning of the U.S. space reconnaissance program and subsided only in 1963, within a year of the Kremlin's having gotten its own reconnaissance satellites off the ground. Each country has been flown over repeatedly by astronauts and cosmonauts of the other side since the manned space programs began, but not at altitudes under a hundred miles and for the express purpose of collecting intelligence.

At what altitude does sovereignty end? What setting of a spaceplane's altimeter would virtually guarantee its safety, and what setting would invite an attack? In considering this, the National Command Authority will most likely decide to avoid the problem altogether by continuing to use the manned vehicles in the same way it uses its Blackbirds, while leaving overflights to the various unmanned spacecraft.

"There are no currently identifiable DOD [Department of Defense] mission requirements that could be uniquely satisfied by a manned space station," Richard D. DeLauer, the under secretary of defense for research and engineering, said in 1983. "Further, no current DOD requirements were found where a manned space station would appear to provide a significant improvement to DOD over alternative methods of performing the given task. Studies to date have identified no unique, cost-effective contributions that man-in-the-loop can make to the execution of military missions such as surveillance, navigation, and communications." Thus did the Pentagon serve notice that it did not favor yet another of NASA's most important projects, a manned space station designed to help keep the embattled space agency in business at a cost currently estimated at $8 billion.

An unmanned space station is another matter, however. Plans for such a station have been in the works for several years, though if they have been finalized, they surely constitute one of the blackest of the NRO's programs. Space engineers have on several occasions acknowledged to the author that an unmanned station is under active consideration by the Defense Department and that, unlike the manned station's roughly equatorial 28-degree inclination, it will travel a polar or near-polar route.

"That kind of orbit is well suited to weather forecasting," one Grumman engineer noted in reference to the unmanned space station's perpendicular flight path relative to the equator.

"And to reconnaissance," someone pointed out. "The polar orbit is a reconnaissance orbit."

"Yeah. That, too," the engineer acknowledged before abruptly changing the subject. Perhaps the unmanned space station is already earmarked to carry the designation KH-13.

As already noted, the vulnerability of reconnaissance and surveillance satellites' uplinks, downlinks and tracking stations to attack or to natural disaster has been a source of concern for a number of years. In the long run, expanding the control points (providing the Consolidated Space Operations Center at Colorado Springs with control of several military satellite systems to take some of the load off Sunnyvale, for example) will not suffice because the number of such expensive sites must necessarily remain extremely limited, and the satellites will therefore remain at considerable risk.

Because of this, as well as the possibility that the satellites themselves will be attacked, Robert Cooper told the AIAA engineers who met in Washington in April 1985, the "umbilical cord" connecting the control facilities on earth to the satellites is going to have to be cut in successive stages until the orbiters are able to take care of themselves to an extent that is now almost unbelievable. Not only are they going to have to be hardened, but perhaps more important, they are going to have to be made to "think" for themselves.

"Currently, satellites are taken care of by smart people on the

surface of the earth," Cooper explained. "Generally, those are people who know about the design of the satellite and who watch it
intensively, twenty-four hours a day. When a fault occurs in any of
our spacecraft, these smart people spring immediately into action.
They diagnose the difficulty in the spacecraft and they determine
actions that can be taken to preserve the mission. With the flexibility
that exists in many of our spacecraft, an almost infinite number of
actions can be taken that will tend to preserve the mission, perhaps
in some degraded form," the head of DARPA added.

"Now," he continued, "in order to put that capability into the
spacecraft, it is either going to be necessary to gather these people
together and take them along in the spacecraft, or to emulate their
capability on board. We have programs now in artificial intelligence
technology that can take expert knowledge and codify it into intelligent machines." Cooper added that enough knowledge will have to
be stored about the design of the satellite and the context of the
mission so that computers on the spacecraft are able to overcome
malfunctions and keep the mission going.

Cooper emphasized that he was not talking about merely loading
the computer's memory with a list of everything that anyone can
think of that could go wrong with the satellite so that specific
corrections could be made to match specific problems. No. Rather,
the computer would have to be programmed to understand as much
about the satellite's design and mission as the people on the ground
so that it can make equally intelligent decisions in the event of some
failure in the system.

Codifying such knowledge will be extremely difficult, the director of the Defense Advanced Research Projects Agency told the
engineers and military officers—difficult, but hardly impossible. He
picked a ballistic missile early warning satellite, such as DSP-647,
as a case in point.

"A typical satellite design that might encompass a sensor of this
complexity might have documentation that described the satellite
and the sensor system completely that would amount to about
10,000 pages of carefully written descriptive material. In order to
provide the context for the mission—that is, why the satellite is
there, what's around it, what are the threats against it, what are the
environmental threats particularly, what kinds of problems are there
with the aiming of the satellite, and that sort of thing—there might
be another 1,000 pages of text or script describing all that in detail.

"And so, if you assign to that about 300 words per page, and about seven letters per word, and one byte per letter, you come out with about 35 gigabytes of information that would have to be stored on the satellite in order to provide the design information and the contextual information for an intelligent machine to assess what was going on aboard the satellite so that appropriate action could be taken," Cooper said. "About 35 gigabytes," he repeated for emphasis. That would be about 35 billion bits of data that could be called up, in any combination, almost instantly.

The system described by Cooper would amount to what the Air Force calls self-repairing controls, research on which is relatively new but is progressing rapidly. This would entail the spacecraft's microcomputers assessing the nature of the malfunction or attack threat and then taking whatever remedial action was necessary to continue the mission while advising the control facility that a serious problem has developed. Were a movable antenna to jam, for example, a self-repairing control system would analyze the problem, study the design of the antenna and its drive components, and then try to get it moving again, perhaps by overriding the drive. Failing that, the computer would weigh the importance of that segment of the mission, and, if necessary, fire the hydrazine thrusters so that the entire spacecraft would reposition itself in such as way that the stuck antenna would point in the right direction.

The sensors and artificial intelligence apparatus aboard the reconnaissance and surveillance spacecraft that will be in orbit in the twenty-first century will be driven by the next generation of computers, the supercomputers that will be capable of ten billion floating point operations a second. As now planned, the supercomputers will control real-time technical collection of intelligence, plus all housekeeping and self-defense functions.

"We're talking, not about factors of two, or three, or ten," Cooper said in regard to the extent that the supercomputers on the satellites will be improvements over existing models. "We're talking about factors of thousands to tens of thousands in computational power."

Recognizing that the United States already has a substantial lead over the Soviet Union in computer technology, the Defense Department has sought to widen it even more by creating a Strategic Computing Program, run by DARPA, with the goal of developing and harnessing machine intelligence for technical intelligence collection, space surveillance, the Strategic Defense Initiative, and other areas within the coming decade.

"The modality by which that is to be accomplished," Cooper

went on, "is to take maximum advantage of current micro-electronics technology, particularly in gallium arsenide, but also in the other technologies available, and to use concurrent processing techniques to drive up the computing power of the current-generation computers by many, many orders of magnitude."

Concurrent processing is a technique in which many microprocessors with various levels of capability are "ganged" so that they all work on the same problem at the same time, speeding computation. The Strategic Computing Program began testing a gang of 128 microprocessors in the summer of 1985. Cooper predicted that one day soon, 64,000 and then a million microprocessors might be tested for concurrent computational capability. If successful, the program will produce on-board arrays of minicomputers with capabilities that are astronomical in both senses of the word.

There is concern within the national technical intelligence establishment, and particularly the Air Force, that America's expanding network of space systems, certainly including its reconnaissance and surveillance satellites, is in varying degrees vulnerable to a generally less sophisticated, but adequate, Soviet attack capability. The spacecraft do not have to cope with air turbulence, weather, severe gravitational effects, and other hazards associated with flight in the atmosphere, so toughness has been sacrificed in all cases for maximum mission capability. Satellites are not only inherently "dumb," but extremely fragile. This gives the would-be attacker a considerable advantage.

Accordingly, there are at least four avenues besides autonomy that are being followed in order to maximize the chances for satellite survival in the event of attack: hardening, maneuvering, deception, and proliferation.

Hardening is the most widely used protective measure and involves any number of techniques employed to protect the spacecraft and its support systems by making them physically resistant to attack. The use of gallium arsenide in place of silicon in the satellite's sensors and computers has already been mentioned, as have metal shielding and the use of protective doors and coated lenses to help block laser attack. Research is also under way to develop solar panels that are more resistant to the effects of nuclear explosions and other radiation than those currently in use. It has also been suggested that, where possible, solar panels be abandoned altogether in favor of nuclear energy, either from isotopes or from reactors. Nuclear power plants not only produce more energy than solar panels but are far less susceptible to the effects of laser radiation, concussion, shrapnel, or pellet barrage. Some U.S. military satellites currently operate with isotopes, though none of them are low-orbiters, since the NRO does not want to risk the sort of embarrassment that the Soviet Union experienced when two of its radar ocean reconnaissance satellites tumbled out of orbit carrying hot fissile material.

Since spoofing and jamming are among the most tempting ways to interfere with satellites because of their ambiguous effects (especially those relating to spoofing), they are particularly worrisome. Besides encryption equipment, which has long been used for both uplink and downlink communications, the next generation of satellites will go into space with beam-hopping antennas, so the data flow will jump from one antenna to another. There will also be rapid changes of frequency, bursting (the transmission of data in short, tightly packed segments), and the use of extremely high frequency wavelengths. EHF signals do not disperse as readily as those on the lower wavelengths, and they are therefore more difficult to jam or intercept. Extremely high frequency transmission travels in such straight lines that anyone wanting to interfere with it must be virtually between the transmitter and the receiving antenna in order to do so.

Maneuvering is considered to be of marginal value at best against co-orbital interceptors and virtually useless against directed energy weapons such as chemical and nuclear-pumped lasers, particle beams, or electromagnetic railguns.

There are several methods by which satellites can try to deceive their attackers, though. One, inherent in the design of the spacecraft itself, involves "stealth," or low-observable, technology. This entails designing the satellites with as many smooth curved surfaces as possible in order to reduce their radar cross section (which is yet another argument for getting rid of the solar paddles and going to nuclear). Skins sheathed in the new "ultrablack" coating will absorb radar pulses rather than reflect them, while protective covers will be used to reduce heat emissions in order to thwart infrared-directed attack systems.

As far back as the 1960s, Air Force B-52 bombers were equipped with an electronic countermeasure known as "range gate-stealing" that allowed them to project their image away from themselves so that they appeared on enemy radar to be where they weren't.

Theoretically, there is no reason why such a system would not work on satellites as well. In the same vein, research has been under way since the late seventies on ways to electronically reduce the spectral signatures of satellites in the regions where Soviet tracking sensors normally operate so that the spacecraft's images are further reduced on the opposition's radar.

Decoys are also under serious consideration. AVCO developed a decoy satellite in the mid-seventies. As conceived by its designers, the system would use a radar warning receiver similar to the "fuzz-busters" that tell SR-71, U-2, and TR-1 crews that they are being tracked for attack, plus an infrared warning indicator that would alert the spacecraft to the fact that something has been shot at it. Then, three things should happen simultaneously: the satellite's thrusters are supposed to maneuver it out of the direct path of the attacking missile; it tries to electronically break its pursuer's tracking lock; and it launches a decoy whose signature is identical with its own. This system can only be used against co-orbital or direct-ascent attack, and its success, of course, would depend on whether the ASAT could be suckered into going after the wrong target.

The last and most devious bit of deception has to do with the use of "dead," or "sleeping," satellites. Perfectly functional spacecraft might be disguised as spent boosters or other discarded orbital junk, as satellites that have been turned off prematurely so as to appear useless, or as vehicles that give the appearance of having suffered total point failure when in fact they are merely being kept dormant until needed.

Proliferation entails increasing the number of satellites doing reconnaissance and surveillance and keeping as many of them as possible out of harm's way. Given the expense involved in building reconnaissance satellites, emulating the Russians in terms of assembly-line production and a rapid launch rate is clearly out of the question. The better alternative seems to be the use of very high orbits—higher than synchronous. The advantage of the synchronous orbit is that it allows a satellite to remain in a nearly fixed position relative to the earth at all times. But this brings disadvantages, too. Spacecraft with fixed positions are particularly easy targets for such ASATs as neighboring satellites that act like communications or navigation platforms but are really space mines waiting to be triggered at the appropriate moment. Placing spacecraft in orbits beyond synchronous—at sixty thousand miles or more, for example—helps to keep them beyond the region in which sudden, successful attack is possible.

If there is a single development on the horizon that signals the beginning of the realization of the air generals' old Flash Gordon reconnaissance fantasy, it has to do with the use of satellites to supply instantaneous intelligence not only to Washington but also to commanders in the field.

Starting sometime within the next decade, space reconnaissance is scheduled to undergo a transformation that, in magnitude, will be on the order of the leap from airplanes to satellites. It is going to be used not only for strategic purposes but also for tactical ones. The future is called TENCAP: Tactical Exploitation of National Capabilities.

Whereas space reconnaissance is currently strategic, in that it collects intelligence that is for the most part considered to be of long-term value (ship construction, missile testing, and so forth) and is funneled directly to Washington for digestion and implementation, tactical intelligence bypasses the national intelligence establishment and goes directly to the forces in the field, where it can be used immediately.

As currently planned, TENCAP will involve the use of the KH-12 and a communications relay satellite named Milstar, which is to replace the SDS spacecraft that now transmit KH-11 imagery. Milstar is supposed to provide worldwide jam-resistant communication links between the National Command Authority and the forces in the field, as well as connecting those forces with one another. It will be the first satellite to incorporate virtually all of the hardening systems for protection against nuclear blast. In addition, it will have the capability to antenna-hop, frequency-hop, and burst-transmit. Its transmission will be encrypted and will use extremely high frequencies. Further, Milstar will be the first nonreconnaissance satellite that is extremely maneuverable.

Seven fully operational Milstars, plus some spares, are to be put into synchronous orbit, beginning in the late 1980s. In their role as part of TENCAP, they are to relay real-time KH-12 imagery directly to Army, Navy, and Air Force field commands without going through Washington. This means that an Army general will be able to get real-time imagery of the enemy's movements, for example, even as they are taking place. Field commanders in combat or in confrontations with opponents will be able to ask the Satellite Control Facility at Sunnyvale or CSOC in Colorado Springs to task the KH-12 for the imagery they require and receive it within minutes by sending the appropriate signal up to Milstar. "They won't have to go to NPIC anymore," according to John Pike of the Federation of American Scientists, who referred to the often long wait for pictures from Washington. "They'll take what they need straight off the bird."

TENCAP's 1984 budget was $77 million; its 1986 budget climbed to $120 million. "As space reconnaissance gets more expensive, they have to broaden the user base, and TENCAP will do that," Pike said. "It's supply-side intelligence."

"In a world where knowledge is power, remote sensing has become a key source of information." That statement could be the credo of the National Reconnaissance Office or the CIA's Office of Imagery Analysis. It could be, but it isn't. Rather, it is the opening sentence of a glossy flier produced by the SPOT Image Corporation of Reston, Virginia, and it heralds the beginning of a new era: that of true commercial reconnaissance.

SPOT (for *Système Probatoire d'Observation de la Terre*) is the name of an imaging satellite developed by the French national space agency in cooperation with companies in Sweden, Belgium, and France. SPOT 1, a boxy machine weighing close to four thousand pounds and carrying an unfurlable solar panel at one end and twin high-resolution cameras at the other, was lofted into orbit by an Ariane booster that took off from Kourou, French Guiana, on the evening of February 21, 1986. It was placed into a circular 516-mile-high orbit whose 98.3-degree sun-synchronous inclination was within a degree and a half of the KH-11's. This means that SPOT 1 makes a complete revolution of the earth every 101 minutes fourteen times a day, and repeats its orbital cycle (the territory over which it passes) every twenty-six days.

But it is not so much SPOT 1's orbital parameters as its sensing system that is particularly noteworthy. The two cameras can record digital color images in three spectral bands with sixty-foot resolution and produce black-and-white pictures having a resolution of thirty feet. The cameras use CCDs and can either store their imagery on tape or dump it immediately. In addition, the mirrors that are used to reflect images into the cameras can be pointed to either side as the spacecraft flies along its ground track. This not only allows it to cover a six-hundred-mile-wide swath of territory, but by recording the same area from different angles on successive orbits, it produces stereoscopic pictures of excellent quality. The first imagery returned by the satellite included scenes of Nice, on the Riviera, in which sharp details of streets and marinas could be discerned.

Until the advent of SPOT, the field of commercial remote sensing was virtually the sole province of the U.S. Landsat satellites that were developed by NASA and first orbited in 1972 as part of its Earth Resources Technology Satellite program. Landsat 4 and 5, which are currently in orbit, are now operated by the Earth Observation Satellite Company (EOSAT) of Landover, Maryland, a private venture of RCA and the Hughes Aircraft Company. Since the space agency was prohibited from putting high-resolution sensors on its Landsats in order to keep it clean—out of the spy business—while protecting the sensibilities of Third World nations that were concerned about spaceborne espionage, the U.S. satellites' best resolution is only about ninety feet. EOSAT is planning to launch a multisensor, polar-orbiting satellite called Omnistar aboard the shuttle toward the end of the decade that should have greatly improved resolution. Such capability will be necessary if EOSAT is to compete with SPOT for remote sensing business.

Remote sensing, however, is an ambiguous undertaking. When it is conducted in order to measure forestland, inventory wheat production, or track schools of tuna, it is called resource management. But when the same cameras are turned on submarine construction facilities at Groton or Severomorsk, or on ballistic missile complexes in South Dakota or Svobodnyy, it becomes reconnaissance. To be sure, the service is marketed as one that is applicable to geology, urban planning, agriculture, forestry, water management and other relatively mundane enterprises. But for a nominal price ($250 to $1,790, depending upon the nature of the pictures), any individual can order high-resolution imagery of anything in the SPOT Image Corporation's growing inventory; if the desired material isn't in stock, SPOT 1's controllers in Toulouse will order the satellite to collect it. On May 1, 1986, for example, SPOT 1 took black-and-white pictures of the smoldering nuclear reactor at Chernobyl at the request of a "commercial client" who wanted data on the environmental consequences of the massive release of radiation. It subsequently imaged the U.S.S.R.'s main nuclear test site at

Semipalatinsk and the space shuttle facility at Tyuratam, both of which made the morning papers.

SPOT's implications are profound because it blurs the distinction between civilian and military observation from space in direct proportion to the clarity of its imagery. The satellite's potential for use as a reconnaissance platform has not been wasted on French intelligence officials, who have already begun tasking it for that purpose and will continue to do so until France's own military intelligence satellite, Helios, is launched in the early nineties.

The Western news media are likely to be another beneficiary of SPOT's reconnaissance capability. Where the press in the United States is concerned, however, this will no doubt raise interesting First Amendment issues as the right to publish or air news comes in conflict with national security considerations and perhaps the rights of individuals as well. Do the news media have the right to show the disposition of U.S. combat units on the eve of an invasion like that of Grenada, of an imminent air strike like the one against Libya, or of U.S.-backed insurgency operations against countries like Nicaragua or Afghanistan? Given the long-standing policy of not revealing satellite imagery of the U.S.S.R. so as not to unduly embarrass the Kremlin, what might Washington's reaction be if Soviet ballistic missile silos are inventoried on the evening news?

The heart of the matter, however, has to do neither with placing U.S. military personnel in greater danger nor with embarrassing Moscow. Rather, it impacts directly—as it always has—on the curtailing of presidential power by limiting options. That is to say, the range of choices a president has with which to respond to any given situation would necessarily be narrowed with the entire country in effect peering over his shoulder at the reconnaissance imagery. Threat inflation, or warning that the enemy is stronger than he really is, constitutes a traditional posture used for increasing defense spending, for gaining concessions in arms control negotiations, for intervention in third-party states, and for other desiderata, irrespective of what the technical intelligence actually shows. But this would be virtually impossible were the media to produce pictures that contradicted the White House in each such instance, thereby diminishing political maneuverability to an extent that could be crippling. (The publication of such pictures would also help keep the administration "honest," of course, but that consideration would bear little weight with whichever party is in power and not much more with an opposition that hopes to gain power at a later date.)

The foreign policy establishment abhors being second-guessed by amateurs, particularly in public.

Meanwhile, SPOT 1 is bound to encroach to some extent on the traditional preserve of military space intelligence, and in the process provide the ordinary citizen with a perspective of the world that only a generation or so ago was taken to be the exclusive domain of comics supermen and angels. And it is just possible that some of those who look at SPOT 1's digitized multicolor stereoscopic orbital imagery, taken from 516 miles in the sky, will also carry within their earliest memory the flickering recollection of those equally remarkable picture postcards made by Julius Neubronner's trained pigeons at the Dresden fair in 1909.

14

Arms Control Verification and National Security

Around 1640, when learning, literature, the fine arts, adroit politics, and the Dutch East India Company's burgeoning trade routes had brought a dazzling golden age to Holland, an obscure artist named Jan Christaenz. Micker made a curious painting of his native Amsterdam.

At first glance, *View of Amsterdam* looks like an elaborate picture-map, complete with legends, done from the perspective of a high, oblique angle. It shows in considerable detail ships in port, churches, rows of narrow tile-roofed houses fronting canals, small bridges, and streets, all surrounded by poldered farmland that had been reclaimed from the North Sea.

But a second, closer look shows that the land at the painting's upper edges has a gentle curve to it, suggesting that Micker had caught sight of the curvature of the horizon itself as he did his work. Even more remarkable, the entire scene, which is mostly sunlit, is richly dappled with the shadows of unseen clouds. The dark puffs range across the small city and out over the green water, whose choppiness suggests the approach of a storm from the sea. It is as though Micker had painted his picture in the basket of a balloon suspended about five thousand feet over the ocean right in front of Amsterdam. But that would have been impossible, of course, since no European is known to have gone aloft in a balloon or anything else in the seventeenth century.

Micker evidently possessed an extraordinary imagination that allowed him to factor in the curvature of the earth and to visualize the cloud shadows he saw on the ground around him from the perspective of a place he had never been. In conceiving *View of Amsterdam*, the artist managed to combine map making with traditional painting in a way that suggests an apparently insurmountable contradiction for the human eye.

"If the observer were high enough to see the curvature of the globe and the shadows of clouds over the city, he would be too high to make out the details of the boats and buildings that the artist has so painstakingly painted," Svetlana Alpers, a professor of art history at the University of California at Berkeley, has noted. " 'A good map is [one] in which one views the world as from another world,' " Alpers quoted a Dutch contemporary of Micker as having observed. "In a sense," the art historian added, "Micker has made such a map. Its idiosyncratic mix of distance and intimacy, of impersonality and visual attentiveness, of art and life, suggests how Amsterdam would have looked seen from a place where no mortal could possibly have been."

In fact, it suggests nothing so much as the combined imagery from area-surveillance and close-look space reconnaissance, which we have just learned how to do. Jan Christaensz. Micker's ethereal fantasy—his picture painted from an impossible place—has come true in real time. The impossible has become routine.

There is an anomaly about space reconnaissance. While the collection systems and the process by which intelligence is extracted from them remain concealed deep in their respective compartments, the product itself—information about the world—is freely dispensed in prodigious quantity. There is so much leaked technical intelligence, in fact, that the general public throughout the West is scarcely aware of the extent of the deluge.

Early in July 1984, for example, *Jane's Defence Weekly*, an authoritative British military journal, ran an article detailing the effects of a series of massive explosions that had occurred in the ammunition depot at Severomorsk, home port of the Soviet Union's Northern Fleet, the previous May. (The aftermath of the accident was photographed by satellites, according to an article originating in *The New York Times*'s Washington Bureau.)

After noting almost parenthetically that the Northern Fleet is believed to have one aircraft carrier, 148 cruisers, destroyers, and other surface vessels, plus 190 of the Soviet Navy's 371 submarines, Jane's provided an extraordinary inventory of the guided missiles that had been lost in the disaster: 580 of 900 SA-N-1 and SA-N-3 surface-to-air missiles, nearly 320 of the facility's 400 SS-N-3 and SS-N-12 long-range ship-to-ship missiles, all or nearly all of about 80 SS-N-22 missiles (which, the article noted, can carry nuclear warheads), and an undetermined number of SS-N-19 anti-ship missiles. In addition, the story said, some SA-N-6 and SA-N-7 surface-to-air missiles were damaged, as were large quantities of spare parts, while the entire stock of submarine-launched ballistic missiles was spared.

Though unheralded by the newspapers that ran the story, and apparently ignored by most readers, the reconnaissance of the devastation and its analysis were pretty amazing stuff. Not only had the Navy been able to assess the damage by picking out individual missiles or fragments of them strewn on the ground or partly embedded in the charred and twisted rubble but, even more impressive, it had known what the normal complement of each type of missile was supposed to be.* If this is also true where other Soviet military installations are concerned, and there is no reason to suppose that technical intelligence at Severomorsk is unique, it indicates that the armed services maintain updated, accurate inventories of their counterparts' weapons stockpiles, even down to relatively small SA-N-1s, which have a range of only about nine miles.

The number of instances in which satellite reconnaissance has figured in news stories is considerable. On July 12, 1982, *The New York Times* quoted administration officials in Washington as saying that, based on satellite intelligence information, Iranian troops had moved close to the Iraqi border and might be able to invade within a matter of days.

Aviation Week & Space Technology reported on March 12, 1984, that the Russians were accelerating work on manned and unmanned heavy boosters, together with extensive work on their space station program, in order to "project Soviet power in space to a level the

---

*It is likely that the imagery from which the missile data were extracted came from a KH-11 and was analyzed at the Naval Intelligence Support Center at Suitland, Maryland, where Samuel Loring Morison worked as an interpreter. Morison was also the U.S. editor of *Jane's*, which may explain how the magazine got the information. He was later convicted of sending three classified KH-11 photographs of the Soviet carrier BLACK COM 2 to *Jane's*.

Soviets hope will outpace the relative technological advantage held by U.S. space systems." The article went on to mention that the Soviet Union was working on a heavy manned space shuttle similar to the one made in America, a heavy space station, and a winged spaceplane, among other programs. "U.S. reconnaissance satellite photography of construction at the Tyuratam launch site shows not only large new launch pads under construction for the shuttle and Saturn-5-class vehicles but the construction of extensive support facilities indicative of those required to maintain a long-term high level of activity. . . . Reconnaissance satellite images of the cryogenic rocket fuel storage areas show them to be much larger than the storage capability at Kennedy [space center] now used for the shuttle but built originally for the Saturn 5 program nearly 20 years ago."

The June 11, 1984, issue of *Time* described how Soviet military units, including tanks, had been thwarted in a major effort to kill or capture an Afghan rebel named Ahmad Shah Massoud. In whatever direction the Soviet tanks turned, *Time* reported, "they ran across rebel-laid land mines. According to Western diplomats in the Afghan capital of Kabul, casualties were so high that gravediggers at the local cemetery worked overtime to bury up to 40 soldiers a day. The mujahedin had some special help that enabled them to resist the formidable assault so well. Three weeks before the Soviet tanks began to roll, American spy satellites detected movements that allowed agents to warn the rebels of the impending attack."

Immediately after assuring the French National Assembly in November 1984 that an agreement to withdraw French and Libyan troops from Chad had been honored by both sides, French President François Mitterrand was forced to admit that the Libyan retreat had in fact slowed to the point of nearly stopping. The disclosure that the French withheld information on the Libyan pullout "followed documentation by the United States State Department, based on satellite photographs, of the continuing Libyan presence in Chad," *The New York Times* reported. "On Tuesday, officials in Washington said most of Libya's 5,500 troops were still in Chad."

More often than not, space reconnaissance is not even mentioned, though its role is implicit. Speaking about the state of Soviet ballistic missiles as they relate to arms control, for example, Lord Carrington, the secretary general of NATO, blithely mentioned in passing during a television interview that the number of SS-20 mobile missiles pointed at Western Europe had recently jumped from 348 to 441. If true,* the figures were amazing not only for their precision but for their connection with weapons that are said by Washington to be particularly difficult to track and inventory because they are moved around on transporters. Yet neither of the journalists who participated in the program saw fit to ask the Englishman where he got his numbers.

But the most detailed inventory and assessment of Soviet weaponry to be made public is issued each year by the Defense Department itself in a lavishly illustrated, richly detailed manual called *Soviet Military Power.* This compendium of Kremlin weaponry, whose first edition in 1981 coincided with the Reagan administration's call to arms, has fattened over the years from 99 pages to 143 in 1985.

Soviet Military Power pinpoints the locations of nuclear warhead stockpiles in the Soviet Union and Eastern Europe, as well as the number and locations of ammunition depots, bridge equipment storage and reserve armor storage depots, and the concentrations of petroleum, oil, and lubricants used by the Soviet military.

It lists by type and performance every fighter, bomber, missile, helicopter, surface ship, submarine, tank, and mobile rocket launcher in the Soviet inventory, as well as total ballistic and cruise missile production. It shows the ABM missile and radar sites around Moscow, and includes a drawing of one of the missiles emerging from its silo. It also depicts the early warning and ballistic missile tracking radar at Abalakova that is alleged to be in violation of the ABM treaty.

The 1985 edition contained not only a drawing showing the Soviet co-orbital ASAT firing its pellets in an apparent test, but also an illustration of one of the weapons on top of an erected booster that is set near railroad tracks leading out from a large shed, under which more ASATs seem to be waiting for a roll-out so that they, too, can be fired.

There are, in addition, many tantalizing details that almost seem to have been inserted as much to impress the reader with American reconnaissance capability as with the magnitude of the Soviet arms buildup: "28,000 of the USSR's 52,000 main battle tanks are oppo-

*Three days earlier, Soviet leader Mikhail S. Gorbachev had maintained at a press conference in Paris that there were 243 SS-20s "on alert" and targeted on Western Europe, while an undisclosed number of others had been taken out of service and "anybody can photograph them." The implication was that he considered U.S. reconnaissance to be routine.

site NATO Europe," it said in one picture caption. "Pontoon bridges and other river-crossing equipment—some 27,000 meters of bridging equipment—have been pre-positioned in Eastern Europe to speed the forward thrust of Soviet tank and motorized rifle divisions in the event of conflict," it said elsewhere.

"In terms of numbers alone, Soviet strategic and tactical air defense forces are impressive," according to the 1985 edition. "Moreover, with the continuing deployment of new systems like the SA-10 SAM and *impending deployment* [italics added] of the SA-X-12, these numbers are increasing along with capability. Currently, the Soviets have nearly 10,000 SAM launchers at over 1,200 sites for strategic defense, along with more than 4,000 launch vehicles for tactical SAMs, subordinated to nearly 445 launch units. More than 1,200 interceptors are dedicated to strategic defense, while an additional 2,800 Soviet Air Forces (SAF) interceptors could be used.

"The deployment of the supersonic MiG-31/FOXHOUND interceptor, the first Soviet aircraft with a true look-down/shoot-down and multiple target engagement capability, continued during 1984," the report added. "The FOXHOUND, comparable in size to the US F-14 TOMCAT, is deployed at several locations from the Arkhangelsk area to the Far East Military District. More than 70 of these aircraft are operational."

Even cruise missiles are listed. *Soviet Military Power* contains a chart comparing five kinds of Soviet cruise missiles with three of their U.S. counterparts, including their respective sizes, range, and number of warheads.*

Soviet Military Power is crammed with extremely hard data that are either substantially incorrect or else are on target. If a significant amount of the material is wrong, those who have prepared the report have exaggerated the Soviet threat, either deliberately or by guessing. And given the precise manner in which the pictures, maps, and charts are presented—being derived from "various US

---

*As Moscow has responded to Washington press conferences with press conferences of its own, it has answered *Soviet Military Power* with its own report, a lackluster pamphlet called *Whence the Threat to Peace*, an amalgam of photographs of U.S. weapons (some pirated from *Aviation Week & Space Technology* and uncredited), charts, and prose, all of which is claimed in the introduction to be factual and unpolemical. This is not quite true, however. A chart depicting who adopted which weapon first, for example, uses a drawing of an intact bomb to represent Soviet nuclear weapons, while their U.S. counterparts are illustrated by a mushroom cloud. The chart rightly credits the United States with having the first nuclear carrier, but errs in showing that the U.S.S.R. has none, since BLACK COM 2 was then well along in construction. The chart also leaves out laser weapons altogether, which were pioneered by the Soviet Union.

sources" and which are "as authentic as possible," according to the report—one would have to suspect that serious distortions are deliberate. If that is true, it means that the Defense Department is grossly exaggerating the extent of the threat posed by the Soviet Union. That would have dire ramifications.

If, on the other hand, the material in *Soviet Military Power* is substantially correct, then there is only one conclusion to be drawn: U.S. space reconnaissance and associated collection methods are extremely good, particularly since, as is common practice, the finest details are withheld to protect the systems that gather the intelligence. For its part, Moscow has denounced *Soviet Military Power* as being unbalanced, but it has never quibbled over the numbers given for Soviet weapons or forces, or over their description and capabilities.

The quality of U.S. technical collection, as indicated by all the news leaks and by the Pentagon's annual threat report, was made explicit by Harold Brown, secretary of defense in the Carter administration, during the SALT II congressional hearings in November 1979:

> Our national technical means enable us to assemble a detailed picture of Soviet forces, including the characteristics of individual systems, by using information from a variety of sources. For example, our intelligence system has enabled us to build a comprehensive understanding of the Soviet ICBM system from design through deployment. We know that the Soviets have four design bureaus for the development of their ICBMs. We monitor the nature of the projects and the technologies pursued at these bureaus. We know which bureau is working on each of the new or significantly modified ICBMs known to be under development. We have a reasonably good idea of when they will begin flight testing of these missiles.
>
> Missile production takes place at several main assembly plants and at hundreds of subassembly plants, employing hundreds of thousands of workers. We monitor the Soviet ICBM deployment areas on a regular basis, observing construction activity, movement of people and materials, and training exercises. We have a good understanding of the organizational and support structure for deployed ICBM units.
>
> We regularly monitor key areas of the Soviet ICBM test ranges. We monitor missile test firings with a wide variety of sensors:

cameras taking pictures of launch impact areas; infrared detectors measuring heat from the engine; radars tracking ICBMs in flight; and radios receiving Soviet telemetry signals (the Soviets use telemetry signals to measure the performance of their test missiles in flight, and we use them to deduce technical characteristics of their missiles). The use of multiple sources complicates any effort to disguise or conceal a violation.

No one can pretend that our intelligence collection capability is perfect, or that there is no room for improvement. No sensor can be expected to catch every Soviet event of interest—but it is just as unlikely that a Soviet cheating program on a significant scale will evade every sensor. I expect the Soviets have a healthy respect for our intelligence capabilities, and that respect will influence their calculations about the costs and possible benefits of cheating.

There seems to be almost universal agreement that U.S. space reconnaissance capability is very good (and to take the former secretary of defense at his word, the Russians evidently think so too). But where arms control verification is concerned, is it good enough?

In order to attempt to answer that question, it is important to make a distinction between treaty monitoring and verification. Monitoring has to do with observing and recording—detecting, identifying, and measuring—as many important developments as possible that take place on denied territory. It is therefore a technical process that happens with or without arms control agreements and is conducted by the intelligence community. Verification, on the other hand, has to do specifically with arms control and is the process in which judgments are made regarding whether the terms of a particular treaty are being observed. It involves making subjective, judgmental decisions based on the intelligence that is collected by monitoring.

Verification—deciding whether the other side is living according to the terms of the agreement—is therefore susceptible to political distortion, since those who do the verifying tend to manipulate the intelligence, consciously or otherwise, so that it appears to bear out their preconceptions; they see what they want to see, as the saying goes. The bomber and missile gaps and the vanished Nicaraguan MiGs are but three cases in point.

Central to the topic of arms control, which is one of the most important and bitterly debated foreign policy issues of the age, is the matter of verification: Can it be done adequately to protect the vital interests of the United States?

The Reagan administration and its adherents have steadfastly maintained that arms control agreements with the Soviet Union are essentially unverifiable and, what is more, that there are numerous well-documented instances of cheating by the Russians on existing treaties. It has been alleged, for example, that among other transgressions Moscow has exceeded the 150-kiloton underground nuclear explosion limit imposed by the threshold treaty, that it has built a huge ABM radar at Abalakova in violation of the ABM treaty, and that it has encrypted missile telemetry and tested two different kinds of ICBMs contrary to the provisions of SALT II. The veracity of the charges aside, they do raise a fundamental contradiction. It is difficult to understand how U.S. technical collection systems can spot these and other instances of alleged treaty violations on the one hand, and at the same time not be equal to the task of providing adequate verification data on the other. If the administration is right about the violations, there is every indication that verification is adequate; if verification is not adequate, as they say, then there is no basis for believing that the Russians have cheated. The argument cannot be had both ways.

The evidence suggests overwhelmingly that the U.S. technical collection system, with its vast network of sensors and multiple redundancies, is adequate for verification. This does not mean that the system is foolproof, that it can be relied upon to spot every instance of cheating. But it is generally conceded that no major weapon has been developed by the U.S.S.R. that has gone unnoticed, unanalyzed, and uncataloged by the United States, and that no nuclear explosion has gone unrecorded and unmeasured.

Opponents of arms control and those who doubt (or who publicly claim to doubt) the nation's verification capability approach the subject from a negative standpoint, which can be summarized in this way: How can it be said that every weapon has been inventoried and every explosion recorded when we don't know what we've missed? "We have never found anything they have successfully hidden," Amrom Katz, one of the fathers of U.S. overhead reconnaissance, has remarked wryly.

It is, of course, impossible to prove a negative. The Soviet Union could have uncounted ICBMs by the hundreds hidden in remote valleys in the Urals or disguised as forest-fire watchtowers in Siberia. It could have laser battle stations, invisible to NORAD, circling the earth at this moment, poised to strike. "It is possible that ten thousand hamburgers a minute are being manufactured in space," Isaac Asimov once observed. "No one can prove they are not being manufactured. But it would simply defy logic." So would the existence of unseen ballistic missiles and unrecorded nuclear weapons tests.

Similarly, the point is often raised that imaging satellites cannot see through clouds or at night, or penetrate buildings. But that contention (which is not entirely correct where clouds and night are concerned) raises this question: What can occur only under cloud cover, at night, or in buildings that could threaten the national security of the United States?

Even pretending that a complex of ICBM silos could be dug from scratch, reinforced, and then loaded with missiles in three or four weeks—which is impossible—what military planner would want to stake the success of the project on unbroken cloud cover for so long a period? And this simplistic scenario ignores agents in the ministries in Moscow who would leak word of the plan, satellites that would record the movement of building materials and missiles from the factories to the site of the new silos, and incessant signals intercepts that would provide a great deal of additional information on what is afoot.

What general staff would predicate the invasion of another country on its army's guaranteed concealment under an unbroken blanket of clouds for two weeks or so, even if imaging was the only means of technical intelligence collection that could thwart the invaders? What, exactly, can happen at night that cannot be discovered in the morning? "An army that can train only at night loses a good deal in effectiveness and sleep, whatever it gains in secrecy," one major study on verification has noted. The cloud and night arguments are simply not credible.

Then there is the impenetrability-of-roofs argument. While roofs cannot be penetrated by cameras and other imaging sensors, what goes into them and what emerges can be closely counted, tracked, and analyzed. No weapon is placed in service by any military organization before it has been thoroughly tested, and testing takes place out of doors. As former Secretary of Defense Brown has indicated,

Soviet tests of major weapons are rigorously recorded by several systems, many of which are redundant. In the case of a ballistic missile test, this includes ground-based radars in Turkey, China, and the Aleutians, shipborne radar, ground-based signals intercepts, airborne sensing, and telemetry and other signals intercepts from space. "No new Soviet strategic systems (and few others) have ever been deployed, without our having known about them in advance. Indeed, we have usually been aware of new systems even before full-scale testing began—and we have monitored the progress of Soviet deployments essentially as they progressed, e.g., we have not had to make major changes later in the estimates of *deployed* forces," according to a study on arms control verification conducted by the Carnegie Endowment for International Peace.

This is not to say that there is no possibility for deception. There are infinite ways to cheat. One type of trick, for example, could entail getting the opposition to look in the wrong place by tossing a tempting bone there while the real action takes place somewhere else. A ballistic missile silo could be deliberately camouflaged just poorly enough so that it would reveal "secrets" that might send CIA and DIA analysts off on the wrong scent. Although such a scheme is intellectually interesting and has no doubt been included in appropriate gaming exercises, it comes with problems. For one thing, considerable expenditure of time and resources would have to be invested in such a subterfuge, so it would have to be judged not cost-effective. Also, those who planned and executed such a scheme could never be certain that those they meant to fool had not seen through the ploy and only appeared to be going along in order to cover the fact that they were also reconnoitering the real target. While there are countless ways in which to attempt deception, then, it is germane to test them for cost-effectiveness and the realistic expectation that they will fool the U.S. national technical means of intelligence collection.

In practice, arms control violations, such as they are, do not involve grandiose feats of strategic concealment or deception so much as they do each side's efforts to occasionally push at the edges of the various agreements to see how much they will give. And the matter of determining what constitutes a treaty violation is a highly subjective one that has caused frequent disagreement, not only between the United States and the Soviet Union, but within the U.S. intelligence community itself.

During the first six years of the Reagan presidency, for example, repeated charges were made, both in appropriate channels and on page one of the morning newspaper, that the Kremlin had violated arms control accords on numerous occasions. For its part, the Kremlin denied all the charges and countered with several of its own.

The Russians were accused of violating the ABM treaty not only by building the giant phased array radar at Abalakova, but by testing a rapid reload capability for their SH-08 hypersonic ballistic missile interceptor, which is prohibited by Article 5. They were further charged with violating the terms of SALT II by deploying two ICBMs—the SS-X-24 and the SS-25—and by encrypting relevant telemetry during ballistic missile tests, both of which are forbidden. A report released by the Reagan administration on February 1, 1985, concluded that the Soviet Union had conducted nuclear test explosions on eight or nine occasions since 1976 that exceeded the 150-kiloton limit imposed by the threshold agreement. The report, which was issued in the public manner of the Reagan White House, neglected to mention that seismic experts in the CIA and the Department of Energy, as well as at several universities, believed that the monitoring system in use at the time exaggerated the strength of underground blasts and, if corrected, would show that Moscow was substantially in compliance with the treaty. Six months later Secretary of State George P. Shultz compounded the problem by rejecting a Soviet proposal to ban all nuclear tests by asserting in the same statement that similar agreements had been violated in the past and that no "proper means" of verifying them existed. If he explained this contradiction, it went unrecorded.

In December 1985, Reagan himself claimed that the Kremlin had violated the terms of SALT II by deploying more intercontinental ballistic missiles and long-range bombers than it did in 1979 when the treaty was signed—2,504. "Such activity is indicative of a Soviet policy inconsistent with the political commitment [of SALT II]," he charged, again in public.

But early in February 1986 the Joint Chiefs of Staff issued its own intelligence assessment of Soviet compliance with SALT II and concluded that the Russians had 2,477 weapons that came under the provisions of the treaty. This, of course, contradicted Reagan. The report also provided another indication of the extent of U.S. monitoring capability by noting that Moscow had reduced its force of SS-11 missiles by 70, while deploying 45 new SS-25s; retiring 15 Bison bombers and adding 10 Bears; withdrawing two Yankee-class submarines that carried 16 ballistic missiles each and two Hotel-class

subs that carried 6 missiles, while adding a Typhoon-class submarine, which carries 20 missiles, and Delta IV submarines, which
can carry a total of 32 missiles.

Administration officials reacted to the Joint Chiefs' report by
saying that the issue of Soviet arms control violations was primarily
political and had no military importance. That was quite true. But
the political aspect of the episode went beyond a mere difference of
opinion between conflicting intelligence reports. It underscored the
manner in which the administration used technical intelligence data
on a highly selective basis in order to shape public and congressional
attitudes toward the Soviet Union and its arms control policy. The
tactic was not lost on Spurgeon M. Keeny, Jr., a former deputy
director of the Arms Control and Disarmament Agency who went
on to become the president of the arms control association, a private
group.

The Joint Chiefs' report confirmed "that the Soviet Union continues to comply with the SALT II treaty by dismantling strategic
systems," Keeny said. "It appears gravely irresponsible," he added,
"for the Administration to have formally charged the Soviet Union
in December with the violation of the SALT II overall numerical
limits when the JCS order of battle now shows them to be well
within the required limits."

For its part, the Kremlin has denied any wrongdoing and leveled
some arms control violation charges of its own. It has maintained
that the Abalakova radar is for space tracking only and that missile
telemetry that is encrypted does not fall within the provisions of
SALT II. Although both explanations are remotely possible, neither
is credible and each depends on the United States maintaining a
degree of trust that is without parallel in the history of arms control.
Moscow also insists that the SS-25 is not new at all, but is actually
a permitted modification of an existing long-range missile, the
SS-13.

And on January 29, 1984—just hours before President Reagan
was scheduled to go on television to announce his plans for a second
term—Moscow made public its own detailed list of alleged U.S.
arms control violations. What was most interesting about the disclosure was not so much the purported violations themselves as the fact
that the Kremlin, evidently exasperated with Reagan's incessant
charges in public of Soviet cheating, had decided that it would have
to respond in kind. Western diplomats said they could not recall
another occasion in recent years when Moscow had released the full

text of a diplomatic note on so sensitive an issue. But the clue as to why it had done so was in the note itself. In one place it accused the United States of "systematically" violating the confidentiality of discussions between the two nations on the observance of strategic arms agreements. Such discussions are supposed to take place within the secure confines of the Standing Consultative Commission, a joint Soviet-American panel that had been set up in 1972 under the terms of SALT I to meet in Geneva for the specific purpose of privately thrashing out alleged violations. But Reagan was betraying the spirit of the SCC and, instead, was playing to Western Europe and the crowd back home. The Politburo, new to American-style public relations grandstanding, was attempting to match the Reagan administration, if not beat it, at its own game.

Specifically, the Kremlin's note charged the United States with several SALT II violations and with some others as well. The placing of Pershing II and ground-launched cruise missiles in Western Europe violated the prohibition against using other states to circumvent the treaty, Moscow charged. The note went on to accuse Washington of violating the ABM treaty by erecting the Shemya phased array radar and conducting research for the Strategic Defense Initiative, of contravening the limited test ban by allowing radioactive particles from underground explosions to escape into the atmosphere, and of violating the threshold treaty by exploding weapons with yields greater than 150 kilotons. It also accused the United States of having illegally covered Minuteman ICBM silos,* and, for that matter, of not even having ratified the agreement in the first place. The Russians had struck back in full public view.

At no time in the history of nuclear arms control, which effectively began in October 1963 with the limited test ban treaty, has there been such a spate of public allegations of treaty violations, coupled with the purported inadequacy of verification methods, as has occurred during the Reagan presidency. The ability of the national

---

*Beginning in 1973, the Russians noticed that Minuteman II silos had been covered with 2,700-square-foot corrugated aluminum and wood structures while they were being hardened and modernized, according to a primer on verification put out by the American Association for the Advancement of Science. Marshall Shulman, director of Columbia University's W. Averell Harriman Institute for the Advanced Study of the Soviet Union, said in a television interview that the silos were covered when the Minuteman IIs were replaced by Minuteman IIIs and remained covered for years. The large covers were eventually replaced by smaller ones at Soviet insistence in the SCC.

technical means of intelligence collection to spot all of the Soviet
Union's violations and provide detailed descriptions of the Kremlin's weaponry for the Defense Department's annually revised cata-
logs on the one hand, while at the same time being held as
inadequate to the task of verifying arms control agreements on the
other, remains one of the abiding contradictions of the Reagan
presidency. But it is not a contradiction without reason.

Seven months and one day into its first term, the administration
delivered a note to Moscow that presaged its stance on arms control
for years to come. The message, conveyed by the then director of
the Arms Control and Disarmament Agency Eugene V. Rostow to
the Soviet chargé d'affaires in Washington, stipulated that any future arms control accords would have to include on-site inspection
and other "cooperative measures," such as an exchange of information on demand and the designation of weapons production facilities. Although Nikita Khrushchev had expressed a willingness to
accept on-site inspection for a comprehensive ban on the testing of
nuclear weapons as far back as the early 1960s and more than a
decade later agreed to an inspection protocol for the peaceful nuclear explosions treaty, Reagan was advised, and correctly, that the
Kremlin did not really like on-site inspection because it found it to
be unnecessarily intrusive and conducive to spying. (This is a shared
belief, however. When on-site inspection in the United States was
raised during preliminary talks to ban all testing, the Carter administration rejected mandatory inspections out of hand.)

In sending the warning to the "evil empire," as he had taken to
calling the Soviet Union, Reagan was serving notice that he intended to be tougher at arms control than his predecessors had been.
The conservatives who had come to power with Reagan had made
no bones about their attitude toward arms control—that it
amounted to little more than a license for the Kremlin to accelerate
its own weapons buildup while the United States naïvely adhered
to the agreements, falling ever further behind. This view was entirely compatible with the new president's own political instincts,
of course, so he embraced it enthusiastically. In making the note
public, however, the Reagan White House was taking one of its first
deliberate steps to assure the electorate that had swept it to power
on a wave of unabashed patriotism that the days of going soft on the
Kremlin, and being bled militarily because of dangerously one-sided
arms control agreements, were at an end.

The note delivered by Rostow that August in effect asserted that

U.S. national technical means of verification, which had been considered by all four of his immediate predecessors to be fully adequate for the conclusion of arms control agreements, were no longer considered to be so and that the whole business of arms control was therefore going to have to be reappraised in a new light.

Eleven months later Reagan formally endorsed the new policy at a National Security Council meeting by announcing that the United States would no longer participate in any international effort to end nuclear testing. Thus, with the turn of a phrase, Ronald Reagan formally abandoned one of the key foreign policy goals of six of his predecessors. This time the news came not in a speech or in another of the baited warnings to the Kremlin that were trumpeted to the American people almost simultaneously but in a leak to a reporter. In a subsequent briefing for other reporters, two straight-faced administration officials (who requested and received anonymous "source" status) led their interviewers to understand that pursuit of the long-sought Comprehensive Test Ban Treaty (CTBT) was being terminated, mostly because of concern that its provisions could not be adequately verified.

The assertion that U.S. technical means of verification are no longer up to the task of guaranteeing compliance with arms control agreements has been stated repeatedly by the Reagan administration, with the result that the new incompetence has become the accepted cornerstone of arms control policy and one of the most important justifications for the renewed arms buildup. If the United States is unable to verify treaties, after all, it means that its strategic reconnaissance system is not up to the task of accurate counting (as the administration claims is the case where cruise and mobile ballistic missiles are concerned), and this in turn means that the nation needs to increase the acquisition of still more arms to offset all of those on the other side that it is now being persuaded it can no longer see.

". . . the Soviets would have a far easier problem of verifying compliance with limitations on the U.S. ASAT system than we would have on the Soviet system," according to the report sent by the Reagan administration to Congress in March 1984 in an effort to gain support for the U.S. system. "For example, a ban on all ASAT systems would require that the Soviet ASAT system be eliminated. The Soviet interceptor is relatively small and is launched by a type of space booster that the Soviets use for other space launch missions. . . . The USSR could maintain a covert supply of intercep-

tors which could be readied quickly for operational use, probably
without risk of U.S. detection." The report added that a ground-
based laser ASAT could also be concealed. "We want to negotiate
in good faith," one senior Reagan administration official complained, but added, "How do we do it when it can't be verified?"

On the afternoon of May 28, 1985, Jack F. Evernden, a research
geophysicist and a leading seismologist with the U.S. Geological
Survey at Menlo Park, California, gave a paper at the American
Association for the Advancement of Science annual meeting in Los
Angeles. Evernden, a gray-haired man with a sharply angular face
that wears a look of implacable dismay, began by apologizing for not
addressing his scientific specialty in the paper he was about to
deliver, which was called "Why Has It Been Impossible to Arrange
a CTBT?"

"Though I once did, I no longer believe that technical considerations have anything to do with negotiations and attainment of new
test ban treaties. Therefore, I will not spend my time today reciting
a litany of seismological lore. Rather, I will express my deeply felt
views on why no progress towards such treaties has occurred in the
past two decades," Evernden said. Here, in part, is what followed
his opening remark:

> In the mid-1960's, while employed by the Department of De-
> fense, I was asked to advise on the technical content of a letter
> written for the signatures of the Joint Chiefs, this letter stating
> that all of the earlier words of the Chiefs in support of a verifiable
> comprehensive test ban treaty were false. It had just been convinc-
> ingly demonstrated for the first time that there were indeed seis-
> mological techniques that could distinguish the seismic waves of
> explosions and earthquakes and there was every reason to believe
> that these techniques would work for smaller events than had as
> yet been investigated.
>
> This demonstration prompted the Chiefs to state flatly that
> they never had been in favor of a CTBT. They had been willing
> to assert that they were only as long as seismologists were incapa-
> ble of monitoring such a treaty, thus providing the Chiefs with
> a convenient shield behind which to hide their real attitudes.
> Upon removal of that shield, they stated the truth; that they were
> then, and would remain, opposed to a CTBT. They would al-

ways opt for bombs rather than for mutual forbearance, under the millennia-old attitude that the only ways to deal with one's enemies are via the doubled fist and the truncheon, and unlimited license to build new engines of war. . . .

The current presidential assertions that the Soviets have probably cheated on the Yield Threshold Test Ban Treaty (YTTBT) are based upon such an incredibly thin thread of seismological argument as to be unobservable even under high magnification. There are many tens of papers in the seismological literature which, taken together, quantitatively deny this presidential assertion and prove without a doubt that available seismological evidence does not support the case for Soviet cheating on the YTTBT. All of the necessary analysis has been in the hands of the U.S. Government for years. Why all of these efforts to obfuscate?

An explanation, a simple one, for all of this irrationality has become apparent to me after years of contending with these issues. And it has nothing to do with one or all governments consciously harboring evil intent. No, the situation is far more dangerous than that. It's simply that when most men, whether liberal Democrat, conservative Republican or Soviet Communist, come to ultimate governmental authority, they are of no better stuff than you and I, and they are oft overwhelmed by the responsibility and complexity of political decision, particularly when such decision must be made on the basis of scientific data that they totally fail to comprehend; data which are multidimensional and highly sophisticated and about which someone with a hidden agenda will always argue there is a dangerous margin of interpretation and possible uncertainty.

When faced with being accountable through the ages to come for the safety of their respective countries during their few years of tenureship, should a President or Premier take the route of the untried, or should he follow the oft-tried and oft-failed, but always defensible and always strongly felt, route of the mailed fist? He is certain that no one can accuse him of weakness if he opts for guns and bombs. Maybe stupidity, but not weakness. That such conduct actually is a sign of a much more profound weakness is a point too subtle for his anxious mind to comprehend.

A government that does not believe in limiting arms, or thinks that the other side is so treacherous that the notion of adequately monitoring such limitation is untenable, ought not enter into arms control agreements. But to cast doubt on the process itself by falsely labeling national technical means of verification as inadequate is to subvert reason to the basest political posturing. To insist that we cannot see what we need to see, while seeing only what we want to see, is to condemn ourselves to live with the demons of our own creation forever. That is how big this is.

Abbreviations and Acronyms

AAF	Army Air Forces
ABM	Anti-Ballistic Missile
ABMA	Army Ballistic Missile Agency
ACSI	Assistant Chief of Staff, Intelligence
AFTAC	Air Force Technical Applications Center
ARPA	Advanced Research Projects Agency
ASAT	Anti-Satellite [weapon]
ASW	Anti-Submarine Warfare
BMD	Ballistic Missile Defense
BMEW	Ballistic Missile Early Warning
BNE	Board of National Estimates
CCD	Charge Coupled Device
CIA	Central Intelligence Agency
COMINT	Communications Intelligence
COMIREX	Committee on Imagery Requirements and Exploitation
COMOR	Committee on Overhead Reconnaissance
COPUOS	Committee on the Peaceful Uses of Outer Space
CSOC	Consolidated Space Operations Center
CTBT	Comprehensive Test Ban Treaty
DARPA	Defense Advanced Research Projects Agency
DCI	Director of Central Intelligence
DDP	Deputy Director for Plans (CIA)
DDS&T	Deputy Director for Science and Technology (CIA)
DEFSMAC	Defense Special Missile and Astronautics Center
DIA	Defense Intelligence Agency
DIP	Digital Image Processing
DSCS	Defense Satellite Communications System
DSD	Defence Signals Directorate (Australia)
DSMP	Defense Satellite Meteorological Program
DSP	Defense Support Program

ECM	Electronic Countermeasures
ELINT	Electronic Intelligence
EMP	Electromagnetic Pulse
EORSAT	Electronic Ocean Reconnaissance Satellite
ERTS	Earth Resources Technology Satellite
EXCOM	Executive Committee
FLTSATCOM	Fleet Satellite Communications [System]
FOBS	Fractional Orbiting Bombardment System
GCHQ	Government Communications Headquarters (Britain)
GEODSS	Ground-Based Electro-Optical Deep Space Surveillance System
GRU	Chief Intelligence Directorate of the General Staff (U.S.S.R.)
HUMINT	Human Intelligence
ICBM	Intercontinental Ballistic Missile
INR	(Bureau of) Intelligence and Research
IOC	Initial Operational Capability
IONDS	Integrated Operational Nuclear Detection System
IR	Infrared
IRBM	Intermediate-Range Ballistic Missile
JCS	Joint Chiefs of Staff
JPL	Jet Propulsion Laboratory
JRC	Joint Reconnaissance Center
KGB	Committee for State Security (U.S.S.R.)
KH	Keyhole
LTBT	Limited Test Ban Treaty
MAD	Magnetic Anomaly Detection
MHV	Miniature Homing Vehicle
MIDAS	Missile Defense Alarm System
MOL	Manned Orbiting Laboratory
MRBM	Medium-Range Ballistic Missile
MSS	Multispectral Scanner
NACA	National Advisory Committee on Aeronautics
NASA	National Aeronautics and Space Administration
NATO	North Atlantic Treaty Organization
NDS	Nuclear Detection System
NFIB	National Foreign Intelligence Board
NIE	National Intelligence Estimate
NISC	Naval Intelligence Support Center
NOAA	National Oceanic and Atmospheric Administration
NOIC	Navy Operational Intelligence Center
NORAD	North American Aerospace Defense [Command]
NPIC	National Photographic Interpretation Center
NREC	National Reconnaissance Executive Committee
NRL	Naval Research Laboratory
NRO	National Reconnaissance Office
NSA	National Security Agency
NSC	National Security Council
NSP	Navy Space Project
NTM	National Technical Means
OBC	Optical Bar Camera
ONR	Office of Naval Research
OSD	Office of the Secretary of Defense
OSO	Office of SIGINT Operations
PHOTINT	Photographic Intelligence

PI	Photo Interpreter
PNIE	Priority National Intelligence Estimate
PNIO	Priority National Intelligence Objective
PSAC	President's Science Advisory Committee
RADINT	Radar Intelligence
RAF	Royal Air Force
RORSAT	Radar Ocean Reconnaissance Satellite
RSO	Reconnaissance Systems Officer
SAC	Strategic Air Command
SALT	Strategic Arms Limitation Talks
SAM	Surface-to-Air Missile
SAMOS	Satellite and Missile Observation System
SCF	Satellite Control Facility
SCI	Sensitive Compartmented Information
SDAC	Seismic Data Analysis Center
SDS	Satellite Data System
SI	Special Intelligence
SIGINT	Signals Intelligence
SIR	Shuttle Imaging Radar
SNIE	Special National Intelligence Estimate
SOSUS	Sound Surveillance System
SPADATS	Space Tracking and Detection System
SPADOC	Space Defense Operations Center
SR	Strategic Reconnaissance
SSTS	Space Surveillance and Tracking System
TAC	Tactical Air Command
TAV	Trans-Atmospheric Vehicle
TCP	Technological Capabilities Panel
TENCAP	Tactical Exploitation of National Capabilities
TECHINT	Technical Intelligence
TELINT	Telemetry Intelligence
TK	Talent-Keyhole
TTBT	Threshold Test Ban Treaty
USIB	United States Intelligence Board

Glossary

Following are some basic definitions of technical terms relating to space reconnaissance and surveillance.

Apogee	The highest point reached by a satellite in an elliptical orbit, and therefore the point farthest away from the earth's atmosphere.
ASAT	Anti-satellite weapon. It can be a co-orbital satellite, a direct-ascent missile, a missile fired from an aircraft, or a directed energy weapon, such as a laser. Electronic "spoofing," such as jamming or misdirecting a satellite, is also considered part of the ASAT inventory.
COMINT	Communication intelligence. The collection, processing, decoding, and analysis of foreign communication traffic sent by radio, telegraph, telephone, or other electromagnetic means.
Eccentricity	The "shape" of an orbit, or how elliptical it is, based on a satellite's apogee and perigee.
ELINT	Electronic intelligence. The collection, processing, decoding, and analysis of foreign noncommunication electromagnetic intelligence, not including that relating to radioactive emanations. Data concerning a Soviet aircraft's radar jamming system would be ELINT.
Ferret	Generally, a class of satellites that measures foreign radar signals from orbits as low as a few hundred miles up to about 30,000 miles. Also used to describe aircraft that feint penetrations in order to trick radar operators into turning on their equipment.
Geosynchronous (or synchronous)	An orbit 22,300 miles above the equator. Satellites in that position do not move relative to the spot on earth over which they orbit.
Ground track	The path on earth over which a satellite travels.
Hardening	Methods used to enhance a satellite's ability to withstand an

attack or radiation bombardment. Metal shielding, gallium arsenide circuits, and laser-resistant lens coatings are three possibilities.

Housekeeping
(or stationkeeping) Any or all of the scores of operations that must be done to keep
a satellite in orbit and performing its mission. These include
turning its thrusters on and off to maneuver it and maintain
three-axis stability, keeping its solar panels pointed in the right
direction, turning sensors on and off if necessary, turning power
on and off, adjusting it to function properly in the earth's
shadow, and so forth. Many satellites, and particularly the low
orbiters, require almost constant attention or they will fail cata-
strophically in a matter of hours.

HUMINT   Human intelligence. The collection of information by spies.

Inclination   The angle of a satellite's orbit relative to the equator. A true
polar orbit is inclined 90 degrees. Intermediate inclinations
cover precisely matching areas north and south of the equator:
a satellite with an inclination of 65 degrees, for example, flies
over every part of the earth below 65 degrees latitude, north and
south.

LASINT   Laser intelligence. Data collected about foreign laser capability.
A U.S. LASINT satellite is currently under development.

Mach   The speed of sound. It varies with altitude, but is generally
calculated at between 640 and 700 miles an hour.

Oblique   Imagery taken at an angle.

Perigee   The lowest point reached by a satellite in an elliptical orbit, and
therefore the point deepest in the earth's atmosphere. Because
of the increased gravitational pull at such relatively low altitude,
satellites fly their fastest, making imaging difficult because of the
speed of the satellite relative to that of the earth. The targets of
imaging satellites are therefore usually overflown either just
before or just after perigee is reached, not during it.

Period   The time it takes a satellite to circle the earth. Low orbiters
generally do it in about 90 minutes, while those in exceptionally
elliptical orbits can take 12 hours or more.

PHOTINT   Photographic intelligence. Although strictly speaking, this has
to do only with traditional film cameras doing standard photog-
raphy, it is generally taken to include electro-optical imaging as
well.

Point failure   The malfunctioning, usually decisively, of a satellite in orbit.

Polar orbit   An orbit that takes a satellite over, or nearly over, the earth's
poles. This means that every spot on earth, or almost every spot,
passes beneath the satellite every day.

RADINT   Radar intelligence. Sometimes used to define intelligence that is
collected, processed, and analyzed about foreign radar. Some-
times used to mean the use of radar to collect intelligence.

Real-time
intelligence   Intelligence that is transmitted as a given event is occurring.

SIGINT   Signals intelligence. The overall designation that includes CO-
MINT, ELINT, TELINT, and most other electromagnetic
intelligence, as distinct from imaging.

Sun-synchronous   An orbit, generally used by weather and imaging reconnaissance satellites, which follows an inclination of about 98 degrees

	and therefore always keeps the satellite's orbital plane the same relative to the sun. This makes it easier to spot change by noting whether the length or position of shadows varies from one day to another.
Tasking	The assigning of reconnaissance targets in some kind of order.
TECHINT	Technical intelligence. Information collected by machines, as opposed to HUMINT.
Telemetry	Performance data about a guided missile, such as fuel consumption, guidance system operation, separation procedure, and speed that is sent to the ground. This is generally done by radio, but it can also be stored on tape inside the missile and either dropped in a capsule or kept on board until impact.
TELINT	Telemetry intelligence. The interception, processing, and analysis of telemetry.
Verification	The determination of whether the signatory to an arms control agreement is living up to its terms. This is always a "political" determination, as opposed to monitoring, which is only the collection of intelligence and is therefore strictly technical.

Notes

1. THE NEED TO KNOW

Page

3–11   Keegan's observations were recorded in a taped interview in June 1984. Additional material on his assessment of the American defense posture appears in "Air Force Ex-Intelligence Chief Fears Soviet Has Military Edge," *The New York Times*, January 3, 1977, and "New Assessment Put on Soviet Threat," *Aviation Week & Space Technology*, March 28, 1977.

11–12   Colby's recollections are from his *Honorable Men*, pp. 294–95.

13   The "gray man" description is from "Ex-C.I.A. Head Now Works for a Nuclear Freeze," *The New York Times*, June 14, 1983.

13–15   Colby's remarks were recorded in a taped interview in April 1984.

15–16   The Abalakova radar (sometimes sited at Krasnoyarsk) was first made public in "U.S. Scrutinizes New Soviet Radar," *Aviation Week & Space Technology*, August 22, 1983, pp. 19–20. It was subsequently reported in "U.S. and Soviet Discuss Whether Moscow Violated Terms of 2 Arms Pacts," *The New York Times*, October 5, 1983.

17   Brown's testimony is in U.S. Congress, Senate Committee on Foreign Relations, *The SALT II Treaty*, November 19, 1979, p. 196.

23   Information on the SI, TK, and Byeman classification systems is from *The U.S. Intelligence Community*, pp. 315–18, and from a highly reliable source who wished to remain anonymous.

24   Lindsey, *The Falcon and the Snowman*, pp. 54–57.

24   Dirks is quoted in Richelson, "The Keyhole Satellite Program," p. 138.

25   MacKinder's ideas are summarized in Padelford and Lincoln, *International Politics*, pp. 53–54.

2. Denied Territory

Page

26–28   Saint-Exupéry, *Flight to Arras*, p. 92 (antiaircraft fire) and pp. 42–43 (fighters).

28   Coutelle's *aérostiers* are described in *The American Heritage History of Flight* (New York: American Heritage Publishing Co., 1962), pp. 54–55.

29   *The Queen of the Air* photograph appears in Stanley, *World War II Photo Intelligence*, p. 18.

29–30   Lowe's exploits are from *The American Heritage History of Flight*, pp. 64–65, and Infield, *Unarmed and Unafraid*, pp. 22–28. The Union captain's report is quoted in Duke and Lanchberry, eds., *The Saga of Flight*, pp. 44–46.

30–31   The 9th Infantry Regiment's kite and camera are described and pictured in Stanley, *World War II Photo Intelligence*, pp. 19–20.

31   Neubronner's pigeons are the subject of a display in the Reconnaissance Museum at Beale Air Force Base, California.

31–32   The Signal Corps Flying School and related developments are treated in Infield, *Unarmed and Unafraid*, pp. 29–30, and in Stanley, *World War II Photo Intelligence*, p. 21.

32–33   Raleigh's observations are from his *War in the Air* (I), p. 250. The primacy of reconnaissance is from p. 260.

33   *The Rand McNally Encyclopedia of Military Aircraft* (Angelucci, ed.) gives good basic descriptions of the various World War I reconnaissance planes, as well as those that came after them.

33–34   German reconnaissance strength in March 1918 and Near Eastern operations are from Peter and Thetford, *German Aircraft of the First World War*, pp. xxxi–xxxvi.

34   Lord Douglas of Kirtleside's technique is from Raleigh, *The War in the Air* (II), p. 89.

34   Camera lenses and film types are from Stanley's *World War II Photo Intelligence*, p. 26. So are details of high-altitude camera problems and their solution.

37   Goddard's Rochester "bomb" is from his *Overview*, pp. 147–49, and the electric flash system is described on pp. 244–45.

38–39   The strip camera's development is from Goddard, *Overview*, pp. 241–44 and p. 308.

39   The Fairchild T-3 is described and pictured in Stanley, *World War II Photo Intelligence*, pp. 136–37.

41–44   Joint Air Exercise No. 4 and the events leading up to it are described in Copp, *A Few Great Captains*, pp. 392–98.

44   Goddard's Mexican reconnaissance is from his *Overview*, p. 377. So is the *Graf Zeppelin* theory.

44–45   German prewar reconnaissance is described at length in Kahn, *Hitler's Spies*, pp. 114–35, and also in Killen, *The Luftwaffe: A History*, pp. 66–67. Von Fritsch's fall is chronicled in Shirer, *The Rise and Fall of the Third Reich*, pp. 314–18.

45–47   The Cotton organization and its leader are described in Babington-Smith, *Air Spy*, especially pp. 7–28. The memorandum is quoted on p. 21.

47–48   Stanley's *World War II Photo Intelligence* delineates the three types of intelligence-gathering units on p. 36.

49   The paint removal and polishing are recounted in Ivie's *Aerial Recon-
          naissance: The 10th Photo Recon Group in World War II*, p. 192.
49   Photoreconnaissance versus tactical reconnaissance is mentioned in
          Stanley's *World War II Photo Intelligence*, p. 61.
49   The Advanced Fighter Reconnaissance Training manual is quoted in
          Ivie's *Aerial Reconnaissance*, p. 15. The near court-martial is in a footnote
          on p. 167. The strafing incident (footnote) is from pp. 62 and 65.
50   B-29 reconnaissance operations against Japan are summarized in *The
          Army Air Forces in World War II* (Craven and Cate, eds.), pp. 163–65.
          The 1928 ground plan is mentioned on p. 164.
50–51   The technical innovations are from Goddard's *Overview*. The infrared
          experiment is mentioned on p. 236. Goddard recalled (on p. 321) an
          interchange with Elliott Roosevelt in which the latter said that a pilot
          using the strip camera "would have to fly so low he'd be mincemeat."
          Baker's lenses are described on pp. 327–28. The radar reconnaissance
          camera is mentioned briefly on pp. 322 and 328 (and see p. 395 for a
          debate between Goddard and Curtis LeMay on the relative merits of
          radar versus optical reconnaissance systems).
51–52   The description of locating the V-1 is in Babington-Smith's *Air Spy*, pp.
          226–29. Photo interpretation is also covered in Chapter 8 of Stanley's
          World War II Photo Intelligence and in the Department of the Air Force's
          Photographic Interpretation Handbook.

3. ASSETS, BLACK AND SKUNKY

Page
54n   Belenoko's account of the attack on Powers is from Barron's *MiG Pilot*,
          p. 182. The same assertion is made in *The Penkovskiy Papers*, which
          claims that 14 SA-2 missiles were fired, shotgun style, at the U-2 and
          that shock waves from a near miss sent it out of control. The book also
          maintains that a MiG-19 was accidentally hit in the fusillade. Powers's
          own account in *Operation Overflight* is necessarily vague; he literally
          didn't know what hit him. U-2 pilots have claimed that MiG-21s pursu-
          ing U-2s during the Cuban missile crisis in 1962 would flame out and
          become ballistic (their engines would stop for lack of air and they would
          lose control to the point of becoming missile-like) at about 62,000 feet,
          after which they would tumble back down, out of control. See Humph-
          ries, "High Flight," pp. 10–12.
55   Khrushchev's speech was reported at length by *The New York Times* on
          May 6. The U.S. admission, which was made by the State Department,
          was reported by the *Times* on May 8. Mention of the fear of surprise
          attack is on p. 1.
56   The advent of the TU-4 and Long Range Air Force are in Prados's *The
          Soviet Estimate*, pp. 38–40.
56, 56n   Soviet V-2 activity and Gröttrup's contractual arrangement are from
          Baker, *The Rocket Team*, p. 320.
56–57   Kistiakowsky's remarks are from an interview with the author that took
          place in August 1981.
57–58   The first Army Air Force's ferrets are briefly described in "The Archan-
          gel *Is* Illuminated," *Journal of Electronic Defense*, February 1984. pp. 24,
          68.
58–59   The early postwar photoreconnaissance and ferret missions operating

out of Alaska and England are described in detail in Richelson's *American Espionage and the Soviet Target*, Chapter 4.

59   Reconnaissance casualties are from Prados, *The Soviet Estimate*, p. 30.

60   The XF-12's interior was described in the Republic Aviation Corp.'s report, *Photographic Installation of the XF-12 Long Range Photographic Reconnaissance Airplane*, especially pp. 7–17.

61   The *Aviation Week* article was "F-12 Based on Fighter Experience," November 10, 1947, pp. 28–30.

61   George Goddard said in his *Overview* that "the jet age had overtaken" the XF-11 and, by implication, the XF-12 as well (p. 360).

61–62   The engineers' prediction is from the Douglas Aircraft Company's "Preliminary Design of an Experimental World-Circling Spaceship" (Report SM-11827), pp. 1–2.

62–63   Moby Dick, the "Murmansk Runs," and the hitchhiking RF-86 are from Prados *The Soviet Estimate*, pp. 29–30.

64–65   The Long Range Detection Program and coverage of the Soviet atomic test program are described in Richelson's *American Espionage and the Soviet Target*, Chapter 4.

66–67   Amory's account of the Canberra penetration is from an Oral History interview, transcript pp. 112–13. The flight is corroborated in Goddard's *Overview*, pp. 388–89.

67   The downed U.S. reconnaissance planes and the Sabre-MiG battle are in "List of Clashes on Planes Given," *The New York Times*, May 6, 1960.

68   Taylor and the Bisons is from Prados, *The Soviet Estimate*, p. 43.

68–69   "Open Skies" is from McDougall, . . . *The Heavens and the Earth*, p. 127. See also Eisenhower, *The White House Years: Waging Peace*, p. 519.

69   The ODMSC's meeting with Eisenhower and related events are from Killian, *Sputnik, Scientists, and Eisenhower*, p. 68.

69   Bissell's remark is from an interview with the author.

70   The composition of the TCP, including Project 3, is listed in declassified organizational charts sent to the author by Dr. Killian.

71n   The Skunk Works' origins are recounted in Johnson, "Development of the Lockheed SR-71 Blackbird," *Lockheed Horizons*, Winter, 1981/82, p. 134.

72n   The RB-57D's mishaps are from Miller's *Lockheed U-2*, pp. 16–17. The collapsed wings are not known to have resulted in any fatalities, but each such accident resulted in the aircraft's being written off.

72   The genesis of CL-282 was described by Johnson to the author. Additional information on it and on the X-16 is in Miller's *Lockheed U-2*, pp. 17–18.

73   Dulles's observation about reconnaissance is from his *The Craft of Intelligence*, p. 67.

73   Killian's remarks about Eisenhower and the Air Force are from an interview with the author. Killian also said that the Air Force was "contemptuous" of the CIA, that enmity had existed between the two throughout the Eisenhower years, and that both the TCP and the president's Science Advisory Committee placed more stock in CIA intelligence reports than in those of the Air Force.

74–75   Bissell's remarks are from an interview with the author.

75–76   The U-2's camera system is treated in some detail in Miller's *Lockheed U-2*, pp. 65–71. Much information about the system and quality of the photographs came from the trial of Francis Gary Powers in August 1960. The relevant part of the court transcript is quoted in Katz, *The Soviets and the U-2 Photos—An Heuristic Argument*, pp. 16–19.

77   Bissell's remarks about the working relationship are from the interview.

77–78   Ben Rich's remarks are from an interview with the author.

78–79   Project Gopher and others are from Richelson's *American Espionage and the Soviet Target*, Chapter 5, and from *The New York Times*, February 6, 1960.

79–80   The early operational history of CIA U-2s is covered in Miller's *Lockheed U-2*, pp. 25–28.

81n   The John Foster Dulles quotation is from Killian, *Sputnik, Scientists, and Eisenhower*, p. 84.

4. THREATS, REAL AND IMAGINED

Page

82   Bush's remarks are quoted in U.S. Senate, *Hearings Before the Special Subcommittee on Atomic Energy* as reproduced in *Hearings Before the Preparedness Investigating Subcommittee*, pp. 822–23.

83   Project Feedback is detailed in Klass, *Secret Sentries in Space*, pp. 81–88, and mentioned in Richelson, "The Keyhole Satellite Program," p. 125. Pied Piper is also defined in both of those sources on the pages given above.

84   Design specifications for General Operational Requirement No. 80 are in McDougall,´. . . *the Heavens and the Earth*, p. 111.

85–86   Agena's details are from *Jane's All the World's Aircraft: 1962–63* (Great Missenden, Bucks, England: Jane's all the World's Aircraft Publishing Co.), p. 399. A full-size Agena is on display in the National Air and Space Museum.

87–88   Reentry procedure for the camera-carrying satellite is from RAND Corp., "A Family of Recoverable Satellites," p. 22.

89–90   Davies's "photographic apparatus" patent is No. 3,143,048, granted on August 4, 1964. In addition to showing schematic drawings of the capsule, there is a diagram of the radio equipment and control system.

91   Billings's description of SAMOS is from Kistiakowsky, *A Scientist at the White House*, p. 45.

92   Johnson himself alluded to Sputnik's representing a "technological Pearl Harbor" in hearings that November. See U.S. Senate, Committee on Armed Services, *Inquiry into Satellite and Missile Programs, Hearings Before the Preparedness Investigating Subcommittee*, pp. 1–2.

92–93   Symington's and Luce's quotations are from Killian, *Sputnik, Scientists, and Eisenhower*, p. 8.

93   Reedy's memorandum is quoted in Prados, *The Soviet Estimate*, p. 64.

93–94   G. Mennen Williams's poem is reprinted in Killian, *Sputnik, Scientists, and Eisenhower*, p. 8.

95   Sedov's predictions and descriptions of experiments are from McDougall, . . . *the Heavens and the Earth*, p. 60; the TCP prediction is from p. 120; RAND's is from p. 147.

95   The U-2 Tyuratam overflight is in Kenden, "U.S. Reconnaissance Satellite Programmes," p. 243.

95   The Turkish SIGINT stations are listed in Bamford, *The Puzzle Palace*, pp. 159–60.

96–97   The ICBM tests are from Prados, *The Soviet Estimate*, p. 79. General
           Walsh's tenure as ASCI is from p. 81.
97   The "flyspeck" anecdote and reference to Dulles's using his own ana-
           lysts is from Wise and Ross, *The Invisible Government*, p. 212.
98   Conflicting projections on SS-6 production are from Prados, *The Soviet
           Estimate*, p. 82.
98*n*   William Colby's opinion is from an interview with the author.
98–99   The breakfast warning is from the author's interview with Kis-
           tiakowsky.
99   The resumption of testing and the Soviet space shots are from Prados,
           The Soviet Estimate, p. 84.
100   Symington's prediction is in Bottome, *The Missile Gap*, p. 97.
100–101   Khrushchev's remarks are quoted in Klass, *Secret Sentries in Space*, pp.
           43–44.
101–2   U-2 targets as outlined by Dulles were originally deleted and classified.
           The relevant remarks were declassified in 1982. See *Executive Sessions of
           the Senate Foreign Relations Committee*, Historical Series, 86th Cong.,
           2nd Sess., 1960, Vol XII, pp. 284–85.
103   The SA-1s and the SA-2 threat is discussed in Prados, *The Soviet Esti-
           mate*, pp. 96–97.
104   National Security Action Memorandum 1846 is from Richelson, "The
           Keyhole Satellite Program," p. 126.
104   The circumstances of Bissell's getting the Corona program were related
           in the interview with the author.
104–5   NSC 5814/1 is described in McDougall, . . . *the Heavens and the Earth*,
           pp. 180–81 and in Richelson, "The Keyhole Satellite Program," p. 126.
           Concern about protection of spacecraft is in McDougall, p. 182; Itek's
           report is mentioned on p. 191.
106   The Khrushchev–de Gaulle interchange is from Prados, *The Soviet Esti-
           mate*, p. 101.
107   The Landsat 5 photograph of Tyuratam appears in Johnson, *The Soviet
           Year in Space: 1984*, p. 7.
107   The article on Pied Piper was "USAF Pushes Pied Piper Space Vehi-
           cle," *Aviation Week*, October 14, 1957, p. 26.
107   Bissell's recollection of the Pied Piper cancellation is from the interview
           with the author.
107   The plan to orbit a primate was dropped at the earliest feasible time.
           Gen. Bernard Schriever, head of the Air Research and Development
           Command (and technically Corona's Air Force co-director) announced
           in August 1961 that "the monkey is out" because it duplicated experi-
           ments conducted by NASA. See "Air Force Abandons Space-Monkey
           Plan," *The New York Times*, August 29, 1961.
107   General Electric Company, *Summary, U.S. Air Force Discoverer Satellite
           Recovery Vehicle Program: I-XIV* (PIB-52), 1960.
107–9   For details of how the program was run, including some astronautical
           experiments, under the supposed jurisdiction of the Space Systems Divi-
           sion, see "Discoverer Becomes Satellite Test Bed," *Aviation Week &
           Space Technology*, September 25, 1961, pp. 99–102.
110   Bissell said in an interview with the author that several of the satellites
           prior to nos. 13 and 14 carried cameras. Herbert Scoville recalled in
           another interview that one pod, which had just missed being caught

in the air, sank out of sight just as the frogmen reached the splashdown site.

111   The imagery of Plesetsk is from Richelson, "The Keyhole Satellite Program," p. 127.

111   In addition to *Aviation Week*'s Pied Piper article in October 1957, *The New York Times* published a story nine days after Powers was shot down claiming that the SAMOS "Spy Satellite" was planned for that autumn (May 9, 1960); the following day *The Wall Street Journal* ran a similar article; *The Times* reported Discoverer 13's successful mission while pointing out that it was "designed as a reconnaissance satellite . . ." and "equipped with a detachable capsule in which exposed film would be returned to earth" (August 14, 1960). Eisenhower was even photographed inspecting the carcass of the retrieved spacecraft.

111   Harry Schwartz, who specialized in interpreting Soviet affairs for *The New York Times* in New York in 1960, reported the *International Affairs* article in "Soviet Warns U.S. On Spy Satellites," November 1960.

5. THE CUBAN MISSILE CRISIS: PICTURES AT AN EXHIBITION

Page

115   Colonel Wright's interpretation of the trapezoids is recounted in Abel, *The Missile Crisis*, p. 26. Schlesinger's hypothesis is in his *A Thousand Days*, p. 797.

116   The USIB is explained in Cline, *The CIA: Reality vs. Myth*, p. 232. (See also Raleigh, *The U.S. Intelligence Community, passim.*)

116–17   The March National Intelligence Estimate, 85-62, is in Prados, *The Soviet Estimate*, pp. 130–31. Khrushchev's assurance is quoted in Abel, *The Missile Crisis*, p. 16.

117   The difficulties of taking satellite pictures of Cuba in 1962 were recounted by Herbert Scoville, Jr., in an interview with the author. Scoville maintained that the imagery was not helpful.

117–18   Marchetti's description of crate-ology is from his *The CIA and the Cult of Intelligence*, p. 263.

118–19   Prados sketches the circumstances surrounding McCone's order and the substance of SNIE 85-3-62 in *The Soviet Estimate*, p. 137.

119–20   Schlesinger's reference to McCone's "presentiment" is in his *A Thousand Days*, p. 799.

122   Bundy's involvement in the Gilpatric-Carter dispute is from an interview with the author.

123   Major Heyser's flight profile is in Miller, *Lockheed U-2*, p. 40.

124   Bundy's reasons for waiting until the morning of the sixteenth to tell Kennedy about San Cristóbal are contained in a memorandum he wrote to Kennedy more than four months after the crisis had ended. The document is excerpted in Sorensen, *Kennedy*, p. 673. Carter's statement about the MRBMs is on p. 675.

126   Robert Kennedy's recollection of the meaninglessness of the photographs is from his *Thirteen Days*, p. 24.

126–27   Bundy's observations about the photographs are from an interview with the author.

127   McNamara's three options and Kennedy's statements are from "Library Releases Cuban Crisis Tapes," *The New York Times*, October 27, 1983.

128   Jinking remains a basic tactical reconnaissance maneuver. In August 1981 the author flew a reconnaissance run in one of the 363rd's RF-4C Phantoms over the 170-mile length of the Jefferson National Forest, almost all of it at low level and involving jinking.

129   General Powell's remarks were made in an interview with the author.

130   Khrushchev's offer is quoted, in part, in Abel, *The Missile Crisis*, pp. 186–87.

135   The Joint Study Group's recommendations and their aftermath are discussed in Prados, *The Soviet Estimate*, pp. 122–24.

135   The National Reconnaissance Office is described in some detail in Richelson's *The U.S. Intelligence Community*, pp. 12–15. Kistiakowsky's observations are from his *A Scientist in the White House*, p. 382.

136   Sylvester's memorandum is quoted in part in Richelson's *The U.S. Intelligence Community*, p. 11.

136   The 239-A and 622-A designations are mentioned in *Ordnance*, September–October 1962, p. 184.

6. ARMS CONTROL AND THE ACCEPTANCE OF "SPIES" IN THE SKY

Page

139   Holystone is mentioned in Richelson, *The U.S. Intelligence Community*, pp. 129–30.

140   Zhukov's commentary is from his "Space Espionage Plans of International Law," *International Affairs*, Moscow, October 1960, as reprinted in *Legal Problems of Space Exploration*, p. 1098, which is quoted by Steinberg in "The Legitimization of Reconnaissance Satellites: An Example of Informal Arms Control," p. 43 (hereafter referred to as Steinberg). Khrushchev's remarks are from the same page. The threats by Khrushchev and Zhukov are from p. 44.

141   Foster Dulles's call for a UN space committee is quoted in part in McDougall, . . . *the Heavens and the Earth*, p. 184.

143   The antipodal bomber is detailed in Sparks, *Winged Rocketry*, pp. 72–87.

143   FOBS is described in some detail in Peebles's *Battle for Space*, pp. 64–69, 72–73, and p. 76.

144   Gavin's contention is from his *War and Peace in the Space Age*, pp. 215–16.

144   White's testimony is from Steinberg (see note for p. 140) p. 42.

144–45   Bold Orion and SAINT are described at length in Stares, *The Militarization of Space*, p. 109 and pp. 112–16, respectively. Peebles's *Battle for Space* also contains useful material on SAINT, including what is purported to be diagrams of the spacecraft and its orbital mode on pp. 100–2.

145–46   The spray paint scheme was described by Nicholas L. Johnson in an interview with the author. Johnson added that littering enemy satellites' flight paths with clouds of tiny debris, which would have caused considerable damage because of the spacecraft's high speed, was also considered. The scheme was abandoned, however, when it was realized that U.S. satellites might plow into the orbiting junk as well.

146n   Blue Gemini is mentioned in Steinberg (see note for p. 140), pp. 130–31 from Milton Leitenberg's paper, "The History of US Antisatellite Weapon Systems," presented at the Cornell/Rockefeller Workshop on Decision Making for U.S. Programs of Military R&D, March 1–2, 1979.

146–48   Early Spring, Hi-Ho, and Programs 505, 437, and 437 AP are from

Stares, *The Militarization of Space,* pp. 117–28. Stares also makes the point, as have others, that there is a "symbiotic" relationship between ABMs and ASATs.

150   Bulganin's letter to Eisenhower is excerpted in *Arms Control and Disarmament Agreements,* p. 36. The provisions of the LTBT and a commentary are on pp. 34–43.

151   Events leading to the Soviet acceptance of U.S. reconnaissance satellites are nicely detailed in Steinberg (see note for p. 140), especially pp. 133–35.

7. THE AIR BREATHERS: BLACKBIRDS AND COBRAS

Page
153*n*   Nationalist Chinese U-2 operations, including losses, are described in Miller, *Lockheed U-2,* pp. 32–33. The claim that nine were shot down is from *Aviation Week & Space Technology,* May 19, 1986, p. 17.

154   Launch costs are from Giffen, *U.S. Space System Survivability,* pp. 13 and 61. The cost of the satellites is from "Secrecy of U.S. Reconnaissance Office is Challenged," *The New York Times,* March 1, 1981, from an interview with John Pike of the Federation of American Scientists, and from a source who wishes to be anonymous.

154   The Titan 34D accident, which was reported as being the first involving one of the superboosters in eighteen years, was reported in "Industry Observer," *Aviation Week & Space Technology,* on September 9, 1985, p. 15, and in greater detail on November 18, 1985, in "Titan 34D Booster Failed Following Premature Shutdown of Aerojet Engine," p. 26. *Aviation Week* put the loss of the booster and payload at "over $150 million." The use of the word "over," of course, makes the estimate suitably ambiguous.

155   Details of Project Suntan are from an interview with Ben Rich, who succeeded Kelly Johnson as head of the Skunk Works. A detailed description of the CL-400 appears in NASA's *Liquid Hydrogen as a Propulsion Fuel, 1945–1959,* pp. 141–68.

157   Kingfisher and the ramjet-powered rubber reconnaissance craft are noted by Kelly Johnson in his article, "Development of the Lockheed SR-71 Blackbird," *Lockheed Horizons,* Winter, 1981/82. pp. 4–5.

158   McNamara's accolade is in "The TFX Unveiled: McNamara Hails It," *The New York Times,* October 16, 1964.

158*n*   Refueling for the attack on Libya is from "U.S. Demonstrates Advanced Weapons Technology in Libya," *Aviation Week & Space Technology,* April 21, 1986, p. 18.

159*n*   The RS/SR and A-11/A-12 mix-ups were corroborated in a letter to the author from Nick Durutta, Lockheed California's public information coordinator.

160   These performance figures are close to the stated design objective, as mentioned in Francillon's *Lockheed Aircraft Since 1913,* p. 421. Also, *Aviation Week & Space Technology*'s annual compendium of world aircraft, missiles, and spacecraft has given the plane's ceiling as 100,000 feet and the U-2's as 90,000 feet (March 18, 1985, p. 146).

160   Heat levels are from Kelly Johnson's "Development of the Lockheed SR-71 Blackbird," p. 4. Glasser's remark is from the interview with the author.

161   Data on the SR-71's radar cross section are from the interviews with
           Johnson and Rich and from interviews at the 9th Strategic Reconnais-
           sance Wing at Beale Air Force Base in June 1984.

161–62   The radar and missile detection system is described in "Radar Detector
           Aboard SR-71 Alerted Pilot to Missile Attack," *The New York Times*,
           August 29, 1981, and also from the Rich interview. The North Korean
           missile firing incident and its immediate aftermath were reported in
           "North Korea Fires Missile at U.S. Aircraft Near DMZ," *The New York
           Times*, August 27, 1981, and "U.S. Expresses 'Serious Concern' Over
           Firing of North Korean Missile," *The New York Times*, August 28, 1981.
           Dean Fischer, the State Department spokesman, maintained that it was
           the first such incident involving an SR-71. But he was incorrect, accord-
           ing to what Kelly Johnson said in an interview with the author.

162–63   Belenko's comments are from Barron's *MiG Pilot*, p. 177.

162   SR-71 doctrine is from the interviews at Beale Air Force Base. Glasser's
           and Behler's remarks are from the interviews.

163   Soviet complaints about SR-71 overflights have been reported, for exam-
           ple, in "Washington Roundup," *Aviation Week & Space Technology*,
           April 16, 1984, p. 17. The Cuban allegation was made on April 26, 1983,
           and reported in "Around the World," *The New York Times*, on April
           27.

163   An SR-71 made two hour-long flights along the length of Cuba on
           October 31, 1985, according to Cuban authorities who were quoted in
           an article in which U.S. officials confirmed that at least one such flight
           had been made to spot weapons that were being routed from the
           U.S.S.R. to Nicaragua. Havana maintained that it was the sixth time that
           U.S. reconnaissance planes had flown over their country in four years
           ("U.S. Says Moscow Ships More Arms to Nicaragua," *The New York
           Times*, November 5, 1985). See also "Soviets Extending Power in Carib-
           bean" (which shows three SR-71 vertical photographs), *Aviation Week
           & Space Technology*, March 28, 1983.

163   Lt. Col. Glasser's and Maj. Behler's remarks were made during inter-
           views at Beale Air Force Base.

164–65   Published photos taken by SR-71s bear out the use of these kinds of
           cameras.

165   Synthetic aperture radar is described in considerable detail in *SAR:
           Fundamentals of Synthetic Aperture Radar System Employing Optical Cor-
           relation*. See also Tsipis, *Arsenal*, pp. 321–25. Curtis LeMay has said that
           SAR can allow an aircraft flying over Omaha to pick out individual
           buildings in Kansas City, a distance of 165 miles (*Aviation Week & Space
           Technology*, May 28, 1984, p. 11). For descriptive material on the aircraft
           in general, see *Lockheed Horizons*, Winter 1981/82; Miller's *The Lockheed
           A-12/YF-12/SR-71 Story*; and three articles in *Aviation Week & Space
           Technology*: "Simulator Displays SR-71 Characteristics (May 10, 1976,
           pp. 93–97), "Detailed Preparations Mark SR-71 Flight," (May 10, 1976,
           pp. 99–100), and "SR-71 Impressive in High Speed Regime" (May 18,
           1981, pp. 46–56).

166   The D-21 was described by Kelly Johnson in an interview with the
           author. It is also mentioned in Francillon's *Lockheed Aircraft Since 1913*,
           pp. 417–18. The A-12–D-21 test program is in Miller, *Lockheed, SR-71
           (A-12/YF-12/D-21)*, p. 3.

167   The SR-71 refurbishing and upgrading operation at Palmdale was wit-
           nessed by the author.

167   Staging from Beale to overseas bases was briefly described to the author
           at Beale. See also Richelson's *The Soviet Target*, Chapter 8, and Crick-
           more, "Blackbirds in Britain."

168–69   Glasser's recollection of the double sunrise is from an interview with the
           author.

169–70   General information on the characteristics and performance of the vari-
           ous RC-135s is in Streetly's *World Electronic Warfare Aircraft*, pp. 38–42.
           See also Streetly, "US airborne ELINT systems, Part 3: the Boeing
           RC-135 family," pp. 460–64.

170n   The Su-15 silhouettes are mentioned in Richelson's *The Soviet Target*,
           Chapter 8.

170–71   The TU-95D intercepts were reported in "U.S. Fighters Escort Soviet
           Military Aircraft," *Aviation Week & Space Technology*, August 6, 1984,
           p. 29.

171   Rivet Joint and Combat Sent missions are from Richelson's *The Soviet
           Target*, Chapter 8.

171   The Soviet radars are from Streetly's *World Electronic Warfare Aircraft*,
           p. 120.

172   Sensors carried on Cobra Ball aircraft were mentioned in a private
           conversation.

8. FOREIGN BASES: A NET SPREAD WIDE

Page

175n   TRSSCOMM on the *Liberty* is described in Bamford, *The Puzzle Palace*,
           p. 219.

176n   Data on the RA-5C are from *The Encyclopedia of World Air Power*
           (London: Aerospace Publishing Ltd., 1980), pp. 303–4.

176   The location of foreign air bases is from Streetly, "US airborne ELINT
           systems, Part 2: the US Air Force," p. 274.

178   The NOIC is described in some detail in Richelson, *The U.S. Intelligence
           Community*, pp. 62–64.

178   The quotation from the defense analyst on the quality of satellite imag-
           ery of Soviet submarines is from Allen and Norman, "The Silent Chase:
           Tracking Soviet Submarines," *The New York Times Magazine*, January
           1, 1984, p. 14.

178   Garwin's explanation of submarine noise levels and the difficulty in
           picking them up is from "Antisubmarine Warfare and National Secu-
           rity," *Scientific American*, July 1972, p. 16.

179–80   Location of SOSUS arrays are indicated in Wit, "Advances in Antisub-
           marine Warfare," pp. 36–37.

180n   FLTSATCOM is sketched in *Fleet Satellite Communications
           (FLTSATCOM) System*, a United States Air Force fact sheet issued by
           the Air Force Space Division in August 1981. A far more comprehensive
           description is given by Ball in *The U.S. Fleet Satellite Communications
           (FLTSATCOM) System: The Australian Connection*.

180   The MIT assessment of SOSUS and antisubmarine warfare in general
           was quoted by Walter Sullivan in "Can Submarines Stay Hidden?" *The
           New York Times*, December 11, 1984.

183–84   An overview of Vela is contained in the *Hearings Before the Joint Com-
           mittee on Atomic Energy, Congress of the United States: Developments in*

the Field of Detection and Identification of Nuclear Explosions (Project Vela) and Relationship to Test Ban Negotiations.

184   Romney's testimony and a detailed description of the Wichita observatory are from the above hearings, pp. 87–128.

184   Dr. Herzfeld's testimony is excerpted in the report by Wilkes and Gleditsch, *Intelligence Installations in Norway: Their Number, Location, Function, and Legality,* p. 51. Data on HF, VHF, and UHF facilities in Norway, together with descriptions of the equipment they use, appear on pp. 17–37. Atmospheric nuclear explosion monitoring and seismic monitoring, both for verification and military "diagnostics," are described on pp. 45–56. The satellite facility at Vetan and its several likely uses are discussed on pp. 37–45. The data on the location of the Chinese detection sites are from a private conversation.

186   By January 1984, U.S. and NATO forces were installing new electronic listening posts along the 1,200-mile-long Norwegian coast. The information came to light in connection with the case of Arne Treholt, a Norwegian Foreign Ministry press representative who was charged with espionage (*The New York Times,* January 29, 1984).

186   The report of Soviet commando activities along the Swedish coast and their likely meaning is from *The St. Louis Globe-Democrat,* August 24, 1984. *The New York Times* carried a shorter version on the same date.

187–89   Ball's book is *A Suitable Piece of Real Estate: American Installations in Australia.* The geographic connection is on pp. 15–16. Reference to the UKUSA Agreement is on p. 27. The quotation about inseparability is on p. 40. The CDAA antenna is mentioned on p. 44 and diagrammed on p. 45. The various COMINT listening posts run by the DSD are mentioned on pp. 40–45.

190–91   Christopher Boyce's reference to having committed espionage almost as a whim is in Lindsey's "To Chase A Spy." Additional material is in *The New York Times,* March 26, 1982. Lindsey's description of Rhyolite's capability is from *The Falcon and the Snowman,* pp. 61–62.

191–92   Soviet telemetry channels and encryption are dealt with in Ball's "The Rhyolite Program," pp. 13–16 and in Richelson's "Technical Collection and Arms Control," pp. 23–26. Rhyolite launches are also discussed in the pages cited.

192   I have been told that Rhyolites continued to be used in modified form.

192   Chalet was first mentioned publicly in "U.S. Plans New Way to Check Soviet Missile Tests," *The New York Times,* June 29, 1979.

192–94   The Magnum launch was copiously reported, in large measure because the Air Force went out of its way to prohibit press coverage. See, for example, "U.S. to Orbit 'Sigint' Craft From Shuttle," *The Washington Post,* December 19, 1984; "Military Mission of Space Shuttle to Be Kept Secret," *The New York Times,* December 18, 1984; "Launching of Shuttle's Secret Satellite Is Rumored" and "On Secret Shuttle, Silence Is Leaden," *The New York Times,* January 27, 1985; and "IUS Meets Mission Objectives on Defense Dept. Shuttle Flight," *Aviation Week & Space Technology,* February 4, 1985, p. 20. Secretary of Defense Caspar Weinberger's assertion that reporting the launch was irresponsible appeared in a story on page one of *The Washington Post* on December 20, 1984. The article that unwittingly carried reference only to Magnum's parking orbit was "Initial Orbit of New Satellite Differed From Usual,"

The New York Times, April 26, 1985. King-Hele et al., *The R.A.E. Table of Earth Satellites* (1985) gives the satellite's final orbit as "probably geosynchronous" on p. 817.

194   Nurrungar's physical layout is described briefly in Ball's *Code 647: Australia and the U.S. Defence Support Program (DSP)*, pp. 20–21.

195   The best account of the fragility of the DSP system is in Ford's "The Button" (which details NORAD's workings in considerable detail), *The New Yorker*, April 1 and 8, 1985.

195–96   Fink's remarks signaling the birth of DSP-647 are in "DOD Plans Multi-Mission Satellite RFP," *missiles and rockets*, May 2, 1966, p. 17. The initial concept and budget information is from "New USAF Satellite to Include Infrared, Photo Scanning Gear," *Aviation Week & Space Technology*, December 26, 1966, p. 23. DSP's basic dimensions and capability are given in Pringle and Arkin, *S.I.O.P.*, pp. 96–97, and in Ball's report *Code 647: Australia and the U.S. Defence Support Program (DSP)*, pp. 4 and 12–13.

197   DSP-647's coverage of the Soviet missile complexes is from Ford's "The Button," p. 58. Its other capabilities are listed by Ball in *Code 647*. The Senate testimony, as cited by Ball, is from Senate Appropriations Committee, *Department of Defense Appropriations for Fiscal 1975*, Part 1, p. 514.

197–98   Ball's Rhyolite-Chalet hypothesis is in *Code 647*, p. 16. Argus is in Lindsey, *The Falcon and the Snowman*, p. 63.

9. THROUGH THE KEYHOLE

Page

199–200   The location of the NRO's Washington and El Segundo offices is from Richelson's *The U.S. Intelligence Community*, p. 14. Its presence in Sunnyvale and at CSOC, both of which physically control satellites, is an obvious necessity. Ties to DS&T, the OSO (which reports to DS&T) and to the Navy Space Project are also from *The U.S. Intelligence Community*, p. 14.

201   NRO's budget data was compiled by John Pike of the Federation of American Scientists and independently corroborated.

202   Budgetary criticism of the NRO was made in "Secrecy of U.S. Reconnaissance Office Is Challenged" and in "KH-11 Overruns Said to Slow Development of Follow-On Spacecraft," *Aerospace Daily*, January 23, 1984, pp. 115 and 119. Pike's "playpen" comment is from an interview with the author.

203   The late Herbert ("Pete") Scoville, Jr., who directed the CIA's Office of Scientific Intelligence during repeated clashes with the Air Force over control of space reconnaissance during the period 1959–61 was particularly critical of Brockway McMillan, who he said was more interested in protecting turf than in perfecting reconnaissance. Others have seconded that remark.

203–5   Killian's reference to the Air Force being contemptuous of the CIA was made during an interview with the author. The composition of the SAMOS Panel and other material relating to it is from Richelson's *The U.S. Intelligence Community*, pp. 12–15. Kistiakowsky's diary entry appears in his *A Scientist at the White House*, p. 382.

205–7   The composition of the NRO's leadership is from Richelson's *The U.S.*

Intelligence Community, pp. 12–13. Bissell's nearly being the NRO's first head is in Richelson, "The Keyhole Satellite Program," p. 130; Bissell provided details, including Dulles's reaction, in an interview with the author. The Charyk and McMillan material is from interviews with Bissell and Scoville. McCone's reason for starting the Directorate for Science and Technology is from Cline, *The CIA: Reality vs. Myth*, p. 223.

210–12   The basic USIB/NFIB structure and purpose is covered in Marchetti's *The CIA and the Cult of Intelligence*, pp. 71–78. Richelson's *The U.S. Intelligence Community* is by far the best source for the entire strategic reconnaissance bureaucracy, told with commendable conciseness (see Chapters 13 and 14 in particular).

212–13   The increased autonomy of the NRO's upper echelons was described by a source who wishes to be anonymous.

213n   The KH-11 malfunction after maneuvering is from "Gulf War Said to Reveal U.S. Intelligence Lapses," *The New York Times*, September 27, 1980.

214–15   KH-5 and KH-6 data are from Richelson's "The Keyhole Satellite Program," p. 133. Reference also is made to them in Klass's *Secret Sentries in Space*, particularly Chapter 14.

215–21   NPIC is mentioned in Richelson's *The U.S. Intelligence Community*, primarily pp. 28–29. Is is also included in a diagram of the composition of the Directorate of Intelligence in Agee, *Inside the Company, CIA Diary* (Chart III); Bamford, *The Puzzle Palace*, p. 189, and Cline, *The CIA: Reality vs. Myth*, pp. 227, 245. The description of the building is based on firsthand observation. Information about the three-echelon distribution process is from the interview with General Keegan, in addition to a source who wishes to be anonymous.

219   Digital equipment used in interpretation, and the process itself, are described in Scribner, Ralston, and Metz, *The Verification Challenge*, pp. 69–74, and in somewhat more detail in Jasani, *Outer Space: A New Dimension in the Arms Race*, pp. 197–214. The latter also gives details of various imaging sensors and some of the ways in which they are used. The individual's role in photo interpretation is outlined in "Satellite Photograph Interpretation."

220n   *Aviation Week & Space Technology*, November 25, 1985, p. 96.

220   The Office of Imagery Analysis is mentioned by Richelson in *The U.S. Intelligence Community*, p. 28, and is diagrammed with its sister offices in *Facing Reality* (Figure 5).

221   Klass's observation about line-of-sight range is in his *Secret Sentries in Space*, p. 190.

221   Keegan's assertion that SIGINT missions outnumber those for imaging by a factor of four is from an interview.

222   Orbital data for the July 6, 1964, PHOTINT-ferret launch, like most other, similar data, are from King-Hele et al., *The R.A.E. Table of Earth Satellites*, a standard reference that reports on all launches and is arranged chronologically.

222–24   The information about the number of ferrets in orbit at one time came out in a conversation with a knowledgeable intelligence officer, as does the material on Jumpseat.

10. REAL TIME:
THE ADVENT OF INSTANT INTELLIGENCE

Page

226–29   Events leading to the meeting with Carter, and the circumstances of the meeting itself, were recounted by Knoche and confirmed by a source who wishes to be anonymous. The time of the meeting is listed on a front page of Brzezinski's *Power and Principle.*

227   Keegan's assertion about the overrun is from the second interview. The problem is also cited in *Aerospace Daily*'s "KH-11 Overruns Said to Slow Development of Follow-On Spacecraft," pp. 115–16, and in Bamford, "America's Supersecret Eyes in Space," p. 53. It is alluded to in *Aviation Week & Space Technology*'s "Space Reconnaissance Dwindles."

227   The KH-11's size, weight, operational flight profile, and general imaging characteristics are from Richelson, "The Keyhole Satellite Program," p. 137; Borrowman, "Recent Trends in Orbital Reconnaissance," *Spaceflight,* January 1982, p. 10; and "Eyes in the Sky: Satellites' Use Growing With Capabilities," *The New York Times,* March 29, 1983. Other material comes from interviews with John Pike and Jeffrey Richelson.

227   Reference to the Byeman code name Kennan comes from an anonymous source. The numerical reference is commonly used for reconnaissance satellites and is used to tell which is which: 5000 refers to all imaging satellites, while 500 means that it is a KH-11, and the last digit or two denotes the particular satellite. The first one up was therefore 5501. The major SIGINT satellites are in the 7000 series.

231   Backfire testimony is in the U.S. Senate Committee on Foreign Relations, *The SALT II Treaty,* pp. 173–82. The DIA's recantation was reported in "Pentagon Reassesses Soviet Bomber," *The New York Times,* October 1, 1985.

231–33   Data on infrared and multispectral scanners are in part from Jasani, *Outer Space: A New Dimension of the Arms Race,* pp. 130–32, Klass, *Secret Sentries in Space,* pp. 143–46, and Richelson, "The Keyhole Satellite Program," 122–23.

232n   The chlorophyll green net is from "Israelis Develop Lightweight Camouflage Netting," *Aviation Week & Space Technology,* April 29, 1985, p. 151.

234   The life of the KH-8 launched on January 21, 1982 is recounted in Richelson, "The Keyhole Satellite Program," p. 135. Richelson asserted that the satellite may have been testing the camera system for the KH-11.

235   Reference to reconnaissance satellite coverage of the accident at Severomorsk is made in "USSR blast demolished key missiles," *The Denver Post,* June 22, 1984, and "U.S. Says Blast Hit Soviet Arms Base," *The New York Times,* June 23, 1984. The nuclear explosion theory is from Drew Middleton's column in *The New York Times,* June 26, 1984.

235   The KH-8's average lifetime and orbital parameters are from "Space Reconnaissance Dwindles," p. 18. It might be noted that as late as 1980, the trade press, including *Aviation Week & Space Technology* on October 6, was reporting that the number of KH-8s was so low that the series was practically expended; the above magazine put the number at four. This does not square with the apparent subsequent launches of the satellite, indicating that there were either more in reserve than indicated by Pentagon sources, or that more were manufactured.

235–36   MOL missions are described in Prados, *The Soviet Estimate*, p. 174. See also Baker, *The History of Manned Space Flight*. The CIA's role in killing the main camera system is from a source who wishes to be anonymous.

237–38   KH-9 technical data comes from Richelson, "The Keyhole Satellite Program," pp. 135–36; Peebles, "The Guardians," pp. 381–83; Kenden, "U.S. Reconnaissance Satellite Programmes," pp. 250–52; Greenwood, "Reconnaissance and Arms Control," pp. 15–18; Greenwood, "Reconnaissance, Surveillance and Arms Control," pp. 10–12; "Recon Satellite Assumes Dual Role," pp. 12–13; and "Big Bird Nears Full Operational Status," p. 17.

240   Material concerning observation of the four SS ICBMs is from Peebles, "The Guardians," p. 384.

240–41   Details on the G-1 are from Baker, *The Rocket*, p. 225. See also the fine U.S. Senate report, *Soviet Space Programs: 1976–1980*, pp. 113–19.

242   Richelson's calculations on Keyhole coverage are from his "The Keyhole Satellite Program," p. 142. The Six-Day War/KH-X material is from p. 136.

244   The quality of KH-11 resolution, and particularly as being the equivalent of the photographic type, is generally acknowledged by experts on CCDs.

244–47   Material on charge-coupled devices is from the interview with Janesick and from Blouke and Janesick, "Charge-coupled Device Image Sensors" and Janesick et al., "The Future Scientific CCD." Use of CCDs in the KH-11 was mentioned in *The Defense Monitor*, Vol. XIV, No. 10, p. 3, and was confirmed by a source who wishes to be anonymous.

245   The subject of improvements to reconnaissance satellites while they are in block series has been distorted at least once in public. During the trial of Samuel Loring Morison in 1985, government prosecutors maintained that the KH-11s on station at that time were unchanged from the first one that went up in 1976. That is untrue, according to one highly knowledgeable former intelligence official who has told the author that the satellites undergo continuous improvement at TRW. *The Washington Post* provided fine coverage of that episode on October 10 and 16, 1985.

247   Nelson made his comments in an interview with the author, and also provided information on active optics.

248   Dimensions of the SS-11 are from *Aviation Week & Space Technology*'s annual air and space compendium, March 12, 1984, p. 165.

248–49   Launch dates for the first five KH-11s are from Richelson, "The Keyhole Satellite Program," p. 137, as are references to their various operations.

249   Reconnaissance of Libya for and after the attack is from *Aviation Week & Space Technology*, April 21, 1986, p. 17. The satellite's blast damage assessment is from "Ukrainian Nuclear Fire Spreads Wide Tragedy With Radiation Cloud," *The Wall Street Journal*, April 30, 1986. The soccer game was reported in "Fire Unlikely to Be Controlled Soon, U.S. Experts Say," *The New York Times*, May 1, 1986. In addition, the *Times* articles on May 2 and 4 make reference to Air Force or satellite "photographs" showing the accident scene.

250   The assertion that KH-11s supplied intelligence during the Falklands war is in White's report "U.S. Satellite Reconnaissance During the Falklands Conflict." It was disputed by a highly knowledgeable source who wishes to be anonymous.

250   The Navy began using Air Force imaging satellites for ocean surveil-
           lance in 1971 while it worked on its own system for tracking foreign
           surface vessels and submarines and listening to them. The original satel-
           lites were probably Agena-Ds that were fitted with infrared scanners
           and phased array radar. The infrared scanners on the satellites (which
           were code-named Program 749) were said to be accurate enough to pick
           out pleasure boats on the Potomac from altitudes of nearly 600 miles.
           The Naval Ocean Surveillance Satellite system (NOSS), which is also
           code-named Classic Wizard, uses passive satellites named White Cloud.
           The technique calls for a "mother" satellite and three subsatellites to
           orbit at a 63-degree inclination at a near-circular altitude of about 700
           miles. The subsatellites are used for triangulation in order to fix the exact
           positions of target ships. Officials at the Naval Research Laboratory,
           which developed White Cloud, were taken aback in October 1984 when
           they learned that souvenir envelopes depicting the four satellites and
           providing some operational details were being sold for one dollar in the
           Johnson Space Center gift shop in Houston. Besides noting that the
           satellites were first launched at Vandenberg on top of an Atlas booster
           on April 30, 1976, the text of the envelopes explained that the satellites
           carry "high-frequency antennas for detecting shipboard radar and com-
           munications signals." See Ball, *Ocean Surveillance* (Reference Paper No.
           87); "Ocean Surveillance System Launched," *Aviation Week & Space
           Technology*, March 10, 1980, p. 18; and "NASA Souvenir Spills Navy
           Satellite Secrets," *Aviation Week & Space Technology*, October 22, 1984,
           p. 20.

250   Richelson's calculations on coverage are from his "The Keyhole Satel-
           lite Program," p. 142. Lapses and manpower shortages are from an
           anonymous source.

11. In the Arena: Cosmos, Spoofing,
and Killer Satellites

Page
252–53   Details of Bright Star are from "Americans Fly into 'Battle' in Egypt
           in Swirls of Dust," *The New York Times*, November 19, 1980. Middle-
           ton's appraisal appeared in his column on November 13.

254–55   Cosmos 1221's and 1218's operational characteristics are mainly from
           "Soviet Satellite Reconnaissance Activities and Trends," pp. 92–93. The
           satellites' orbital characteristics are in King-Hele et al., *The R.A.E. Table
           of Earth Satellites: 1957–1980*, pp. 624–25.

255   Johnson's remarks are from an interview with the author.

256   Soyuz dimensions and orbital characteristics are from Baker, *The His-
           tory of Manned Space Flight*, p. 285. Data on specific Cosmos modifica-
           tions and other details are from Clark, "Aspects of the Soviet
           Photoreconnaissance Satellite Programme," pp. 169–72. See also John-
           son, "Trends of the Soviet Photographic Reconnaissance Pro-
           gramme," pp. 295–302.

257   Sources for the Titan 34D accidents and their effect are cited in the notes
           for Chapter 12.

258   Reference to the operation of six satellites simultaneously is from John-
           son, *The Soviet Year in Space: 1984*, pp. 11–12.

259   Wheelon's list of satellite vulnerability to tracking is from his "Anti-
           Satellite Weapons and Space Warfare," a paper given at the New York

Academy of Sciences conference on High Technologies and Reducing the Risk of War, May 7, 1986.

259–60 Countermeasures against ASATs were addressed at the same conference by Steve Fetter and Michael M. May in "Protecting U.S. Space Assets From Anti-Satellite Weapons."

260 Gallium arsenide's properties are described in "Varian Developing Gallium-Arsenide Solar Cell," *Aviation Week & Space Technology,* December 2, 1985, p. 199, and "Gallium Arsenide: A Technology Comes of Age," *Defense Science & Electronics,* October 1985, pp. 37, 38, and 43. The "ultrablack" coating is from *Aerospace America,* November 1985, p. 1 ("Aerospace Spotlight").

260–61 Electromagnetic pulse is treated in some detail in Glasstone and Dolan, *The Effects of Nuclear Weapons,* especially in Chapter XI. Nicholas Johnson has drawn the distinction between EMP and SGEMP. See also Broad, "The Chaos Factor," pp. 41–49, and Stein, "Electromagnetic Pulse—the uncertain certainty," pp. 52–56.

261 Garwin's remark was made at a conference called Strategic Defense: Technical Problems and Prospects, on October 12, 1983.

261 Orbital data on Cosmos 1643 is from Johnson, *The Soviet Year in Space: 1985,* p. 18. The deduction concerning capsule ejection is from the Johnson interview.

261–62 The real-time hypothesis was made by the North American Aerospace Defense Command and by Geoffrey Perry of Great Britain's Kettering Space Observer Group as reported in "USSR Boosts Reconnaissance Capabilities," p. 15. That article also noted that the Russians had developed a system in which a reconnaissance satellite could be launched, checked out, and then kept "dormant" for ten days before being turned again. The technique would allow the satellites to be stored, thereby conserving fuel, electrical energy, and other "consumables" until they were needed.

263 The Russian Mars probes are mentioned in Burgess, *To The Red Planet,* p. 29, and Oberg, *Red Star in Orbit,* pp. 39, 42, and 45. Mariner 10's mission to Mercury and Venus is detailed in Murray and Burgess, *Flight to Mercury.* Caloris imagery and related data are on pp. 100–3.

266 Mark's statement is from an interview with the author.

267–68 Material on the first three types of Soviet SIGINT satellites is from Ball, "Soviet Ears in the Ether: A Guide to Soviet Signals Intelligence (SIGINT) Capabilities and Operations" (draft), April 1984, pp. 50–53.

268 The advent of Cosmos 1603 was reported in "Huge Soviet Satellite's Maneuvering Elicited Special U.S. Tracking Effort," *The New York Times,* January 15, 1985. Its orbital characteristics are from King-Hele et al., *The R.A.E. Table of Earth Satellites: 1983–1984,* p. 806.

268 The demise of Cosmos 1714 was reported in Washington Roundup, *Aviation Week & Space Technology,* January 6, 1986, p. 15.

269–70 EORSATS and RORSATS are detailed annually in Johnson, *The Soviet Year in Space* and in Ball, "Soviet Ears in the Ether," pp. 53–54.

270 The intricacies of Soviet ocean reconnaissance operations are detailed in Johnson, "Orbital Phasings of Soviet Ocean Surveillance Satellites," pp. 113–17.

270 The Romashka reactor is described in "U.S. Assesses Hazard of Cosmos Fuel," *Aviation Week & Space Technology,* January 31, 1983, p. 20, as well as in two previous articles in that magazine (September 7, 1964, and October 26, 1964).

271–72   The Cosmos 954 episode and its aftermath is recounted in Borrowman, "Soviet Orbital Surveillance—the Legacy of Cosmos 954."

272   Cosmos 1402's end was reported in "Russian Satellite Falls Harmlessly Over Indian Ocean," *The New York Times*, January 24, 1983. Johnson's observations are from an interview with the author. See also "Despite Dangers for Nuclear Satellites, Their Allure Persists for Superpowers," *The New York Times*, January 25, 1983.

272   The fate of Cosmos 1625 was reported in "Soviet Intelligence Satellite Fails, Reenters Over Europe," *Aviation Week & Space Technology*, February 4, 1985, p. 21.

273–74   McGarrity's remarks are from "Soviets Orbit Large New Military Electronic Intelligence Satellite," *Aviation Week & Space Technology*, January 14, 1985, p. 20.

274   The orbital parameters of Cosmos 1402 and 1405, as well as the Chinese satellite, were randomly chosen from the pages of *Aviation Week & Space Technology* (September 20, 1982, p. 18); such reports are carried by the magazine several times a year and are based on official Air Force releases generated by NORAD.

274–76   Information on the Space Surveillance Center and SPADATS was gathered during a tour of the facilities on June 21, 1984, and from "Center Set for Soviet Space Monitoring," *Aviation Week & Space Technology*, March 28, 1983, pp. 56–57 (particularly related to the Space Defense Operations Center). See also "Soviets Orbit Large New Military Electronic Intelligence Satellite," *Aviation Week & Space Technology*, January 14, 1985.

275   GEODSS data is from the United States Air Force Fact Sheet 80-036 of June 2, 1980, and from "USAF Upgrades Deep Space Coverage," *Aviation Week & Space Technology*, February 28, 1983, pp. 57–58, and "GEODSS Photographs Orbiting Satellite," *Aviation Week & Space Technology*, November 28, 1983, pp. 146–47.

275–76   The Teal Amber and Teal Blue operations are in Powell, "Photography of Orbiting Satellites," pp. 82–83.

277   The *Space Threat Environment Description* was seen by the author in the Space Surveillance Center.

277   The four types of Soviet ASATs are listed in the Executive Branch's *Report to the Congress on U.S. Policy on ASAT Arms Control*, and in greater detail in *The Soviet Year in Space: 1984*, pp. 36–38. A table detailing all twenty ASAT tests appears in Johnson, *The Soviet Year in Space: 1982*, p. 26.

278   The fusing problem was noted in Johnson, *The Soviet Year in Space: 1982*, which cited *Aviation Week & Space Technology*.

278n   Marcia Smith's observation is from her *Antisatellites (Killer Satellites) Issue Brief Number IB81121*, p. 4. Hans Mark's statement is from the interview with the author.

279   The case against ASAT has been made in many forums, among them Wheelon's "Anti-Satellite Weapons and Space Warfare," pp. 45–55 (which also provides fine descriptions of the various systems); the Union of Concerned Scientists' *Anti-Satellite Weapons: Arms Control or Arms Race?*; and Pike's *Verification and Anti-Satellite (ASAT) Weapons: An FAS Staff Review*. James E. Oberg argues for a U.S. ASAT in "Andropov's Orbiting Bombs," while Nicholas Johnson assesses ASAT's role in war in "The U.S. must now play catch-up with Soviet satellite technology," pp. 66–74.

The Soviet ASAT program is amply described in Baker, *The Shape of Wars to Come*, pp. 115–20.

279–81   The U.S. system is chronicled in Peebles, *Battle for Space*, pp. 77–102. See also "Weapon Against Satellites Ready for Test," *The New York Times*, August 23, 1983, and "USAF Vehicle Designed for Satellite Attack," *Aviation Week & Space Technology*, January 14, 1985.

The weapon's initial test was covered in "Air Force Reports First Test Firing of Space Weapon," *The New York Times*, January 22, 1984.

280   The fate of P78-1 was chronicled in "Working Solar Monitor Shot Down by ASAT," *Science*, October 4, 1985, pp. 44–45. See also "McDonnell Douglas F-15 Launches Asat in Third USAF Test," *Aviation Week & Space Technology*, October 21, 1985, p. 19.

281   The Soviet laser ASAT is described in *Soviet Military Power 1984*, pp. 35–36 (which includes a sketch of one being fired straight up). The laser-induced "temporary anomalies" is from Johnson's *The Soviet Year in Space 1984*, p. 37. General Hartinger's comments are from "Space Command Seeks Asat Laser," *Aviation Week & Space Technology*, March 21, 1983, p. 18. See also "Safeguarding Our Military Space Systems," *Science*, April 18, 1986, pp. 336–40, and the Congressional Office of Technology Assessment's *Anti-Satellite Weapons, Countermeasures, and Arms Control*.

282n   The "Captain Midnight" spoof was reported in "Tapes Studied for Clues in HBO Interference," *Aviation Week & Space Technology*, May 5, 1986, p. 28.

282–83   Spoofing is addressed in Giffen, *U.S. Space System Survivability: Strategic Alternatives for the 1990s*, p. 26.

283   Johnson's remark is from an interview with the author.

12. RECONNAISSANCE AS POLITICS: NICARAGUA AND THE MISSING MiGs

Page

285   The retaking of satellite imagery is from a source who wishes to be anonymous.

286–89   The transcript of Hughes's press briefing accompanies "U.S. Offers Photos of Bases to Prove Nicaragua Threat," *The New York Times*, March 10, 1982. The interview with Ramírez is in the same edition.

291   The Punte Huete tour was reported in "Nicaragua Confirms It Is Building Military Airport," *The New York Times*, August 17, 1984. See also "U.S. Warns Nicaragua on Airport," *The New York Times*, August 18, 1984.

291   Ortega's reference to the MiGs is in "Nicaraguans to Get MIG Fighters," *The New York Times*, September 20, 1984.

293   The initial *New York Times* article appeared at the bottom of page one ("U.S. Fears MIG's Are Bound for Nicaragua") on November 7, 1984.

294   The warning to Moscow, Nicaragua's denial, Reagan's and Bush's comments, and related material appeared in two articles in *The New York Times* on November 8: "U.S. Warns Soviet It Won't Tolerate MIGs in Nicaragua" and "Nicaragua Says No Jet Fighters Are Being Sent."

294   The secretary of state's reference to Moscow's denial is in "Shultz Indicates Soviet Has Denied Shipping Fighters," *The New York Times*, November 9, 1984.

294   Invocation of the Monroe Doctrine is in "U.S. Aides Broaden Warnings to Nicaragua," *The New York Times*, November 9, 1984.

294–95   The SR-71 flights were mentioned in various articles about the episode. See in particular "Sonic Booms Shake Cities in Nicaragua for the Fourth Day," *The New York Times*, November 12, 1984.

295   Scoville's testimony is quoted in Marchetti, *The CIA and the Cult of Intelligence*, p. 271.

296   The two officials were quoted in a *New York Times* editorial, "The Peril of the Missing MIGs," November 15, 1984.

13. INTO THE FUTURE: HALO, SPOT, RADAR FARMS, AND OTHER EXOTIC ASSETS

Page

297   Richelson's observation is from the interview.

298   Mission 41-C material is from *Space Shuttle Mission 41-C*, March 1984 (NASA press kit) and from the following: "Orbiter Crew Restores Solar Max," *Aviation Week & Space Technology*, April 16, 1984, pp. 18–20; "Tight Pace Challenges Solar Max Repair," *Aviation Week & Space Technology*, March 26, 1984, pp. 42–51; and "Two on Shuttle Repair Defects of Ailing Craft," *The New York Times*, April 12, 1984. See also "Balky Black Box Key to Operation," *The New York Times*, April 12, 1984.

298   Abrahamson was quoted in "Nuts and Bolts of Interstellar Repair," *The New York Times*, April 15, 1984. Crippen was quoted in "Fixed Satellite Reset in Orbit; Shuttle Ready to Land Today," *The New York Times*, April 12, 1984.

298–99   The 41-G mission is described in "Shuttle Plan Emphasizes Earth Survey," *Aviation Week & Space Technology*, September 24, 1984, pp. 38–47 (including reference to the KH-11's orbital refueling capability), and from *New York Times* articles: "2 Aboard Shuttle Get Go-Ahead to Try a Satellite Refueling Test," October 11, 1984, and "Astronauts, Freed from Technical Woes, Turn Attention to Earth," October 10, 1984.

299–300   Mission 51-A was described in the following *Aviation Week & Space Technology* articles: "Satellite Retrieval Linked to Precise Orbit Control," November 5, 1984, pp. 66–70; "Satellite Retrieval Succeeds Despite Equipment Problem," November 19, 1984, pp. 16–19, and "Astronauts Deploy, Retrieve Satellites," November 19, 1984, pp. 20–25. *New York Times* coverage included: "Astronauts Snare Errant Satellite for the First Time," November 13, 1984; "Second Satellite in Space Rescued by 2 Astronauts," November 15, 1984, and "Shuttle Returns After a Triumph in Space Rescues," November 17, 1984 (the last containing Broad's and Moore's quotations).

301   Repair and refurbishment of the Space Telescope is mentioned in *Space Telescope*, p. 38.

301   Aldridge's letter to General Welch is quoted in "USAF, NASA Discuss Shuttle Use for Satellite Maintenance," *Aviation Week & Space Technology*, December 17, 1984, p. 15.

302–3   Space Launch Complex No. 6 is described in Karas, *The New High Ground*, pp. 45–46, and in "Shuttle Launch Facilities Built at Vandenberg," *Aviation Week & Space Technology*, August 6, 1984, p. 53.

303   The Titan 34D explosion on August 28 received scant attention in *The New York Times* three days later ("Titan Explodes After Takeoff at

California Launching Site"). Another short report in the "Industry Observer" section of *Aviation Week & Space Technology* on September 9 called it "the most significant U.S. space mission failure in years." For a more comprehensive report on the accident, see "Titan 34D Booster Failed Following Premature Shutdown of Aerojet Engine," *Aviation Week & Space Technology*, November 18, 1985.

304   The Carter administration's decision to use only shuttles for national security payloads is in Wheelon's "Anti-Satellite Weapons and Space Warfare," p. 8.

304   Air Force involvement in pursuing CELVs before the Challenger accident is in "Defense Dept. to Retain Expendable Launchers as Backup to Shuttle," *Aviation Week & Space Technology*, March 18, 1985, p. 115.

304–5   The Titan 34D explosion of April 18 was chronicled in "Titan Explosion Cripples Launch, Surveillance Capability," *Aviation Week & Space Technology*, April 28, 1986, pp. 16–19. That article said that the Titan's payload had been a KH-9, an assertion that was confirmed in a private conversation. Both *The New York Times* and *The Washington Post* suggested in articles on April 19 and 24, respectively, that the cargo had been a KH-11. The cause of the accident is from "Titan Solid Booster Failure Caused Vandenberg Accident," *Aviation Week & Space Technology*, p. 24.

305   Stares's comment is from *The New York Times* initial article, "Titan Rocket Explodes Over California Base," April 19. The description of the accident scene is from that article and from "Titan Accident Disrupts Military Space Program," *Science*, May 9, 1986, pp. 702–4.

305   Colby's prediction is from his *Honorable Men*, p. 461.

307–9   The KH-12 is briefly mentioned in "Monitoring the Soviet Military," *The Defense Monitor*, Vol. XIV, No. 10, 1985, p. 3. Additional material came from the interview with John Pike and from a source who wishes to be anonymous.

307–8   Missions 4 and 4Y are outlined in "Baseline Reference Mission Descriptions," *The Space Transportation System Security Classification Guide*, Table 3.1, section 3, p. 2.

308   The KH-12's additional fuel capacity can be inferred from its extended orbital life. The succession of increased total weight is from an interview with Robert Windrem.

309   The planned move of KH-12/shuttle operations to Cape Canaveral is from "KH-12 Reconnaissance Satellite Planned for Kennedy Launch," *Aviation Week & Space Technology*, June 23, 1986, p. 17.

310–12 Robert Cooper's remarks are from a paper he delivered on April 9, 1985, at the AIAA annual meeting: "New Generation Space Surveillance."

311–12 Teal Ruby is described in "Tests Confirm Teal Ruby Design," *Aviation Week & Space Technology*, December 26, 1983, pp. 8–9, and "Rockwell Tests Model of Teal Ruby System," *Aviation Week & Space Technology*, January 23, 1984, p. 52. It also figures in an advertisement run by Rockwell International in *Aviation Week & Space Technology* on July 16, 1984, p. 53. HALO is briefly described in Baker, *The Shape of Wars to Come*, p. 162.

312   Fletcher's remarks were contained in a statement he made before the Subcommittee on Research and Development, Committee on Armed Services of the House of Representatives, on March 1, 1984 (mimeo., pp. 6 and 8). The Defense Technologies Study Team's report is described

in some detail in "Study Urges Exploiting of Technologies," *Aviation Week & Space Technology*, October 24, 1983, pp. 50–57.

313   The SIR-B imagery of Canada, New England, and Mount Shasta is described in "Astronauts, Freed from Technical Woes, Turn Attention to Earth," *The New York Times*, October 10, 1984. The ocean experiment is the subject of a report, "A Comparison of SIR-B Synthetic Aperture Radar Data with Ocean Internal Wave Measurements," *Science*, June 20, 1986, pp. 1529–31.

313   John Ford's remarks are from an interview with the author.

313   Space-based radar is described in Calder's "Space-based Radar Comes Over the Horizon," pp. 112–14. See also "Use of Space Shuttle for Remote Sensing Research: Recent Results and Future Prospects," *Science*, December 3, 1982, pp. 993–95 and the accompanying article, "Shuttle Imaging Radar Experiment," pp. 996–1003; and Elachi, "Radar Images of the Earth from Space," pp. 54–61. Vertical/horizontal digital radar imaging was reported in "New Power Lets Computer Depict Images Invisible to Eye," *The New York Times*, September 2, 1986.

314   Air Force-DARPA radar research is described in "Technology Effort Lays Advanced Radar Base," *Aviation Week & Space Technology*, November 15, 1982, p. 56.

314   The satellite Anthony Kenden pondered in "A New U.S. Military Space Mission" could have been a phased array radar satellite.

314   SSTS is mentioned in "USAF Reviews Surveillance System Technology," *Aviation Week & Space Technology*, March 5, 1984, p. 62. It was the Space Based Surveillance System.

315–16 TAV material is in "USAF Spurs Spaceplane Research," *Aviation Week & Space Technology*, March 26, 1984, pp. 16–17; Marshall, "NASA and Military Press for a Spaceplane," pp. 105–7; "DARPA Plans Supersonic Ramjet Technology Program," *Aviation Week & Space Technology*, May 6, 1985, p. 111; and "The Aerospace Plane," *Defense Science 2004+*, February/March 1986, pp. 10–16. The Lockheed press release is from the company's Burbank office and is dated June 4, 1984.

316   The Aeronautical Systems Division official and the consultant are quoted in "USAF Studies Transatmosphere Vehicle," *Aviation Week & Space Technology*, November 7, 1983, pp. 44–45.

316–17 DeLauer's comments are from a paper he delivered at the AIAA/NASA symposium, "Space Station: Policy, Planning and Utilization," conducted in Arlington, Va., July 18–20, 1983, and reproduced in a book of the same title, p. 40.

317   The Grumman engineer was Dr. David J. Larson, who made the remark in answer to a question during a field trip by graduate students from New York University.

317–20 Robert Cooper's remarks are from a paper he delivered on April 9, 1985, at the AIAA annual meeting: "New Generation Space Surveillance."

320–21 Advanced solar panels, beam-hopping antennas, and frequency changes are in "USAF Pushes Survivability of Satellites," *Aviation Week & Space Technology*, September 24, 1984, pp. 71–72.

321   The current use of nuclear power is from a source who wishes to be anonymous.

322   Decoys are in "USAF Pushes Satellite Survivability," *Aviation Week & Space Technology*, March 28, 1977, pp. 52–53.

323   Milstar information is from a United States Air Force fact sheet put out by its Space Division and dated February 1983. Additional material is

from "Pentagon Neglects Satellite Defenses," *Science*, May 18, 1984, and "Milstar to Employ Centaur Upper Stage," *Aviation Week & Space Technology*, January 2, 1984, pp. 21–22.

323–24   TENCAP began as an aerial reconnaissance program and is mentioned in passing in Richelson, *The U.S. Intelligence Community*. Its space dimension is from the interview with John Pike.

324   The SPOT quotation is from the company's flier "Satellite-Based Remote Sensing." Technical data on the spacecraft is from Courtois and Weill, "The SPOT Satellite System," pp. 495–99. The first launch was reported in "Civilians Use Satellite Photos for Spying on Soviet Military," *The New York Times*, April 7, 1986 and in "First Image from SPOT," *Science*, March 28, 1986, p. 1504.

325   SPOT coverage of Chernobyl was reported on the NBC Nightly News on May 1, 1986, and in *Aviation Week & Space Technology* on May 12, 1986, p. 24. See also "Photos Said to Show New Activity at Main Soviet Nuclear Test Site," *The New York Times*, August 4, 1986, and "Soviet Space Shuttle Facilities at Tyuratam Imaged by French Spot," *Aviation Week & Space Technology*, September 1, 1986, pp. 42–43. Its use by French military intelligence is from "Industry Observer," *Aviation Week & Space Technology*, May 26, 1986, p. 13.

14. ARMS CONTROL VERIFICATION AND
NATIONAL SECURITY

Page
328–29   *View of Amsterdam* is reproduced with Alpers's commentary in "Shadows of Unseen Clouds," *The Sciences*, November/December, 1984, pp. 32–33. The original is in the permanent collection of the Amsterdam Historical Museum.

329–30   The *Jane's* was quoted at length in "Soviet Naval Blast Called Crippling," *The New York Times*, July 11, 1984. See also "U.S. Says Blast Hit Soviet Arms Base," *The New York Times*, June 23, 1984.

330   The Iranian invasion story was "Iranian Army Poised for Invasion of Iraq, U.S. Officials Assert," *The New York Times*, July 12, 1982.

330–31   The Soviet space program story was "Soviets Strive to Outpace U.S. Technology in Space," *Aviation Week & Space Technology*, March 12, 1984, p. 111.

331   Satellite coverage of Afghanistan is from "Caravans on Moonless Nights," *Time*, June 11, 1984, p. 38.

331   The count of Libyan troops in Chad was in "French Say Libyans Remain in Chad," *The New York Times*, November 17, 1984.

331–32   Carrington's appearance was on October 7, 1985.

332n   Gorbachev's figures are in the excerpts from his and François Mitterrand's press conference, *The New York Times*, October 5, 1985.

333   Soviet air defenses and the capability of the Foxhound are in the U.S. Defense Department's *Soviet Military Power* (1985), pp. 48–49. Cruise missiles are on p. 35.

333   The chart is in Military Publishing House's *Whence the Treat to Peace*, p. 7. The assertion that the U.S. Defense Department's *Soviet Military Power* is unbalanced was reported in "Moscow Says the Pentagon Booklet Is Unbalanced," *The New York Times*, September 30, 1981.

334–35   Brown's remarks are in *The Salt II Treaty: Report of the Committee on Foreign Relations, United States Senate*, pp. 196–97.

335   The difference between monitoring and verification is in Meyer's "Verification and Risk in Arms Control," pp. 112–13.

338   The report is *Challenges for U.S. National Security,* p. 43. The statement about following Soviet strategic systems development is on p. 44.

339   The Abalakova radar is from "U.S. Scrutinizing New Soviet Radar," *Aviation Week & Space Technology,* pp. 19 and 20.

339   The rapid reload ABM test is from "Soviets Test Defense Missile Reload," *Aviation Week & Space Technology,* August 29, 1983, p. 19.

339   The SS-25 violation is from "Weinberger Claims New SS-25s Violate SALT 2," *Aviation Week & Space Technology,* October 28, 1985, p. 22.

339   The report of Soviet violations of the TTBT was reported in "Administration at Odds over Soviet Cheating," *Science,* May 10, 1985, pp. 695–96.

339   Shultz's contradictory statement was made in Helsinki on the occasion of the tenth anniversary of the Helsinki accords and was reported in "Shultz Rejects Test Ban," *The New York Times,* July 30, 1985.

339–40   Reagan's assertion that the Soviet Union had gone over the SALT II limit and the JCS estimate are from "Joint Chiefs Find No Soviet Cheating," *The New York Times,* February 8, 1986. Keeny's comments are included.

340–41   Moscow's note of January 29, 1984, was reported in "Moscow Accuses U.S. of Violating Arms Agreements," *The New York Times,* January 30, 1984.

341   The Standing Consultative Commission's structure and workings are detailed in Article XIII of the ABM part of the SALT I agreement, as reproduced in *Arms Control and Disarmament Agreements,* pp. 141–42. See also Talbott, *Deadly Gambits,* pp. 228–30.

341*n*   The Minuteman silo covers are noted in Scribner, Ralston, and Metz, *The Verification Challenge,* p. 99. Shulman's remark was made on the MacNeil/Lehrer Newshour on January 16, 1986.

342   The insistence on on-site verification is from "U.S. Tells Soviet Any Arms Pact Must Include On-Site Verification," *The New York Times,* September 2, 1981. The Soviet stance on on-site is mentioned in Joel Wit's article on the op-ed page of the *Times,* April 5, 1983.

343–44   The ASAT report is the mimeo. sent to Congress on March 31, 1984, by the executive branch, pp. 3–4. The administration official was quoted in "Antisatellite Arms Ban Is Unlikely," *The Washington Post,* February 27, 1984.

344–45   Evernden's seismological work regarding arms control appears in Sykes and Evernden, "The Verification of a Comprehensive Nuclear Test Ban." See also Hafemeister, Romm, and Tsipis, "The Verification of Compliance with Arms-Control Agreements," and von Hippel, Albright, and Levi, "Stopping the Production of Fissile Materials for Weapons."

Sources

Books

Abel, Elie. *The Missile Crisis.* New York: J. B. Lippincott, 1966.

Agee, Philip. *Inside the Company: CIA Diary.* London: Allen Lane, 1975.

Air Force, Department of. *Photographic Interpretation Handbook.* Washington, 1954.

Angelucci, Enzo, ed. *The Rand McNally Encyclopedia of Military Aircraft.* New York: Military Press, 1980.

Arms Control and Disarmament Agency, U.S. *Arms Control and Disarmament Agreements.* Washington, D.C., 1980.

Babington-Smith, Constance. *Air Spy.* New York: Harper & Brothers, 1957.

Baker, David. *The History of Manned Space Flight.* New York: Crown Publishers, 1981.

———. *The Rocket.* New York: Crown Publishers, 1978.

———. *The Shape of Wars to Come.* Cambridge: Patrick Stephens, 1981.

Ball, Desmond. *A Suitable Piece of Real Estate: American Installations in Australia.* Sydney: Hale & Iremonger, 1980.

Bamford, James. *The Puzzle Palace.* Boston: Houghton Mifflin Co., 1982.

Barron, John. *MiG Pilot: Lt. Victor Belenko's Final Escape.* New York: Reader's Digest Press, 1979.

Beschloss, Michael R. *Mayday: Eisenhower, Khrushchev and the U-2 Affair.* New York: Harper & Row, 1986.

Bottome, Edgar. *The Missile Gap.* Rutherford, N.J.: Fairleigh Dickinson University Press, 1971.

Brzezinski, Zbigniew. *Power and Principle.* New York: Farrar, Straus & Giroux, 1983.

Burgess, Eric. *To the Red Planet.* New York: Columbia University Press, 1978.

Cline, Ray S. *The CIA: Reality vs. Myth.* Washington: Acropolis Books, Ltd., 1982.

Colby, William E. *Honorable Men: My Life in the CIA.* New York: Simon & Schuster, 1978.

Copp, DeWitt S. *A Few Great Captains.* Garden City, N.Y.: Doubleday & Co., 1980.

Craven, Wesley Frank, and James Lea Cate, eds. *The Army Air Forces in World War II,* Vol. V. Washington, D.C.: Office of Air Force History, 1983.

Duke, Neville, and Edward Lanchbery, eds. *The Saga of Flight.* New York: Avon Books, 1961.

Dulles, Allen. *The Craft of Intelligence.* New York: Harper & Row, 1963.

Eisenhower, Dwight D. *The White House Years: Waging Peace, 1957–1960.* Garden City, N.Y.: Doubleday & Co., 1965.

Francillon, René J. *Lockheed Aircraft Since 1913.* London: Putnam., 1982.

Gavin, James M. *War and Peace in the Space Age.* London, Hutchinson, 1959.

Gerard, Merille, and Pamela W. Edwards, eds. *Space Station: Policy, Planning and Utilization.* New York: American Institute of Aeronautics and Astronautics, 1983.

Glasstone, Samuel, and Philip J. Dolan, eds. *The Effects of Nuclear Weapons.* Washington: Department of Defense and the Energy Research and Development Administration, 1977.

Goddard, George W. *Overview.* New York: Doubleday & Co., 1969.

Gray, Peter, and Owen Thetford. *German Aircraft of the First World War.* London: Putnam, 1962.

Gunston, Bill. *Spy Planes and Electronic Warfare Aircraft.* New York: Arco Publishing, Inc., 1983.

Infield, Glenn B. *Unarmed and Unafraid.* London: Macmillan Co., Ltd., 1970.

Ivie, Thomas G. *Aerial Reconnaissance: The 10th Photo Recon Group in World War II.* Fallbrook, Calif.: Aero Publishers, Inc., 1981.

Jasani, Bhupendra, ed. *Outer Space—A New Dimension in the Arms Race.* London: Taylor & Francis, 1982.

Kahn, David. *Hitler's Spies.* New York: Macmillan Publishing Co., 1978.

Karas, Thomas. *The New High Ground.* New York: Simon & Schuster, 1983.

Kennedy, Robert F. *Thirteen Days.* New York: W. W. Norton Co., 1969.

Killen, John. *The Luftwaffe: A History.* London: Frederick Muller Ltd., 1967.

Killian, James R. *Sputnik, Scientists, and Eisenhower.* Cambridge: MIT Press, 1982.

King-Hele, D. G., J. A. Pilkington, H. Hiller, and D.M.C. Walker. *The R.A.E. Table of Earth Satellites, 1957–1980.* London: Macmillan Press Ltd., 1981.

Kistiakowsky, George B. *A Scientist at the White House.* Cambridge: Harvard University Press, 1976.

Klass, Philip J. *Secret Sentries in Space.* New York: Random House, 1971.

Krass, Allan S. *Verification: How Much Is Enough?,* London: Taylor & Francis, 1985.

Lindsey, Robert. *The Falcon and the Snowman.* New York: Pocket Books, 1979.

Marchetti, Victor, and John D. Marks. *The CIA and the Cult of Intelligence.* New York: Dell Publishing Co., 1974.

McDougall, Walter A. . . . *the Heavens and the Earth: A Political History of the Space Age.* New York: Basic Books, 1985.

Meyer, Cord. *Facing Reality: From World Federalism to the CIA.* New York: Harper & Row, 1980.

Miller, Jay. *Lockheed SR-71 (A-12/YF-12/D-21).* Arlington, Tex.: Aerojax, Inc., 1985.

———. *Lockheed U-2.* Austin, Tex.: Aerofax, Inc., 1983.

Murray, Bruce, and Eric Burgess. *Flight to Mercury.* New York: Columbia University Press, 1977.

Oberg, James E. *Red Star in Orbit.* New York: Random House, 1981.

Ordway, Frederick I., and Mitchell R. Sharpe. *The Rocket Team.* New York: Thomas Y. Crowell, 1979.

Padelford, Norman J., and George A. Lincoln. *International Politics.* New York: Macmillan Co., 1954.

Peebles, Curtis. *Battle for Space.* New York: Beaufort Books, 1983.

Penkovskiy, Oleg. *The Penkovskiy Papers.* Garden City, N.Y.: Doubleday & Co., 1965.

Powers, Francis Gary. *Operation Overflight.* New York: Holt, Rinehart & Winston, 1970.

Prados, John. *The Soviet Estimate.* New York: Dial Press, 1982.

Pringle, Peter, and William Arkin. *S.I.O.P.: The Secret U.S. Plan for Nuclear War.* New York: W. W. Norton, 1983.

Raleigh, Walter. *The War in the Air.* London: Oxford University Press, 1922.

Richelson, Jeffrey T. *American Espionage and the Soviet Target.* New York: William Morrow & Co., 1987.

————. *The U.S. Intelligence Community.* Cambridge, Mass.: Ballinger, 1985.

Saint-Exupéry, Antoine de. *Flight to Arras.* New York: Harvest/HBJ Books, 1942.

Schlesinger, Arthur M., Jr. *A Thousand Days.* New York: Houghton Mifflin Co., 1965.

Scribner, Richard A., Theodore J. Ralston, and William D. Metz. *The Verification Challenge: Problems and Promise of Strategic Nuclear Arms Control Verification.* Boston: Birkhäuser, 1985.

Shirer, William L. *The Rise and Fall of the Third Reich.* New York: Simon & Schuster, 1960.

Sorensen, Theodore C. *Kennedy.* New York: Harper & Row, 1965.

Sparks, Maj. James C. *Winged Rocketry.* New York: Dodd, Mead & Co., 1968.

Stanley, Col. Roy M. *World War II Photo Intelligence.* New York: Charles Scribner's Sons, 1981.

Stares, Paul B. *The Militarization of Space.* Ithaca, N.Y.: Cornell University Press, 1985.

Streetly, Martin. *World Electronic Warfare Aircraft.* London: Jane's Publishing Co. Ltd., 1983.

Talbott, Strobe. *Deadly Gambits.* New York: Alfred A. Knopf, 1984.

Taylor, John W., and David Mondey. *Spies in the Sky.* New York: Charles Scribner's Sons, 1973.

Tsipis, Kosta. *Arsenal.* New York: Simon & Schuster, 1983.

Turner, Stansfield. *Secrecy and Democracy.* New York: Houghton Mifflin Co., 1985.

Wise, David, and Thomas B. Ross. *The Invisible Government.* New York: Random House, 1964.

————. *The U-2 Affair.* New York: Random House, 1962.

Yost, Graham. *Spy-Tech.* New York: Facts on File, 1985.

JOURNALS AND REPORTS

Ball, Desmond. *Code 647: Australia and the U.S. Defence Support Program (DSP),* Reference Paper No. 82. Strategic and Defence Studies Centre, Australian National University, July 1982.

————. *Ocean Surveillance,* Reference Paper No. 87. Strategic and Defence Studies Centre, Australian National University, November 1982.

————. "Soviet Ears in the Ether: A Guide to Soviet Signals Intelligence

(SIGINT) Capabilities and Operations" (mimeo.). Strategic and Defence Studies Centre, Australian National University, April 1984.

———. "The Rhyolite Program" (mimeo.). Strategic and Defence Studies Centre, Australian National University, November 1981.

———. *The U.S. Fleet Satellite Communications (FLTSATCOM) System: The Australian Connection,* Reference Paper No. 69. Strategic and Defence Studies Centre, Australian National University, July 1981.

———. *The U.S. Vela Nuclear Detection Satellite (NDS) System: The Australian Connection,* Reference Paper No. 70. Strategic and Defence Studies Centre, Australian National University, October 1981.

Beal, R. C., et al. "A Comparison of SIR-B Directional Ocean Wave Spectra with Aircraft Scanning Radar Spectra," *Science,* June 20, 1986, pp. 1531–35.

Blouke, Morley, and James R. Janesick. "Charge-coupled Device Image Sensors." Paper delivered at the Technical Means of Verification of Compliance with Arms Control Agreements Conference, February 1984.

Borrowman, Gerald L. "Recent Trends in Orbital Reconnaissance," *Spaceflight,* January 1982.

———. "Soviet Orbital Surveillance—the Legacy of Cosmos 954," *Journal of the British Interplanetary Society,* February 1982.

Center for Defense Information. "Monitoring the Soviet Military," *The Defense Monitor,* Vol. 14, No. 10, 1985.

Challenges for U.S. National Security (Final Report). Panel on U.S. Security and the Future of Arms Control. Carnegie Endowment for International Peace, 1983.

Clark, Phillip S. "Aspects of the Soviet Photoreconnaissance Satellite Programme," *Journal of the British Interplanetary Society,* April 1983.

Courtois, Michael, and Gilbert Weill. "The SPOT Satellite System," *Monitoring Earth's Ocean, Land, and Atmosphere from Space—Sensors, Systems, and Applications,* New York: American Institute of Aeronautics and Astronautics, 1985.

Defense Department, U.S. *Soviet Military Power,* 1981, 1983, 1984, and 1985.

Douglas Aircraft Company. "Preliminary Design of an Experimental World-Circling Spaceship," Report No. SM-11827, May 2, 1946.

Executive Branch, U.S. Government. "Report to the Congress on U.S. Policy on ASAT Arms Control" (mimeo.), March 31, 1984.

Fetter, Steve, and Michael M. May. "Protecting U.S. Space Assets from Anti-Satellite Weapons," presented at the High Technologies and Reducing the Risk of War conference, New York Academy of Sciences, May 7, 1986.

Gasparovic, J. R., et al. "A Comparison of SIR-B Synthetic Aperture Radar Data with Ocean Internal Wave Measurements," *Science,* June 20, 1986, pp. 1529–30.

General Electric Company, Missile and Space Vehicle Department. *Summary, U.S. Air Force Discoverer Satellite Recovery Vehicle Program: I-XIV,* PIB-52, 1960.

Giffen, Robert B. *U.S. Space System Survivability: Strategic Alternatives for the 1990s,* Monograph Series No. 82-4. Washington, D.C., The National Defense University, 1982.

Godson, Roy, ed. *Intelligence Requirements for the 1980's: Clandestine Collection,* No. 5. National Strategy Information Center, Washington, 1982.

Greenwood, Ted. "Reconnaissance, Surveillance and Arms Control," *Adelphi Papers,* No. 88. International Institute for Strategic Studies, 1972.

Janesick, James R., et al. "The Future Scientific CCD," Jet Propulsion Laboratory, Pasadena, Calif., undated.

Johnson, Nicholas L. *The Soviet Year in Space.* Colorado Springs: Teledyne Brown Engineering, 1983, 1984, 1985.

———. "Orbital Phasings of Soviet Ocean Surveillance Satellites," *Journal of Spacecraft and Rockets*, March–April 1982.

———. "Trends of the Soviet Photographic Reconnaissance Programme," *Journal of the British Interplanetary Society*, August 1980.

Katz, Amrom. *The Soviets and the U-2 Photos—An Heuristic Argument*, RM-3584-PR. RAND Corp., March 1963.

———. *Verification and Salt: The State of the Art and the Art of the State*. Washington: The Heritage Foundation, 1979.

Kenden, Anthony. "A New U.S. Military Space Mission," *Journal of the British Interplanetary Society*, October 1982.

———. "U.S. Reconnaissance Satellite Programme," *Spaceflight*, July 1978.

McRoberts, Joseph J. *Space Telescope*. Washington: National Aeronautics and Space Administration, 1982.

Meyer, Stephen M. "Verification and Risk in Arms Control," *International Security*, Spring 1984.

Military Publishing House. *Whence the Threat to Peace*, Moscow, 1984.

Peebles, Curtis. "The Guardians," *Spaceflight*, November 1978.

———. "Satellite Photograph Interpretation," *Spaceflight*, April 1982.

Pike, John. *Verification and Anti-Satellite (ASAT) Weapons: An FAS Staff Review*. Washington, D.C., Federation of American Scientists, 1983.

Powell, Joel W. "Photography of Orbiting Satellites," *Spaceflight*, February 1983.

RAND Corp. *A Family of Recoverable Satellites*, RM-2012. November 12, 1957 (abridged and reissued in March 1984).

Republic Aviation Corp. *Photographic Installation of the XF-12 Long Range Photographic Reconnaissance Airplane*. Farmingdale, N.Y., undated.

Richelson, Jeffrey T. "The Keyhole Satellite Program," *Journal of Strategic Studies*, June 1984.

———. "Strategic Reconnaissance and National Style" (mimeo.), 1985.

———. "Technical Collection and Arms Control." Paper presented at the Conference on Verification and Arms Control, UCLA Center for International and Strategic Affairs, Los Angeles, January 25, 1984.

Sloop, J. L. *Liquid Hydrogen as a Propulsion Fuel, 1945–1959*, N79-16994. Washington, D.C., National Aeronautics and Space Administration, 1978.

Smith, Marcia S. *Antisatellites (Killer Satellites)*, Issue Brief Number IB 81123. Washington, D.C., Congressional Research Service, April 6, 1983.

Steinberg, Gerald M. "The Legitimization of Reconnaissance Satellites: An Example of Informal Arms Control Negotiation" (doctoral dissertation, Cornell University), 1981.

Stoertz, Howard, Jr. "Monitoring a Nuclear Freeze," *International Security*, Spring 1984.

Trachtenberg, Marc. "The Influence of Nuclear Weapons in the Cuban Missile Crisis," *International Security*, Summer 1985.

———. "White House Tapes and Minutes of the Cuban Missile Crisis," *International Security*, Summer 1985.

Union of Concerned Scientists. *Anti-Satellite Weapons: Arms Control or Arms Race*. Cambridge, Mass., 1983.

U.S. Congress, House, Committee on Arms Services. *Department of Defense Authorization of Appropriations for Fiscal Year 1985 (H.R. 5167)*, Part 4. 98th Cong., 2nd sess., February–March 1984.

U.S. Congress, Joint Committee on Atomic Energy. *Developments in the Field of Detection and Identification of Nuclear Explosions (Project Vela)*. 87th Cong., 1st sess., July 1961.

U.S. Congress, Office of Technology Assessment. *Anti-Satellite Weapons, Counter-measures, and Arms Control,* Washington, D.C., September 1985.

U.S. Congress, Senate, Committee on Aeronautical and Space Sciences. *Soviet Space Programs, 1962–65; Goals and Purposes, Achievements, Plans, and International Implications.* 89th Cong., 2nd sess., December 1966.

U.S. Congress, Senate, Committee on Armed Services. *Inquiry into Satellite and Missile Programs Before the Preparedness Investigating Subcommittee.* 85th Cong., both sess., 1958.

U.S. Congress, Senate, Committee on Commerce, Science, and Transportation. *Soviet Space Programs: 1976–80.* 97th Cong., 2nd sess., December 1982.

U.S. Congress, Senate, Committee on Foreign Relations. *The Salt II Treaty.* 96th Cong., 1st sess., November 1979.

von Hippel, Frank, and Barbara G. Levi. "Controlling the Source: Verification of a Cutoff in the Production of Plutonium and Highly-Enriched Uranium for Nuclear Weapons." Paper presented at the annual meeting of the American Association for the Advancement of Science, May 24, 1984.

Wheelon, Albert D. "Anti-Satellite Weapons and Space Warfare." Paper presented at the High Technologies and Reducing the Risk of War conference, New York Academy of Sciences, May 7, 1986.

White, Max. "U.S. Satellite Reconnaissance During the Falklands Conflict" (Undated mimeo.). Earth Satellite Research Unit, Department of Mathematics, University of Aston, England.

Wilkes, Owen, and Nils Petter Gleditsch. *Intelligence Installations in Norway: Their Number, Location, Function, and Legality.* Oslo: International Peace Research Institute, 1979.

Magazines

The following are of considerable importance but do not represent all of the articles that were used. The others are fully cited in the Notes.

"Alaskan Stations Track Discoverer Satellite," *Aviation Week,* August 31, 1959.

Allen, Thomas B., and Norman Polmar. "The Silent Chase: Tracking Soviet Submarines," *The New York Times Magazine,* January 1, 1984.

"The Archangel *Is* Illuminated," *Journal of Electronic Defense,* February 1984.

"Big Bird Nears Full Operational Status," *Aviation Week & Space Technology,* September 25, 1972.

Bamford, James. "America's Supersecret Eyes in Space," *The New York Times Magazine,* January 13, 1985.

Broad, William J. "The Chaos Factor," *Science 83,* January–February 1983.

Calder, James A. "Space-Based Radar Comes Over the Horizon," *Aerospace America,* January 1984.

Chapman, John. "New Eyes for NATO," *Military Technology,* October 1983.

Crickmore, Paul. "Blackbirds in Britain," *Aeroplane Monthly,* December 1983.

"Defense Dept. to Retain Expendable Launchers as Backup to Shuttle," *Aviation Week & Space Technology,* March 18, 1985, p. 115.

"Discoverer Becomes Satellite Test Bed," *Aviation Week & Space Technology,* September 25, 1961.

"Discoverer Success Speeds AF Plans," *missiles and rockets,* August 22, 1960.

"DOD Plans Multi-Mission Satellite RFP," *missiles and rockets,* May 2, 1966.

Elachi, Charles. "Radar Images of the Earth from Space," *Scientific American,* December 1982.

Elachi, C., et al. "Shuttle Imaging Radar Experiment," *Science,* December 3, 1982.

"F-12 Based on Fighter Experience," *Aviation Week,* November 10, 1947.

Fink, Donald E. "Simulator Displays SR-71 Characteristics," *Aviation Week & Space Technology*, May 10, 1976.

———. "U-2s, SR-71s Merged in One Wing," *Aviation Week & Space Technology*, May 10, 1976.

Ford, Daniel. "The Button," *The New Yorker*, April 1 and 8, 1985.

"Ford Developing Expert System to Aid Satellite Fault Repair," *Aviation Week & Space Technology*, May 12, 1986, p. 89.

Garwin, Richard L. "Antisubmarine Warfare and National Security," *Scientific American*, July 1972.

Garwin, Richard L., Kurt Gottfried, and Donald L. Hafner. "Antisatellite Weapons," *Scientific American*, June 1984.

Greenwood, Ted. "Reconnaissance and Arms Control," *Scientific American*, February 1973.

Hafemeister, David, Joseph J. Romm, and Kosta Tsipis. "The Verification of Compliance with Arms Control Agreements," *Scientific American*, March 1985.

"How Hawaiian Station 'Hula' Tracks Orbiting Discoverer," *missiles and rockets*, April 18, 1960.

Humphries, Orin. "High Flight," *Airpower*, July 1983.

Johnson, Clarence L. "Development of the Lockheed SR-71 Blackbird," *Lockheed Horizons*, Winter, 1981/82.

Johnson, Nicholas L. "Soviet Satellite Reconnaissance Activities and Trends," *Air Force Magazine*, March 1981.

———. "The U.S. must now play catch-up with Soviet satellite technology," *Military Electronics/Countermeasures*, April 1983.

"KH-11 Overruns Said to Slow Development of Follow-on Spacecraft," *Aerospace Daily*, January 23, 1984.

"KH-12 Reconnaissance Satellite Planned for Kennedy Launch," *Aviation Week & Space Technology*, June 23, 1986, p. 17.

Lindsey, Robert. "To Chase a Spy," *The New York Times Magazine*, October 2, 1983.

Marshall, Eliot. "NASA and the Military Press for a Spaceplane," *Science*, January 10, 1986.

May, Michael M. "Safeguarding Our Military Space Systems," *Science*, April 18, 1986, pp. 336–40.

"New Assessment Put on Soviet Threat," *Aviation Week & Space Technology*, March 28, 1977.

"New USAF Satellite to Include Infrared, Photo Scanning Gear," *Aviation Week & Space Technology*, December 26, 1966.

Oberg, James E. "Andropov's Orbiting Bombs," *Reason*, December 1983.

"Recon Satellite Assumes Dual Role," *Aviation Week & Space Technology*, August 30, 1971.

Ropelewski, Robert R. "SR-71 Impressive in High-Speed Regime," *Aviation Week & Space Technology*, May 18, 1981.

"Satellite pictures show Soviet CVN towering above Nikolaiev shipyard," *Jane's Defence Weekly*, August 11, 1984.

Settle, Mark, and James V. Taranik. "Use of Space Shuttle for Remote Sensing Research: Recent Results and Future Prospects," *Science*, December 3, 1982.

Smith, R. Jeffrey. "Titan Accident Disrupts Military Space Program," *Science*, May 9, 1986, pp. 702–4.

"Soviets Hike Reconnaissance Pace," *Aviation Week & Space Technology*, July 4, 1966.

"Soviets Orbit Large New Military Electronic Intelligence Satellite," *Aviation Week & Space Technology*, January 14, 1985.

"Space Reconnaissance Dwindles," *Aviation Week & Space Technology*, October 6, 1980.

Stein, Daniel L. "Electromagnetic pulse—the uncertain certainty," *The Bulletin of the Atomic Scientists*, March 1983.

Streetly, Martin. "US airborne ELINT systems, Part 2: the US Air Force," *Jane's Defence Weekly*, February 18, 1985.

——. "US airborne ELINT systems, Part 3: the Boeing RC-135 family," *Jane's Defence Weekly*, March 16, 1985.

"Study Urges Exploiting of Technologies," *Aviation Week & Space Technology*, October 24, 1983.

Sykes, Lynn R., and Jack E. Evernden. "The Verification of a Comprehensive Nuclear Test Ban," *Scientific American*, October 1982.

"Titan Explosion Cripples U.S. Launch, Surveillance Capability," *Aviation Week & Space Technology*, April 28, 1986, pp. 16–19.

"Titan Solid Booster Failure Caused Vandenberg Accident," *Aviation Week & Space Technology*, May 5, 1986, pp. 24–25.

"Titan 34D Booster Failed Following Premature Shutdown of Aerojet Engine," *Aviation Week & Space Technology*, November 18, 1985.

"U.S. Fighters Escort Soviet Military Aircraft," *Aviation Week & Space Technology*, August 6, 1984.

"U.S. Scrutinizes New Soviet Radar," *Aviation Week & Space Technology*, August 22, 1983.

"USAF Spurs Spaceplane Research," *Aviation Week & Space Technology*, March 26, 1984.

"USSR Boosts Reconnaissance Capabilities," *Aviation Week & Space Technology*, January 21, 1985.

Velocci, Tony. "Strategic reconnaissance/surveillance," *Military Technology*, October 1983.

von Hippel, Frank, David H. Albright, and Barbara G. Levi. "Stopping the Production of Fissile Materials for Weapons," *Scientific American*, September 1985.

Welling, William. "The Aerospace Plane: Quick Responsiveness for the Pacific Basin," *Defense Science 2004+*, February/March 1986.

Wit, Joel S. "Advances in Antisubmarine Warfare," *Scientific American*, February 1981.

NEWSPAPERS

As with magazines, only articles of major importance are listed below. Others are listed in the appropriate places in the Notes.

"Air Force Ex-Intelligence Chief Fears Soviet Has Military Edge," *The New York Times*, January 3, 1977.

"Arms Verification Issue at Heart of U.S. Debate," *The New York Times*, November 24, 1985.

"Can the Arms Tangle be Unknotted?" *Newsday*, January 4, 1985.

"Debate Over Nuclear Ban: Can U.S. Spot Cheats?" *The New York Times*, March 8, 1983.

"Ex-C.I.A. Head Now Works for a Nuclear Freeze," *The New York Times*, June 14, 1983.

"Eyes in the Sky: Satellites' Use Growing with Capabilities," *The New York Times*, March 29, 1983.

"Imperfect Science, Important Conclusions," *The New York Times,* July 28, 1985.

"Joint Chiefs Find No Soviet Cheating," *The New York Times,* February 8, 1986.

"Library Releases Cuba Crisis Tapes," *The New York Times,* October 27, 1983.

"Moscow Accuses U.S. of Violating Arms Agreements," *The New York Times,* January 30, 1984.

"Moscow Denies It Violated Arms Pacts," *The New York Times,* October 21, 1984.

"Pelton's 'Top Secret' Intelligence Not So Secret," *The Boston Globe,* June 5, 1986.

"Photos Did No Damage, Ex-C.I.A. Official Testifies," *The Washington Post,* October 16, 1985.

"Satellite Unchanged From Manual Bought by Soviets, U.S. Officials Say," *The Washington Post,* October 10, 1985.

"Secrecy of U.S. Reconnaissance Office Is Challenged," *The New York Times,* March 1, 1981.

"Soviet Arms Breach Charged," *The New York Times,* October 11, 1984.

"Study Says Soviet Broke Arms Pacts," *The New York Times,* September 12, 1984.

"Titan Rocket Explodes Over California Base," *The New York Times,* April 19, 1986.

"U.S. Again Asserts That Soviet Broke Arms Agreements," *The New York Times,* December 12, 1985.

"U.S. Aide Says Soviet Has Kept Most Arms Pacts," *The New York Times,* January 10, 1986.

"U.S. and Soviet Discuss Whether Moscow Violated Terms of 2 Arms Pacts," *The New York Times,* October 5, 1983.

"U.S. Is Challenged on Soviet Radar," *The New York Times,* March 15, 1985.

"U.S. Offers Photos of Bases to Prove Nicaragua Threat," *The New York Times,* March 10, 1982.

"U.S. Says Soviet Complies on Some Arms Issues," *The New York Times,* November 24, 1985.

"U.S. Says Soviet Violates ABM Treaty," *The New York Times,* February 2, 1985.

"U.S. Says Soviet Violates Treaty with a Missile," *The New York Times,* October 23, 1985.

"U.S. Sees New Soviet Arms Violation," *The New York Times,* May 12, 1983.

INTERVIEWS

Maj. Robert Behler	June 11, 1984 (T)
Charles Beichman	June 18, 1984 (T)
Richard M. Bissell, Jr.	May 23, 1984 (T)
McGeorge Bundy	June 28, 1984 (T)
Moustafa T. Chahine	June 18, 1984 (T)
William E. Colby	April 17, 1984 (T)
Lt. Col. Jerry Glasser	June 11, 1984 (T)
James E. Gunn	May 14, 1984 (T)
James Janesick	June 14, 1984 (T)
Clarence L. Johnson	January 26, 1983 (T)
Nicholas L. Johnson	June 22, 1984 (T)
Amrom Katz	June 16, 1984 (T)
Gen. George J. Keegan, Jr.	September 16, 1981
	June 2, 1984 (T)
James R. Killian, Jr.	February 11, 1985 (T)
George B. Kistiakowsky	August 12, 1981
E. Henry Knoche	July 1, 1985 (t)
Edwin Land	October 27, 1984 (t)
Hans Mark	May 6, 1985
Harold E. Nash	May 27, 1984 (T)
Jerry Nelson	June 6, 1984 (T)
John Pike	June 27, 1983 (T)
Gen. Cecil W. Powell	August 25, 1981
Ben Rich	June 19, 1984 (T)
Jeffrey T. Richelson	April 18, 1984 (T)
Herbert Scoville, Jr.	April 12, 1984 (T)
Gen. Paul D. Wagoner	June 21, 1984 (T)

(T) Taped
(t) Telephone

Index

ABOUT THE AUTHOR

WILLIAM E. BURROWS has written about aviation and space for more than two decades. He has reported for *The New York Times*, *The Washington Post*, *The Wall Street Journal*, and *The Richmond Times-Dispatch*, and is the author of three previous books: *Richthofen*, *Vigilante*, and *On Reporting the News*. Mr. Burrows's articles have appeared in *Foreign Affairs*, *The New York Times Magazine*, *Harper's*, *The Sciences*, and *Harvard Magazine*.

Mr. Burrows holds two degrees in international relations from Columbia University and is at present a professor of journalism and director of the Science and Environmental Reporting Program at New York University.